SCHOOL OF
ORIENTAL AND AFRICAN STUDIES
UNIVERSITY OF LONDON

*Historical Writing on the Peoples of Asia*

# HISTORIANS OF CHINA AND JAPAN

*Edited by*

W. G. BEASLEY

*Professor of the History of the Far East*
*University of London*

AND

E. G. PULLEYBLANK

*Professor of Asian Studies*
*University of British Columbia*

LONDON
OXFORD UNIVERSITY PRESS
NEW YORK   TORONTO

88122

*Oxford University Press, Ely House, London W.1*

GLASGOW   NEW YORK   TORONTO   MELBOURNE   WELLINGTON
CAPE TOWN   SALISBURY   IBADAN   NAIROBI   DAR ES SALAAM   LUSAKA   ADDIS ABABA
BOMBAY   CALCUTTA   MADRAS   KARACHI   LAHORE   DACCA
KUALA LUMPUR   SINGAPORE   HONG KONG   TOKYO

SBN 19 713521 8

*First published* 1961
*Fourth impression* 1971

PRINTED BY PHOTO-LITHOGRAPHY AND MADE IN GREAT BRITAIN AT
THE PITMAN PRESS, BATH

# PREFACE

Between the years 1956 and 1958 the School of Oriental and African Studies, University of London, held a series of study conferences to survey and evaluate the course and character of historical writing on the peoples of Asia. The subject is large and to bring it down to manageable parts the method of analysis by region was adopted; and South Asia, South East Asia, the Near, Middle, and Far East were in turn examined. In historical depth the survey of each region extended from the period of the early empires and literatures, through the age of Western dominance and the freedom movements down to the present day. Writings in both Western and Asian literatures were analysed.

The conferences brought together the leading authorities in these studies from Asia and the West and had the effect of making them more keenly aware not only of the underlying assumptions, predilections and prejudices of past writers but also of their own standpoints as historians. These investigations, which are continuing, have an enhanced value because they are taking place at a time when historians are seeking to rewrite Asian history and the peoples of Asia and the West are adjusting their relationships.

In preparing for each conference the same methods were used. Seminar groups, including a judicious balance of mature scholars and younger historians in training from Asian and Western countries, were established to analyse in detail the papers which had been prepared according to an agreed, comprehensive plan by the prospective members of the forthcoming conference. The business of the conferences therefore consisted not in reading papers but in attempting to solve the problems thrown up by the seminars.

We are greatly indebted to the School of Oriental and African Studies which provided the funds to organize a conference on historical writing on the peoples of the Far East.

In the view that the papers which were submitted to the conferences possess an intrinsic and comparative value the School of Oriental and African Studies has generously provided funds for their publication and, suitably edited and introduced, they will appear under the following editors: Professor W. G. Beasley and Professor E. G. Pulleyblank (China and Japan); Professor D. G. E. Hall (South East Asia); Professor B. Lewis and Dr. P. M. Holt (The Near and Middle East); Professor C. H. Philips (India, Pakistan, and Ceylon).

*School of Oriental and*                              C. H. PHILIPS
*African Studies*

# CONTENTS

vii

# Contents

# 1. INTRODUCTION

The contributions presented in this volume were originally designed to provide a body of material for discussion at a conference, not a complete survey of historical writing about China and Japan. Since the conference took place there has been an opportunity to supplement the original list of papers by the addition of those by Professor Demiéville and Mr. Gray. To both of them the editors would like to express special thanks for their co-operation. Similarly, the authors of other papers have been able to revise their contributions in the light of the discussions which took place in London in July 1956. For this reason, if no other, it has seemed unnecessary to present any account of those discussions here. Rather, the editors, in preparing this introduction, have felt free to offer their own personal observations on the subjects with which they deal. They gladly acknowledge their debt to what is written in the papers and what was said at the meetings—not only by the authors of the papers, but also by a number of other scholars who attended them—but they would not wish it to be thought that the statements and speculations which follow are in any sense the 'findings' of the conference. The editors accept, each in his own field,[1] the same responsibility for their respective shares of the introduction as for their contributions elsewhere in the volume.

## (a) Chinese historical writing

The recording of the past which we call history has developed independently into a major intellectual activity not more than three times. The European historical tradition looks back to its Greek and Roman origins. Islam developed its history, unlike its philosophy, apparently uninfluenced by Greek models. And lastly, China produced an historical literature, peculiar both in its merits and in its limitations, but unique in the volume of its output and the length and continuity of its record. If one is to understand rightly the problems of historiography and the part that it has played in the development of human civilization, it is obvious that one must take into account all three traditions, but there are formidable barriers in the way of achieving such a comprehensive perspective. Western historiography, transformed during the nineteenth century, spreads with other

[1] The section of the introduction dealing with Chinese writing is by E. G. Pulleyblank, those dealing with Japanese and Western writing by W. G. Beasley. Mr. A. Fraser, of the School of Oriental and African Studies, has given much valuable help with proofs.

elements of western civilization to every part of the world as a part of 'modernization', and even if only in the form of grossly vulgarized 'historicist' doctrines—Marxist and otherwise—western historical ideas become widely disseminated. The Chinese tradition on the other hand (I am not of course concerned here with the Islamic) remains culture bound. It is by no means dead, but since traditional Chinese civilization as a whole is being engulfed and transformed by the impact of the West, there is comparatively little impulse among Western historians to recognize the past achievements of Chinese historiography or to consider the relevance of its very different tradition for comparison with their own.

It must be admitted that even if that impulse existed and western historians did wish to come to an understanding of Far Eastern historiography there would be great difficulties in the way. Little has been translated. Moreover, historiography is so intimately a part of traditional Confucian culture and so conditioned by the nature of Chinese society that one must penetrate rather deeply into that culture and society before one can really comprehend it. It requires to be interpreted by persons who are able to some extent to adopt two points of view at the same time. They must be specialists thoroughly versed in Chinese studies and at the same time sufficiently aware of the interests and preconceptions of Western historians to interpret what they find in a way that will be meaningful to their intended audience. There have been a few attempts to bridge this gap but the task largely remains to be done. The authors of the articles on Chinese historiography in this collection would not claim to have accomplished it but their intention has been to contribute towards this end.

Chinese civilization is by no means as old as popular legend would have it, and indeed the beginnings of its literary tradition are roughly equivalent in age to those of Greece. Mr. van der Loon discusses in his introductory paper the origins in the separate states into which China was divided down to 221 B.C. of the first chronicles, developing out of the records of diviners and ritualists. Through the connection, supposed or genuine, of Confucius with the editing of the chronicles of his native state of Lu, Chinese historiography came to be fraught with a solemn ethical function, the duty of expressing 'praise and blame', that was to hang over it, often to its detriment, throughout its subsequent development. The pre-imperial period also saw the beginning of other types of writing that contributed to the development of history, for instance the keeping of genealogical records in aristocratic families. The laconic but wonderfully vivid collection of history and legend from the feudal states that was later rearranged as a commentary to the Spring and Autumn Annals and became known as the Tso Tradition was the inspiration of many of China's greatest historians in later ages. Already in the pre-imperial period had grown up the practice of quoting historical precedents as a means of persuasion in philosophical discussion and this no doubt gave an impetus to the collection of anecdotes associated with historical personages and events. Finally, at the beginning of the imperial period comes Ssu-ma Ch'ien (*c.* 145–85 B.C.) who stands as a watershed, gathering together and summing up the traditions of the past, and in his great history of China down to his own day, the Records of the Historian, providing the unsurpassed model for the long line of Standard Histories which has stretched on after him in an unbroken line to the twentieth century.

Professor Hulsewé takes up the story discussing Ssu-ma Ch'ien's methods and comparing his work with the second Standard History, the *Han shu*, or History of the Former Han Dynasty, of Pan Ku. Certain respects in which the latter differed from its model, notably its restriction to a single extinct dynasty, the nomenclature of certain of its sections and other points of detail, were imitated by later Standard Histories. Moreover, though it was begun privately and was the work of an individual, or rather of a single family of historians, in being brought to completion under official auspices it foreshadowed the official historiography of later times.

After the collapse of the Later Han dynasty at the end of the second century A.D. there followed a period of several centuries during most of which China was divided into two or more fragments. At this time there was a considerable amount of historical writing, only a small portion of which survives in its original form. The methods and ideas of history writing in this period have not been dealt with by any of the papers here presented. There were, however, several important developments. It was at this time that history first became recognized as an autonomous subject of study. Self-consciousness about literature of all kinds greatly increased and with it came ideas about history as a genre. The writing of history still retained the mixture of private initiative and official patronage that had characterized it in Later Han.

Then came the reunification of China and the establishment of the T'ang dynasty at the beginning of the seventh century. With the restored empire there was an upsurge in officially sponsored historiography, at first devoted to the compilation of definitive Standard Histories for the preceding centuries and then to the gathering of material for the 'National History' of the T'ang itself and its periodic working up into finished form. From this period onward the composition of Standard Dynastic Histories was with only one exception no longer the work of single individuals but the task of groups of historians working in the History Office, an official governmental organ. The principles and methods used in this work from the T'ang to the Ming are the subject of Professor L. S. Yang's paper. He discusses first the various types of archival material that were drawn upon and the ·preliminary Diaries of Activity and Repose, Records of Current Government, Daily Records, Veritable Records, etc., which were based

upon them and which constituted the material for the dynastic histories.
In T'ang, it seems clear, the Veritable Records and successive versions of
the National History were public property but later they became, as he
shows, secret governmental archives available in principle to authorized
persons only.

Official historiography in China, Professor Yang goes on to show, had
as its purposes the maintenance of continuity and the provision of useful
reference material for statesmen in need of precedents. It is one of the most
remarkable things about the Chinese tradition of historiography how successive dynasties regarded it as their duty to compile the history of preceding dynasties from the material left by these predecessors and how on
the other hand they seemed to regard the making of a definitive history of
their own time as the business of their successors. In the composition of
histories we find certain perennial, often conflicting, ideas expressed—
'truthful record' as opposed to 'appropriate concealment', 'praise and
blame' as opposed to objective statement. Professor Yang shows how they
were followed or violated in the actual composition of Standard Histories.
He shows that a high standard of critical acumen and historical sense was
reached in the Sung dynasty only to be succeeded by a more rigid and
unimaginative pedantry from Yüan and Ming onwards in keeping with
the prevailing scholastic temper of those times. At the same time, however,
there were increasing elaboration and refinement in the actual techniques
of official historiography.

Professor Wolfgang Franke gives us a case study of this later official historiography in his paper on 'The Veritable Records of the Ming Dynasty
(1368–1644)'. Whereas for earlier times we do not generally possess the
materials composed in the History Office during a dynasty but only the
finished product in the form of the Standard History later compiled from
them, in the case of the Ming we possess the Veritable Records of each
reign and so are much less dependent on the Ming History composed under
the Manchus. Professor Franke's detailed description of the careful rules
and procedures laid down for the Veritable Records and on the other
hand, the political pressures which influenced their composition and
affected them even after they had received official approval and were
theoretically to be kept inviolate under seal reveals much about both the
theory and the practice of Chinese official historiography.

Apart from the basic annals of the emperors, the two most important
sections of the Standard History pattern as invented by Ssu-ma Ch'ien
and continued by his successors were the monographs or treatises which
deal with distinct subjects such as the calendar, astronomy, economics,
administrative geography, etc., and the *lieh-chuan* which mainly consisted
of biographies of individuals. Each of these sections underwent development and gave rise to separate forms of history writing outside the Stan-

dard history pattern. These two types of writing are discussed by Dr. Balazs and Dr. Twitchett respectively.

Chinese history was written, says Dr. Balazs, by bureaucrats for bureaucrats. Its purpose was to provide collections of the necessary information and precedents required to educate officials in the art of governing. Nowhere is this more clearly shown than in the treatment of bureaucratic institutions in the monographs of the Standard Histories and in works such as encyclopaedias and compendiums. The monographs in the Standard Histories deal with the main fields of activity of the bureaucrat and, as Dr. Balazs shows, one can trace in the changing emphasis in the monographs from the first Standard History to the most recent, the changes in the preoccupations of the bureaucrats in the same period. The interest in ritual, cosmology and omens which is very prominent in Han diminishes in later times and is replaced by emphasis on the practical business of administration—civil service organization, criminal justice, taxation and currency, etc. While the monographs in the dynastic histories fell victim to the same dead stereotyping that infested official historiography as a whole and tended to consist merely of chronologically juxtaposed excerpts and resumés from official documents without any attempt at analysis or synthesis, certain individuals of genius such as Tu Yu and Ma Tuan-lin made the history of institutions a vehicle for more penetrating historical studies in which they expressed personal views. Unfortunately the penalty of success was imitation under official auspices and the continuations of Tu Yu's and Ma Tuan-lin's institutional encyclopaedias, though useful as collections of material, are as dead and wooden as other forms of official history writing.

The origins of biography in China are obscure. There is no known source or precedent for Ssu-ma Ch'ien's biographical accounts arranged as 'traditions' (*chuan*) appended to the 'basic annals' (*pen-chi*) of the emperors, after the manner of the 'traditions' attached to the Spring and Autumn Annals. As Dr. Twitchett shows, however, the close resemblance between the *Shih chi* biography form and the earliest extant epitaphs on stone (first century A.D.) suggests that a model for this type of writing existed. Dr. Twitchett describes in detail the way in which material for biographies was gathered, selected, and written up in the History Office in later times and shows the close connection that existed between this type of official writing and works of private piety such as family biographies and epitaphs. He shows that biography in China was written with different conceptions from those of the west. The individual existed enmeshed in a network of social relationships and an account of his life was necessarily devoted to showing how he fulfilled the roles which these relationships placed upon him, above all the role of official. Heroic poetry and tragedy, which have exerted such an influence in moulding Western conceptions of biography, were absent in China and the patterns on which 'lives' were fashioned were fragmented and episodic, like a Chinese novel, conforming nevertheless to a unified view of an ethical universe and man's destiny in it.

Although official history is bound to take the centre of the stage in any account of Chinese historiography this does not mean that there was any lack of privately composed works as well. Indeed, as we have seen, the main genres of official history originated from private initiative as in the case of the first of the Standard Histories, Ssu-ma Ch'ien's Records of the Historian. When we speak of private history writing, however, we refer in the main to works of more modest dimensions—accounts of short periods or single events, memoirs, collections of anecdotes, etc. To deal with all this varied writing during the whole 2000 years of imperial China would be out of the question in a work of this scope. Professor Herbert Franke has, however, described the private historiography of a limited period, that of the Mongol rule in the thirteenth and fourteenth centuries. Conditions were not unfavourable for such writing, for oppressive as the foreign rulers might be in some respects they were not in a position to exercise the same degree of supervision on Chinese literary output as was normal under a native dynasty. Not a few works were written in which Sung loyalty was openly expressed. Professor Franke lists and describes numerous privately written works from this time which contain information of a historical kind. As he points out, since the authors of 'private' works of history were themselves literati and either potential or actual bureaucrats there is a strong similarity in outlook between this 'private' writing and Chinese official historiography; though private authors might be free of some of the restraints that inhibited the history official. Buddhist historiography is therefore of especial interest since it alone lay outside the confines of Confucian orthodoxy, and Professor Franke devotes a special section to it.

After these all-too-brief and summary accounts of the main genres of history writing we turn to consider what Chinese historians thought about their activity and their critical methods. Self-consciousness about the writing of history increased, as has been said, in the Northern and Southern Dynasties (fourth to sixth centuries) and reached a climax in T'ang (seventh to ninth centuries) with the institution of the History Office. It was at this time that Liu Chih-chi wrote his Generalities on History (*Shih-t'ung*) in which he expressed his views on how history should be written and criticized the way previous historians had or had not conformed to these principles. It is a work of great interest which enables us to see the conceptions that lay behind Chinese history writing and to appreciate the critical attitude and historical sense with which a great Chinese historian went about his work.

Liu Chih-chi, who was notorious for his iconoclastic attitude even to the most revered classics, came at the beginnings of the critical and philo-sophical movement which culminated in the scholarship and philosophy of the Sung dynasty (960–1279). Rationalistic criticism of received tradi-tion on the one hand and speculative philosophy on the other reached a high point in these centuries and it is no accident that they also produced some of the most mature works of historical scholarship. Perhaps the greatest of all was Ssu-ma Kuang's Comprehensive Mirror for Aid in Government (*Tzu-chih t'ung-chien*), a history of China in annalistic form from 403 B.C. to A.D. 959. We are fortunate in possessing a considerable amount of information about its compilation which enables us to appreci-ate the high standards of criticism that were applied to the selection and comparison of the material. It represents probably the limit that could be attained without breaking through the framework of scissors and paste compilation, a thing that even Ssu-ma Kuang was unable to achieve.

In the trough of the Ming period (1368–1644) history fared no better than other forms of intellectual activity, but the shock of the Ming col-lapse and the Manchu conquest caused a reaction against metaphysical theorizing. The work of the text-critical school which developed in the seventeenth century under the leadership of Ku Yen-wu was directly stimulated by the desire to turn scholarship to practical ends and streng-then the nation. Although in their reaction against the orthodoxy of Sung neo-Confucianism the text-critical school looked back to Han commenta-tors on the classics and became known as the School of Han Learning, they were really continuing the work of Sung philologists. But both in classical studies and in history, their criticism achieved new rigour and objectivity and, as Mr. Gray points out, they laid a foundation of exact scholarship to which all students of China's past are still deeply indebted. Moreover, in Chao I (1727–1814), we find a man who could see beyond the isolated details and make the kind of inductive generalizations about trends of social and institutional history that modern historians seek to establish.

In general, however, it would be true to say that Ch'ing historical studies were strong on the criticism of points of detail and weak on synthesis. It was left to a follower of neo-Confucianism, Chang Hsüeh-ch'eng (1738–1801) to react against this tendency and to propound, in the first treatise on history since Liu Chih-chi, general ideas about the nature and meaning of history which for the first time tried to break out of the traditional mould and approached a conception more like our modern one. Professor Demiéville, who was invited to the London conference but was unfortu-nately unable to attend in person, has sent us his paper on Chang Hsüeh-ch'eng, in whom he has long had a great interest. Chang, whose ideas were little appreciated or understood in his own day and forgotten after his death only to be revived in the present century, was a vital personality as well as a profound and original thinker. Professor Demiéville likens him to Giambattista Vico. Unfortunately he was not able to carry out his plan for a synthetic history of the Sung period, so we cannot tell how he would have interpreted his own ideas in practice.

The shock of the Western impact on China after the Opium War was even greater than that of the Manchu conquest but it was not until the end of the century that it led to the beginnings of a reappraisal of China's past by Chinese scholars. Only the most tentative conclusions are yet possible about the subsequent half-century of historical thinking and scholarship, intimately bound up as they have been with the revolutions in thought and attitudes, no less than in politics and society, through which China has been passing. To have made no reference to this period might, however, have left the quite untrue impression that China's tradition of historical studies ceased at the end of the eighteenth century. Mr. Gray, who was not at the conference, was therefore asked to contribute a paper on this subject and this concludes the section.

Mr. Gray stresses the vitality and continuity of China's own scholarly tradition in the twentieth century. The scepticism of the Ch'ing period provided a secure springboard for the even more radical revision of accepted ideas that came about through a widening vision of the world in which China no longer occupied the whole stage. Nor did twentieth-century scholars, working on newly discovered and newly recognized source-materials, have much to learn in the way of philological techniques from Europe. Political revolution, on the other hand, and the new ideas from outside that accompanied it, inevitably led to radically new points of view being expressed about China's past and to impassioned controversies between them. K'ang Yu-wei, the leader of the Reform Movement of 1898, in his revival of the New Text School, was facing both ways, for he sought to bolster up Confucianism by showing that it was really a revolutionary doctrine in keeping with the progressive ideas of nineteenth-century Europe. After the failure of the movement his younger associate, Liang Ch'i-ch'ao, in exile in Japan, went considerably farther in rejecting the Chinese tradition and adopting ideas from the west. He was the leading Chinese publicist of modernization in the first two decades of the twentieth century but in the end he retreated into a defensive rejection of 'materialism' in favour of the supposed superiority of China's spiritual heritage. He turned from politics to academic studies and produced some of his best historical writings.

The real political awakening of China came only after the end of the First World War. Liberalism and pragmatism, advocated by Hu Shih, fought a losing battle with Marxism, and the thirties were highlighted by polemics on the interpretation, in Marxist terms, of the nature of Chinese society and its past. Meanwhile, new source-materials such as the oracle bones of An-yang, the wooden slips of the north-west frontier, and the manuscript finds on paper at Tun-huang and elsewhere in Central Asia, the opening up of the palace archives at the fall of the empire, the recognition of the importance of popular forms of literature and art, all these things have greatly enlarged the scope of historical scholarship. We may conclude the story of China's writing of her own history at this point without attempting to assess the trends of study and thought both within the People's Republic and outside it in the mid-twentieth century.

Needless to say the papers here presented do not cover every aspect of Chinese history writing, though there is, I think, at least passing mention of all the major branches. It is regrettable that more has not been included about some things such as historical geography, local gazetteers and other works of a local character, archaeology, etc. The authors will, however, probably be less concerned about this lack of comprehensiveness than about the overall impression that will be conveyed to the European historian. Have we succeeded in giving him a correct impression of how the Chinese thought about history and the part history played in their civilization? I cannot of course answer this question, though I should hope that some communication will have been made.

Remembering the discussions that took place at the London conference and having now re-read the papers, I may perhaps suggest from a personal point of view certain ways in which the total picture may perhaps be inadequate and one-sided. I wonder, for instance, whether we have sufficiently conveyed to the reader the passionate interest which the Chinese had in their history. The quoting of historical precedents and drawing of lessons from past events was no mere perfunctory exercise and this point might have been stressed by examples such as the controversy about the correct succession of dynasties (*cheng-t'ung*). Or one could have used the example of Wang Fu-chih's (1619–92) On Reading the Comprehensive Mirror (*Tu T'ung-chien lun*) and On Sung (*Sung lun*) to show how political ideas could be expressed in the form of judgements on historical events. History largely took the place of mythology for the Chinese and provided an inexhaustible fund of episodes on which the story-teller, the novelist, and the dramatist could draw. The historical imagination which we miss so much in the dry-as-dust 'objective' records of official history could give itself free rein and we can begin to understand how the Chinese could be so attached to the stories of their past. The relation between history and fiction has been touched upon by one or two of the authors. It deserves fuller treatment.

All such matters, however, will have to be left to others or to other occasions.

## (b) *Japanese historical writing*

For much of its history Japanese culture has been part of a pattern which evolved in, and remained centered on, China. The same can be said of Japanese historical writing. It has therefore seemed legitimate to devote rather less space to Japan than to China in this volume. Equally, and for the same reasons, there is a tendency, when discussing the historical writing of Japan, to compare it constantly with that of China, to measure it by the degree of its adherence to or departure from Chinese models. Even in the modern period, in which China does not to the same degree act as a cultural focus, the reactions of the two countries to Western influence provide a similar basis for comparison and contrast. Much of the discussion at the conference for which these papers were prepared was concerned with this problem. So, too, are many of the remarks which follow.

In surveying Japanese historical writing in the period ending about the middle of the nineteenth century, one can conveniently divide it according to the language in which works were written, that is, to treat separately those written in Chinese and those in Japanese. As one would expect, works written in Chinese in Japan reflect a larger measure of Chinese influence than the rest. Indeed, the earliest of them, the *Rikkokushi*, or Six National Histories, which are the subject of Mr. Robinson's first paper, belong to the period of conscious imitation of things Chinese in the eighth and ninth centuries and follow the lines of Chinese official historiography as closely as their compilers found possible. That they took the form of annals, without the full range of biographies and monographs to be found in a Chinese Standard History, seems to have been due initially to lack of material. In other respects, differences were dictated by political structure. In establishing the first of a series it was possible to start with myth and bring the narrative down to any convenient point of recent time, but subsequent writers, continuing the story, faced the necessity of identifying suitable periods to study. In China, the dynasty provided the obvious segment, reasonably compact and manageable. In Japan, there was only the one dynasty in the whole of recorded time. Thus the historian had to adopt other criteria, usually the reign of a single Emperor or an arbitrarily chosen group of successive reigns. In this respect the second and subsequent works comprising the Six National Histories are more akin to the Veritable Records (*shih-lu*) or National Histories (*kuo-shih*) of China than to the Standard Histories themselves.

Differences in political development also provide another kind of contrast between the two countries. In China, the work of the official historian was an inherent part of the function of the State, reflecting certain philosophical assumptions which were closely linked with government, and the historian himself was a member of a bureaucracy which had real power. In Japan, despite the policy of sinicization which was followed during the period covered by the Six National Histories, these conditions never fully obtained. The official historian of Japan had neither the same standing nor the same function as his Chinese counterpart. Moreover, his activities ceased as soon as institutional change brought a system of government which was both effective and non-Chinese. In the period of Fujiwara dominance, still more in the feudal period which followed, Chinese political models were abandoned in Japan. Thereafter, until the seventeenth century, there were only isolated examples of historical writing in the Chinese language.

The resumption of Chinese practice in the Tokugawa era was by no means confined to historical literature. Nor was it entirely accidental. The restoration of law and order after centuries of intermittent civil war, the existence of a strong central authority, accompanied none the less by a high degree of independence in provincial administration under the great feudal lords, even the nature of the ruling samurai class, which rapidly changed from a military into a bureaucratic elite, all these things combined to form a kind of society to which Chinese experience was more directly relevant than at any earlier time, this despite the continuing emphasis on birth and hereditary status in Japan. Confucianism became the dominant philosophy, officially encouraged and supported. The samurai Confucian scholar became a familiar component in both central and local government. He habitually wrote in Chinese and turned to China for ideas, so much so that to many the word 'history' signified that of China rather than Japan. It is not surprising that the result was a historical literature comparable in range, form, and quality, even literary quality, with that of a Chinese dynasty. The History of Japan (*Dai Nihon Shi*), produced by the scholars of Mito, had many of the virtues and of the defects of, say, Ssu-ma Ch'ien's Records of the Historian (*Shih chi*). The Bakufu's *Honchō Tsugan* (Comprehensive Mirror of Japan) signalled the revival of official historiography, which was continued throughout the period, while a host of lesser works appeared, varying from individual attempts at compiling the equivalent of a Standard History to summaries of national history in chronicle form, collections of biographies, or accounts of limited topics and single events. Even Chinese techniques of textual study were imported and applied. In fact, this second stage of sinicization was more far-reaching and more complete than anything achieved at the time of the Six National Histories.

On the other hand, the Tokugawa scholars also inherited—though they often ignored it—a different tradition, stemming from a literature written in Japanese. It is possible to argue that this started with the *Kojiki* (Records of Ancient Matters) at the beginning of the eighth century, but the language of this work is hybrid and its immediate influence was inconsiderable. A better starting point is the eleventh century, with the emergence of the so-called 'historical tales' (*rekishi-monogatari*), of which Mr. Robinson writes in his second paper. These clearly formed part of a widespread move away from strictly Chinese canons towards something less highly developed but indigenous: in political institutions, Fujiwara control and feudal tenure; in religion, 'popular' Amidist Buddhism, linked with the development of a simplified script; in literature, vernacular prose, the outstanding example of which is the Tale of Genji. The 'historical tales', in fact, used some of the techniques of the novel. Yet they were not historical novels in the Chinese sense. Though they might make use of dialogue and anecdote, they were avowedly a substitute for an official historiography which had ceased to exist, not a popularization of more formal work. The most famous of them, the *Ō-kagami* (Great Mirror), was even cast in the annals-biography form of a Standard History.

Of more lasting influence than the 'historical tales' was another kind of writing, stimulated by the emergence of feudal rule. This is discussed in the second and third of the papers dealing with Japan. The earliest examples were the *Gukanshō* (Miscellany of Ignorant Views) and the *Jinnō Shōtōki* (Records of the True Descent of the Divine Emperors), dating from the thirteenth and fourteenth centuries respectively. In form they had certain similarities to the Chinese survey histories of men like Ssu-ma Kuang or Chu Hsi. They also made extensive use of Chinese historical ideas, though these were modified to suit a Japanese context. But what most distinguished them was their preoccupation with a problem essentially Japanese: the relationship between an Emperor, who did not rule, and his hereditary officials, Kampaku or Shōgun, who did. Work of this type reached its highest point of development in the Tokugawa period, with Arai Hakuseki's *Dokushi Yoron* (Views on History), which not only set out a periodization of Japanese history based on changes in the nature and location of political authority, thereby establishing a pattern still used by many modern writers, but also moved some way towards an emphasis on cause and effect in its presentation of material. The result was something not far removed from a causal narrative, though some essential features of the chronicle remained.

Dr. Blacker's paper on Rai Sanyō illustrates a different element in the same tradition. Sanyō's Unofficial History of Japan (*Nihon Gaishi*), though not comparable with the work of his predecessors in the matter of historical technique, excelled them in literary reputation and popular appeal. Indeed, it was not only influenced by, but was also capable of exerting an influence on, contemporary politics, once the position of the Emperor became again a question of immediate relevance, as it did in the middle of the nineteenth century. The controversies of this period also brought into prominence earlier works of similar outlook, like Kitabatake's Records of True Descent and the Mito History of Japan.

Despite the interest of these developments, traditional Japanese historiography, taken as a whole, was neither so continuous nor so impressive as that of China. For the most part it made use of the same forms of expression; and even where this was not so, it was strongly rooted in Chinese thought. Yet, while it produced nothing entirely new or different, it was independent enough to evolve variations of its own where subject-matter made this necessary, showing a degree of flexibility in this respect that absolves it from the charge of slavish imitation and does much to explain the readiness with which Japanese historians later adjusted to the ideas of the West. This is to say no more than that Japanese historiography varied from that of China in much the same degree as Japanese culture generally adhered to or departed from Chinese models. Still, a survey of it helps to focus the attention on certain key periods of development. The first of these comes in the eleventh and twelfth centuries, when there was a shift away from Chinese practice, at least as it had been received in Japan till then, in the varied spheres of literature, religion, and political institutions. The relationship between the different parts of this process deserves more study than it has hitherto received. At a detailed level, in the field of literature, it is not clear what was the precise connection between the 'historical tales' on the one hand and the novels or diaries on the other. Similar problems are raised when one turns to the seventeenth century. Changes in the feudal structure, the enforcement of national seclusion (*sakoku*) and the revival of Chinese influence in the country's intellectual life are all more or less contemporary developments which need to be related to each other.

Turning to the modern period, Japanese experience clearly differed greatly from that of China, in terms of the speed and effectiveness with which the two countries reacted to their contacts with the civilization of the West. Japan's comparative openness to change is logical enough. It was, after all, an essentially Chinese culture that was being challenged and, even under the Tokugawa, Japan was not so fully wedded to it. But so general a statement still leaves much to be explained. It is impossible to enter fully into this problem here, even in the limited context of historical writing, but the two papers by Mr. Numata and Dr. Borton provide a basis for some discussion of it. Mr. Numata traces the development of official historiography in modern Japan, with which was associated certain Western techniques of historical investigation, both being linked initially with Tokyo University. Dr. Borton deals rather with a twentieth-century topic, the writing of economic history, mostly by the scholars of Kyōto University. This exemplifies a final stage in which Western methods and outlook were accepted almost in their entirety. Unfortunately, it has not been possible to include papers on certain other aspects of modern Japanese historiography, especially in the Meiji period, which would serve to fill out the picture. The brief sketch which follows might help to indicate some of the directions which further study could take.

In historical writing, as in much else, the Meji period represented a break with the past. From a tradition based largely on the methods and outlook of Chinese scholarship there was a gradual move in the direction of so-called 'scientific' historiography of the Western type. Accompanying this was an expansion of the historian's field to include cultural, social, and economic topics. Yet these changes were neither immediate nor complete. The first twenty-five years of the period, until about 1893, saw the continuation of much that was old and only the first tentative introduction of the new, while some elements from earlier historical writing have continued to exercise an important influence well into the twentieth century.

In these early years a number of general histories were still being written in the chronicle style, often in Chinese. Moreover, some of the Tokugawa period books continued to be widely read, especially Rai Sanyō's Unofficial History of Japan: between 1876 and 1884 alone five supplements to it were published, as well as a number of commentaries and summaries. The late Tokugawa interest in early history was continued, reinforced now by contemporary politics, in that the new structure of government evolved after 1868, however revolutionary in practice, was in theory a restoration of political relationships existing before the rise of feudalism. This gave the study of the ancient world a new appeal. From similar and more compelling motives came an interest in the immediate past. As a subject for writing, the overthrow of the Tokugawa and the creation of a new regime attracted chiefly the attention of those who had themselves participated in events, or their immediate descendants and adherents. Initially, therefore, the emphasis was on the anti-Tokugawa movement. With the passing of time, however, voices were also raised in defence of the Bakufu, or at least of some of its leaders. Fukuchi Genichiro's *Bakufu Suibō Ron* (Views on the fall of the Bakufu) in 1893 and Katsu Awa's *Bakufu Shimatsu* (Account of the Bakufu) three years later are the outstanding examples.

The history of the feudal period in general, which had attracted the attention of so many Tokugawa scholars, was virtually ignored in these years. This is not surprising. While the collapse of feudalism had an obvious contemporary relevance, its rise and development were an academic subject, the study of which had to wait until the twentieth century (and is even now, perhaps, the least advanced of all, despite the progress made since 1945). To Japan of the early Meiji period, indeed, already in the initial stages of a vast programme of modernization, the historical experience of the West was of far greater interest. It was from this fact that the new developments in historiography very largely took their origin.

As part of a general interest in things Western, a number of translations appeared in Japan of Western historical writing. Initially such books were translated for the sake of their content, but some of them, as examples of a form of historical writing quite different from the Sino-Japanese tradi-

tion, soon had an influence on the methodology of Japanese scholars dealing with the history of their own country. Among the earliest and most
influential were the works of Guizot (first translated in 1872) and those of
Buckle (translated in 1875). Their treatment of European and of English
history respectively not only served as models of the causal narrative, but
also brought home to some Japanese the fact, as Fukuzawa Yukichi wrote
in 1875, that previous writers had been concerned 'not with the history of
Japan, merely with the history of Japanese governments'.

It was the extension of the field of history to include subjects other than
kings-and-battles which characterized the early Meiji school writing
*bummei-shi*, the history of civilization or enlightenment. Although Fukuzawa
Yukichi was the leader of the group, which dubbed Japan half-civilized
in terms of western material and political progress, it was Taguchi
Ukichi who first applied this approach to the writing of Japanese history.
His *Nihon Kaika Shōshi* (Short History of Japan's Modernization), in six
volumes, published between 1877 and 1882, remains a landmark in
Japanese historiography despite its many inaccuracies and suspect interpretations. Its identification and discussion of general trends is evidenced
in its chapter headings: chapter I, for example, deals with Japan from the
Shintō origins to the spread of Buddhism; Chapter II runs from the introduction of Chinese ideas to the decline of Kyōto; Chapter III describes
the development of feudalism in the provinces up to the establishment of
the Kamakura Bakufu; and so on. This arrangement by topics reflects
the influence of Guizot and Buckle, though in periodization and general
structure the book is not unlike Arai Hakuseki's *Dokushi Yoron*. Where
Hakuseki was preoccupied with political events, however, Taguchi
Ukichi, out of a desire to measure Japan's development against a world
(i.e. Western) scale of what constituted civilization, put his emphasis on
such matters as art, religion, and national customs.

For some fifteen years the writing of *bummei-shi* flourished, though much
of the work done consisted merely of extracting from the ancient chronicles
and other records such information as related to cultural, as distinct from
political, history. Many such books were no more than chronicles with a
specialized subject-matter. Meanwhile, the use of the causal narrative was
also spreading, even to those who did not accept the philosophical principles of Fukuzawa and Taguchi, as also was a recognition that history
need not concern itself exclusively with political and military events. By
the end of the nineteenth century, one can say, despite wide variations of
personal approach, the actual presentation of history to the reading public
tended to be more often in the new than in the old form.

By that time, moreover, new influences were making themselves felt at
a different level. The earliest changes had concerned only the form of
presentation of historical writing; but with a wider knowledge of European

writings on methodology, especially of the German tradition stemming from Ranke, Japanese scholars began to use also the new techniques relating to the collection and investigation of historical data. These techniques, introduced into the Imperial University at Tokyo round about 1890, found ready acceptance, especially among those scholars who had maintained the earlier traditions of textual criticism and analysis known as *kōshōgaku*. The emphasis on accuracy and the use of original sources, to which this process contributed, became linked with the idea of 'impartial', or 'scientific', historical writing. This is a subject dealt with at greater length by Mr. Numata.

As evidence of the extent to which western methodology had penetrated Japanese academic circles, one might cite the controversy concerning the philosophy of history which raged in the years 1898–9. This took the form of a series of articles published in volumes x and xi of *Shigaku Zasshi* (Journal of Historical Studies), the monthly periodical founded by the historians of Tokyo Imperial University in 1889. From these articles it became clear that there already existed a number of views about the nature and function of history—all of them paralleled in similar disputes in the West—ranging from the purist assertion that the historian's primary task must be the collection of accurate data, to the philosophical argument that this process must be subordinate to the eventual aim of identifying laws governing historical change in general terms, i.e. laws relevant to all ages and all geographical areas. Inoue Tetsujiro, for example, in an article published in October 1898, inclined to the latter view. In the following year, Uchida Ginzō argued that both processes were essential and their development must go hand in hand. By contrast, the editorial group from Tokyo, including Shigeno Yasutsugu, urged the purist approach; and although they admitted (grudgingly, perhaps) that the historian must attempt to establish causal relationships between his facts, they insisted that anything more than this belonged to the field of philosophy, not of history.

What matters about this controversy, for our purpose, is not the nature of the particular views expressed, but the fact that, taken together, they reflect an attitude to historical writing very different from that prevailing in Japan some fifty years earlier. Clearly, in historiography, as in so many other things, Western culture had entered Japan not as unity but as variety. Nor should one seek explanations for the development only in the field of scholarship, still less confine one's search to the history of historical writing. To explain it fully would mean explaining the whole process of the Westernization (or modernization) of Japan, for historical studies were but part of this larger whole. One might, however, cite a number of ancillary factors which seem of relevance. Certainly the policies of the Meiji government, for example, contributed largely to the development of

Japanese historical studies. Establishment of a modern educational system provided an institutional framework within which the historian became a professional and a specialist, while the new curricula, emphasizing practical subjects (which included law and geography as well as science and technology) furnished him with academic surroundings predominantly Western in their origin. It is not surprising that Western historical method was imported with the rest. At the same time, government policy gave the study of Japanese history a secure place in the new educational order. In the process of building up a consciousness of national unity, history played its part together with 'ethics' (*shūshin*) and Shintō ceremony, especially after about 1890, when there came a reaction against the uncritical acceptance of Western ideas and habits which had marked the previous decade. Official encouragement reinforced tradition and helped to make history one of the major academic activities of the new universities. Yet the price paid for this patronage was a heavy one. On the one hand, historical scholarship became involved in political controversy: in a sense, the *bummei-shi* of Fukuzawa and Taguchi was itself linked with opposition to the government. On the other, certain topics themselves became subject to tabu, notably any which involved a realistic study of the historical role of the Imperial house. Government policies, in fact, while they stimulated historical writing generally, thereby helping indirectly to bring improvements in technique, tended also to impose restrictions at the level of interpretation.

Developments in the field of publishing were also of some importance. Widespread use of movable type made possible the printing of historical records which had previously been accessible only to the few. It also enabled the historian to reach a larger reading public—itself emerging as a result of compulsory education—with consequential changes in his presentation of material. In the late Meiji period, Japanese finally replaced Chinese as the normal language for historical writing. The chronicle gave way to narrative and description.

In historical writing, as in politics, industry, foreign relations and many other fields, the second half of the Meiji period, between about 1890 and 1912, saw the first really significant fruits of changes which had been initiated earlier. The attempts to write official history (in the Chinese language and in chronicle form) were now at last abandoned. Government-sponsored organizations turned their attention instead to the publication of historical records, a practice which has continued in the twentieth century and spread to private groups and individuals. In 1890 Shigeno Yasutsugu and two of his colleagues at Tokyo produced an outline history in seven volumes entitled *Kōhon Kokushi Gan* (Draft Survey of Japanese History). Within the next few years Fukuchi Genichiro, Yoshida Tōgo and Katsu Awa wrote studies of Tokugawa history. In 1896 came Takekoshi

Yosaburo's *Nisengohyaku Nen Shi* (History of 2,500 years). All these books showed some degree of Western influence in their presentation of material, while Takekoshi, modelling himself upon Macauley, sought to bring together both the new scientific treatment of evidence and also the more comprehensive range of subject-matter—social, economic, religious and cultural, as well as political—which had characterized the *bummei-shi* school.

Some ten years later there came another new departure with the publication in 1907–8 of Waseda University's *Dai Nihon Jidai Shi* (Japanese History by Periods). This work was arranged in ten volumes, divided chronologically, each being written by a specialist in the period concerned, and was avowedly an attempt to provide an accurate and detailed study, a task thought to be beyond the competence of a single individual, by enlisting the services of a group. This practice has remained common in Japan, though in recent years the tendency has been rather to collect a number of articles into a single volume than to produce multi-volume works. It was accompanied, also in 1908, by Kuroita Katsumi's *Kokushi no kenkyū* (A Study of Japanese History). Kuroita not only gave an appraisal of Japan's cultural development, with detailed references to earlier writing, but also discussed in general terms such topics as historical literature and bibliography, historical geography, genealogy, and chronologies. His was, in fact, as much a handbook and work of reference as it was a history of Japan.

This emergence of specialization, both in periods studied and in historical techniques, stemmed largely from an emphasis on the scientific approach to historical writing. In the same years a different kind of specialization was also beginning to take shape. So far, despite the work of men like Taguchi and Takekoshi, the historian's chief interest had been in the story of Japan's political development. An account of social or economic trends might find a place as part of a general survey, but there had not been any clear separating out of these aspects of history to constitute a subject of specialized study with its own disciplines and techniques. Much the same, of course, might be said of historical writing in Europe at the time. Both in Europe and Japan, concentration on this new field belonged chiefly to the twentieth century. It was, as Dr. Borton shows, from about 1920 on that Japanese writing on economic history assumed major importance, under the leadership of such scholars as Uchida Ginzō, Honjō Eijirō, and Tsuchiya Takao, thereby adding to historiography a new dimension. New questions were asked and new material became relevant in the search for answers to them. In the process, the emphasis between different factors in the total historical pattern was sharply modified.

Though this was to the good, there was another side to the medal. The

story of Japan's past became still more fragmented, not only by chronological division but also now by types of subject-matter. Many historians,
moreover, accepting theories of economic determinism, looked with contempt on those who persisted in writing about politics and were in turn
criticized by them. Some, especially among the Marxists, became preoccupied with theory almost to the exclusion of data. Others, the so-called
'academic' school, turned their whole attention to amassing factual knowledge with little or no thought of its possible applications. Disputes between and within the different groups were accentuated by university
loyalties and perpetuated by the strong bonds existing between student
and teacher, so that some of the more vigorous controversies have now
lasted more than a quarter of a century. One could even argue that the
first result of introducing Western ideas was not so much to modify the
accepted picture of Japanese history as to produce a series of different—
and discrete—versions of it.

Something of the same kind can be said of Japan's response to the West
in other contexts, too. It is not only in historical writing that there has been
a period of confusion and experimentation, giving one the impression of an
effort at once determined and diffuse. Nor is it surprising that there should
have been such a period. The attempt to master a culture as varied as that
of the West could never have brought results had the approach been
entirely controlled and single-minded. The process was a complex one—
and is not yet fully understood, though it has become increasingly attractive to historians as a subject of study. As a small but interesting part of this
whole, Japanese historiography of the last hundred years is something
which still needs much more detailed treatment than it has been possible
to give it in this volume.

*(c) Western historical writing on China and Japan*

Since Western writing has so far contributed relatively little to our total
knowledge of Chinese and Japanese history—and that in a few specialized
fields—no attempt has been made here to give a comprehensive account
of it. The papers presented on this subject, like others in the volume, are
intended to provide some examples which might serve as a basis for discussion. Two of them deal with historians of particular periods: that by
Professor Boxer with European writing (Portuguese, Spanish, French and
Dutch) of the sixteenth to eighteenth centuries; that by Mr. Hudson with
British writing of the late nineteenth and twentieth centuries.[2] Professor
Lattimore's paper is of a different kind, comprising a critical survey of the

[2] A further contribution, concerning Western writing on China in the nineteenth and twentieth
centuries, was prepared for the conference by Mr. O. P. N. B. van der Sprenkel. This paper,
unfortunately, is not available for publication; but I would like to express my indebtedness to
it for material on which a number of the observations in this section of the introduction are
based. [W.G.B.]

literature on a single topic, the social history of Mongol nomadism, ranging in time from Gibbon to the present day, which provides an opportunity for some brief consideration of Russian writing in one of its aspects. Had it been possible to expand this part of the volume, it would clearly have been desirable to have had a more extended treatment of Russian histories dealing with China and Japan, as well as of German, French, and American work, whether in the form of papers on the various national traditions or of papers on the historiography of special topics. Even so, the papers now printed, together with the discussions arising from them at the conference for which they were prepared, furnish material for some tentative observations of a general kind. The following remarks will seek briefly to state a few of them as they appear to the present writer.

Until very recent times, most specialist books on China and Japan in Western languages were written by men who had lived and worked in the Far East. In the sixteenth, seventeenth, and eighteenth centuries, the period dealt with by Professor Boxer, the Jesuit missionaries dominate the field. In the nineteenth and early twentieth centuries the Jesuits were followed by others: Protestant missionaries, diplomats, journalists, and those who went to teach in schools or universities. All these men had one thing in common, that their writing originated from an interest in and knowledge of the area. The fact had important consequences. It meant, for example, that their work was not exclusively history in the academic sense. For some, history was but part of a whole which embraced also government, law, economics, geography, literature, art. For others it arose as the product of an initial interest in language or philosophy. In fact, the subject of study was a country or its culture, not specifically or solely its history. The concept of 'sinology' still exists as a reminder of this outlook.

Personal experience also had its effect in influencing the nature of the subjects studied. Apart from accounts of contemporary or near-contemporary events, like the Taiping Rebellion in China and the Satsuma Rebellion in Japan, much of the history written was designed to explain society as it existed in the writer's time or to describe the immediate background of events which had occurred within his own knowledge. Equally, there was a strong emphasis on the history of Western relations with the area. Indeed, such subject-matter occasionally swamped all other material even in books which were avowedly general histories. On the other hand, a number of books appeared dealing with the earliest history of the two countries. In the case of China, these seem to have been motivated, at least in part, by a desire to provide historical background for the study of philosophy. In Japan, they sprang largely from an interest in language or political institutions.

In some respects Western writing has been more akin to the historiography of China and Japan than to that of the West itself, especially in interpretation and choice of subject-matter. The reasons for this can be readily conjectured. Writers, because they were living in the Far East, tended to be open to some of the same influences as their Chinese and Japanese contemporaries and to choose the same topics for study: the emphasis on early and on recent history, for example, with a consequent neglect of the periods that lie between, is common to both. A further explanation is to be found in the dependence of the Western historian on the findings of scholars in the country or countries which he studied. Sometimes he worked with Chinese or Japanese collaborators and assistants. Even where this was not so, language difficulties usually forced him to rely on modern works in Chinese or Japanese, rather than on a wide range of original source-materials,[3] with the result that, consciously and unconsciously, he often accepted their viewpoint as well as their factual information. This is evident even in a man like James Murdoch, despite the militantly 'Western' nature of the comments with which he besprinkles his narrative.

These remarks are not intended to imply that all Western writing on Far Eastern history has been worthless. Much of it has been useful, some of it very good indeed; but for the most part it has been valuable as a means of introducing the subject to the Western reader, rather than in the stricter sense of making 'a new contribution to knowledge'. Moreover, it has not served as a channel for the introduction of new techniques of historical writing into China and Japan. These have been derived, as a rule, directly from the West's writing on its own history, from Ranke, Buckle, and Guizot, rather than from Cordier or Murdoch.

When one turns to the twentieth century, it is possible to identify the beginnings of a change in the nature of Western writing, stemming from changes in the political relationships between China, Japan, and the West. The earliest European visitors to the Far East had been much impressed by what they found there. The Jesuits, as Professor Boxer points out, wrote in terms of great admiration of Chinese institutions, in particular, and this was reflected in many of the books which were based on their reports. In the nineteenth century, however, the economic and political dominance of the Western Powers and the evidence of decay in Chinese and Japanese society led to different attitudes. This was the age of catchwords like 'the heathen Chinee' and 'the cycle of Cathay', with their implied contempt for a culture which was static, or decadent, or at least did not exemplify the viorous growth which seemed characteristic of that of Europe. By this estimate, Far Eastern history was not a subject worth serious study. It was left to the men who went there—and few of them

---

[3] It may have been one of the attractions of early history that the original materials were more limited in bulk and therefore more readily used by a Western scholar handicapped by slowness in reading. However, this is offset to some extent by the greater difficulty of the texts themselves.

could avoid being either complacent or patronizing about it. It is this which has been designated the 'imperialist' phase, in historical writing as in international relations.

Towards the end of the century there were two developments which heralded a new approach. First was Europe's discovery—re-discovery, perhaps—of Chinese and Japanese art, which gave an impetus and respectability to historical study of it. Second was the rapid emergence of Japan to a position of international importance and prestige. The next fifty years saw the creation and destruction of a vast Japanese empire, while in China revolution was followed by civil war and again by revolution, bringing in the end a powerful regime apparently as capable of threatening Western interests as Japan had been. The Far East was suddenly important—and far from static. As a consequence, it became increasingly a matter of concern in Western countries and, by natural extension, in Western universities. Since 1930, still more since 1945, there has been a rapid increase in the number of university teachers in Europe and the United States specializing in Chinese and Japanese subjects, including history.

The work produced in this latest period has differed in a number of ways from what went before. The authors no longer live and work in the countries about which they write, though they usually manage to visit them for purposes of study. They are also more conscious than their predecessors of being 'academic', a gain in the quality of detachment which may well be balanced by a loss in that of human experience. The periods studied have shown little change. There is still a general preoccupation with the most recent and the most remote, though there is also a growing appreciation of the need for more detailed investigation of what went between. The dependence on Chinese and Japanese scholarship also remains, but it is collective rather than individual—dependence on a university rather than a teacher, on a library rather than a book. This reflects the most conspicuous change of all, the emphasis on training, technique, research, professional expertise. The characteristic book is the monograph: detailed, critical, and limited in topic. In fact, for the first time Western scholars are subjecting the history of China and Japan, so far as difficulties of language and the accessibility of materials permit, to the same kind of study as has already been applied to that of their own countries. This is clearly to the good. Yet it involves certain dangers. Isolated monographs—and their number must remain comparatively small—the exact purpose and significance of which can only be fully understood in the light of a knowledge of existing literature in Chinese or Japanese, can be appreciated only by the specialist. The more technical their terminology and manner of presentation,.the more this is true. They need to be supplemented, therefore, by a range of more general studies, dealing at reasonable length with particular periods or topics, which would serve to fill the gap between the research monograph at one extreme and the survey history at the other. Such books are not only necessary to the historian for his own reference. They are also of wider importance, for without them there is some risk of pursuing the search for 'new knowledge' to the exclusion of a second task, fulfilled by earlier Western writers on Far Eastern history, namely, that of interpreting the subject to the Western reader.

## 2. THE ANCIENT CHINESE CHRONICLES AND THE GROWTH OF HISTORICAL IDEALS

### P. VAN DER LOON

*University Lecturer in Far Eastern History, University of Cambridge*

Until recently the period of Chinese history which corresponds to the first millenium B.C. has, at least in the West, received far closer attention than the eighteen hundred following years. As a result, Chinese historiography has been judged by the most ancient records or by later comprehensive histories rather than by those later works which deal with one dynasty or part of a dynasty. It was not until the Sung period that historiography reached that admirable standard of accuracy and critical sense the study of which would render justice to the high quality of Chinese historiography taken as a whole. Measured against that standard, the products of the Chou and Han periods are very inferior. Not only is Chinese history before the establishment of the Empire in 221 B.C. less well attested, not only are the sources fewer and often imperfectly preserved, but later historians, in their selection, although not perhaps their presentation, of historical material, while still paying homage to the examples of antiquity, greatly surpassed the ancient chronicles and the earliest so-called Standard Histories.

Yet there can be no doubt that the unbroken tradition of Chinese historiography was founded on aims and ideals set in the ancient period. A study of how these ideals developed seems therefore worthwhile. I shall dispense with a detailed description of the ancient chronicles, but try to show how, as time went on, new elements enriched the recording of the past. Having thus restricted the theme of this paper, I need not dwell upon the origin of historical sources in a wider sense. They can be traced back to c. 1300 B.C., but the link between the earliest materials, consisting of inscriptions on oracle-bones and on bronze, on the one hand, and annalistic records on the other, although often postulated, has not been conclusively proved.

The first comprehensive history of China, the *Shih chi*, or Records of the Historian, written about 100 B.C., has in the chapter devoted to the state of Ch'in the following entry: 'In the thirteenth year (of Duke Wen, corresponding to 753 B.C.) they for the first time appointed scribes, in order to record events. Among the people there were many who were reformed.' It is relevant to note that the annals of the state of Ch'in were among the sources used in the *Shih chi* and that without doubt the entry was based on fact. In 753 B.C. this state was still very young; the appointment of scribes came soon after the establishment of the state. In the older states such scribes certainly existed much before this time. It is impossible exactly to describe the functions of these officials, but their duties comprised divination, the recording of court events and the keeping of archives. Among the records they kept, 'annals' (*chi*) and 'genealogies' (*shih*) are best attested. There are numerous references in Chou-time sources to both categories; and some still existed when the *Shih chi* was written and formed source material for it. At present we have only the famous Spring-and-Autumn Annals (*Ch'un-ch'iu*) of the state of Lu, which cover the period 722–481 B.C., and fragments of the annals of Wei (the Bamboo Annals, *Chu-shu chi-nien*) extending from high antiquity to 298 B.C. The form of these annals was apparently not always the same: those of Wei and Ch'in of which we have direct knowledge recorded the events only under the year as a whole, whereas the annals of Lu are arranged by season and month and often give the exact day as well. In both cases, however, the information provided is extremely terse, summarizing in one sentence each court event, military expedition, eclipse of the sun, etc.

In view of the subsequent development of Chinese historical writing, the question will be asked whether the compilation of these earliest annals had a moral aim, that of frightening the bad and encouraging the good. The additional sentence quoted above, 'Among the people there were many who were reformed', would seem to bear this out. A moment's reflection, however, yields a different answer. This sentence obviously expresses the conviction of a later scribe that the keeping of annals since 753 B.C. had been beneficial, rather than the hope of the first scribe of Ch'in that his activities would have a good effect. That such statements were subsequently added to the original entries is also clear from another example in the same annals: 'In the twentieth year of his reign (678 B.C.), Duke Wu died. He was buried at P'ing-yang in the district of Yung. For the first time human victims were made to follow a dead person in the grave. Those who were thus sacrificed numbered 66 persons.' We know from archaeological evidence that this cannot have been the first time that human sacrifices were made, but that on the contrary they soon became less frequent. Later philosophers rationalized this custom by explaining isolated cases as incipient barbarism instead of survivals of barbarism. Moralizing interpretation of annals, like that of songs,[1] tends to obscure their original function. The task of the scribe was probably of a ritual character, and historiography was closely linked with the fortune of the ruling houses. Their success was thought to depend on the ritual in the ancestral temple and on the regular succession of the seasons, to be registered in the calendar. The sole contribution these annalists made towards the development of historiography is the chronological framework they employed.

[1] See Arthur Waley, *The Book of Songs*, pp. 335–7.

Side by side with the annals there existed an oral tradition. We do not know when the legends, stories and anecdotes deriving from this oral tradition were first written down or by whom. References in ancient works to functionaries who were in charge of this kind of material are vague, and it seems improbable that we owe these writings to the official scribes as such. The richest mine of historical and folkloristic information on the Chou period that has been preserved is the so-called Tso Tradition (*Tso chuan*). It fully displays that genius for evoking a clear image in its intimate detail that has always remained a characteristic of Chinese story-telling. However, it is very difficult to unravel the complications of the composition and transmission of this book. For one thing, it seems certain that the wealth of names and concrete facts in it were partly based on the annals of various Chinese states between the eighth and fifth centuries B.C., thus preserving much in these annals that would otherwise be lost. It is also possible to isolate certain original cycles of stories from the artificial form in which the Tso Tradition has been cast. If we do so, it becomes apparent that there is a bias in favour of some states and that the work certainly has political aims as well. More significantly, we find interwoven with the stories many philosophical ideas, ranging from plain moralizing to cosmological speculation, that by themselves are evidence that this chronicle was not composed before 300 B.C. Historical ideas in the work are therefore hardly dateable, but its character as a combination of exact facts derived from written sources and details based on oral tradition marks a distinct phase in the growth of historical writing.

The long gestation of the sole major chronicle that has survived has made me anticipate the period which has always been considered decisive for the formation of the ideals of Chinese historiography. I mean the period of Confucius and his disciples. The belief that Confucius was responsible for some form—later scholastic opinion is not agreed on what form— of editing of the Spring-and-Autumn Annals of his native state occurs already in the writings of Mencius and was therefore current in the fourth century B.C. It was held that these annals were a book of judgements, in which praise or blame was allotted to those concerned in each historical event. Such moral judgements were not given explicitly but were expressed by a discriminating use of terminology. To give only one example: when a prince was killed, the personal name of the prince would be recorded if he had been bad, but the name of the murderer if *his* action was disapproved of. Not only were moral judgements included, but there was a purpose behind the terminology throughout the Spring-and-Autumn Annals. In this way a textbook of political ethics came into being, which needed a great deal of interpretation if the judgements were to be understood. Confucius, however, provided his disciples with oral explanations, which were later on written down in what were called Traditions, having varying degrees of orthodoxy. There exist three of these Traditions, two of which are almost exclusively concerned with the word-for-word exegesis of the text. The third Tradition was arbitrarily combined with the historical work or works mentioned earlier and became known as the Tso Tradition. The resulting text may thus be said to consist of a compilation of historical writings artificially fitted into the framework of the Spring-and-Autumn Annals of Lu.

All the works supposed to have been edited by Confucius were afterwards declared to be canonical books, and questions of authenticity have been obscured by centuries of quasi-theological controversies. However important for the history of Chinese thought, I believe that for our immediate purpose neither the dating of the Traditions nor even the exact historiographical role played by Confucius is the most important question to concentrate on. It will perhaps be more revealing to place the Spring-and-Autumn Annals and its commentaries against the background of the ideological climate of the period in which they were composed, and to understand the ideologies in their turn from changes in society.

How did the different atmosphere in historical writing come about? Why did moralizing and other rational interpretation replace the original ritual character of historiography? A traditional answer would be to point to the invasions of the barbarians with their lower cultural standards and the resulting need for the Chinese to assess their own heritage. Or one might say that the central authority of the Chou kings with their pre-eminent ritual function was waning, while various regional states increased in importance by swallowing up their neighbours. Attempts to explain the rise and fall of states would then be an evident consequence. Confucius was a member of the lower nobility, which in this time, when larger political units crystallized, lost in influence. Employed as a schoolmaster, he sought his ideal in the past and commended the sages of old, since whose time, he said, degeneracy had set in. He spoke of the real gentleman, who by study and social sense improves himself and his environment, study meaning the ceaseless investigation of the moral lessons taught by the liberal arts: the songs, ritual, music, and the old documents.

Convincing though this explanation seems for the rise of moralistic historiography, it is nevertheless one-sided. In the first place, it was not until three or four generations after Confucius that Mencius connected him with the Spring-and-Autumn Annals, and we do not even know for sure that Mencius referred to the same text as the one we have now. Secondly, the ideal of the correct use of terminology is almost certainly later than Confucius and probably arose in the same milieu as the controversies on the relation between words and reality, a topic so hotly discussed by the Sophists in the fourth century B.C. Much of what has been specifically ascribed to the Confucians was common to the other schools of thought. There is, for example, the large-scale euphemerization of ancient myths, often with a distinct ideological tendency, like the story of the legendary Yao of whom the Mohist school said that he had handed over the empire to Shun, because Shun was more capable than his own son. The attribution of a political idea or reform to ancient sages was a normal expedient used by different philosophical schools to promote what was in reality a novel policy. I do not suggest that the citation of historical precedents, which has always remained a characteristic of Chinese thinking, only began at this time, but it probably became more pregnant than before. In short, the development of historical ideas should not be exclusively linked with any particular school, but is a more general process. If any further example be needed, I may refer to the classificatory way of thinking which was soon to run through all forms and trends of Chinese articulate reasoning, including historical speculation.

I can do no more here than indicate some of the changes that took place in Chinese society from about the sixth century onwards. I have already mentioned the territorial expansion of regional states, which was facilitated by the invention of new military techniques and later on by the introduction of mounted archery. Especially noteworthy is the outward expansion of states on the periphery of the Chinese cultural area into 'barbarian' territory. In contrast to the indirect rule that had in the old states been largely exercised through the nobility, in these conquered marches a direct administration was created with some kind of bureaucracy. The use of iron was spreading and irrigation made a higher yield possible in agriculture. Strict territorial divisions were established, not only for the purpose of defence but also for the efficient levy of land-tax, which became gradually based on produce. If we finally add the emergence of individual land-tenure and the increasing importance of trade, it will be clear how tremendous were the changes which made themselves felt between the sixth and the fourth centuries B.C.

It was during this period that all the well-known philosophical schools arose and flourished. Most of their controversies were concerned with the solution of practical problems of a political or economic nature. That they all compared their own situation with real or fictitious situations in the *past*, rather than with other contemporary societies, may perhaps be partly explained by the relative isolation of the Chinese world. It may be remarked that Confucius stands only at the beginning of the transformation from ritual to rationalized thinking, and that even Mencius, with, for example, his insistence on hereditary emoluments for the ruling class, was a conservative. For our purpose, however, it is not so important to trace the change in historical thinking to one man as to underline, in general, the conscious application from about 400 B.C. of social and moral norms to historiography. Facts were no longer solely presented in their chronological sequence, but brought (and often forced) into a moral system which showed some form of causality and postulated historical laws.

The text and the commentaries of the Spring-and-Autumn Annals have always been kept strictly separate, and this arrangement has had a great influence on later historiography. It was believed that the opinion of the historian should never be mixed up with the facts presented. 'Praise and blame' was therefore usually expressed in an epilogue. But there is no doubt that the moral judgements were often not confined to explicit comments, but also, notwithstanding the claim to let the facts speak for themselves, expressed through the selection of the material. This necessarily biased selection is, of course, not found in Chinese historiography alone, any more than the frequent categorical affirmation or the exclusion of conflicting evidence when there was room for doubt.

I shall pass over the historical sources provided by the collections of fictitious conversations between princes and their ministers. Nor shall I dwell on the interesting theories which were developed by Tung Chung-shu during the second century B.C., as these are concerned with a philosophy of history rather than historiography. But something must be said about the new factor in the recording of history after China had become a centralized and bureaucratic empire. This new factor was a systematic historiography capable of transmitting the experience of statecraft. Ssu-ma T'an and his son Ssu-ma Ch'ien wrote the first general history of China, which is now known as the *Shih chi*, or Records of the Historian.[2] As regards the form of their work, they largely employed existing methods of presenting historical material. Thus the first part of the *Shih chi* comprises annals, going back to the distant past, and recording in a matter-of-fact way a long series of concrete court events. For the earlier periods the authors contented themselves with copying long extracts of ancient works without much change. The dynasty under which they lived themselves is treated much more fully. Here they quoted verbatim a large number of carefully dated documents from the archives, such as imperial edicts and memorials which the ministers had submitted to the throne. Another part of the book contains what were called 'traditions', dealing mostly, but not exclusively, with the lives of statesmen, scholars and other important persons. While these chapters can be conveniently labelled as biographies, a critical examination of their contents confirms that they often consist of material that, because of its anecdotal or romantic character, must have originated from oral tradition.

A third major division of the *Shih chi* does not bear any resemblance to previous historical works. This part gives eight short historical treatises on more or less technical subjects, ranging from music and the calendar to

[2] For a further discussion of the *Shih chi* see the paper by A. F. P. Hulsewé, below, pp. 34–37.

hydrography and political economy. All these subjects were of extreme importance for the functioning of the imperial administration.

Judging the work as a whole, although the author's opinion is occasionally brought out and he displays at times a healthy scepticism, as a rule he simply reproduces his sources in the original wording and does not try to go behind them. After the fall of the Former Han dynasty, Ssu-ma Ch'ien's example was followed by the author of the *Han shu*, or Han Documents (History of the Former Han Dynasty), and after him in all the so-called Standard Histories.[3] The three main divisions are always annals, biographies, and treatises, but more and more the ideal is sought in strict adherence to written, preferably official, sources. Non-verifiable elements, such as speech, are dropped, and the result is an impersonal account, a Government White Paper, compiled with scissors and paste but hardly digested or interpreted.

But all these considerations must give way to a final question: how did Chinese historiography achieve that fullness and accuracy which all scholars who work with these compilations come to admire? Was it due only to Confucian ideology, insisting as it did on truth, albeit not an objective truth? Or is it the bureaucratic function of historiography which we should underline, and could anything but unswerving faithfulness to institutions, to precedents and to the written document be expected from officials? Was there not also some contribution to these ideals from the countless scholars who developed and maintained exacting standards of textual authenticity?

All generalizations on Chinese historiography, including the ones in this paper, are open to grave doubt. Western scholars have perhaps tended too much to make comparisons with European histories written in the nineteenth and twentieth centuries instead of those of earlier times. They have insisted that Chinese historiography does not connect individual facts, but have forgotten the innumerable essays and memorials where a historical perspective is provided. Moreover, when criticizing the tendentious character of a particular work or group of works, we should remember that such loss is usually compensated by the fullness of the material, especially if private historical writing is taken into account. And after all, the tension between 'praise and blame' and objective truth was not confined to China. It is still with us.

[3] The development of the Standard, or Dynastic, Histories is dealt with in some detail in the papers which follow; see especially those by A. F. P. Hulsewé, pp. 31–43, and Yang Lien-sheng, pp. 44–59.

# 3. NOTES ON THE HISTORIOGRAPHY OF THE HAN PERIOD

## A. F. P. HULSEWÉ

*Professor of Chinese Language and Literature, University of Leiden*

In the ups and downs in the history of the Chinese people, the foundation in 221 B.C. of the centralized empire ruled by bureaucratic officials forms one of the sharpest breaks. This event marks the culmination of a long historical process of progressive centralization: from a multitude of city states to many regional states, from many regional states to a small number of territorial states, and from these to the single all-embracing empire. It is also the expression of a social change, from a society sharply divided between a hereditary nobility and their villeins or serfs, to a more complex community consisting of all the emperor's subjects, likewise divided, but by less clearly marked lines, between a progressively more privileged bureaucracy closely connected with the landowning men of property, and the great multitude of farmers, no longer at the beck and call of noble masters but now subject to taxation and to statute-labour duty, both for public works and for military service. In this new society the merchants play their part, although the extent of their influence is as yet not quite clear.

Centralization is the order of the day: the whole newly unified country is administered by officials appointed by the imperial central government; orders from the capital determine the call upon levies of many thousands or tens of thousands. When the pressure from the alien tribes on the North-west frontier becomes too strong, the emperor's commands set huge armies in motion, armies which subdue enormous regions, far beyond the pale of the Chinese community.

The empire was founded when in 221 B.C. the king of the ancient state of Ch'in had finally overcome the last of the other states which had opposed his imperialist designs. When he died in 211 B.C., his weak-minded son was unable to continue his father's strong government and before long the Chinese domain was torn by rebellion and civil strife. From the ensuing struggles the peasant-leader Liu Chi, meanwhile advanced to the status of king of Han, eventually emerged victorious around the beginning of the second century B.C. as the ruler of the reunited realm, the Han empire.

The new 'bourgeois' society under its new political organization engendered among many other things a new way of writing history, an historiography which was in many respects radically different from the earlier forms of chronicling important events.

The following notes are to be considered as brief remarks on the historiography of the Han period (206 B.C.–A.D. 221), centred on the two works concerning the Former Han dynasty, viz., the *Shih chi* (Records of the Historian) and the *Han shu* (History of the Former Han Dynasty), particularly on the latter. On the *Shih chi* a great deal has been said by Edouard Chavannes,[1] whilst the History of the Later Han Dynasty (*Hou Han shu*) has been extensively studied by Hans Bielenstein.[2] Much of what they have said applies *mutatis mutandis* to the *Han shu*. The historiography of the *Han shu* has been treated in a mediocre doctor's thesis by Miss Lo Chen-ying[3] with nothing like the acumen shown by the two scholars mentioned above. And the world is still waiting for Professor Dubs to publish his *Introductory Volume* which is to contain 'a discussion of the texts'[4] and where we may expect the learned author's views on the historiographical principles involved.

On the Chinese side an enormous amount of attention has been paid to the Han histories. However, the majority of the Chinese scholars through the ages have been primarily concerned with problems of textual criticism, philological explanation and antiquarian elucidation, so that they continue up to the present the long line of commentators who have devoted their energies to these texts since the second century of our era. Others, for example the first scholar who pondered the general problems of historiography, the famous Liu Chih-chi (661–721) in his Generalities on History (*Shih-t'ung*),[5] have touched on problems of a more general nature. But until recently one of the very few scholars to write more extensively on these more general and technical problems of the Han histories was Chao I (1727–1814), who did so in the first three chapters of his *Notes on the Twenty-two Histories*.[6]

Of modern studies devoted to the general problem connected with the History of the Former Han, as distinct from textual problems,[7] I only

---

[1] E. Chavannes, *Les mémoires historiques de Se-ma Ts'ien* (Paris, 1898), i. After the presentation of this paper and, in fact, after its final revision, there appeared a full-length book devoted to Ssu-ma Ch'ien and the historiography of the *Shih chi*, viz. B. Watson's *Ssu-ma Ch'ien, Grand Historian of China* (Columbia, U.P., New York, 1958).

[2] H. Bielenstein, *The Restoration of the Han dynasty* (Stockholm, 1953).

[3] Lo Tchen-ying, *Une famille d'historiens et son oeuvre; les formes et les méthodes historiques en Chine* (Lyon, 1931).     [4] H. H. Dubs, *The History of the Former Han Dynasty*, i, p. ix.

[5] See the paper by E. G. Pulleyblank, below, pp. 136–51. In *Oriens Extremus*[4] (1957), pp. 5 ff. and 125 ff., Byongik Koh has published 'Zur Werttheorie in der chinesischen Historiographie auf Grund des *Shih-t'ung* des Liu Chih-chi (661–721)'.

[6] *Nien-erh shih cha-chi*, first printed in 1799; cf. A. Hummel, *Eminent Chinese of the Ch'ing period* (Washington, 1943), p. 75.

[7] For textual problems the fundamental work remains, of course, Wang Hsien-ch'ien's *Han-shu pu-chu* (Additional comments on the *Han shu*) (1900), although it is often useful to refer back to the authorities he quotes. Wang's *magnum opus* was added to on many points of detail by Kanō Naoyoshi in a series of articles in the Kyōto series of the journal *Tōhō gakuhō* and, quite recently, in the extensive (662 pages!) *Han-shu k'uei-kuan*, 'Remarks on the *Han shu*', by Yang Shu-ta (Peking, 1955); and by Shih Chih-mien in *Hsin-ya hüseh-pas* I/2 and II/1 (Hongkong, 1956).

know the verbose and none too pertinent *Studies on the Shih chi and the Han shu* by Cheng Hao-sheng,[8] apart from rather concise references to these texts in a few histories of Chinese historiography.[9]

When we look through the bibliographical chapter of the History of the Former Han Dynasty[10]—the History of the Later Han Dynasty does not include such a chapter—and even more when we consider the long list of unfortunately lost historical works composed during the two Han dynasties and enumerated in the exhaustive bibliographical compilation of Yao Chen-tsung,[11] we cannot but say that the Han period saw a great advance in historical writing. Judging by the texts which have come down to us the advance was not merely in quantity, but also in quality. The primitive forms of rather incoherent annals like the Spring and Autumn Annals (*Ch'un-ch'iu*) of the feudal state of Lu[12] and the so-called Bamboo Annals (*Chu-shu chi-nien*) of the state of Wei,[13] on the one hand, and the disjointed collections of tales and anecdotes like the so-called Tso Tradition (pertaining to the Spring and Autumn Annals),[14] the Discourses of the States, and the Stratagems of the Warring States,[15] on the other, all these have been either vastly improved or replaced by better co-ordinated frames. Moreover, new forms seem to have arisen only in the Han period. As in so many other respects, the unified new empire under the Han also produced new methods in the field of historiography, methods and forms which were to remain standards of emulation for the succeeding two thousand years.

However, of all the historical writings of the Han period which are known to have existed, only a few have come down to us and those which we can consult today are of unequal value and completeness. They are the *Shih chi*, the *Han shu*, the *Han chi* (The Chronicles of the Han Dynasty), and the *Tung-kuan Han-chi* (The Chronicles of the Han from the Eastern Pavilion),

[8] *Shih Han yen-chiu* (Studies on the *Shih chi* and the *Han shu*) (Commercial Press, Shanghai, 1933), 170 pages; this book has the advantage of quoting extensively from a great many authors who gave an incidental opinion on these two works (which will be cited hereafter as *SC* and *HS* respectively).

[9] e.g., Wei Ying-chi, *Chung-kuo shih-hsüeh shih* (Chinese historiography) (Shanghai, Commercial Press; 1941[1], 1947[2]), pp. 80–82; Li Tsung-t'ung, *Chung-kuo shih- hsüeh shih* (Chinese historiography) (Taipeh, Formosa, 1955), pp. 23–35.

[10] *HS* 30.          [11] *Erh-shih-wu shih pu-pien*, ii, 1457, 1564 ff., 2348 ff.

[12] Translated by James Legge, *The Chinese Classics*, vol. v, pts. 1 and 2. For a discussion of the early writings mentioned here, see the paper by P. van der Loon, above, pp. 24–30.

[13] This curious name was given to this text in about A.D. 280 when it was found in a pillaged tomb; see e.g. E. Chavannes, op. cit., i, p. clxxxviii sq., and Kanda Kiichirō, *Shinagaku setsurin* (1933), p. 1039. The present text, translated in the Prolegomena to James Legge's translation of the *Shu-ching*, or Book of Documents (Chinese Classics, vol. iii, pt. 1, pp. 105 sq.), has been corrupted and falsified; Wang Kuo-wei has partly reconstructed the ancient text from early quotations, see his *Ku pen Chu-shu chi-nien chi-chiao*, 'Textual criticism of the ancient Bamboo Annals' in his collected works. Wang's work has again been amended and improved by Fan Hsiang-yung in his *Ku-pen chu-shu chi-nien chi-chiao ting-pu* (Shanghai, 1957).

[14] Translated by J. Legge in *The Chinese Classics*, vol. v, pts. 1 and 2.

[15] Neither the Discourses (*Kuo-yü*) nor the Stratagems (*Chan kuo ts'e*) have been adequately translated.

D

respectively. Among these, the third is but a reorganized extract of the second, whilst of the erstwhile voluminous fourth merely a fraction has survived.[16] So, although the *Han chi* often proves to be a useful instrument to check parallel passages in the *Han shu*, it is the latter which is the most valuable source for the history of the Han period, i.e. of the Former Han. For the Later Han period we have to rely in the main on the *Hou Han shu* which was compiled centuries later—though mainly based on the *Tung-kuan Han-chi*—and which therefore falls outside the scope of the present paper; moreover, it has been extensively analysed in Bielenstein's splendid chapters on the historiographical methods followed in that work, referred to above, chapters which need not be repeated.

Between the two first-mentioned texts the relationship is extremely close, but here we are confronted with a difficulty which has not yet been solved. It amounts to this: the *Han shu* seems to have been largely based on those parts of the *Shih chi* which deal with the Han period and at present the two texts agree more or less perfectly. However, the *Shih chi* is known to have been cut down by imperial order when the *Han shu* had been completed and at a period when it is hardly likely that it was available in many copies to the outside world. It is therefore not impossible that those sections of the *Shih chi*—or at least parts of these—which deal with the Han period were reconstructed from the *Han shu* text at a later date. If this could be proved, the *Shih chi* would lose considerably in value as an independent source of information for Han history.

But this is putting the cart before the horse, nor is this negative facet the most important point in Han period historiography. The salient fact is that we possess two voluminous historical works written in Han times[17] which have been transmitted in quasi-complete form. So it behoves us to consider what it is they bring, in what way they are different from earlier works and in how far they became a standard for later generations.

The name *Shih chi*, 'the Records of the Historian', is the title given towards the end of the second century A.D. to a text known earlier as 'the Writings of His Honour the Grand Astrologer', *T'ai-shih kung shu*. The text consists of 130 chapters on the history of China from the earliest ages to the author's lifetime, i.e. to the beginning of the first century B.C. As a result of additions and interpolations made immediately upon the work's completion and the death of its author, it is—and it presumably will remain—impossible to establish definitely when the original was finished, particularly also because the date of the author's death is unknown. Many studies have been devoted to this complicated problem without a definite

---

[16] Cf. H. Bielenstein, op. cit., pp. 10 ff.

[17] Ku Chieh-kang's punctuated edition (1936) of the *Shih chi* text without commentaries fills three large octavo volumes with a total of 2153 pages, and if the old computations are correct which count 'more than 500,000 words' in the *Shi chi* and 'more than 800,000' in the *Han shu*, the latter work would come to about 3500 pages or five volumes.

solution being reached; for the time being the 'nineties of the first century B.C. remains the best approximation.[18]

The first impetus for the writing of this history came from Ssu-ma T'an, a court astrologer who eventually became Grand Astrologer and who died in 110 B.C., but the actual work was done by his son, Ssu-ma Ch'ien, who in time came to occupy his father's office and who is also known for his active participation in the reform of the calendar in 104 B.C.

Again, as in the case of the History of the Later Han Dynasty, we are fortunate in that a great Western scholar has devoted his attention to the problems connected with the genesis of the *Shih chi*. In the introduction to his translation of the first forty-seven chapters of this work, Edouard Chavannes has extensively discussed Ssu-ma Ch'ien's aims and methods.[19]

In the first place it deserves notice that he—and perhaps his father—seems to have compiled his history as a private person, in spite of the fact that as court astrologer it must also have been his official task to note and to co-ordinate the acts of his ruler and the phenomena of nature, particularly those in the sky, which was the duty of the ancient astrologer-recorders as exemplified by the early annalistic works.[20] This does not mean to say that Ssu-ma Ch'ien held opinions different to those of his age on the scientific and religious tenets concerning the inter-relationship and the interaction between human society and the world of nature; the contents of his annalistic chapters and his inclusion of a special monograph on astrological astronomy and on sacrifices alone prove the contrary. But apart from his implicit belief in the educative function of history he seems to have been moved by a desire to glorify his own age[21]—without, however, becoming uncritical: his disapproving attitude towards the ruler he served, emperor Wu (140–87 B.C.), aroused the censure of his successors.

The *Shih chi* (Records of the Historian) consists of 130 chapters, divided into five groups, or rather four: 1. the imperial annals, 2. the tables, 3. the treatises, 4. the hereditary noble houses of the local rulers of pre-dynastic China, and 5. the Memoirs, mostly consisting of biographies. Of these, the annals and the descriptions of the noble houses possess virtually the same structure, both being annalistic treatments of events. As such these two groups are nothing new, as annalistic works had existed since olden times. Nevertheless, in Ssu-ma Ch'ien's hands they were greatly extended, both in detail and in the scope of the information they provide.

---

[18] For a summary of opinions both on the fate of the text and on the dates, especially by Wang Kuo-wei, see F. Jäger, 'Der heutige Stand der *Shi-ki*-Forschung', in *Asia Major* (1933), ix, 21–37.

[19] E. Chavannes, op. cit., i, pp. xlvii–lxi, cxxxvi–cxcvi.

[20] On this subject cf. the concise and very acceptable survey in Li Tsung-t'ung, *Chung-kuo shih-hsüeh shih* (Chinese historiography) (Taipeh, Formosa, 1955), pp. 1–10. See also H. O. H. Stange, 'Die älteste chinesische Literatur', in *Asia Major*, Neue Folge I (1944), pp. 125 ff.

[21] Cf. E. Chavannes, op. cit., i, p. lix.

This is especially true for the later imperial annals, in which vivid descriptions of events have been inserted, although the absolute veracity of many of these 'conversation-pieces' may be doubted in view of the results of Bielenstein's investigations into similar passages occurring in the History of the Later Han Dynasty.[22]

The tables are in certain respects the systematization of Han period genealogical material in a form known before his time, but in others they are a new venture, particularly the attempt at synchronization of the histories of the former territorial rulers and of the confused events between 206 and 202 B.C. which led to the establishment of the Han dynasty. Completely new, also, seems his chronological list indicating the time in office of important ministers.

The Treatises are, it would seem, an absolute innovation; they deal with important subjects like the calendar, irrigation, economic developments, rites and music, astrology, and sacrifices. They are systematic descriptions, chronologically arranged whenever possible, of institutions which were considered to be of primary importance to the ruler for his right government of the realm. They demonstrate, at their best, the Chinese version of the view that *historia docet*. However, in making this remark we should not forget one circumstance—and this applies to the whole work—which is overlooked too often when the *Shih chi* is considered as the first of the imposing series of 'dynastic histories'. It so happens that the latter were all written *after* the disappearance of the dynasty whose history they relate, whereas the *Shih chi* was written during the heyday of the Han period and devotes more than half of its pages to a description of it.

Finally, the Memoirs or 'organized traditions' represent likewise a new departure in historical writing. In the field of biography the novelistic tale about the deeds of certain prominent persons was evidently not unknown in earlier ages,[23] but here the traditions about famous individuals have been brought together systematically. It is here in particular that Chavannes' remark applies: 'La critique de Se-ma Ts'ien ne s'exerce presque jamais d'une manière apparente. Il ne discute pas la valeur des écrits dont il se sert . . . il cite les témoignages qu'il croit bons; il passe sous silence ceux qu'il condamne.'[24]

Included among the Memoirs are the descriptions of the foreign peoples with most of whom China had entered into closer contact during the lifetime of the author. These descriptions are inserted in a seemingly haphazard fashion, except the one on the Huns, which is made to follow the biography of the famous general Li Kuang.[25]

[22] Bielenstein, op. cit., pp. 50–60; cf. also pp. 73 ff.

[23] Cf. Henri Maspero's famous study, 'Le roman de Sou Ts'in', in *Etudes asiatiques* (1925), ii, 127–41; see also J. B. Hightower, *Topics in Chinese literature* (Cambridge, Mass., 1950), pp. 16 ff.

[24] E. Chavannes, op. cit., i, p. clxxxii.

[25] Li Kuang's biography is found in ch. 109, the description of the Huns is in ch. 110.

Summarizing the above we can say that Ssu-ma Ch'ien produced a history of China extending from antiquity up to his lifetime, presenting his material partly in the traditional form of annals, though with considerable improvements, and partly in completely new forms, organizing the material around a number of institutions (the Treatises) or around persons (the Memoirs).

These forms, old and new, were adopted by Pan Ku when he set himself the task, a century and a half later, of writing the history of the Former Han period, i.e. of the two centuries between the founding of the Heavenly Han late in the third century B.C. and its restoration by a scion of the imperial Liu family after the fall of the 'usurper' Wang Mang in A.D. 23.

In a great many respects the History of the Former Han Dynasty (*Han shu*) has been modelled after the example of the *Shih chi*, both in form and in content, with the obvious difference that Pan Ku, because he confined himself to the history of the Han, disregarded ancient history (with one curious exception: the Table of Ancient and Modern Personalities, in which the 'moderns' are completely lacking and the whole object of which has been seriously criticized by earlier Chinese scholars). Nevertheless, differences are far from lacking, but in order to discuss these we shall have to turn first to the origin of the *Han shu*.

Pan Ku's Autobiographical Account in the *Han shu*, and in particular the Memoirs devoted to him and to his father in the History of the Later Han Dynasty (*Hou Han shu*),[26] contain indications concerning the motives which prompted Pan Piao and his son Pan Ku to undertake this work. The Autobiographical Account is very short on the subject, as Pan Ku merely states that 'during the sixth generation of the Han emperors an astrologer-and-subject—viz., Ssu-ma Ch'ien—recalled their merits and virtues, privately composing imperial annals which he compiled at the end of the 'hundred Kings' and negligently ranked with the Ch'in and Hsiang (Yü, i.e. with the overthrown previous dynasty and the great antagonist of the founder of the Han dynasty). After the *t'ai-ch'u* period (104–101 B.C.) there is a gap, there being no recordings. Therefore (I) have searched among and compiled from the previous records and I have strung together and collected what I have heard and thus I have related 'The Texts of the Han (dynasty)', which take their beginning with the Eminent Founder (206–195 B.C.) and end with (emperor) Hsiao-p'ing (A.D. 1–6) and the execution of Wang Mang (A.D. 23).'[27] In the earlier part of this chapter, when describing the life of his father Pan Piao,[28] he does not mention that the latter had completed a whole book on the history of the Han dynasty! This we only learn from the History of the Later Han, where Pan Piao's interest in history and his historiographical activities are mentioned.[29]

[26] *HS* 100 B. 1a, *Hou Han shu* Mem. 30. 2a–4a, 7b ff. (*Hou Han shu* is hereafter cited as *HHS*).
[27] *HS* 100 B. 1a.     [28] *HS* 100 A. 11b.     [29] *HHS*. Mem. 30. 2a.

There it is said that Pan Piao was dissatisfied with the vulgarity and inadequacy of the accounts of later times which had been attached to the *Shih chi*, and that he 'in continuation collected matters neglected by earlier historians and from aside threaded in different reports, making the Later Traditions (*Hou chuan*) in several tens of chapters'.[30] The text continues immediately with the following words: 'In this connection he pondered over the preceding history (or histories) and criticised and corrected their good points and failures. His Summary Discussion says . . .' and then, after some remarks on Chou time and Early Han historians, there follows a lengthy critical attack on Ssu-ma Ch'ien and his *Shih chi*, winding up by saying that in these Later Fascicles he would carefully examine these points.[31] On his father's death in A.D. 54 'Pan Ku considered that his father (Pan) Piao's continuation of the former history (or histories) was not detailed enough; thereupon he hoarded his energy and sharpened his thought, wishing to complete his work'. Then follows the well-known story how Pan Ku was denounced for 'privately refashioning the history of the state',[32] how emperor Ming had him released from prison due to Pan Ku's brother's intercession and also because the emperor had been impressed by the work, which the local officials had confiscated and forwarded to the throne. Once liberated, he was given an appointment and ordered to work on a history of the founding of the *Later* Han! Only then 'the emperor thereupon again made him finish and complete the documents he had formerly written'. The next phrases have been taken bodily from the Autobiographical Account in the *Han shu*. Neither of these two texts warrant the absolute conviction that Pan Ku copied the *Shih chi*; it is of course quite possible, and in fact rather likely, that the *Shih chi* is to be included among the 'previous records' which Pan Ku says that he investigated, but in themselves these two passages cannot be said to provide clear proof for this assumption.[33] As to Pan Piao's efforts, Pan Ku does not mention them in the place where we would expect him to do so, i.e. in the Autobiographical Account; nevertheless, as Chinese scholars have pointed out, the text of the *Han shu* contains a few passages indicating plainly that they are due to Pan Piao.[34] Ying Shao in the second century even believed that the Annals of the emperors Yüan and Ch'eng—covering the period between 48 and 8 B.C.—were wholly the work of Pan Piao.[35]

If, in view of the above, the share of Ssu-ma Ch'ien's *Shih chi* and of Pan

---

[30] Liu Chih-chi (661–721) in his *Shih-t'ung* reports that this work consisted of 65 fascicles (*Shih-t'ung t'ung-shih* 12. 7b in the Ssu-pu pei-yao ed.).

[31] *HHS* Mem. 30A. 4a; see Chavannes, op. cit., i, pp. ccxix ff.          [32] *HHS* Mem. 30A. 7b.

[33] The great attack on the authenticity of the present *Shih chi* was made by Ts'ui Shu in his *Shih-chi t'an yüan* (Investigation into the origins of the *Shih-chi*), 1918.

[34] The eulogies appended to the annals of the emperors Yüan and Ch'eng in the *Han shu*, chapters 9 and 10, and to the biographical chapters 73, 84, and 98.

[35] This opinion of Ying Shao's is quoted in the commentary to the eulogy of chapter 9.

Piao's *Hou chuan* in Pan Ku's work cannot be assessed, we do know, on the contrary, that certain chapters are not due to his pen, at least not completely. For the History of the Later Han Dynasty reports in the biography of Pan Ku's learned sister Pan Chao[36] that on Pan Ku's death in A.D. 92 'its (viz., the *Han shu's*) eight tables and the treatise on astronomy had not yet attained their completion' and that therefore Pan Chao was ordered by emperor Ho to proceed to the imperial archives 'to follow in his traces and complete it'. In this she was some time later assisted by Ma Hsü, elder brother of the well-known Confucian and commentator of the classics, Ma Jung.[37] As indicated by several scholars,[38] the compilation of the *Han shu* proves to have extended over a period of nearly eighty years, calculating from the earliest beginnings by Pan Piao some time after A.D. 36 to the death of Pan Chao some time between 110 and 121.[39] It seems that, unlike the *Shih chi*, the History of the Former Han Dynasty did not suffer any considerable accretions, although the remarks by Dubs concerning the possibility that at a later time an inauspicious solar eclipse was inserted in the annals of the emperor Kao ought to make us careful.[40] On the other hand, it ought to be noted that Hsün Yüeh's *Han chi* (Chronicles of the Han Dynasty), which is supposed to be based virtually exclusively on the Former Han history (*Han shu*), does contain a few matters not in the text of the present *Han shu*, nor in the version of this text as used by Ssu-ma Kuang in the eleventh century.[41] Here the possibility exists at least that these passages were lost during the manuscript transmission of the *Han shu*. In a few places the *Han shu* text is palpably defective, as for example in the annals of emperor Yüan.[42]

I believe that one may say with justification, that Ssu-ma Ch'ien undertook the compilation of the Records of the Historian (*Shih chi*) as a private venture and that Pan Piao did the same when he wrote his Later Traditions (*Hou chuan*). Again, when Pan Ku started to revise and to extend his father's work, he did so as a private person, otherwise he could never have been accused of 'privately (or "stealthily") rewriting the history of the state' (*ssu kai-tso kuo-shih*). But when afterwards he continued to work in this field, he did so at the express desire of emperor Ming, having already gained formal access to the palace archives in connection with the compilation—together with others—of the annals of the founder of the Later Han and of the Memoirs concerning the other figures who had played a

---

[36] *HHS* Mem. 74. 3b.

[37] *HHS* Mem. 74. 3b and *Hou Han chi* 19. 3b (*SPTK* ed.) by Yüan Hung (320–76).

[38] Most recently by Li Tsung-t'ung, op. cit., p. 32.

[39] Cf. N. L. Swann, *Pan Chao, foremost woman scholar of China*, p. 50.

[40] See H. H. Dubs, *History of the Former Han Dynasty*, i, 166.

[41] Li Tsung t'ung, op. cit., p. 34, refers to Ma Tuan-lin, *Wen-hsien t'ung-k'ao*, ch. 193 s.v. *Han chi* (Commercial Press edition, p. 1631, col. 1).

[42] *HS* 9. 7b. Dubs, op. cit., ii, 319. I suggest that the words 'chancellor Yü Ting-kuo' have been omitted there.

role in the latter's victorious struggle for power during the 'twenties and 'thirties of the first century A.D. In other words, when he wrote the *Han shu*, or History of the Han Dynasty (i.e. the Former Han), he did so with official sanction, and in this respect it is curious, to say the least, to see how he applies the word *ssu*, 'privately, stealthily', which had been used against him personally, to the historiographical activities of Ssu-ma Ch'ien.[43] I can find no explanation for the use of the word *ch'en* '(Your) servant', in the few passages from Pan Piao's work and referring to the latter personally; Pan Ku does not use this term to designate his forbears who served the Former Han emperors, nor does he use it when referring to his father or to himself. Are we perhaps to assume that Pan Piao wrote his Later Traditions under official orders and that this is one of the reasons why his son Pan Ku could be accused of rewriting the history *of the State?*

However, it is difficult, I believe, to distill from the text of the *Han shu* any particular attempt to glorify the rulers of the Former Han Dynasty. When necessary, their faults are discussed and even in conspicuous places, like the 'eulogies' which summarize the chapters to which they are appended and which contain the author's judgement. Emperor Wu, for example, is praised in the 'eulogy' of the annals of his reign for his efforts for the glorification of Confucianism, but his military exploits which led to the establishment of Chinese power in Central Asia and in the as yet non-sinicized South are not mentioned. However, the 'eulogy' to the next chapter speaks about the meritorious efforts of the next emperor's regent and chief helper, Huo Kuang, to restore the national economy after 'the evil after-effects of (emperor) Hsiao-wu's extravagance, when after the military campaigns (the empire) within the four seas was emptied and wasted and the population had been diminished by one half'.[44] Another instance of criticism of the Han emperors is the detailed treatment of emperor Ch'eng's weak-minded acquiescence in the murder of his infant sons, in the chapter devoted to the empresses and concubines of the various emperors.[45]

A final example of Pan Ku's critical attitude towards the Han emperors is especially noteworthy. The rulers of the Later Han were not descendants of the last ruling emperor, but could only claim descent from emperor Ching, who had died in 140 B.C.[46] Now the two darkest blots on the history of their forbear are frankly mentioned, i.e. both his weakness in permitting the execution of his staunchest supporter Ch'ao Ts'o in 154 B.C. and his jealous hatred of his later chancellor Chou Ya-fu whom he caused to be executed.[47] Even if Pan Ku did nothing but copy these passages from the

---

[43] *HS* 100B. 1a.          [44] The eulogies at the end of ch. 6 and 7.

[45] *HS* 97B. 11a ff.; see M. C. Wilbur, *Slavery in China during the Former Han Dynasty* (Anthropological Series, Field Museum of Natural History, vol. 34; 1943), pp. 424 ff.

[46] Cf. Bielenstein, op. cit., pp. 96 and 98.

[47] *HS* 49. 24a and 40.28a; cf. Dubs, op. cit., i, 294 and 297–9 (cf. p. 326).

*Shih chi* into his own text, he showed an independent attitude towards the ruling family by doing so. I do not think that this frankness affords any reason to call Pan Ku's work 'subsidized history' and to say that the *Han shu* is only 'an Imperial political history of the reigning family', as Sargent has done.[48] Dubs was quite right when he refuted this view.[49]

As to the material which Ssu-ma Ch'ien and Pan Ku used for their respective histories, it has been pointed out often enough how, beside existing historical works,[50] they used all kinds of official documents.[51] The texts demonstrate clearly how these authors inserted imperial edicts and official memorials into their works, quoting them at great length. Some biographies consist even for the greater part of memorials handed in by the subject of the biography. Another type of official material consists of reports,[52] and in some cases we get the inescapable impression that the authors extract or quote verbally from the documents of a lawsuit.[53]

Another important source of information were the Diaries of Activity and Repose (*ch'i chü chu*). The first mention of this type of diary which covered 'the activities of the emperors, not only their public ones, but also their private activities within the palace',[54] occurs in the History of the Later Han concerning the diary for emperor Ming,[55] and the modern scholar Chu Hsi-tsu has therefore tried to prove that it was the earliest one ever composed.[56] This has, however, been rightly refuted[57] and it seems clear that the *chu-chi*, the 'recorded notes'[58] of the court-astrologers are the forerunners of the diaries. These 'notes' are mentioned a number of times in the chapter on portents in the *Han shu*, and this serves to prove quite another point, demonstrating again the close relationship between the astrologer and the historian, who has to keep a record of the signs in the heavens—and on earth, for that matter—and the actions of the ruler. The same attitude of mind is exemplified by the whole chapter on the portents and by the care with which the portentous phenomena are recorded in the annals. The firm belief of the age in the 'signs' provided by nature is also abundantly shown by the many imperial decrees and official memorials occasioned by the occurrence of portentous events.

A very different type of material used by the authors of both the *Shih chi*

[48] C. Sargent, 'Subsidised History', in *Far Eastern Quarterly* (1944), iii, 143.

[49] H. H. Dubs, 'The reliability of Chinese Histories', in *Far Eastern Quarterly* (1946) vi.

[50] *Inter alia* by Chavannes, op. cit., i, pp. clvii ff., and Bielenstein, op. cit., p. 15.

[51] Cf. Chavannes, op. cit., i, p. clvii, Bielenstein, op. cit., p. 44, and the remarks on p. 38 above.

[52] *HS* 63.20a and 97B. 11a; cf. Wilbur, op. cit., pp. 370 ff. and 424 ff.

[53] See my *Remnants of Han law*, p. 71, and cf. *HS* 44.9a ff., *SC* 118.6b ff., and *HS* 60.12b; cf. Wilbur, op. cit., pp. 366–7.

[54] Bielenstein, op. cit., p. 22. Concerning such Diaries in general, see the paper by W. Franke, below, pp. 61–66.

[55] *HHS* Ann. 10A. 9a–b.          [56] In two articles in *Kuo-hsüeh chi-k'an*, ii (1930).

[57] By Bielenstein, op. cit., p. 22, and Li Tsung-t'ung, *Chung-kuo shih-hsüeh shih* (Chinese historiography), p. 74.

[58] Treated extensively in Chu Hsi-tsu's first article, *Kuo-hsüeh chi-k'an* (1930), ii, 397 sq.

and the *Han shu* is found in the biographies of many of the men who helped the founder of the Han dynasty to gain the throne.[59] This material is a copy—or, in view of the scarcity of details concerning persons and places, an abstract—of the registers which noted the valiant deeds of these men. They contain a careful numerical account of the places captured and the enemy officers and men killed or made prisoner. The existence of such records is known for later times;[60] here they must have served to demonstrate the reasons why the leaders concerned were enfeoffed as marquises by emperor Kao.

Although on the whole the *Shih chi* and the *Han shu* are very similar— if we confine ourselves to those parts of the *Shih chi* which are concerned with the history of the Han period—both in structure and in content, there are several differences.

In the first place the *Han shu* annals start with those of the founder of the dynasty and the description of the life of his great antagonist Hsiang Yü has been confined to a Memoir, whilst in the *Shih chi* this chapter is inserted as Annals before the Annals of the first Han emperor. But more important than this purely formal difference is the extension of the number of Treatises in the *Han shu*; these have been increased *inter alia* by a treatise on penal legislation, introduced by some brief remarks on the army,[61] a treatise on portents, and a treatise on the administrative divisions of the empire, based on the census of A.D. 5. Ssu-ma Ch'ien's table of important events[62] has been radically changed and reorganized so as to form an additional treatise, containing a description of the official organization and a chronological list of the occupants of the most important ministries.[63]

A difference in outlook between the two historians is shown by the introductions and 'eulogies' to several chapters, even when the factual contents of the chapters are practically identical.[64] Here Ssu-ma Ch'ien proves to be more of a political realist with an interest in economics, whilst Pan Ku appears to be rather a strict Confucianist.[65] This is quite in agree-

[59] e.g. in *Han shu* 39 (biographies of Hsiao Ho, Ts'ao Shen), 40 (Chou Po), 41 (Fan K'uai), etc. The information—apart from occurring in the corresponding *Shih chi* chapters—is also briefly summarized in the Tables, where the reason for the enfeoffment is given. This point is also noted by Chao I, *Nien-erh shih cha-chi* 1.11b–12a.

[60] Cf. *HS* 50.8a (*SC* 102.7b); it is clear from the text itself and it is again explained by Ju Shun (fl. 221–65) by means of a quotation from Han time 'Military Law', that the merits of the officers and soldiers were noted and reported to higher authority.

[61] See my *Remnants of Han Law*, pp. 314–16 and 321–9.

[62] *SC* 22, Chavannes, op. cit., iii, 186–200.                                       [63] *HS* 19.

[64] e.g. *SC* 122–*HS* 90 and *SC* 129–*HS* 91, containing biographies of 'harsh officials' and 'rich men' respectively; a translation of *SC* 129–*HS* 91 is to be found in N. L. Swann, *Food and Money in Ancient China* (Princeton, 1950), pp. 413–64. An easy comparison is made possible by Sung Hsi, *Cheng-shih lun-tsan* (Judgements and Eulogies in the Official Histories) (Taipeh, Formosa, 1954), i, 1–94.

[65] See Utsunomiya Kiyokichi, *Kan-dai shakai keizai-shi kenkyū* (Studies on the social and economic history of the Han-period) (Tokyo, 1955), pp. 168–202.

ment with the different periods in which they lived: the one in the time of growth and development under emperor Wu (140–87 B.C.), the other during the period of containment and formalization and of incipient socio-economic decay, towards the end of the first century A.D.

The great innovation which took place in the later Han period is the appointment of scholars to the post of historian; the work of the ancient court astrologers who at the same time were chroniclers comes to an end, or rather the elaboration of their data is transferred to a group of outsiders. And so we see Pan Ku, who as a private person had started to write a history of the Former Han dynasty, ordered to take part in the compilation of annals and biographical memoirs of the founders of the Later Han.[66] This work was continued, with occasional lapses, up to about A.D. 177; it came to be called the *Tung-kuan Han chi* (The Chronicles of the Han from the Eastern Pavilion), after the building in which the historians were put to work. As stated above, only part of this voluminous work remains.[67] However this may be, the appointment of Pan Ku and others as official historians in the first century A.D. forms the starting point of a development which was to lead eventually to the establishment of a Bureau of Historiography in T'ang times in the seventh century.[68]

Another development took place in a different sphere: the emergence, or rather renewal, of the purely annalistic history. Annals had been the form of the first truly historical works and Ssu-ma Ch'ien had also retained annals as an integral *part* of his *Shih chi*. However, presumably as the result of the desire for abridged and synoptical works,[69] the large *Han shu* was condensed by Hsün Yüeh (148–209). In this condensation the material was also rearranged according to a continuous annalistic frame, in which information from the biographies and treatises was inserted. The example of these *Han chi* or Chronicles of the Han Dynasty was frequently followed later, the finest example of this type of extended annals being the Comprehensive Mirror for Aid in Government (*Tzu-chih t'ung-chien*) by the splendid historian and statesman, Ssu-ma Kuang (1019–86).[70] The *Han chi* itself has come down to us virtually undamaged; it is a useful tool to check statements in the *Shih chi* and the *Han shu*, and as far as I am aware no special study has been devoted to it.

[66] See above, p. 38.      [67] See Bielenstein, op. cit., pp. 10 sq.

[68] For the stages of this development see e.g. Wei Ying-chi, *Chung-kuo shih- hsüeh shih* (Chinese historiography) (1947), pp. 31–60; for the establishment of the T'ang bureau see R. des Rotours, *Le traité des fonctionnaires et le traité de l'armée* (Leiden, 1947), i, 199 ff.

[69] See Li Kuei-yao, 'Shih-chi chüeh-i' ('Doubts concerning the Shih-chi'), in *Tsing-hua Journal* (1927), iv, 1176.

[70] See Otto Franke, 'Das *Tse tschi t'ung kien* und das *T'ung-kien kang-mu*, ihr Wesen, ihr Verhältnis zu einander und ihr Quellenwert', in *Sitzungsberichte der Preussischen Akademie der Wissenschaften*, Phil. hist. Klasse (1930), iv, and Achilles Fang, *The Chronicle of the Three Kingdoms* (Cambridge, Mass., 1952), i, Introduction. The work of Ssu-ma Kuang is discussed in the paper by E. G. Pulleyblank, below, pp. 151–66.

# 4. THE ORGANIZATION OF CHINESE OFFICIAL HISTORIOGRAPHY: PRINCIPLES AND METHODS OF THE STANDARD HISTORIES FROM THE T'ANG THROUGH THE MING DYNASTY

## LIEN-SHENG YANG

*Professor of Far Eastern Languages, Harvard University*

### 1. *Introduction*

Of the twenty-four Standard Histories (*cheng-shih*) recognized under the Ch'ing dynasty, the last nine cover the period from the T'ang dynasty through the Ming.[1] There are two histories (the Old and the New) for the T'ang dynasty, two (the Old and the New) for the Five Dynasties period which followed the T'ang, and one for each of the later dynasties, the Sung, Liao, Chin, Yüan, and Ming. Taken together as a series, these nine histories represent official records of the dynasties which governed the whole or a considerable part of China at one time or another between 618 and 1644. A study of the principles and methods of these Standard Histories, therefore, should throw some light on the organization of Chinese official historiography.

These nine histories share a few distinct features. First, each Standard History was written, or rather compiled, under the following dynasty or a later one. This seems natural enough and may appear to merit no comment. The significance of this fact, however, lies in the continuous employment of the practice: the compilation of an official history for a defunct dynasty confers or at least implies recognition, and these nine histories cover at least as many alien dynasties as Chinese.[2]

Another feature is that the compilation normally was done by a Commission or Bureau, that is, a group of historians officially assigned to the task; the sole exception is the New History of the Five Dynasties (*Hsin Wu-tai-shih* or *Wu-tai shih-chih*), which was the private work of a single historian, Ou-yang Hsiu. These, then, were imperially sponsored undertakings, in contrast to the Standard Histories covering the pre-T'ang period, which were usually begun as a private or semi-private project of an individual or of a family of historians. Official compilations were pre-

[1] For bibliographical references, see 'Notes on the Dynastic Histories', by Professor L. C. Goodrich, included in Lien-sheng Yang, *Topics in Chinese History* (1951), pp. 32–38.

[2] Liao, Chin, Yüan, vs. T'ang, Sung, Ming. The middle three of the Five Dynasties were also non-Chinese.

dominant from the T'ang dynasty on; the change has been generally accepted as a landmark in the history of Chinese historiography.[3]

A third feature is that, like the earlier Standard Histories, these nine works are all in the so-called annal-biography (*chi-chuan*) style or, to be more analytical, the composite style:[4] a history in this style normally contains two to four standard divisions which are mutually complementary. The composite annal-biography style is often contrasted with the chronicle (*pien-nien*) style, which has been used for many important and influential historical works but never for the Standard Histories. The association of composite style and Standard History was so firm that as early as T'ang times the former term was used to define the latter.[5]

These characteristics will lead us to an investigation into the principles and methods used in the nine Standard Histories under discussion, but before entering upon this discussion I wish to make a few remarks on the sources of the histories, especially the official records preserved from the defunct dynasty. Principally these were series of short-term histories covering the successive reigns within the dynasty, one series tending to be used as partial source for another. The primary official record was the *ch'i-chü chu*, the Diary of Activity and Repose, of each emperor, kept by official historians especially assigned to this task. The successive Diaries of Activity and Repose, supplemented by other materials, chief among which were the *Shih-cheng chi* or Records of Current Government prepared by the chief ministers or their subordinates, served as the major source for compilation of the *Jih-li* or Daily Records; these in turn became the primary source of the *Shih-lu* or Veritable Records of the emperor. Both the Daily Records and the Veritable Records were in the chronicle style; biographies of important persons, however, were supplied in the entries which recorded their deaths.[6] Biographical information could be drawn both from official and from private sources, such as an epitaph or a family history. On the basis of these works and other government compilations such as the Collected Statutes known as *hui-yao* or *hui-tien* (under the Yüan dynasty, the *Ching-shih ta-tien*), certain dynasties had their official historians compile a *Kuo-shih*, State or National History, which was in the composite style.

[3] Cf. Naitō Torajirō, *Shina shigaku shi* (1949), pp. 236–40; Chin Yü-fu, *Chung-kuo shih-hsüeh shih* (1944), pp. 73–74, 97–98.

[4] I am indebted to Dr. C. S. Gardner for the term 'composite style'.

[5] This association, however, was not made by the T'ang historiographer Liu Chih-chi, whose concept of *cheng-shih* covered a much wider range of histories in both annal-biography and chronicle styles. For a discussion of the term *cheng-shih*, see Liu I-cheng, *Kuo-shih yao-i* (1948), pp. 50–51. The historiographical work of Liu Chih-chi is discussed in the paper by E. G. Pulleyblank, below, pp. 136–51.

Such biographies are not found in the Veritable Records of the Manchu (Ch'ing) dynasty, which probably constitute the only exception to the rule. On this point, see the paper by D. C. Twitchett, below, pp. 100–1. The Veritable Records, especially those of the Ming dynasty, are discussed more fully in the paper by W. Franke, below, pp. 60–77.

These official records, from the Diaries of Activity and Repose to the National History in process under a still reigning dynasty, were often extremely voluminous. Normally only an official copy and a secondary copy (*fu-pen*) were made, and they were not to be consulted by any unauthorized person. In other words, such records constituted secret national archives.[7] The only major exception was the Collected Statutes, which were printed and made available to officials and scholars. It should be borne in mind that these official accounts, especially the Veritable Records, might go through revision once, twice, or even three or four times before transmission to the following dynasty. Invariably such revision would be by imperial order, and nearly always for political reasons. The unrevised version was not, however, to be destroyed as long as the dynasty lasted, because there was always a chance that an emperor might order still another revision, which would call for consultation of all the earlier versions. This was especially the case with the Veritable Records of the Sung emperors.

Such official records, when available, made it so easy for the Commissions to compile the Standard History of a past dynasty that in some cases the work was completed in an amazingly short time. It took only two years and a half to put together official histories of the Sung, Liao, and Chin dynasties, ordered in the Yüan period; and after the fall of the Mongol régime itself, only about a year was required for compilation and revision of the Yüan History. Most of the other Standard Histories took somewhat longer, the most drawn out being the preparation of the Ming History, which occupied several decades (1678–1739). All the Standard Histories, however, drew heavily on the official records preserved from the dynasty in question. This debt is generally acknowledged by the official historians themselves; far from discrediting them, in keeping with Chinese tradition this kind of copying would enhance their standing as dependable recorders.[8]

## 2. *Principles*

Among the principles embodied in the Standard Histories, most important are those involving the questions Why and How. In answer to the question Why, the two main principles are that of continuity of the record and that of transmission of useful reference.

The principle of continuity received special emphasis whenever the dynasty under which an official history was being prepared was of a different ethnic group from that of the defunct dynasty. In a memorial recommending a historical project to cover the preceding Liao and Chin

---

[7] For example, see rules concerning secrecy of the Veritable Records and the National History in Sung times as given in *Sung hui-yao kao* 70, 'Chih-kuan' 18.66a and 77b.

[8] C. S. Gardner, *Chinese Traditional Historiography* (1938), pp. 69–70.

dynasties, the Yüan scholar Wang O (who became a *chin-shih* at the head of the list in 1224, under the Chin dynasty) wrote: 'Since antiquity, a state can be destroyed but not its history. In general the history of the preceding dynasty has been compiled by its successor, because judgment and evaluation can become impartial only with later generations.' The date of this memorial probably was 1261. Wang O's statement was quoted by contemporary and later writers and became rather famous.[9] However, he was not the first to express such a principle. About ten years before, Liu Ping-chung had already proposed to the Mongol authorities the compilation of a history of the Chin dynasty. 'That a state is destroyed but its history preserved,' he said, 'has been the normal way since antiquity.'[10] In the year 1276, after the fall of the Southern Sung capital Lin-an, the Yüan commander Tung Wen-ping expressed the following opinion: 'A state can be extinguished, but not its history. The sixteen rulers of the Sung dynasty reigned over the empire for more than three hundred years. Records of their official historians are kept in their Bureau of History. These should be collected for institutional purposes.' Thereupon more than fifty books of Sung history and similar records were procured and sent to the Yüan History Office.[11]

Early in the year 1369 Ming emperor T'ai-tsu, founder of the dynasty, told the court: 'Recently, upon the fall of the Yüan capital (Peking), we obtained the Veritable Records of its thirteen rulers. Although their state has been destroyed, its events should be recorded. Moreover, history marks success and failure and offers lessons of encouragement or warning, so that it should not be abandoned.'[12] Sixteen Yüan scholars, then in retirement, were thereupon invited to take part in the projected compilation. When the completed work was presented to the throne later in the same year, these words of T'ai-tsu were paraphrased in a memorial by the chief minister Li Shan-chang, who directed the project.

Upon the eventual fall of the Ming dynasty, the Manchu emperor ordered the compilation of a history for it—merely following a well-established tradition, almost a matter of course.

Obviously, the maintenance of this principle of continuity was of considerable propaganda value for the dynasty that was in the saddle. In the first place, the official preparation of a history of the fallen dynasty could be interpreted as showing generosity on the part of the new rulers. Most important, it would help to establish a predecessor-successor relationship and confer on the new dynasty the so-called *cheng-t'ung* or orthodox line of succession. Such justification was particularly desirable because the major dynasties in the period came to power mostly by conquest or revolution. Earlier dynasties, from the Ts'ao Wei through the T'ang, had for the most

[9] Wang Hui, *Ch'iu-chien hsien-sheng ta-ch'üan wen-chi* (*SPTK* edition), 82.11a–b, 93.3b.
[10] *Yüan shih* 156.6b.     [11] *Yüan shih* 157.5a.     [12] *Ming shih-lu*, Hung-wu 37.1a–b.

part followed the practice of arranging abdication, which made the transition at least nominally legitimate and apparently peaceful.

Another propaganda value of compiling a history of the preceding dynasty lay in its attraction to the literati who had remained loyal to it. The compilation of a good history was considered the duty of such a loyalist, because it was just about the last service he could render to the dynasty, much as a filial son would feel in writing a biography of his late father. It was therefore difficult for loyalist scholars to decline an invitation to participate in the historical project, and their acceptance often broke the ice for further collaboration with the new dynasty. Determined loyalists, however, recognized the danger and drew their own lines of limitation. The Yüan scholar Yang Wei-chen, when asked to assist in compilation of the Yüan History under the Ming, wrote a poem in which he compared himself to an old widow who declined to remarry in spite of poverty.[13] The Ming emperor permitted him to retire after rendering some assistance. When the Manchus invited scholars to participate in the Ming History project, the famous Ming loyalist Huang Tsung-hsi, who was recognized as the leading authority on Ming history, refused to go to Peking to take active part, though he agreed to consultation by correspondence. His friend Wan Ssu-t'ung, another leading historian, went to Peking, but only as personal adviser to the Director of the Commission. Although the work Wan did was practically that of editor-in-chief, he never accepted any official position or salary from the Ch'ing government. He spent altogether twenty-four years in Peking, leaving his family in the South.[14] In 1679, when Wan was about to leave for Peking, Huang Tsung-hsi wrote three poems to see him off.[15] These expressed Huang's concern over the Ming History but at the same time indicated his unwillingness to participate in the compilation; they also praised Wan's erudition and at the same time warned him against further collaboration. Huang also alluded to the famous 'old widow' poem of Yang Wei-chen.

Another principle related to the question Why is that of useful reference. The concept of using history as a mirror and a source of lessons goes back to antiquity, and this utilitarian view remained throughout the centuries, as evidenced in the words of Ming T'ai-tsu quoted above. In the case of the nine Standard Histories, with which we are primarily concerned here,

[13] The poem entitled 'Lao k'o-fu yao' (another version gives the title as 'Chen-hsien-fu yao') can be found in *Yüan shih hsüan*, first series, section H, 51a–b. Also see *Ming shih*, 285.3a.

[14] Chang Hsü, 'Wan Chi-yeh yü *Ming shih*', *Tung-fang tsa-chih* 33.14 (1936), 83–90.

[15] *Nan-lei shih-li* (*SPPY* edition) 2.15b–16a. Another poem written by Huang for Wan ten years later, in 1689, is found in *Nan-lei shih-li* 4.12b of the *SPPY* edition but not in the *SPTK* edition, which includes only the three earlier poems. Huang Yün-mei, in his article on the compilation of the Ming History in *Chin-ling hsüeh-pao* 1.2 (1931), 330–1, has correctly quoted the poems separately. Li Chin-hua, in his *Ming-shih tsuan-hsiu k'ao* (1933), pp. 46–47, where he makes use of Huang Yün-mei's study, fails to locate the fourth poem and erroneously puts the four poems together as if they were written at the same time.

this principle seems to be slightly secondary. In imperial China these later official histories were chiefly used for occasional reference, rather than as common reading material. For purposes of education the Classics, of course, were considered by far the most important subject, and when it came to history, most people would turn to the Comprehensive Mirror for Aid in Government (*Tzu-chih t'ung-chien*) by Ssu-ma Kuang, the Outlines and Details based on the Comprehensive Mirror (*T'ung-chien kang-mu*) by Chu Hsi, or the various later compilations which tend to combine abridgements of the works by Ssu-ma Kuang and Chu Hsi.[16] In general these works are in the chronicle style, are relatively compact in terms of the period of coverage, and are quite abundant with comments and moralizations by the historians, other scholars, and the emperor himself. Shortened histories of this type were available in inexpensive editions and were widely used by students. Demand for editions of the last nine Standard Histories came mainly from scholars specializing in history. In the case of the New T'ang History and of the New History of the Five Dynasties, these were read also for the literary style of the author, Ou-yang Hsiu; their circulation probably was exceeded, among the Standard Histories, only by the first four—*Shih chi, Han shu, Hou Han shu*, and *San-kuo chih*[17]—which also enjoyed literary as well as historiographic reputation. Still, the relative popularity of Ou-yang Hsiu's two histories does not alter the general picture. This situation, not generally realized by modern students of Chinese history, is of considerable significance: the small circulation of the later official histories undoubtedly limited their influence in general education.

Relative to the question How, most significant are two pairs of conflicting principles: the principle of truthful recording versus that of ethical partiality or appropriate concealment (*hui*), and the principle of praise and blame (*pao-pien*) versus that of collective judgement.

The principle of truthful recording is traceable to antiquity. In the ancient chronicle, Tso Tradition (*Tso chuan*), for instance, we read about several respectable historians in the period of the Spring and Autumn Annals who were loyal to their duty of truthful recording to the point of sacrificing their lives.[18] The concept was clear that in keeping the record, the historian was responsible to all-under-heaven and to future generations. When the famous Records of the Historian (*Shih chi*) of Ssu-ma Ch'ien was praised by other Han scholars, as a 'veritable record', it was just about the highest compliment a historian could expect.[19] The independence of the

[16] For example, the *Kang-chien ho-tsuan* and the *Yü-p'i T'ung-chien chi-lan* in various editions. On the Comprehensive Mirror, see the paper by E. G. Pulleyblank, below, pp. 151–66.

[17] i.e. the Records of the Historian, History of the Former Han Dynasty, History of the Later Han Dynasty, and History of the Three Kingdoms. On the first three of these, see the paper by A. F. P. Hulsewé, above pp. 31–43.

[18] James Legge, *The Ch'un Ts'ew, with the Tso Chuen*, pp. 290, 514–15.

[19] Bernard S. Solomon, *The Veritable Record of the T'ang Emperor Shun-tsung* (1955), p. xxiii.

historian has been considered so glorious a tradition that a modern Chinese scholar has proudly called it *shih-ch'üan*, 'the authority of history'.[20] To relieve the imperial recorder from anxiety, there was a remarkable tradition requiring the emperor not to read the Diaries of Activity and Repose of his own reign, a tradition referred to several times in the T'ang and Sung periods.[21] Even under the alien Liao dynasty there were two Ch'i-tan historians who refused an imperial request to present the Diaries. The Liao emperor, however, would not tolerate such disobedience, but gave each of the two recorders two hundred lashes and discharged them.[22]

Unfortunately, violation of the independence of the historian came not only from alien rulers but from Chinese emperors as well. The emperor might refrain from reading the Diaries of his own reign, but other historical materials prepared for the ruling house from its own records or those of the defunct dynasty were invariably presented to the Throne for approval. The presentation was often made with considerable ceremony, and the approval would lead to handsome rewards for members of the Commission.[23] The requirement of imperial approval, together with the tradition that the Supervisor of the Commission or the Director of the project was almost always a chief minister, made political influences on the result inevitable. In theory it was possible for the chief minister to represent vested interests other than those of the emperor, and it is conceivable that he might even serve as a checking force against imperial power. Clear illustrations of such cases, however, are not easily found in history. With the increase of despotism in Ming and Ch'ing times, imperial influence on historical compilation became even more prominent. Imperial instructions were issued from time to time to the Historical Commission, sometimes at the request of the Supervisor.[24] These instructions, covering specific as well as general points, were probably welcomed by obedient compilers because their own responsibilities could thereby be reduced.[25]

[20] For a discussion of rules of compilation for the Veritable Records, see Liu I-cheng's article 'Shu shih-lu li' in *Kuo-shih-kuan kaun-k'an* 2.1 (1949), 1–9.

[21] Chao I, *Nien-erh-shih cha-chi* (1902 edition), 19.2b. On *ch'i-chü chu*, see Gardner's *Chinese Traditional Historiography*, pp. 88–89.

[22] Karl A. Wittfogel and Fêng Chia-shêng, *History of Chinese Society, Liao (907–1125)* (1949), pp. 468, 503, 610. On page 610, middle of column 1, *for* beating an official *read* beating two officials.

[23] For example, see *Sung hui-yao kao* 70, 'Chih-kuan' 18. 62a–b and 64a–66b for ceremonies connected with presentation of Veritable Records and the awards. According to Hung Mai, who was an official historiographer under the Southern Sung, members of the Bureau of History tended to space out evenly in time the presentations of such official compilation, sometimes by withholding work already accomplished, in order to maximize the rewards.

[24] Altogether 17 decrees are collected in Liu Ch'eng-kan, *Ming-shih li-an*, chapter 1, and also in Li Chin-hua, *Ming-shih tsuan-hsiu k'ao*, pp. 7–9.

[25] Huang Yün-mei, *Chin-ling hsüeh-pao* 1.2 (1931), 349–60. On this general subject, see also the paper by W. Franke on the Veritable Records of the Ming dynasty, below, pp. 60–77.

Directly contradictory to the principle of truthful recording, that of appropriate concealment is also traceable to antiquity. According to the Kung-yang and Ku-liang Commentaries to the Spring and Autumn Annals, Confucius in writing or editing these annals of the state of Lu purposely concealed disgrace or mistakes of three categories of persons: the honourable (*tsun-che*), the closely related (*ch'in che*), and the worthy (*hsien-che*), effecting such concealment by euphemism or by sheer omission.[26] Whether or not the tradition was actually derived from any practice or teaching of Confucius himself, it clearly reflects the Confucian ethical system, which is marked by a certain amount of particularism. These three categories of persons, together with five others, are also mentioned in penal codes where they are the basis of the Eight Deliberations (*pa-i*), as the eight kinds of people who should receive special consideration from the courts.[27]

Doubtless realizing the incompatibility of the principles of truthful recording and of appropriate concealment, official historians mentioned the former much more frequently than the latter. Instances of concealment, nevertheless, are beyond enumeration. They can be found in all stages of the historiographical process—in the National Histories (*kuo-shih*) compiled by the preceding dynasty for itself, and in the various official and private records on which the National Histories were based. In theory, concealment at one level could be corrected in another, since the 'honourable', the 'closely related', and the 'worthy' might not include the same persons in the eyes of different generations. But by intent or otherwise, old concealments were usually perpetuated and new ones perpetrated. The eighteenth-century scholar Chao I devoted several articles to examples of concealment in Standard Histories, a practice of which he was generally critical.[28] With regard to the Ming History, however, which was completed in his own time, he made no remarks on concealment—which fact in itself may be considered an illustration of the principle of concealment. Although the Ming History has been accepted as a work of high quality prepared with great care, it would be remarkable indeed if it should be found to depart utterly from this well-established tradition. Scholars of the Republican era, for instance, have criticized the Ming History for its glaring omission of references to early contacts with the Manchus.[29] On the other hand, in the view of the Ch'ing compilers it was fitting to avoid bringing out the fact that the Manchus were formerly subjects of Ming China.

[26] *Ch'un-ch'iu Kung-yang chu-su* (*Shih-san ching chu-su* ed.) 6.5a–.6a–b, 11.7a, 12.6b, 23. 5b–6a; *Ch'un-ch'iu Ku-liang chu-su* (*Shih-san ching chu-su* ed.) 8.7a, 14.1b. See also Burton Watson, *Ssu-ma Ch'ien, Grand Historian of China* (1958), pp. 94–97.

[27] See Jean Escarra, *Le Droit chinois* (1936), pp. 15, 255.

[28] See his *Nien-erh-shih cha-chi* 6.42b–44a, 9.22b–23a, 13.1a–b, 21.21b–22b, 27.28b–29a, 29.48b–29a.

[29] Meng Sen, *Ming tai shih* (1957), pp. 1–3; Chin Yü-fu, *Chung-kuo shih-hsüeh shih*, p. 119. For criticisms of the Ming Veritable Records, see the paper by Wolfgang Franke, below, pp. 66–73.

Chao I also pointed out an interesting method of concealment out of regard for the worthy, apparently employed in the New T'ang History and in the Ming History:[30] to wit, in the case of a man who was all but perfect in morality, his minor shortcomings were not mentioned in his biography but in other places. Chao I praised this principle as one of generosity and recommended it as a general rule in historical writing. Its justification was based on the assumption that this was an honest attempt on the part of the historian to encourage morality while respecting the principle of truthful record.

In matters of judgement, the principle of praise and blame again is traceable to antiquity. According to tradition it was carried out by the manner and emphasis of the record as well as by personal comment of the historian. Most famous of all is the allegedly implicit comment through choice of words, as illustrated in the saying with regard to the Spring and Autumn Annals, 'A word of praise is comparable to bestowing a princely robe; a word of blame is as severe as capital punishment.'[31] Such implicit comment can of course become explicit when the conventions are explained, although commentators may differ in their interpretation of the hidden reasons for praise or blame.[32] Explicit comments are occasionally found in Tso's Commentary (*Tso chuan*) to the Spring and Autumn Annals, introduced by the words *chün-tzu yüeh*, 'the gentleman says . . .' which may indicate a personal opinion of the historian or may purport the view of a class of gentlemen. In the Standard Histories, comments at the end of a chapter normally begin with such words as *shih-ch'en yüeh*, 'the official historian says', *tsan-yüeh*, 'the eulogy reads', or *lun-yüeh*, 'the discussion reads'; such comments are generally called *lun-tsan*, 'discussion' or 'eulogy'.

Application of the principle of praise and blame naturally constituted part of the 'authority of history', which was maintained to some extent from Han times on. But conscious application of the principle was made systematically and on a large scale only by the Sung scholars, notably by Ou-yang Hsiu in his New History of the Five Dynasties and Chu Hsi in his Outlines and Details based on the Comprehensive Mirror. Ou-yang Hsiu often explained his principles of recording in the *lun* or discussion at the end of a chapter and also in the so-called Commentaries of Hsü Wu-tang, which were actually from Ou-yang's own hand.[33] Chu Hsi's rules of recording probably constituted the most detailed system ever devised for a Chinese history. It contains, for instance, as many as fifteen articles about different methods and wording for recording 'attacks and campaigns' (*cheng-fa*), with nearly ninety points of detail.

[30] Chao I, *Nien-erh-shih cha-chi* 31.2b.

[31] K'ung Ying-ta, in the preface to his *Ch'un-ch'iu cheng-i*. Cf. the paper by P. van der Loon, above, pp. 24–30.

[32] For example, see Legge's *The Ch'un Ts'ew* . . ., Prolegomena, pp. 38–49, 58–59, 70–71.

[33] Liu I-cheng, *Kuo-shih yao-i*, pp. 177–80.

This characteristic of Sung historiography was in harmony with the spirit of Neo-Confucianism as a new and creative intellectual movement, because, like the bold assertion of a new school as orthodox bearer of the truth, it required the same kind of confidence and imagination to write history in a style that would appear to be suitable only from the hand of a sage.

In Yüan, Ming, and Ch'ing times, however, orthodox Neo-Confucianism became a restrictive force rather than a source of intellectual fermentation. Its ethics became more and more authoritarian in nature. In historiography, this is reflected in the comment (*lun-tsan*) sections of Standard Histories, which tend to offer more eulogy than discussion. In the case of the Yüan History, the whole *lun-tsan* category was simply omitted. In general, judgement by the individual was no longer considered desirable; instead, he was encouraged to represent the 'impartial' concensus of his time. In the imperial decree issued to the Commission for the Ming History, the K'ang-hsi emperor emphasized that the official history of the defunct dynasty should be written with such fairness as to win the people's hearts;[34] and that, for this reason, no petty criticism of the Ming emperors should be allowed. A similar caution was furnished in the following words by a compiler of· the Ming History:[35] '(Official) compilation of history is different from private writing. In private writing it is permissible to use one's personal views as a basis. When a history is compiled by imperial order, it is necessary to integrate the collective, impartial judgment of the empire. One should not trust his own opinion and indulge in criticism.'

The influence of this attitude towards history is considerable. As aptly remarked by Charles S. Gardner in his *Chinese Traditional Historiography*, 'an assumption of complete objectivity underlies the whole Chinese conception of historical writing'. It may be added that with the introduction of the principle of collective judgement under the more recent dynasties, the interpretation of 'objectivity' became still more rigid.

### 3. *Methods*

If the above discussion of principles tends to reduce the modern student's confidence and interest in the Chinese official histories, the unfavourable impression can perhaps be balanced somewhat by a review of their methods. These may be divided into two parts: methods concerning commissioned compilation, and methods concerning the annal-biography style.

Commissioned compilation of histories was introduced on a large scale in the first reigns of the T'ang dynasty. Almost immediately, weaknesses of this method of historiography were discovered. In his famous Generalities on History (*Shih-t'ung*), Liu Chih-chi bitterly attacked the system, of which he himself was a victim. In a letter addressed to Hsiao Chih-chung,

---

[34] Liu Ch'eng-kan, *Ming-shih li-an*, 1.2a–8b.  [35] Ibid., 4.3a.

Supervisor of the National History, and other officials, Liu listed five things which had made it impossible for him to work effectively as an official historiographer.[36] First, in old times historical recording normally had been the responsibility of an individual historian. The Historical Commission, on the other hand, arranged participation by many members, who tended to look to each other and hesitated to record anything on their own initiative. Secondly, the two Han dynasties had facilitated compilation by putting government records at the disposal of their historians; the T'ang practice was for the official historiographers to collect their own materials, and this was found entirely unsatisfactory. Thirdly, the T'ang History Office was located within the area of the Imperial palaces, presumably to prevent undue contacts with the outside. Actually, most of the imperial historiographers completely ignored the rule of secrecy and were quite ready to broadcast any new praise or criticism that had just been put on record. If the entries concerned influential persons, how could the official recorder not hesitate? Fourthly, the ancient historians had enjoyed independent authority in the conduct of their own work; under the later system of ministerial supervision, Supervisor A might order strict truthful recording while Supervisor B might emphasize concealment of faults and mistakes. Whose orders was the recorder to follow? Fifthly, the overall supervision ought to include the laying down of general principles of compilation and the assignment and distribution of tasks; failure in these functions permitted evasion of duties and waste of time. Obviously, most of the five handicaps Liu Chih-chi mentioned arose from the assignment of the compilation to a commission. The last may be considered the key to the whole problem.

After an official history was completed, its critics often found points of inconsistency, duplication, inaccuracy, and omission. The famous Corrections of Errors in the New T'ang History (*Hsin T'ang shu chiu-miu*) by Wu Chen included as many as twenty categories of such points. Errors might reflect poor scholarship, but on the other hand they might well result from hasty completion, or from a lack of co-ordination within the commission. It became more and more obvious that to surmount these difficulties it was a necessary procedure to lay down general policies and rules governing the compilation and to see that they were carried out.

In the cases of the Histories of the Liao, Chin, and Sung Dynasties, and of the Yüan History, the primary goal seems to have been a quick finish, and this was achieved. Instrumental was the fact that the rules of compilation for these histories were few and clear-cut. Another helpful factor was effective, if sometimes high-handed, supervision and editing. According

---

[36] This letter is included in the last chapter of the *Shih-t'ung*. Professor William Hung is engaged in ·riting an extended monograph on Liu Chih-chi and his *Generalit..s on History*, with important portions of this work translated and annotated. Cf. ..ne paper by E. G. Pulleyblank, below, pp. 136–51.

to his biography, when Ou-yang Hsüan was appointed Director of the Liao, Chin, and Sung Histories he laid down general rules of compilation to be observed. Some of the official historiographers, we are told, were quarrelsome, ostentatious, or biased; Ou-yang Hsüan did not bother to argue with them, and simply made changes in their draft chapters when these were presented to him for editing.[37] Among the four or five other Directors at least one, Chang Ch'i-yen, did much the same thing.[38] This authoritarian method apparently contributed to the quick completion of the work. Similarly, when the Yüan History was compiled in 1369 major decisions about the rules were made by one authority, the Emperor himself.[39] Among other things he stipulated that the language need not be in traditional literary style, so that as much of the History as possible could be based on Yüan documents, many of which were written in the vernacular.

Coming down to the Ming History, accumulated experience paid off not in speed but in the quality of the work. Among the well-thought-out rules of compilation proposed by various scholars for its compilation we may cite for example the eight principles succinctly phrased by P'an Lei:[40]

(1) Materials should be collected on a broad basis.
(2) Investigation of documents should be made critically.
(3) Responsibilities should be distributed.
(4) Rules of recording should be standardized.
(5) Recording should be truthful.
(6) Discussions should be impartial.
(7) Time should be allowed generously.
(8) The History should not be voluminous.

The last two principles were more important than they might appear at first, because without them it would be difficult to give effect to the others. These rules of P'an Lei's, together with proposals and discussions of other scholars, were found so useful that in the early years of the Republic a member of the Commission for the Ch'ing History collected and published them in eight volumes, the first being devoted to words on the subject by the emperors Shun-chih, K'ang-hsi, Yung-cheng, and Ch'ien-lung.[41]

Progress in methods of handling the annal-biographical style was made partly through recognition of the mutually complementary nature of the different major divisions of the composite history. Another mode of progress was the creation—or the discontinuation—of chapters of special nature, such innovations being in some cases the result of the most careful

---

[37] *Yüan shih* 182.5b.                              [38] *Yüan shih* 182.3a.
[39] Sun Ch'eng-tse, *Ch'un-ming meng-yü lu* (Ku-hsiang-chai edition) 13.9b–10a.
[40] Liu Ch'eng-kan, *Ming-shih li-an*, 4.6a–9a.
[41] This is the *Ming-shih li-an*, referred to above. The preface is dated 1915.

deliberation. The model of the composite style was set up in Han times in Ssu-ma Ch'ien's Records of the Historian (*Shih chi*) and Pan Ku's History of the Former Han Dynasty (*Han shu*), each of which were divided into four major sections: annals, tables, treatises, and biographies. This model, however, was not immediately followed in its entirety. Of the thirteen Standard Histories covering the period from Later Han to Sui, only six contain treatises and not a single one contains tables. In fact, tables are criticized rather severely in Liu Chih-chi's Generalities on History (*Shih-t'ung*), at least in one chapter (the criticism is somewhat modified in another chapter).[42]

The situation becomes different with the more recent nine histories, of which all include treatises and seven (or eight, if one counts the chapter 'Chih-fang k'ao' in the New History of the Five Dynasties as a table rather than as a treatise on geography) contain tables. Thus the fourfold composite style eventually became firmly established. The value of tables, however, was recognized only gradually; they are lacking in the Old T'ang History and in both the Old and New Histories of the Five Dynasties. One obvious advantage of tables is their economy of space; for instance, persons of relatively little importance can be listed at the appropriate points in tables.

In the introductory section to this paper it has been pointed out that the National Histories (*kuo-shih*) prepared by the reigning dynasties for their own realm were also in the composite style. In the Sung period, until the last decades of the Southern Sung, the National History contained only three major divisions: annals, treatises, and biographies. In the year 1203 the Emperor approved a proposal to include chronological tables in the National History.[43] In the proposal it was stated that as a rule the National Histories for the various reigning dynasties did not contain tables. However, an entry in the encyclopaedia *Yü-hai* says that in the fourth year of Cheng-ho (1114) the *Cheng-shih* or Standard History for Emperor Che-tsung (not, of course, a Standard History in the now usual sense of the term) was presented to the throne, including imperial annals, tables, treatises, biographies, and tables of contents, in all 210 chapters.[44] If this is correct, the fourfold composite style was already in use in the National History towards the end of the Northern Sung period.

As for addition or omission of chapters of special nature, we may take as illustrations the several tables on imperial visits, tribes and lineages, and dependent states which appear in the Liao History, and the table on diplomatic envoys in the Chin History.[45] Special chapters in the Ming

---

[42] *Shih-t'ung t'ung-shih* 3.1a–2b, 16.12b–13b.    [43] *Sung hui-yao kao* 70, 'Chih-kuan' 18.60a–b.
[44] *Yü-hai* (1883 edition) 46.50b–51a; also given in *Sung hui-yao kao* 70, 'Chih-kuan' 18.77a, where the year of presentation, however, is given (probably through error) as the fourth year of Hsüan-ho (1122).    [45] Chao I, *Nien-erh-shih cha-chi* 27.21b.

History include a table of the Seven Ministers (the Presidents of the Six Boards and the Censors of the Left and Right), the biographies of the *t'u-ssu*, 'local chieftains', and the biographies of the *liu-k'ou*, 'wandering bandits'.[46]

The special chapters devoted to *tao-hsüeh*, 'orthodox Confucian thinkers', in the Sung History are of special interest. This category, separate from the traditional category *ju-lin*, 'Confucian scholars' (the use of which was also continued in the Sung History), was set up to honour the thinkers of the Ch'eng-Chu school, including predecessors and continuers of this line in Sung times. It seems likely that the new category was created for the Sung National History in the last part of the Southern Sung period when the teachings of Chu Hsi became firmly established as orthodox, and it was adopted by the Yüan historiographers in preparing the Sung History. In the early reigns of the Ch'ing dynasty there was a hot debate about whether there should be a similar chapter entitled 'Tao-hsüeh' in the Ming History. Among those against its inclusion were the eminent scholars Huang Tsung-hsi and Chu I-tsun, who succeeded in leading the Commission to a negative decision. Both these men were very erudite in their classical learning, but it is understandable that neither Huang, who was mainly a historian, nor Chu, chiefly a literary man, would have much appetite for the petty doctrinal differences maintained by one Neo-Confucian school against another. It may be added that, as an impartial historian, Huang Tsung-hsi in his intellectual history of the Ming period (*Ming-ju hsüeh-an*, 'Fan-li' or 'Rules of compilation') did make the observation that hair-splitting distinctions constituted a remarkable feature of Ming thinking.

## 4. *Conclusion*

From the above discussion one may arrive at the conclusion that as far as basic principles are concerned, Chinese official historiography reached its apex in the Sung period and from that time on became stagnant, in the sense of becoming more restricted and less creative in its productions. On the other hand, in methods and techniques it appears to have continued to progress, reaching its apex only in early Ch'ing times from this point of view. It should not be ignored, however, that Sung historiography, in addition to its notable concern with principles, also broke new ground in matters of method of technique. For instance, in revised versions of Veritable Records and National Histories coloured inks were used to indicate different texts—for example, original text in black, deleted text in yellow, and additional text in red.[47] (True, the use of coloured inks to

[46] These special chapters in the Ming History are commended by Huang Yün-mei in *Chin-ling hsüeh-pao* 1.2 (1931), 336–7. Cf. O. B. van der Sprenkel, 'High Officials of the Ming. A Note on the Ch'i Ch'ing Nien Piao of the Ming History', *BSOAS* 14.1 (1948), 87–114.

[47] *Yü-hai* 48.11b, 15b–16a.

differentiate texts is a practice traceable to much earlier times; one might mention T'ao Hung-ching, who in A.D. 500 used this device in his edition of the famous medical treatise *Pen-ts'ao*.[48] But not until the Sung period was it used effectively in historiography.)

The great Sung historian Ssu-ma Kuang, whose work has been so highly admired and influential, introduced two features in his Comprehensive Mirror for Aid in Government (*Tzu-chih t'ung-chien*). One was the 'long draft' (*ch'ang-pien*), the very comprehensive and detailed version prepared as basis for producing his published history chiefly through editing, rewriting, and condensation. The other was the 'examination of divergencies' (*k'ao-i*), that is, critical notes in which disparate versions of the same event are given and the ground of choice indicated. The long draft of the Comprehensive Mirror, known to be several times longer than the final product, unfortunately is no longer preserved. The 'Examination of Divergencies', however, is included in the commentaries in several editions of the work, and is also available as a separate book. Impressed by its critical nature, Dr. Gardner has found it appropriate to modify his generalization that 'Unfortunately, Chinese practice does not require reproduction of rejected alternatives.'[49] This qualification could also be based on the histories written in different coloured inks described above. In addition, it should be pointed out that inclusion of divergent versions and indication of reasons for those chosen or rejected were already features of the long draft of the Comprehensive Mirror, as clearly shown in instructions given by Ssu-ma Kuang to an associate compiler, Fan Tsu-yü, who was responsible for the T'ang section of the long draft.[50] Further evidence is the fact that in the *Hsü Tzu-chih t'ung chien ch'ang-pien* or Long Draft of a Continuation of the Comprehensive Mirror for Aid in Government, by Li Tao, which was said to be a close imitation of Ssu-ma Kuang's original, we also find occasional notes examining divergencies.

A worthy successor of Ssu-ma Kuang, Li Tao also deserves the credit of introducing a filing-cabinet system. According to a Southern Sung source,[51] to keep in order materials for his Draft Continuation (which has become an indispensable work on Sung history) Li Tao had made for him ten wooden chests, each containing twenty drawers. Each drawer was marked with a year of the sexagenary cycle, so that the two hundred drawers represented two hundred successive years. Information on the

---

[48] For a bibliographical study of the T'ao Hung-ching edition of the *Pen-ts'ao*, see K. Watanabe in *Tōyōgakuhō*, Kyoto, vol. 20 (1951).    [49] *Chinese Traditional Historiography*, p. 65.

[50] Detailed instructions are given in a letter from Ssu-ma Kuang to Fan Tsu-yü (*tzu* Meng-te) found in *Ssu-ma Wen-cheng kung ch'uan-chia chi* (1741 edition), 63.7b–10a, but not in the *SPTK* or *SPPY* edition of Ssu-ma Kuang's collected works. Some doubt has been cast on the authenticity of this and certain other letters ostensibly from Ssu-ma Kuang, but the contents of this letter seem to speak for its being genuine. See Chang Hsü, *T'ung-chien hsüeh* (1948), pp. 37–44 and 126–7. The letter is translated by E. G. Pulleyblank, below, pp. 160–4.

[51] Chou Mi, *Kuei-hsin tsa-chih, hou-chi* (in *Chin-tai mi-shu*, ts'e 168), 25b.

events of each year was filed in the appropriate drawer and eventually put in strict chronological order by month and day. This neat arrangement was considered an excellent model of operation.

Such innovations enhance further the importance of Sung historiography,[52] which naturally formed a part of the renowned cultural achievements of the Sung Dynasty. After all, the writing of history, official or otherwise, is but one kind of intellectual activity and can hardly dissociate itself from other kinds related to it. To produce a truly great history requires not only erudition and critical scholarship, but also considerable literary talent and, not least of all, a philosophical outlook. In any time when most intellectual activities are at a low ebb, it is indeed exceptional if historiography alone can be creative.

[52] For a general discussion of the development of historiography in the Sung period, see Naitō Torajirō, *Shina shigaku shi*, pp. 241–320.

# 5. THE VERITABLE RECORDS OF THE MING DYNASTY
## (1368–1644)

WOLFGANG FRANKE

*Professor, Director of the Seminar in the Language
and Culture of China, Hamburg University*

## TABLE OF EMPERORS OF THE MING DYNASTY

| Posthumous Name | Style | Date of reign |
|---|---|---|
| T'ai-tsu | Hung-wu | 1368–1398 |
| Hui-ti | Chien-wen | 1399–1402 |
| T'ai-tsung (Ch'eng-tsu)[1] | Yung-lo | 1403–1424 |
| Jen-tsung | Hung-hsi | 1425 |
| Hsüan-tsung | Hsüan-te | 1426–1435 |
| Ying-tsung | Cheng-t'ung | 1436–1449 |
| Ching-ti | Ching-t'ai | 1450–1456 |
| Ying-tsung | T'ien-shun | 1457–1464 |
| Hsien-tsung | Ch'eng-hua | 1465–1487 |
| Hsiao-tsung | Hung-chih | 1488–1505 |
| Wu-tsung | Cheng-te | 1506–1521 |
| Shih-tsung | Chia-ching | 1522–1566 |
| Mu-tsung | Lung-ch'ing | 1567–1572 |
| Shen-tsung | Wan-li | 1573–1619 |
| Kuang-tsung | T'ai-ch'ang | 1620 |
| Hsi-tsung | T'ien-ch'i | 1621–1627 |
| Ssu-tsung | Ch'ung-chen | 1628–1643 |

1. *The sources of the Veritable Records*

From the most ancient times down to our own century, historiography has been carried on in China carefully and without interruption. After printing became widely used, from the tenth century on, printed texts—in particular those of historical importance—became more and more voluminous. For the period up to about the end of the first millennium A.D., the official dynastic histories (Standard Histories: *cheng-shih*) are the chief sources for historical research, but for subsequent periods primary sources become increasingly available. It is particularly for the period after the downfall of Mongol rule in the middle of the fourteenth century that the existence of primary historical sources considerably diminishes the importance of the official histories which are only a secondary source.

[1] The posthumous name T'ai-tsung was changed in 1538 to Ch'eng-tsu.

Although the official history of the Ming dynasty (*Ming shih*) is considered as one of the most carefully compiled and thus most reliable works of this kind, it often provides only incomplete information. Furthermore, the rather condensed, short texts of the official history are often very difficult to understand completely. Any serious historical research worker has therefore to consult basic sources of earlier date, which exist in great number for the Ming dynasty. The so-called Veritable Records (*Shih-lu*) are one of the most important sources of this kind.[2] But even the Veritable Records are not the most primary source. Usually they were compiled by a special committee after the death of each emperor and were based on the collection of all kinds of documents written during his reign. The most important of these documents were the so-called Diaries of Activity and Repose (*Ch'i-chü-chu*), which record in detail all governmental actions of the emperor and all matters dealt with in official imperial audiences. Special officials were responsible for the recording of these Diaries, which represent the basic original product of Chinese official historiography, whereas the Veritable Records and the Standard History represent respectively the second and the third stage of historiographical work.[3]

Chinese historical writing traces the institution of the Diaries of Activity and Repose to as far back as the Chou dynasty (*c.* 1050–249 B.C.). The earliest reference to the function of the officials who in later periods recorded them is often taken to be a passage in the Book of Rites (*Li-chi*): 'His (i.e. the emperor's) actions were written down by the Recorder of the Left, and his utterances by the Recorder of the Right.'[4] For example, Ku Yen-wu (1613–82) writes: 'As to the rulers of old times, the Recorder of the Left wrote down the actions and the Recorder of the Right wrote down the utterances in order to prevent mistakes and to make known to the kings of later times [the actions and utterances of their predecessors]. The origin of the office of recording the Diaries of Activity and Repose reaches back very far.'[5] This statement shows clearly the traditional Chinese conception of the task of the historiographer: to restrain the ruler from irresponsible or criminal actions by recording minutely and imperturbably all affairs coming to his knowledge. For no ruler would care to have actions of this kind transmitted to future generations. Thus in China, from ancient times down to the end of the traditional political system, the historiographer always had a position of particular importance. Not a few

[2] A detailed list of the existing Veritable Records for thirteen emperors of the Ming Dynasty with the years covered and the dates of compilation is given in the present writer's 'Preliminary Notes on the Important Chinese Literary Sources for the History of the Ming Dynasty (1368–1644)', pp. 11–14, and still more complete in 'Zur Kompilation und Überlieferung der Ming Shih-lu', pp. 12–31. For bibliographical data on these and other works referred to in footnotes, see the list given at the end of this article.

[3] For a general account of the process by which the Standard Histories were compiled, see the article by Yang Lien-sheng, above, pp. 44–59.

[4] Legge, *Sacred Books of the East*, xxviii, 2.     [5] *Jih-chih-lu* 18, ed. Wan-yu-wen-k'u, vi, 102.

of them had to pay for the conscientious carrying out of their duties with heavy penalties or even with death at the hands of an enraged and vengeful emperor. The same concept is to be found in the monograph on literature in the Standard History of the Sui dynasty (reigning 589–618), the earliest definition of the character of the Diaries available: 'The Diaries of Activity and Repose record utterances and actions, movement and repose of the ruler. In the Commentary to the Spring and Autumn Annals it is said: "The rulers movements must be written down. If there be written what was not according to the laws, how will descendants regard it?"[6] The recorder of the Interior mentioned in the Rites of the Chou Dynasty (*Chou-li*) was in charge of the king's orders, and afterwards wrote an additional copy which he safeguarded. That is the office [of the recorder of the Diaries].'[7]

The earliest Diaries of Activity and Repose known in historical writing by this name (*Ch'i-chü-chu*) date from the time of the emperor Ming of the later Han period (A.D. 58–75). Later Diaries are mentioned for nearly all periods of Chinese history. The earliest and only record of this kind prior to the end of the sixteenth century still preserved deals with the 357 days preceding the official accession to the throne of the first emperor of the T'ang Dynasty, Li Yüan, in A.D. 618. It comprises three chapters with the title 'Diary of Activity and Repose of the foundation of the Great T'ang Dynasty' (*Ta-T'ang ch'uang-ye ch'i-chü-chu*) and was later reprinted several times. It is not surprising that with the exception of this work all other Diaries dated earlier than the later Ming period have been lost, since they were not written for publication. Generally they had to be burnt after the completion of the Veritable Records for the reign of one emperor, and it was only by chance that some specimens evaded destruction.

Following the pattern of previous dynasties, Chu Yüan-chang, the founder of the Ming Dynasty, put some higher officials in charge of the recording of such Diaries as early as in 1364, four years before his ascent to the throne. Later these officials were chosen from the Hanlin Academy, re-established in 1367. The National History Office (*Kuo-shih kuan*), formerly an independent governmental institution, became attached to the Hanlin Academy in the Ming period. The importance of the function of the recorders is stressed by the fact that they were not subordinate secretaries, but were always chosen from the middle ranks of higher officials. Thus they had not only succeeded in the highest academic examination but had also been selected for the Hanlin Academy, having achieved particular distinction in this examination. No details are known about the work of the recorders of the Diaries of Activity and Repose during the first years of the new dynasty, for nothing of their records has

[6] Chuang-kung 23rd year. Legge, *Chinese Classics*, V, 1, p. 102.
[7] *Sui shu*, Ching-chi chih 33, 10b (ed. Wu-chou t'ung-wen). *Chou-li* 26, 31; Biot II, 118.

been preserved. Their functions soon ceased altogether, though the date and the reason for this discontinuation are unknown. Probably the post was abolished during the Hung-wu period, perhaps even later, during Chien-wen or Yung-lo, but certainly not later than 1421, the date of the removal of the capital from Nanking to Peking. In the following period, down to the beginning of Wan-li (1573), no such Diaries were kept. A number of memorials presented by leading officials asked for the re-establishment of regular recording of them, showing that the lack of this practice was widely felt. Although the emperor consented several times to propositions of this kind, nothing was done. Only after a long memorial by the leading statesman of the time, Chang Chü-cheng, was it definitely decided to resume the practice in Wan-li 3 (1575).

The very detailed memorial of Chang Chü-cheng,[8] like most other proposals of this kind, refers to the institution of the Recorder of the Left and the Recorder of the Right in ancient times and stresses that without the Diaries of Activity and Repose no reliable source for the compilation of the Veritable Records would be available, as was the case with the compilation of the Veritable Records by Chang Chü-cheng for the two preceding emperors. Chang Chü-cheng proposed that the duties of the officials in charge of historiographical recording be laid down in accordance with the following eight points:

1. Among the different duties of the historiographical officials, the recording of the Diaries of Activity and Repose was the most important one. One official, changed daily, was to record the Diaries at each Imperial audience and also to write down the complete texts of all Imperial edicts (*sheng-yü*), proclamations (*chao*), commands (*ch'ih*), patents (*ts'e-wen*), etc., as well as of the memorials (*t'i-kao*) of the Grand Secretariat. After secret consultations with the emperor, the Grand Secretaries should at once give the necessary information to the official in charge of the Diaries. Furthermore, six elderly and learned historiographical officials should be ordered to record regularly the memorials presented to the Throne by each of the Six Boards. These officials should be free of all other duties and only be responsible for the exact recording of the memorials of their respective boards.

2. Prescriptions concerning time and place of work for the officials responsible for the recording of Diaries of Activity and Repose in the presence of the emperor.

3. Prescriptions concerning the manner in which the texts of Imperial edicts and of different kinds of memorials were to be passed on till they

---

[8] Dated 27.2. Wanli 3 (7 April 1575). For the complete text cf. Collected Works of Chang Chü-cheng (*Chang Wen-chung kung ch'üan chi*, tsou-shu 4, ed. Commercial Press, Kuo-hsüeh chi-pen ts'ung-shu), pp. 53–56. For a less complete text cf. *Shen-tsung shih-lu* 35, 15a–18b (printed edition).

reached the National History Office. All official writings passed through the Grand Secretariat, to which the National History Office was attached.

4. Since these records would only provide the material for the later compilation of the Veritable Records, exactness was of greater importance than a refined and beautiful manner of writing. Imperial utterances must be recorded literally and should not be put into literary style. In the texts of the memorials only insignificant matters of minor importance might be left out; only passages difficult to understand owing to unclear wording might be slightly improved. Otherwise all texts were to be recorded without alteration. Causal connections and temporal sequence were to be made clearly evident. The content must not be changed or modified in any circumstances. The historiography officials were strictly prohibited from expressing their own opinions or 'praise and blame' (*pao pien*).

5. Directions concerning buildings to be assigned to the National History Office and the utensils to be used by the historiographical officials.

6. Prescriptions concerning the safekeeping of the records. At the end of each month the manuscripts written by the historiographical officials were to be bound into seven volumes, one comprising the Diaries of Activity and Repose and six others the materials from the Six Boards. On the cover of each volume, year and month, as well as the name or names of the historiographical official or officials responsible, were to be noted. The complete volumes were to be sent to the Grand Secretariat for inspection and be sealed there in a small chest. At the end of a year, the volumes of that period were to be taken out of the small chests in the presence of the historiographical officials and all twelve together re-sealed in a larger chest. After that sealing, the volumes should not be touched again.

7. Prescriptions concerning the copying-clerks needed for the work of the historiographical officials.

8. For the first two years of Wan-li and the first months of the third year, the texts of Diaries of Activity and Repose and of the memorials of the Six Boards should be recorded after the event in accordance with existing documentary material.

The emperor approved these proposals by Chang Chü-cheng and apparently orders were given that they be carried out, since most of them are contained in the Collected Statutes of the Ming (*Ming hui-tien*). [9] A number of fragmentary manuscripts of the Diaries of the Wan-li, T'ai-ch'ang, and T'ien-ch'i periods are kept in several libraries in Tokyo and Tientsin. A comparison of some passages with the appropriate passages in the Veritable Records shows that as a rule the accounts given in the Diaries of Activity and Repose are much more detailed and accurate than those in the Veritable Records.

[9] Ch. 221, 7a–9a (Wanli Palace ed.).

The Diaries of Activity and Repose record only matters mentioned in the official Imperial audiences. Important political discussions between the emperor and the small circle of leading statesmen were dealt with during the T'ang and Sung Dynasties in special minutes, called Records of Current Government (*Shih-cheng chi*) or similar names. These Records of Current Government were also basic material for the compilation of the Veritable Records and were not written for publication. Only three chapters of such Records of the Sung period, dated sixth, seventh, and eighth month Chien-yen 1 (1127), are still preserved, under the title 'Records of Current Government of the Chien-yen period' (*Chien-yen shih-cheng chi*). There also exist several other writings of a similar type, partly from the Ming period, but these do not represent official records. They were written privately by the officials concerned.[10] In the above-mentioned memorial by Chang Chü-cheng, the matters which in other periods had been dealt with in the Records of Current Government were assigned to the Diaries of Activity and Repose.

Finally, one may mention also the Daily Records (*Jih-li*) as a type of preparatory work for the Veritable Records. It seems that such Daily Records, based upon the Diaries of Activity and Repose and the Records of Current Government, were compiled over a period of several years. From the time of the first Ming emperor it is known that in Hung-wu 6 (1373) a committee selected from members of the Hanlin Academy was ordered to compile 'Daily Records of the Great Ming' (*Ta-Ming jih-li*). The work was carried through under supervision in a special part of the Imperial Palace strictly closed to the outside world. Early in the morning the members of the committee went together to their working-room; there they got their food and left only in the evening to retire together to their dormitory, likewise carefully separated from the outside world. During the period of nearly nine months[11] until the completion of the work, none of the collaborators was permitted to get into touch with people from the outside. The whole enterprise was kept strictly secret in order to prevent interested people from trying to influence the compilers. These were required to base their work only on the written material available. This was in accordance with regulations issued by the emperor, which also stated that after its completion the work was to be inspected by the emperor and safeguarded in a metal chest, a copy being deposited in the Imperial Library.[12] When completed it comprised one hundred chapters and covered the period from the insurrection of Chu Yüan-chang to the end of Hung-wu 6 (11 February 1374).[13] The preface written by the officials directing the compilation states clearly that the Daily Records were to

[10] Shen Te-fu, *Yeh-huo pien* 8, 25b–26a (ed. 1869).
[11] From 4.9. Hungwu 6 (20 September 1373) to 1.5.7 (11 June 1374).
[12] Mi-shu chien.        [13] Huang Tso, *Han-lin chi*, ch. 13, Hsiu jih-li pao-hsün.

serve as basic material for the later compilation of the Veritable Records.[14] The rigorous secrecy observed again shows the importance placed on recording the governmental actions of the emperor accurately and without inference for transmission to later generations.

As mentioned above, Diaries of Activity and Repose were recorded only for the reigns of the first and the last emperors of the Ming Dynasty, covering at most one hundred years. On what were the Veritable Records for the remaining one hundred and seventy-five years of that dynasty based? As can be seen in a number of contemporary reports and official orders, the so-called Historical Materials (*shih-shu*), 'copies of summaries of endorsed memorials' of the Six Boards and of the other metropolitan government institutions[15] specially prepared for the National History Office, were used in the first instance as basic materials. Furthermore, officials were sent out to the capitals of provinces and districts with special orders to collect material for the compilation of the Veritable Records. One result of such a tour, carried through by Tung Ch'i-ch'ang in 1622, was for example the 'Selected Collection of Memorials of the Wan-li Period which were not made Public but Retained in the Imperial Palace', presented to the throne by the latter.[16] Further important materials for the compilation of the Veritable Records were contributed by the Metropolitan Gazette (*ti-pao* or *t'ang-pao*), official information circulated among the different government boards. Originally written in manuscript, after 1638 it was printed for circulation in movable type. It was the predecessor of the official paper known from the later Ch'ing period as the Peking Gazette.[17]

## 2. *The Veritable Records in the criticism of later historians and the process of compilation of the Veritable Records*

One might have expected that it would be those Veritable Records of the Ming period for which Diaries of Activity and Repose had been available which would be the most exact and detailed. Nevertheless, critical statements of the late Ming and of the Ch'ing period do not confirm this supposition. Indeed, just the opposite is true: the Veritable Records for T'ai-tsu, as well as those for Shen-tsung and Kuang-tsung, were in fact specially denounced as inadequate. Several authors of the Ming period, like Wang Ao, Cheng Hsiao, Lang Ying, Shen Te-fu,[18] and others, con-

---

[14] *Ming wen tsai*, ch. 34 (ed. Commercial Press, Kuo-hsüeh chi-pen ts'ung-shu), p. 354.

[15] Cf. J. K. Fairbank in *HJAS* (1940), v, 60.

[16] Cf. W. Franke, 'Preliminary Notes . . .', No. 106.

[17] Fairbank, loc. cit., p. 61.

[18] Wang Ao (1450–1524), *Chen-tse ch'ang-yü* ed. Chi-lu hui-pien 125, 12b–13a. Cheng Hsiao (1499–1566), *Chin-yen* 103, ibid., 145, 2b. Lang Ying (late fifteenth to middle sixteenth century), *Ch'i-hsiu lei-kao*, ed. Kuang-i shu-chü (1936), i, 111. Shen Te-fu (1578–1642), *Yeh-huo pien* 2, 37b–38a.

demn the Veritable Records of the Ming as a whole. The criticism by T'an Ch'ien, the author of the *Kuo-ch'üeh*[19] can be regarded as comparatively lenient. He writes:

Historiography relies upon the Veritable Records only. The Veritable Records show the exterior facts, but they do not show the inner connexions. Moreover, Yang Wen-chen [i.e. Yang Shih-ch'i] did not avoid missing the facts in [writing of] the events of the expulsion [of Emperor Hui-ti]; and Chiao Mi-yang [i.e. Chiao Fang] also disgraced the truth in many cases when [recording] the glorious time of T'ai-ling [i.e. Emperor Hsiao-tsung]. The compilers of [the Veritable Records of] Shen-tsung and Hsi-tsung were all the creatures of rebellious eunuchs.[20]

The criticism of Wang Shih-chen (1526–90) is comparatively balanced, but he too passes strictures upon the defects of the Veritable Records:

The national historiography never failed in its task to such an extreme degree as under our dynasty. Only when the events passed needed no more concealment [i.e. after the death of a ruler] did the Grand Secretariat and the Hanlin Academy receive the order to compile the Veritable Records. The old memorials from the Six Divisions [of the Censorate, competent for the affairs of the Six Boards] were taken and the former records from the Boards and from the Court [of the Censorate] were consulted; and that was all. The records of utterances and actions by the historiographers of the Left and of the Right [i.e. the Diaries of Activity and Repose] are missing. Thus [the compilers of the Veritable Records] had no material upon which they could rely, and therefore they were not in a position to write. As to national disgraces and imperial faults there was reason for evasiveness and they did not dare to write. But the worst of all was that those in charge of writing had their private sympathies and aversions therein; thus even if there was material to rely upon and nothing to evade they did not wish to write; and therefore if they wrote, it did not correspond to the facts.[21]

But despite this strong criticism, later on Wang Shih-chen acknowledges the unique value of the Veritable Records:

The official historians are unrestrained and are skilful at concealing the truth; but the memorials and laws they record and the documents they copy cannot be discarded. The unofficial historians express their opinions and are skilful at missing the truth; but their verification of right and wrong and their abolition of taboo of names and things cannot be discarded. The family historians flatter and are skilful in exceed-

[19] 'Preliminary Notes . . .', No. 23.
[20] Quoted from Yao Ming-ta, *Shao Nien-lu nien-p'u* (Commercial Press, Chung-kuo shih-hsüeh ts'ung-shu, 1934), pp. 16–17.
[21] *Shih-ch'eng k'ao-wu* I, in *Yen-shan-t'ang pieh-chi* 20, 1a.

ing the truth; but their praise of the merits of [the] ancestors and their manifestations of their achievements as officials cannot be discarded.[22]

The historians of the Ch'ing period show a more positive attitude towards the Veritable Records than those of the Ming. Probably the longer interval between their lifetime and the events dealt with in the Records enable them to get a more objective and better balanced judgement. In this way Hsü Ch'ien-hsüeh (1631–94), one of the chief compilers of the Standard History of the Ming Dynasty, wrote:

> . . . Of the Veritable Records of the Ming, those for the reigns of Hung-wu and Yung-lo are most arbitrary and summary. Most detailed are those for Hung-chih, but the brush of Chiao Fang in distributing praise and censure has in many cases distorted the facts. Most careless are those for Wan-li, and not a single one of the statements written by Ku Ping-ch'ien [Supervisor of compilation of the Shen-tsung *shih-lu*] can be selected as adequate. Only [the Veritable Records for] the reign of Chia-ching are skilled and clear in their statements, keeping the balance between detailed and summary [description]. The Veritable Records for Jen-tsung, Hsüan-tsung, Ying-tsung and Hsien-tsung are superior to those of Wen Huang [i.e. T'ai-tsu]. Those for Cheng-te and Lung-ch'ing are inferior to those of Shih-miao [i.e. Shih-tsung]. That is a general judgement about the Veritable Records for the successive reigns. Family records and non-official histories are not wholly reliable; it is necessary to take the Veritable Records as the fundamental source, and other works for additional reference. [Proceeding in this way] there will probably be no defect. Who endeavours to carry out extensive research cannot rely upon the words of only one author.[23]

These and other comments show that the partiality of some of the compilers according to their personal sympathies and aversions are the chief argument for censuring the Veritable Records. But since the Veritable Records are for the most part made up from the texts of official documents and from dry reports about government actions, the selection of which follows detailed regulations, the chances for the author to express his personal opinion are fairly limited. No criticism raises the reproach of deliberate forging of documents; thus the opportunity for the expression of a personal opinion existed only in the distribution of accents and in carefully concealed hints of praise and blame. Moreover, some documents—even against the regulations—could either be completely suppressed, or condensed in a way distorting the original meaning. If the documents themselves—memorials, for example—contained erroneous statements, correction of these was not the duty of the compilers. Unintentional errors are by no means a rarity in the Veritable Records.

[22] Ibid., 1b.    [23] Hsü Chien-an hsiu-shih t'iao-i in *Ming-shih li-an* 2, 10a.

The sympathies and aversions hinted at in the Veritable Records are not limited to the distribution of praise and blame according to the common standard of Confucian political ethics, as generally recognized and applied by all Chinese historiographers, but are also closely connected with the numerous groups and personalities struggling against each other in daily political life. The fact that such political controversies could affect the Veritable Records was due to the position of the National History Office and to the structure of the compiling committee. Whereas in former periods the National History Office had for the most part a fairly independent position and the compilers were persons not directly involved in actual policy, during the Ming period the Grand Secretaries, who were chiefly responsible for all important political decisions, were likewise in charge of the compilation of the Veritable Records and the National History Office was attached to the Grand Secretariat. After the Hsüan-te period, the Grand Secretaries were *ex officio* Supervisors of Compilation (*tsung-ts'ai*). They had to fix the regulations for compilation work and to check the drafts prepared by the Compilers (*tsuan-hsiu kuan*) belonging to the Grand Secretariat or to the Hanlin Academy. A very important place was held by the Vice-Supervisors of Compilation (*fu tsung-ts'ai*), selected from the Secretaries (*hsüeh-shih*) of the Grand Secretariat. Although in theory they had no decisive authority, in practice they carried out the permanent immediate supervision of the compilation work, whereas the Grand Secretaries had many important duties and could only occasionally give attention to compilation. The Inspectors of Compilation (*chien-hsiu*), nominally senior even to the Supervisors, apparently did not have much influence on the work. They had to be selected from the holders of the highest ranks of the nobility (duke, *kung*; or prince, *hou*) granted for military achievements on behalf of the Empire. Particularly during the middle and later period of the Ming Dynasty, the Inspectors seem to have been personalities of only minor importance, not generally known and chosen for this position merely because of the noble rank they had inherited from their ancestors. In some cases the office of Inspector of Compilation remained in the same family for several generations.

It is evident from the organization of the compilation of the Veritable Records in Ming times that it was regarded as an important political task which explains not only the fact that Veritable Records under preparation were revised if an important change took place among the Grand Secretaries, but also the fact that in some cases even Veritable Records already completed and sealed were against all custom and regulation opened again and rewritten. The Veritable Records for T'ai-tsu were handled in this way. The first compilation was undertaken and completed during the reign of Chien-wen, grandson and successor of Emperor T'ai-tsu. It is quite obvious that the Prince of Yen, fourth son of T'ai-tsu and uncle of

Chien-wen, who usurped the throne in 1402, could not leave untouched the Veritable Records for the reign of his father, since they declared his nephew as the rightful successor to the throne and consequently himself as a rebel, thereby transmitting a statement of his own usurpation to later generations. Thus he ordered the rewriting of them. After the completion of the new draft the old text is said to have been burnt. But even this new draft, completed in a few months, was not satisfactory to the emperor. A few years later he remarked that the compilers had not had a correct attitude towards their work, and that they had completed it too quickly, at the expense of thoroughness. Thus after seven years' work the third draft was finally completed, the only one transmitted. Already in the middle of the Ming period it was known as the only existing one. This final draft has been severely criticized for its numerous errors. As early as the seventeenth century Ch'ien Ch'ien-i (1582–1664) in an extensive study discussed and corrected many of its faults.[24]

Of doubtful origin are the Veritable Records for the reign of Chien-wen. According to some reports the Records of Events (*Shih-chi*) for this period were added to the Veritable Records for T'ai-tsu during the Wan-li period. They are not contained in the existing copies of these Veritable Records, but they constitute the first nine chapters of those for T'ai-tsung, having in some copies the sub-title 'Record of the events of the removing of troubles by order of Heaven' (*Feng-t'ien ching-nan shih-chi*), under which designation the usurpation of the throne by the Prince of Yen was described. Since these chapters give the style Chien-wen—not officially used before Wan-li—it is not clear whether they were compiled together with the other parts of the Veritable Records for T'ai-tsung or at a later date.

Similar problems are raised in regard to the Veritable Records for the reign of Ching-ti, enthroned after his imperial brother was taken prisoner by the Mongols in 1449. After a reign of eight years he was dethroned by a *coup d'état* in favour of his brother, returned from the Mongols; and a few days later he died. In the Veritable Records for Ying-tsung, covering the three reigns from 1436 to 1464, the records of Ching-t'ai (ch. 187–262) are as detailed as those for the preceding and for the following period, but they have the characteristic subtitle 'Annex concerning the wrong emperor, the rebellious Prince of Ch'eng' (*Fei-ti Ch'eng-li-wang fu-lu*) and separate chapter-numbers 5–91. As regards the contents, even the critical events during the enthronement of the emperor Ching-ti are recorded in a generally objective way and the leading part played by Yü Ch'ien at this time is clearly recorded. It was he who in these critical weeks saved the Ming Dynasty from an early downfall after the emperor Ying-tsung was taken prisoner by the Mongols. Yü Ch'ien was killed during the *coup d'état*

[24] *T'ai-tsu shih-lu pien-cheng*, 5 chüan. Cf. 'Preliminary Notes . . .', No. 1.

in 1457 on an empty pretext. This comparative impartiality of the Veritable Records for Ying-tsung is attested by the fact that even the earlier critics did not censure this section in particular, as they did the records dealing with the Chien-wen period. In a memorial of the end of the sixteenth century asking for the compilation of separate Veritable Records for the emperors Hui-ti and Ching-ti, its author, Shen Li, does not mention any deficiency of the contents as reason for his proposal, but only stresses the formal argument that the reigns of emperors recognized in later times as legitimate should be dealt with in separate Veritable Records and should not be attached to those of other emperors.[25]

The most serious controversies took place concerning the Veritable Records of Kuang-tsung, the emperor with the shortest reign (only four months) during the Ming period. They were stimulated by the political struggles which became more and more violent after the beginning of the seventeenth century. The chief opponents in these struggles were an influential group of eunuchs on the one side and the strictly Confucian Tunglin party on the other. The emperor was obviously their victim. The Veritable Records of his reign were compiled first under the supervision of personalities near to the Tunglin party. But soon their enemies, under the leadership of the notorious eunuch Wei Chung-hsien, became more and more powerful, eventually instigating a persecution of the Tunglin party and the execution of a large number of its prominent members and partisans. At the end of 1625 the victorious clique around Wei Chung-hsien succeeded in getting an imperial order for the compilation of a kind of White Book, under the title 'Important Statutes of Three Reigns' (*San-ch'ao yao-tien*).[26] With distinct bias it records documents and events in such a manner as to justify the policy of the anti-Tunglin group and of the all-powerful eunuch Wei Chung-hsien, especially with regard to the so-called 'three great affairs' (*San ta an*) concerning the succession to the throne of Emperor Shen-tsung. The work was finished in the following year. Thereupon the Veritable Records for Kuang-tsung, already completed in 1623 and safeguarded in the Historical Archives, were unsealed and revised according to the 'Important Statutes of Three Reigns', together with those for Shen-tsung not yet finished. This unusual action only has a counterpart in the revision of the Veritable Records for T'ai-tsu under Yung-lo, but in the latter case the emperor himself was the *spiritus rector* of the procedure, whereas in the former it was instigated by a group of eunuchs, the emperor himself playing only a passive part. A similar action was proposed during the Chia-ching period with regard to the Veritable Records of Hsiao-tsung, compiled under supervision of the Grand Secretary Chiao Fang. The critics are unanimous in condemning Chiao Fang for distortion of facts and for defamation of people in his ill favour, so a

[25] *Li-pu chih kao* 97, 8a–11b.     [26] Cf. 'Preliminary Notes . . .', No. 109.

proposition for revision was not entirely without reason. This was recognized by the emperor also, but nevertheless he declined the suggestion.[27] In the case of the Veritable Records for Kuang-tsung the emperor apparently neither had the will nor the authority to prevent the revision aimed at by the eunuchs. Even a memorial presented by the courageous censor Li Hsi-k'ung, opposing the revision by quoting a number of distorting changes made by the revising compilers, had no success. Only when, after the death of emperor Hsi-tsung, Wei Chung-hsien and his followers had been wiped out, the Tunglin party had been rehabilitated, and the 'Important Statutes of Three Reigns' had been burnt, was the matter raised. This was in a memorial by Wen Chen-meng. He pointed out that the Veritable Records for Kuang-tsung, completed and presented to the throne in 1628, had been revised according to the 'Important Statutes of Three Reigns'; and he stressed the importance of taking this matter up again by enumerating five points on which the facts had been distorted.[28] Thus the emperor ordered a new and final revision. Probably all copies of these Veritable Records still preserved are of this twice-revised third and final draft. All these controversies likewise had reference to the last part of the Veritable Records for Shen-tsung, but all revision of these took place before the compilation was completed. They were completed and presented to the throne as late as 1630.

Besides these two cases of official rewriting of Veritable Records already completed and safeguarded in the archives, one more known case of private interference with the Veritable Records has to be mentioned. In the preserved copies of the Veritable Records of the emperor Hsi-tsung, last but one of the dynasty, the records of several months of the years T'ien-ch'i 4 and 7 (1624 and 1627) are missing. This deficiency was noticed as early as the first years of the Manchu dynasty, when preparations for the compilation of the official history of the Ming dynasty were started. According to a contemporary report,[29] these parts are said to have been eliminated during the early Shun-chih period by Feng Ch'üan, a renegade of the Ming. Feng Ch'üan had been a partisan of Wei Chung-hsien and had taken an influential part in the compilation of the 'Important Statutes of Three Reigns' and in the persecution of the Tunglin party. He put himself at the disposal of the Manchus as early as 1644 and was nominated by the conquerors as Grand Secretary in the following year. Thus having secured access to the Historical Archives, he took the opportunity of

---

[27] *Yeh-huo pien*, Appendix 1, 20b–21a. A number of such distorting records in the Hsiao-tsung shih-lu has been corrected by Wang Shih-chen in his *Shih-ch'eng k'ao-wu*, contained in *Yen-shan-t'ang pieh-chi*, ch. 20–30. Cf. Wu Han, *Chi Ming shih-lu*, pp. 424–6.

[28] *Ssu-ch'ao ta-cheng lu* ('Preliminary Notes . . .', No. 110), ed. Kuo-hsüeh wen-k'u, pp. 38–42; Sun Ch'eng-tse, *Ch'un-ming-meng yü-lu* 13, 18b–26a.

[29] Chu I-tsung, *Shu liang-ch'ao ts'ung-hsin-lu hou* in *Pao-shu-t'ing chi* 45, 12a (ed. Ssu-pu ts'ung-k'an).

secretly removing and destroying the parts containing passages disadvantageous to himself, when in the same year the Veritable Records were unsealed for the preparation of the official history. This explanation for the missing parts in the Veritable Records of Hsi-tsung has been adopted by later scholars and never seriously questioned.[30]

3. *The transmission of the existing copies of the Veritable Records*

The Veritable Records were not destined for publication. After the termination of the compilation two manuscript copies of the Veritable Records were presented to the emperor in an exactly prescribed official ceremony. Thereupon the original copy (*cheng pen*) was put under seal in the Grand Secretariat—later in the Imperial Historical Archives (*Huang shih ch'eng*)—and was not allowed to be taken out again. It provided the fundamental source for the compilation of the official history by later generations. The duplicate copy (*fu pen*) was for reference, being at the disposal of the Emperor, of the Grand Secretaries, and of the historiographical officials, and was likewise deposited in the Grand Secretariat. In order to guarantee secrecy all drafts and preliminary copies were burnt at a specified place in the interior of the palace in the presence of all officials who had participated in the compilation. In 1492 the Grand Secretary Ch'iu Chün proposed in a lengthy memorial—as far as is known, for the first time—making a new copy of the Veritable Records and safeguarding it in a building to be specially constructed for this purpose. After enumerating the original copies of the Veritable Records of six emperors preserved in the Grand Secretariat, he wrote:

> Moreover, in the Grand Secretariat another copy is kept for each reign. Besides these no other copies exist. Since there are no implements of metal and stone for the safe-keeping of books and furthermore no arrangements for Palace Archives to store the duplicate copies, I am exceedingly anxious [about the safekeeping of the books] and wish to ask Your Majesty to set up separately at a place near the Palace Library[31] within convenient reach a higher-storied building. For its construction no wood should be used, but it should be built of brick in the same way as the common people have so-called cellars for the safe-keeping of important papers and books against unexpected troubles. [Furthermore] I ask for an imperial command to the literary officials of the Grand Secretariat to deliberate [the issue of] an order to the clerks doing work in the Grand Secretariat: if they have some spare time as regards their duty in the dispatching of papers and documents, and if it does not

---

[30] Cf. *Eminent Chinese of the Ch'ing Period*, i, 240–1.

[31] The Palace Library (*Wen-yüan ko*) and the Grand Secretariat were located in the same building and both names were often used without distinction. Cf. E. Schierlitz, 'Das Wen-yüan-ko der Mingzeit', *M.S.* III (1938), pp. 542–4.

interfere with their original official duties, they should prepare another copy of the Veritable Records for the successive reigns in divided parts. No date for the completion should be fixed. When the copies are ready they should be packed into chests of copper and deposited on the upper floor of the building.[32]

This memorial remain~d without practical effect. It was not until more than forty years later that the emperor agreed to a renewed proposition by the Grand Secretary Chang Fu-ching (1475–1539) and issued an edict ordering the copying of the Veritable Records onto paper of strong quality. The copy was to have the same size as the *T'ung-chien kang-mu*, probably in the Imperial edition printed in the Palace Press (*Ching-ch'ang*). It was not necessary that each month should cover exactly one volume, as was the case in the original copy, but each volume had to have the same size. A special committee was nominated, in the same way as for the compilation of the Veritable Records, to take charge of the copying work, with Inspectors, Supervisors, etc. At the same time the construction of a special building for the safekeeping of the Veritable Records was ordered, as earlier proposed by Ch'iu Chün. The building got the name Imperial History Archives (*Huang shih ch'eng*). Two years later the completion of the copy was announced. It was presented to the emperor in an official ceremony and was sealed up the next day in the new Archives in the presence of the emperor. It is not known what happened to the old manuscript from which the copy had been made. In 1588 emperor Shen-tsung, asking for the old copy, got the answer that it had once been brought to the inner palace for consultation by his predecessor and later stored again in the Imperial History Archives. But a thorough investigation made it evident that it could not actually be discovered. Thus people said it may have been burnt during the Chia-ching period after the completion of the copy, in the same way as the drafts used to be burnt. In that case it could not have been in existence in the Lung-ch'ing period. The Duplicate Copies of the Grand Secretariat were dirty and damaged by permanent use and could not be presented to the emperor. Therefore an edict was issued ordering the copying of the Duplicate Copies. The new copy was to be of a small and handy size, the old one being too big and unsuitable for permanent use. Early in 1591 the work was completed.

It is worth noting that as far as is known this copy for the first time wrote the new posthumous name Ch'eng-tsu instead of the old T'ai-tsung. The copy of the original manuscripts made during the Chia-ching period still had T'ai-tsung, since it was completed two years before the posthumous name of this emperor was changed. Thus the writing of T'ai-tsung or of Ch'eng-tsu can be taken as a criterion for the possible origin of the still

[32] *Hsiao-tsung shih-lu* 63, 7b–8a; *Li-pu chih kao* 46, 8b–9b.

extant manuscripts of the Veritable Records. Probably all texts writing Ch'eng-tsu lead back directly or indirectly to the Wan-li copy of the Duplicate Copy, unless later copyists have changed T'ai-tsung into Ch'eng-tsu, which is not very likely. The texts writing T'ai-tsung—as far as they still date from Ming times—probably lead back to the early Duplicate Copy, the later whereabouts of which are unknown, or to drafts, which actually may not always have been completely destroyed. Later texts writing T'ai-tsung may have been copied from the copy in the Imperial History Archives during the early Ch'ing period. The explicit notice of missing parts of the Veritable Records for Hsi-tsung and of those for the Ch'ung-chen period as a whole indicates that during the early Ch'ing period the copy in the Imperial History Archives was still in existence. But since that time it has been completely lost. Not a single volume is known to be transmitted. Almost the same is the case with the new Duplicate Copy. As far as known only the Tōyō Bunko in Tokyo is in possession of one volume of the Veritable Records of Ch'eng-tsu possibly originating from this set.

Down to the middle of Wan-li, i.e. to the end of the sixteenth century, the Veritable Records seem to have been kept secret from the public. It was only after the above-mentioned copying of the Duplicate Copy that drafts of the Veritable Records or sections of them went into circulation outside the palace to any great extent. Gradually, wealthy families became ambitious of owning a copy of the Veritable Records and prices paid for them rose steadily. Owing to such demand, the texts of the Veritable Records were often copied. Since these copies were chiefly made for commercial and not for purely academic purposes, the copying often lacked the necessary care and accuracy. Moreover, in many cases owners of the Veritable Records personally connected with or particularly interested in the events have modified, condensed, or supplemented the text according to their own judgement. Further copies made from texts dealt with in this way, of course, deviated more or less from the original text. This applied in particular to the Veritable Records for the reigns from Shih-tsung down. In most cases the sometimes rather considerable divergences in the existing manuscripts of the Veritable Records can probably be explained in this way. Nearly all of them are copies privately made during the later Ming or the Ch'ing period.[33] One single volume, probably an exception, has been mentioned above. Furthermore, the main copy of the National Library of Peking—in safe keeping at the Library of Congress since the beginning of the Sino-Japanese War and reproduced in microfilm—is thought to be probably an official copy made in the early Ch'ing

---

[33] Most of the existing manuscript copies are described and as far as possible identified by the present writer in 'Zur Kompilation und Überlieferung der Ming Shih-lu' and in 'Weitere Beiträge zur Kompilation und Überlieferung der Ming Shih-lu'. These notes need not to be repeated here.

period for use in the compilation of the official history of the Ming. A statement that it is the official Duplicate Copy of the Grand Secretariat of the Ming cannot be substantiated. Apart from several complete or incomplete manuscripts—two of them in Europe at Cambridge and in Paris —a printed edition has been available since 1940. It is a photo-lithographic reprint of the manuscript copy formerly kept in the Kiangsu Provincial Library in Nanking, being a modern copy of the manuscript owned by the private library Chia-yeh-t'ang, dating from the late Ming or early Ch'ing period. It was later in the possession of the Institute of History and Phililogy of the Academia Sinica, now probably in Taiwan. Despite the fact that this printed edition has false characters on nearly every page and that it is inferior to some ancient manuscript copies, it can be taken as the standard edition because it is widely available.

BIBLIOGRAPHY

1. *Books and Articles in Western Languages*

L. Aurousseau in *BEFEO* (1912), xii, 72–75.

Wolfgang Franke, 'Zur Kompilation und Überlieferung der Ming Shih-lu', *Sinologische Arbeiten* (Peking, 1943), i, 1–46.

— 'Weitere Beiträge zur Kompilation und Überlieferung der Ming Shih-lu', *Sinologische Arbeiten* (Peking, 1944), ii, 1–29.

— 'Nachtrag zur Kompilation und Überlieferung der Ming Shih-lu', *Sinologische Arbeiten* (1945), iii, 165–8.

— 'Preliminary Notes on the Important Chinese Literary Sources for the History of the Ming Dynasty (1368–1644)', *Studia Serica Monographs*, Ser. A, No. 2 (Chengtu, 1948).

Charles S. Gardner, *Chinese Traditional Historiography* (Cambridge, Mass., 1938).

L. Carrington Goodrich, 'A Note on the Ta Ming Shih Lu', *TP* (1940), xxxvi, 81–84.

A. C. Moule, Chung Kei-won, *The Ta-Ming Shih-lu* (Cambridge and Princeton), ed. by J. J. L. Duyvendak, *TP* (1940), xxxv, 289–329.

Yanai-Inaba-Matsui, 'Beiträge zur historischen Geographie der Mandschurei', vol. i (*Veröffentlichungen der Historisch-geographischen Studien-Abteilung der Süd-mandschurischen Eisenbahn AG. No. 1*, Hrsg. von K. Shiratori).

2. *Books and Articles in Chinese and Japanese*

Asano Chūin, 'Min jitsuroku zakkō', *Kita Asia gakuhō* (October, 1944), iii, 254–85.

Chao Shih-wei, 'Shih-lu k'ao', *Fu-jen hsüeh-chih* (Peiping, 1936), v, 1/2, 46–51.

Chu Hsi-tsu, 'Han T'ang Sung ch'i-chü-chu k'ao', *Kuo-hsüeh chi-k'an*, ii, 4 (Peiping, December 1930), pp. 629–40.

Hsieh Kuo-chen, *Wan Ming shih-chi k'ao* (Peiping, 1933), chüan 4.

Imanishi Shunjū, 'Min no kikyochū ni tsuite', *Shirin* xix, 4 (1934), pp. 701–20, and xx, 1 (1935), pp. 191–8.

Li Chin-hua, *Ming-tai ch'ih-chuan-shu k'ao*, ed. Harvard-Yenching Institute (Peiping, 1932).

Li Chin-hua, *Ming-shih tsuan-hsiu k'ao*, YCHP Monograph 3 (Peiping, 1933).

Lo Hsiang-lin, 'Ta T'ang ch'uang-yeh ch'i-chü-chu k'ao-cheng', *Shih hsüeh chi-k'an* (1936), ii, 115–45.

Matsuura Kasaburō, 'Shinyō toshokanzō Minjitsuroku ni tsuite', *Manshū gakuhō* (Hsinking, 1941), vi, 63–85.

Mitamura Taisuke, 'Minjitsuroku no dembon ni tsuite', *Tōyōshi kenkyū*, viii, 1 (1943) pp. 20–30.

Oda Shōgo, 'Hantō genson no Kōmin jitsuroku ni tsuite', *Seikyū gakusō*, xiii (Sōul, 1933), pp. 137–53, and xiv (1934), pp. 96–98.

Pien Hung-ju, 'Hsieh-pen Ming Shih-lu t'i-yao', *Tung-pei ts'ung-k'an* 3 (Mukden, 1930).

Shimada Yoshimi, 'Minjitsuroku no kankō ni tsuite', *Shokō* No. 140 (Dairen, September 1942), pp. 1–3.

T'ao Yüan-chen, 'Wan-li ch'i-chü-chu', *Wen-shih tsa-chih*, iv, 7/8 (Chungking, 1944), pp. 54–56.

*Tōyō rekishi daijiten*, ii, 144/5, iii, 153/4, iii, 481/2.

Wu Han, 'Chi Ming shih-lu', *CYYY* (1948), xviii, 385–447. Reprinted in the author's *Tu shih cha chi* (Peking, 1956), pp. 156–234.

## 6. L'HISTOIRE COMME GUIDE DE LA PRATIQUE BUREAUCRATIQUE (LES MONOGRAPHIES, LES ENCYCLOPÉDIES, LES RECUEILS DE STATUTS)

### E. BALAZS

*Directeur d études, Ecole Pratique des Hautes Etudes, Paris*

1. *Introduction*

Quel est le trait distinctif de l'historiographie chinoise si on l'oppose dans sa totalité à celle de l'Occident? C'est son caractère stéréotypé, répondra l'historien occidental, après mûre réfléxion et se libérant de ses préjugés dans la mesure du possible. Il entendra par stéréotypé deux choses, apparemment contradictoires: d'une part, le manque du trait personnel—l'individu est absorbé dans et disparait derrière le groupe, dont il n'est qu'un échantillon; et d'autre part, l'absence d'abstraction qui permettrait une synthèse—le détail concret prédomine et malgré sa nature répétitive bouche la vue aux généralisations. Cette double négativité—qui n'est un défaut que dans l'optique occidentale—demande une explication.

Le découpage de l'histoire en tranches dynastiques; l'existence d'une historiographie officielle, salariée et dépendante; l'art traditionnel de la citation, lourd héritage du génie de la langue—voilà les trois facteurs principaux, me semble-t-il, qui ont entravé en Chine l'éclosion d'une historiographie comparable à la nôtre.

L'art traditionnel de la citation, aujourd'hui encore en honneur, consiste à ne jamais résumer un document, mais de le citer. Et puisque il serait à la fois fastidieux et impossible de le citer entièrement, on en reproduit les mots-clés. L'historien qui veut rendre le contenu essentiel d'un document, ne le traduira jamais en ses propres paroles, mais tâchera toujours de faire un choix significatif dans le texte même qu'il découpera phrase par phrase, mot par mot, en le réduisant à un petit nombre de caractères marquants et expressifs. Cette façon de faire des extraits authentiques, mais tronqués, cet art de s'exprimer avec économie, par et aux dépens de l'original, n'est possible que grâce à langue chinoise (caractères-idéogrammes, rôle minime de la grammaire, concision naturelle de la langue écrite).[1] Exercice ingénieux, l'art de la citation à la chinoise est aussi une servitude redoutable. Car il englue l'esprit dans le déjà dit et tue toute création; il favorise la lettre aux dépens du sens; il gonfle les

---

[1] Pour de nombreux exemples de ce procédé, voir A. Fang, *The Chronicle of the Three Kingdoms* (Cambridge, Mass., 1952); cf. aussi la confrontation typographique d'un texte original et de ses extraits dans *MSOS* 36 (1933), 2 et suiv.

textes traditionnels et la tradition des textes en une immense mer de papier et d'encre qui couvre toute spontanéité. Copier—copier habilement, ingénieusement, mais toujours copier—étouffe à la longue les cerveaux.

Si la langue est le véhicule indispensable de l'art de citer, elle n'est pas seule en cause. Certes, la magie du verbe (la charge de signification autonome et d'art dont chaque caractère écrit est porteur) y est pour beaucoup. Mais la piété, le respect devant tout ce qui est écrit, ont sans doute puissamment contribué à l'habitude de ne pas toucher aux textes sacrosaints. Chacun élevé dans la récitation des textes appris par coeur a inconsciemment, instinctivement horreur de changer ce qui a été dit et si bien dit (quand il s'agit des classiques). Et puis, c'est si commode! On se pare du prestige du grand écrivain, on se dispense de penser et la besogne est vite faite.

Le résultat inévitable du rabâchage traditionaliste est la verbosité. Emporté par les flots torrentueux de ses sources, l'historien quelconque ne pourra se hisser au niveau de la concision de ses modèles classiques. Ayant l'habitude de réciter et de ré-citer, il tendra vers la prolixité du raconteur d'anecdotes. Par exemple, il ne dira pas: 'au même moment trois révoltes paysannes ont éclaté dans le Sud de la province.' Il dira: 'le jour $j$, du mois $m$ la $n$-ième année de la période $p$–$r$, Chang X, fils de Chang Y, s'est emparé du sous-préfet Z . . .', et la même chose pour Li et pour Wang. Personne ne nie le prix de ces informations. Mais, justement, le luxe des noms et des titres que se paie notre auteur, le fera la plupart du temps renoncer aux détails concrets significatifs. Si le document original qu'il utilise précisait le nombre des terres possédées par le paysan et le sous-préfet, on peut parier que les deux chiffres disparaîtront ou bien que le premier deviendra 'peu' et que le deuxième sera remplacé par un cliché dans le genre 'ses champs s'étiraient sans discontinuer'. Bref, le procédé de la citation retiendra le détail schématique et sacrifiera le détail significatif.

Sans pouvoir nous attarder sur la question très importante, dans quelle mesure la manie de copier favorise les clichés, disons au moins que le côté 'copiste' de l'historien chinois—faire passer les documents par des moutures successives de citations—est inséparable de sa fonction d'historiographe officiel.

L'office des historiographes, entretenu par le pouvoir dynastique, a en effet comme premier devoir d'enregistrer les faits et gestes de l'empereur, les actes du gouvernement, de noter au jour le jour les événements de la vie publique, de recueillir et de conserver rapports et documents, et de constituer des archives.[2] Qu'il aboutisse ou non à condenser par étapes, ces matériaux en une histoire du règne, cette tâche éminemment conservatrice

[2] Cf. dans ce volume les articles de Yang Lien-sheng, 'The organization of Chinese official historiography', et de W. Franke, 'The Veritable Records of the Ming Dynasty (1368–1644)'.

passe avant celle qui consiste à écrire l'histoire de la dynastie précédente. Car juger, tirer les leçons morales du passé pour le présent, n'est possible que sur pièces, en connaissance des documents (et l'Histoire, selon la conception chinoise, perdrait tout sens si l'on ne pouvait en tirer des instructions et des directives pour agir). Avant d'assumer le rôle du juge, il faut donc instruire le procès du présent, en fournissant aux générations futures les dossiers de l'époque (plus ou moins complets, plus ou moins retouchés dans le moulin à citations). La devise de Confucius lui-même— 'Transmettre!'[3]—préside à cette activité: en principe, chaque document a une valeur intrinsèque de témoignage devant l'éternité; conserver son nom et léguer ses traces à la postérité assure une survie au moins égale au culte des ancêtres. D'où le devoir quasiment religieux d'enregistrer les faits.

Si l'amour excessif des textes est en soi positif, il est difficile de nier que l'entassement de faits bruts et de sources remaniées n'avance ni l'analyse, ni la synthèse du processus historique. Mais le côté à coup sûr le plus négatif des offices d'archivistes et d'historiographes était leur caractère étroitement dynastique. En dépit du postulat contraire et d'honorables exceptions, ils étaient payés pour glorifier leurs maîtres et pour vilipender la dynastie défunte. Ecrire l'histoire selon la recette moralisatrice 'louer ou blâmer' (*pao-pien*) était relativement facile quand il s'agissait d'une dynastie ou d'un règne de longue durée. Les fondateurs lointains ou les puissants morts depuis longtemps, on pouvait les magnifier et critiquer sans gêne; d'autre part, la décadence des derniers empereurs d'une dynastie allait de soi, comme était axiomatique la nécessité de leur arracher le 'mandat du Ciel', en les forçant d'abdiquer ou par un acte de révolte, devenu en cette occurrence signe de suprême loyauté. Avoir deux poids et deux mesures selon le succès ou l'échec des prétendants, selon la légitimité de telle ou telle maison, selon l'influence de la famille de tel ou tel personnage, n'était pas le moindre défaut de l'historiographie officielle. Les inextricables contradictions logiques qui en résultaient, ont toujours nécessité de périlleux exercices d'acrobatie mentale, malgré les conventions tacites et l'acception de l'axiome 'right or wrong, my dynasty (my family)'.

Le plus grand mal n'était pas cependant la dépendance des historiens-fonctionnaires du pouvoir du jour, ni leur manque d'objectivité—ils ont souvent fait preuve d'un degré d'objectivité remarquable dans leur condition—mais l'existence même d'un tel office: impossible d'échapper au cadre dynastique. La nécessité de penser l'histoire en termes dynastiques, de découper le flux des évènements en tranches nettement séparées, a rendu un piètre service aux historiens chinois, en leur octroyant l'optique des cloisons étanches. De plus, le principe cyclique et le manque de continuité ont nettement fait pencher la balance en faveur de la collection

---

[3] *Lun-yü*, vii, 1 (Legge 195; Waley 123).

incohérente de petits faits isolés et découragé la recherche des rapports, de la connexion et de l'enchaînement des faits. Arriver à une vue d'ensemble demandait donc un très grand effort.

Il était difficile pour les historiens chinois de se rendre compte des entraves au développement de leur art, que je viens d'esquisser, et presque impossible d'enlever ces obstacles qui relèvent, en dernière analyse, de la nature même de la société dans laquelle ils vivaient, du caractère spécifique de la couche dirigeante qui l'a dominée pendant plus de deux millénaires et dont ils étaient les interprètes.

L'étroitesse du cadre dynastique fut néanmoins assez tôt ressentie[4] et souvent discutée dès que Ssu-ma Kuang (1019–86) ait eu le courage de dépasser cette limite, en écrivant son célèbre Miroir Complet pour aider à gouverner (*Tzu-chih t'ung-chien*), première histoire générale de la Chine depuis les Mémoires Historiques (*Shi chi*) de Ssu-ma Ch'ien. Cependant, ni Ssu-ma Kuang, ni à sa suite Yüan Shu (1131–1205), ne réussirent à faire éclater la forme traditionnelle d'annales (*pien-nien*). Leurs mérites respectifs sont ailleurs. Le premier inaugura l'historiographie critique,[5] tandis que le second fut le créateur d'une forme d'histoire qui tâche de donner un récit complet d'un sujet, d'une question ou d'une série d'évènements liés par leur substance (*chi-shih pen-mo*). Il est caractéristique que cette forme, qui rapproche le plus du type occidental, soit hybride: les ouvrages du type *chi-shih pen-mo* ne font en somme que regrouper les chroniques par matières, en maintenant l'ordre strictement chronologique à l'intérieur de ces groupes. Il est significatif aussi que les progrès acquis dans ce domaine sous les Sung (960–1279) soient restés sans lendemain.

Il y avait encore une autre possibilité de se libérer du carcan dynastique. La manière d'envisager l'histoire sous l'angle des permanences impersonnelles—choses, structures, constitutions—qui fut le propre d'une partie intégrante des histoires officielles, on pouvait la développer jusqu'à ses conséquences logiques. Le toujours lucide Ma Tuan-lin (*c.* 1250–1325) a bien ressenti ce problème. Dans la préface (*c.* 1317) à sa grande encyclopédie, à laquelle nous reviendrons, il dit: 'Depuis Pan Ku (l'auteur de l'Histoire des Han Antérieurs, *c.* A.D. 90) et ses successeurs, depuis qu'on écrit l'histoire en tranches dynastiques, il n'y a pas de principe général qui fournirait une explication d'ensemble et un lien de continuité.' Puis, reconnaissant les mérites de l'oeuvre de Ssu-ma Kuang, qui couvre plus de 1,300 ans d'histoire, il poursuit: 'Cependant, ce livre est précis pour l'ordre et le dèsordre, l'ascension et le déclin, mais sommaire quant aux statuts et

---

[4] Au moins dès Liu Chih-chi (661–721) et son *Shih-t'ung* (710). Sur Liu Chih-chi et Ssu-ma Kuang, voir la contribution de E. G. Pulleyblank, ci-dessous, pp. 135–66.
[5] Je pense surtout à son 'Examen des divergences' (*K'ao-i*), partie intégrante du *Tzu-chih t'ung-chien*.

institutions . . . Or, à mon avis, ordre et désordre, ascension et déclin, sont des faits sans continuité, sans rapports réciproques (*pu hsiang yin*) . . . (Tandis que) statuts et institutions ont réellement une continuité, des rapports de réciprocité.'[6]

Autrement dit, l'histoire événementielle, dominée par la contingence, est sans grand intérêt. La véritable histoire, digne de ce nom, qui permet de déterminer une suite, une continuité, une sorte d'évolution ou de développement, n'est que l'histoire institutionnelle. Cette interprétation exagère à peine la pensée de Ma Tuan-lin. Car, dans la même préface, il cite le mot de Chiang Yen (444–505): 'Rien n'est plus difficile dans l'historiographie que d'écrire des monographies', et ajoute: 'en effet, les monographies s'attachent aux statuts et sont impraticables à quiconque n'est pas familiarisé depuis longtemps avec les institutions.'[7]

On se demandera comment Ma Tuan-lin est arrivé à cette conception relativement moderne. Pour répondre à cette question, il faut faire un long détour, car il est évident que son raisonnement suppose une longue durée historique aussi bien qu'une accumulation considérable d'expériences par des générations d'historiens.

### 2. *Les monographies*

En face de l'énorme masse de la littérature historique chinoise on doit d'abord se poser la question, décisive pour toute littérature, qui écrit pour qui? Qui est l'auteur et qui sont ses lecteurs? La réponse est nette: l'histoire est écrite *par des fonctionnaires pour des fonctionnaires*. Cette règle générale connaît peu d'exceptions jusqu'aux temps modernes. Les écrivains libres eux-mêmes étaient des fonctionnaires (en retraite) ou voulaient s'engager dans la carrière; d'autre part, toute la production historique (y compris l'histoire anecdotique, généalogique, romancée, régionale et encyclopédique) s'adressait au même public, un public de lettrés, composé de fonctionnaires ou de fonctionnaires futurs. D'où communauté d'intérêts entre auteurs et lecteurs—conséquence qui va de soi, mais dont il convient de souligner la très grande portée. Ayant à peu près la même éducation, le même système de références, une vue du monde, des goûts, des fonctions et des intérêts communs, ceux qui écrivent et ceux qui lisent l'histoire communient sans aucune difficulté. Or ce fait, déjà important pour toutes les branches de l'histoire, devient capital dans le cas des institutions politiques, économiques et sociales, qui touchent de près le régime. Non seulement l'accent qu'on met sur certains thèmes en dépend, mais les sujets mêmes qu'on traite. Certains sujets s'imposent tout naturellement dans l'univers des fonctionnaires, d'autres sont éliminés ou tabou. Le

---

[6] *Wen-hsien t'ung-ka'o*, préface de l'auteur (ed. *Shih-t'ung*, 1935), 3a.
[7] Ibid., 3c; cf. Cheng Ch'iao, préface au *T'ung-chih*, 2a.

choix des sujets dépend à la fois des préoccupations de l'époque,[8] ce qui permet une certaine variation limitée, et de la pérennité des tâches de la classe dirigeante, ce qui oblige les historiens de traiter les mêmes problèmes, le plus souvent sous le même titre traditionnel.

On peut discerner quatre genres dans cette branche spéciale de l'historiographie chinoise. Ce sont dans l'ordre chronologique de leur apparition: les monographies, les encyclopédies, les recueils des statuts et les monographies locales. En vérité, les histoires locales (*fang-chih*) forment une classe à part. Aussi n'ai-je pas l'intention d'en parler ici. Il faut remarquer cependant que dans leur cadre géographique (régional ou local), elles reproduisent le traitement monographique de certains sujets traditionnels, créant s'il le faut de nouvelles catégories, et qu'elles representent le dernier mot de l'historiographie traditionnelle, sa négation et son aboutissement.

Ssu-ma Ch'ien, le père de l'historiographie chinoise, fut aussi le premier à donner à l'histoire sa division quadripartie en annales (*chi*), récits biographiques (*lieh-chuan*), tableaux (*piao*) et monographies. Il a donné à ces derniers le nom de *shu* (qu'on peut traduire par écrit, livre, document, traité ou dissertation), titre qui fut remplacé dès le (*Ch'ien*) *Han-shu* de Pan Ku (A.D. 32–92) par *chih*. Ce terme définitif, sans doute très ancien, signifie d'abord 'enregistrement', 'description', et dans un sense plus général 'histoire'. Ce n'est qu'à partir de Pan Ku que le mot devient le nom du genre.

De quoi traitaient ces premiers essais? On y trouve sous forme embryonnaire ou à un état déjà élaboré presque tous les titres des monographies ultérieures. Il n'est pas possible de suivre ici de près la génèse de tous le traités et d'attribuer sa part créative à chaque historien. Le problème est très complexe et mériterait une étude approfondie. Nous nous contenterons de faire quelques remarques au sujet de l'ordre de leur présentation, en donnant un schéma des sujets traités et un tableau chiffré de l'ordre des préoccupations, de l'ordre traditionnel de préséance.

On peut affirmer sans crainte de se tromper que ce furent les anciens Rituels (en grande partie conservés dans les livres classiques) qui servirent de modèle aux premières monographies. Aussi les traités sur les rites (*li*) et la musique (*yüeh*) occupent-ils la première place. La raison en est sans doute l'existence des Rituels, mais plus encore l'influence grandissante du confucianisme sous les Han: ces questions étaient les plus élaborées, les règles de comportement (cérémonies et coutumes) et les prescriptions de la hiérarchie étant considérées comme primordiales pour le maintien de

---

[8] En vérité, dans une mesure très limitée. L'exemple le plus instructif à cause de son caractère exceptionnel est l'essai sur le bouddhisme et le taoïsme (*Wei-shu* ch. 114: *shih-lao chih*), qui pour cette raison n'apparaît pas dans notre tableau. Autre exemple; le traité de l'organisation tribale dans le *Liao-shih*.

l'ordre social. Chaque fois qu'on rencontre le titre 'rites', il faudrait donc tenir compte des trois aspects (religieux, coutumier et social) du caractère *li*. Le côté religieux se prolonge dans les chapitres traitant des sacrifices et des grandes cérémonies d'Etat (*chiao-ssu* ou *chi-ssu*) tandis que le coutumier se voit accroître par des monographies particulières consacrées au cérémonial de la cour (*li-yi*), aux règlements somptuaires, insignes et uniformes (*yü-fu* ou *ch'e-fu*).

A la deuxième place (mais l'ordre traditionnel fut plus tard interverti)[9] nous trouvons les sujets qu'on peut dénommer les 'sciences' de la nature: les observations des phénomènes du Ciel et de la Terre et les règles qui en découlent, indispensables pour l'agriculture. Ce sont les chapitres sur le calendrier ou calcul du temps (*lü-li*), et sur l'astronomie (*t'ien-wen*). Si le mérite d'avoir été pionnier dans ce domaine revient sans conteste à Ssu-ma Ch'ien, à la fois historiographe et astronome de la Cour disposant d'une longue tradition écrite de ce métier (il donna d'ailleurs à son traité astronomique le titre combien révélateur de 'Fonctionnaires du Ciel'), il est aussi naturel que Pan Ku subit l'influence de la spéculation cosmologique de son époque et inaugura la large rubrique des phénomènes extraordinaires (*wu-hsing*, les 'cinq éléments'): inondations, sécheresses et d'autres 'signes et présages'.

Pour ce deuxième groupe de traités, il faudrait attendre les Sung pour voir naître le besoin d'élargir l'éventail des sciences. Mais ceci reste exceptionnel: le pli des traditions est déjà trop rigide.[10] Il faut donc insister sur les guillemets de 'sciences' et souligner leur stade pré-scientifique, purement empirique et fortement entaché de croyances superstitieuses.

Si toutes les monographies—on pourrait même dire toute l'histoire—étaient conçues comme un *guide de la pratique gouvernementale*,[11] les problèmes de l'administration proprement dite devaient occuper une place centrale. Connaître les rouages de la machine de l'Etat était indispensable pour ses serviteurs. Savoir comment fonctionne l'appareil de l'administration civile et militaire, quels sont les titres, les attributions et la hiérarchie des fonctionnaires (*pai-kuan* ou *chih-kuan* à partir des Han Postérieurs, et *ping*, monographies du système militaire, à partir des T'ang); connaître les avenues du pouvoir, les conditions et les modalités du choix, de la formation et de l'avancement des fonctionnaires (*hsüan-chü*), le système de

---

[9] Les 'sciences' sont à la première place dans: *Wei-shu, Chin-Shu, Chiu Wu-tai shih, Sung-shih, Chin-shih, Yüan-shih, Ming-shih* et *Ch'ing-shih kao*.

[10] Cheng Ch'iao (1104–62) consacre un de ses sommaires (*lüeh*, autre nom pour *chih*, terme qu'il réserve pour le titre de son encyclopédie: *T'ung-chih*) aux plantes et aux bêtes—parmi d'autres innovations sur l'onomastique, la linguistique, la cartographie et l'archéologie. Ce qui ne signifie nullement l'inexistence des sciences naturelles à cette époque, mais leur absence dans les traités traditionnels.

[11] Rappelons le titre définitif de l'ouvrage de Ssu-ma Kuang: 'Miroir complet *pour aider à gouverner*'. Le titre original est non moins significatif sur un autre plan: *T'ung-chih*, 'Histoire générale', titre qu'adoptera Cheng Ch'iao pour son encyclopédie.

l'éducation et, dès les T'ang, les arcanes des examens—à toutes ces questions d'un intérêt vital pour les élites, le lecteur trouvait réponse dans les traités respectifs.[12] De même, pour préparer le fonctionnaire à son ministère, il était nécessaire de l'initier à la géographie en général et à l'administration territoriale de l'empire en particulier (*ti-li*), de le familiariser avec le système hydrographique, les questions des transports et de la canalisation (*ho-ch'ü*). Il fallait également lui donner des notions de l'économie politique (*shih-huo*) et des institutions légales (*hsing-fa*), pour l'habituer à l'exercice de ses fonctions dans l'administration fiscale et judiciaire. Il va de soi que ce troisième groupe de monographies, traitant des institutions de l'Etat, avait tendance à se gonfler au fur et à mesure de l'aménagement de l'Etat et de la consolidation de ses assises bureaucratiques.

Finalement, pour arrondir les connaissances du lettré—et on ne peut jamais assez insister sur le fait que chaque fonctionnaire était par définition un lettré—il était opportun de lui mettre entre les mains un guide bibliographique. Ces bibliographies (*i-wen* ou *ching-chi*), qui n'étaient autre chose que le catalogue des livres de la bibliothèque impériale—pendant longtemps la seule, et toujours la plus grande bibliothèque de l'empire—permettaient une orientation rapide dans toutes les branches de la littérature. La compilation des bibliographies dépendait des circonstances: elle était particulièrement à propos lorsque le rédacteur cumulait les fonctions d'historiographe et de bibliothécaire impérial et aux moments où, les livres écrits ou imprimés s'accumulant après de longues périodes creuses défavorables aux collections, un nouvel inventaire était indiqué.

Bien que l'ordre des monographies soit différent dans chacune des histoires officielles, la division en groupes ne nous paraît pas arbitraire. Au contraire, un classement semble correspondre parfaitement à la conception générale qui est à la base de la répartition des matières traitées. Ce groupement commode en quartre classes nous permet aussi de réunir en un seul tableau toutes les histoires officielles qui contiennent des monographies et de donner une idée de leur importance relative. Les pourcentages calculés sur la base du nombre des chapitres (et non pas, comme il faudrait pour plus de précision, des pages) ne sont qu'approximatifs. Les chiffres sont toutefois suffisamment éloquents pour illustrer certaines tendances.

On trouvera donc dans le tableau ci-dessous d'abord le titre, la date de la rédaction et le nombre total des chapitres (*chüan*) des histoires officielles; puis, le nombre absolu et le pourcentage des monographies (sur le total des chapitres); enfin, le pourcentage de chaque classe à l'intérieur de la partie monographique.

---

[12] L'introduction à la rubrique de l'organisation bureaucratique (*chih-kuan lei*) dans le Catalogue Impérial de 1782 (*Ssu-k'u ch'üan-shu tsung-mu t'i-yao*, ch. 79, ed. Commercial Press, II, 1667) dit: 'En effet, l'établissement des fonctions est la base de toutes les institutions.'

Les rubriques sont les suivantes:
  I. *Rites, coutumes* (rites, cérémonial; musique et liturgie; sacrifices; insignes et uniformes)
 II. *'Sciences'* (astronomie-astrologie; calendrier; phénomènes extra-ordinaires, cataclysmes)
III. *Institutions gouvernementales* (étatiques)
    1. Administration civile et militaire; choix des fonctionnaires (examens); éducation.
    2. Géographie administrative.
    3. Economie (administration fiscale).
    4. Lois (administration judicaire).
 IV. *Bibliographie.*

### TABLEAU DES MONOGRAPHIES DES HISTOIRES OFFICIELLES

| | | *Nombre des chapitres* | | | *Répartition des monogr. entre les classes (%)* | | | | | | |
| | | | | | i | ii | iii | | | | iv |
| *Titre* | *Date* | Total | Mon. | Mon. % | | | 1 | 2 | 3 | 4 | |
|---|---|---|---|---|---|---|---|---|---|---|---|
| Shih-chi | B.C. 90 | 130 | 8 | 6·5 | 49·5 | 30 | | | 4·5 | 17 | |
| Han-shu | A.D. 90 | 120 | 18 | 15 | 16·5 | 44 | | 16·5 | 11 | 5·5 | 5·5 |
| Hou-Han-shu (*) | 300 | 130 | 30 | 23 | 26·6 | 40 | 16·6 | 16·6 | | | |
| Sung-shu | 488 | 100 | 30 | 30 | 49·9 | 36·5 | 6·6 | 13·3 | | | |
| Nan-Ch'i shu | 537 | 59 | 11 | 19·1 | 36·4 | 36·4 | 9 | 18·2 | | | |
| Wei-shu | 554 | 136 | 20 | 14·7 | 25 | 40 | 5 | 15 | 5 | 5 | |
| Chin-shu | 644 | 130 | 20 | 15·4 | 30 | 45 | 5 | 10 | 5 | 5 | |
| Sui-shu | 644 | 85 | 30 | 35·3 | 33·3 | 26·6 | 10 | 10 | 3·3 | 3·3 | 13·3 |
| Ch. T'ang-shu | 945 | 200 | 30 | 15 | 40 | 20 | 10 | 13·3 | 6·7 | 3·3 | 6·7 |
| Ch. Wu-tai shih | 974 | 150 | 12 | 8 | 33·3 | 25 | 16·6 | 8·3 | 8·3 | 8·3 | |
| T'ang-shu | 1060 | 225 | 56 | 25 | 27 | 26·6 | 14·5 | 14 | 9 | 2 | 7 |
| Sung-shih | 1345 | 496 | 162 | 32·7 | 35·2 | 22·8 | 18·5 | 8 | 8·6 | 1·9 | 5 |
| Liao-shih | 1345 | 115 | 32 | 27·8 | 31·2 | 9·6 | 31·2 | 15·6 | 6·2 | 6·2 | |
| Chin-shih | 1345 | 135 | 39 | 29 | 41 | 10·3 | 23 | 10·3 | 12·8 | 2·6 | |
| Yüan-shih | 1370 | 210 | 58 | 27·6 | 24·3 | 17·2 | 27·6 | 15·5 | 8·6 | 6·8 | |
| Ming-shih | 1736 | 332 | 75 | 22·6 | 29·4 | 20 | 16 | 17·3 | 8 | 4 | 5·3 |
| Ch'ing-shih kao | 1927 | 536 | 142 | 26·4 | 16·9 | 24·7 | 18·3 | 28·2 | 7 | 2·1 | 2·8 |

\* Date des monographies.

Quelles sont les conclusions à tirer de cette statistique? Rappelons d'abord les facteurs qui faussent le tableau: nombre des chapitres au lieu des pages; la quantité variable des monographies change outre mesure les rapports entre les classes établies par nous; mettre, comme nous l'avons fait délibérément, cérémonial et insignes sous 'rites', grossit démésurément le groupe rituel et amoindrit le groupe institutionnel. En dépit des inconvénients de cette méthode grossière, on peut aisément constater certaines tendances: *diminution de la place qu'occupent les rites* (de la moitié à un tiers environ) *et les 'sciences'* (de deux cinquièmes à un cinquième); *augmentation de l'importance des matières institutionnelles* en général (du simple au double), et des chapitres sur les fonctionnaires et de la géographie en particulier (du simple au triple). En d'autres termes, nous assistons à un déplacement du centre de gravitation de l'irrationnel vers le rationnel, du rituel au fonctionnel, du spéculatif au concret. Bref: sécularisation, rationalisation, bureaucratisation. Ces tendances seront confirmées par la composition des encyclopédies et des collections de statuts.[13]

Quelle est la valeur des monographies? La réponse sera différente selon qu'on adopte le système des concepts de l'époque dont elles sont l'expression ou qu'on se place à un point de vue moderne. L'utilité des traités pour le lecteur pour qui ils ont été conçus est indéniable: c'est le compendium de toutes les connaissances accessibles et nécessaires au lettré-fonctionnaire moyen. De toutes les connaissances, c'est-à-dire un peu de chaque connaissance qui pouvait être utile à un honnête homme (*chün-tzu*) dans l'exercice de son métier. Et ce métier, ne l'oublions pas, n'était point le savoir spécialisé, ni les connaissances techniques particulières, mais la science de gouverner. Le but, pleinement atteint, de l'instruction générale dispensée par les traités n'était nullement de former des érudits mais des hommes d'Etat, des administrateurs informés de toutes les activités gouvernementales, des membres utiles d'une classe dirigeante.[14]

L'idéal d'une culture générale et d'une formation politique qui soustend tous les traités sans exception explique aussi leur style, leur technique. Les introductions visent moins d'épuiser une question que d'en donner un abrégé, baigné dans la philosophie orthodoxe et émaillé de citations classiques. La partie principale se présente comme un précis de recettes, illustrées d'exemples historiques. Plus le sujet est technique, plus l'auteur aura recours aux sources originales dont il incorporera de longs passages à son texte, se bornant au rôle d'un rédacteur, coupant par ci, ajoutant par là, embellissant parfois, toujours selon l'art de citation cher aux compilateurs chinois et dont nous avons parlé dans l'introduction de ce papier.

[13] Cf la vue différente de J. Gernet, 'Economie et action humaine en Chine', *Critique* (Paris), No. 103 (Décembre 1955), p. 1099.

[14] A peu près comme les leçons de piano ou de chant données naguère aux jeunes filles de bonne famille en Europe ne comptaient pas en faire des artistes mais des épouses, des dames accomplies.

Cela revient à dire que les traités se présentent comme une mosaïque de textes et de bribes de textes: des extraits textuels de calendriers, de calculs astronomiques et mathématiques, de rituels, de textes liturgiques, de lois, de recensements—et d'innombrables mémoires, requêtes, pétitions. Ce dernier point est très important, non seulement en raison de la masse de ces textes, mais parce que leur quantité détermine la valeur passée et actuelle des monographies. En effet, citer tant de mémoires au trône, tant de rapports, était dans la nature des choses: les pièces officielles étaient en même temps la source principale dans une société bureaucratique et l'exercice de style le plus prisé dans une société lettrée.

Or, cet aspect bureaucratique et lettré à la fois de la manière de citer les textes originaux définit la valeur des monographies pour l'historien moderne. Plus que les traités contiennent des textes anciens et moins qu'on aît accès aux documents originaux, plus grand sera le prix des matériaux qu'ils mettent à notre disposition. Souvent les monographies constituent notre source unique pour la connaissance des institutions. Toutefois, on ne peut exploiter toute leur richesse qu'en confrontant continuellement les citations tronquées avec les autres textes contemporains (les annales et les biographies) et surtout les documents originaux conservés ailleurs (monuments archéologiques, inscriptions, codes, collections de statuts, oeuvres complètes des écrivains, etc. . . .). Cette méthode, déjà payante pour l'époque des Han et des Six Dynasties, est de rigueur à partir des T'ang où sources indépendantes et textes parallèles se multiplient. Ajoutons que quelquefois les traités peuvent contenir des informations ou des documents qui ont échappé aux compilateurs des sources plus complètes (comme par exemple les annales véridiques, *shih-lu*, ou les recueils *hui-yao*).

Enfin, en dehors de leur présentation et de leur perspective historique qu'il sera toujours utile à l'historien moderne de connaître, les monographies restent pour nous le cadre le plus commode à remplir et comme la charpente de toute histoire sérieuse à venir. C'est pourquoi il vaudrait mieux d'en tirer le plus grand parti—par des études, des traductions intégrales ou partielles, des commentaires, des indexes—au lieu de se perdre en des projets chimériques et parfaitement inutiles concernant la traduction totale des vingt-quatre histoires officielles. Le poids mort en chinois suffit.

### 3. *Les encyclopédies*

L'abondance et la variété des encyclopédies chinoises appellent quelques observations générales. On peut distinguer selon l'usage auquel elles sont destinées plusieurs sortes d'encyclopédies: les inventaires de connaissances ou encyclopédies générales; les lexiques de composition littéraire; les manuels de sciences politiques; et, finalement, les collections de textes, conservatoires d'érudition. Tous ces genres se touchent, bien entendu, et ont un dénominateur commun: le goût de la citation et de la classification. La propension de l'esprit chinois à la pensée par catégories—les encyclopédies s'appellent à juste titre 'livres de classification' (*lei-shu*)—et à la compilation par citations textuelles n'explique que la méthode commune de cette vaste branche de la littérature.[15] Leur floraison à partir des T'ang (618–906) a des raisons historiques particulières.

Ce sont les examens pour le choix des fonctionnaires qui ont créé une demande et une offre croissante pour des manuels commodes de toutes les connaissances utiles en vue des épreuves. La nécessité d'écrire des essais et des poèmes selon un canon traditionnel fit sentir le besoin d'anthologies de modèles, de thèmes, de stylistique, de versification; l'obligation de connaître les livres classiques et les histoires, surtout les parties ayant trait aux questions de gouvernement, au sens le plus large du mot, l'obligation aussi d'écrire un pensum et de répondre à des questions concernant des problèmes politiques et administratifs, firent désirable la parution de manuels contenant un résumé et un abrégé historique de tous les sujets, classés par catégories.

Si nous disons que les examens d'un caractère littéraire et bureaucratique ont donné une forte impulsion à la production d'encyclopédies, il revient au même d'affirmer que la production en séries de lettrés-fonctionnaires a orienté l'historiographie vers la compilation de compendiums d'économie politique. Examens et manuels ne sont qu'une expression complémentaire de la fonctionnarisation de la société chinoise.

L'idéal d'une culture générale—humaniste, littéraire et politique—qui préside à la formation des lettrés-fonctionnaires, explique du reste l'horizon commun des monographies historiques et des encyclopédies, tant générales que spécialisées. Pour s'en rendre compte, il suffit d'examiner la table des matières de ces dernières.[16] Ce qui est un signe des temps, c'est l'accroissement de l'intérêt aux sciences politiques, aux problèmes économiques, à l'histoire des institutions. Il faudrait vraiment être aveugle pour ne pas voir un rapport entre la crise du milieu du VIIIe siècle et la gestation de cette littérature.

La première des encyclopédies d'économie politique, aujourd'hui perdue, 'Institutions gouvernementales', *Cheng-tien* (*c.* 740, en 35 ch.), fut l'oeuvre de Liu Chih, fils de Liu Chih-chi (661–721), un des plus grands historiens de la Chine.[17] La filiation de l'ouvrage me paraît aussi carac-

[15] Voir Teng-Biggerstaff, *An Annotated Bibliography of Selected Chinese Reference Works* (Cambridge, Mass., 1950), 106 et suiv.

[16] Ibid., p. 110: 'The following is a rough summary of contents . . . of most later encyclopedias: celestial phenomena, geography, emperors and empresses, human nature and conduct, government, rites, music, law, officialdom, ranks of nobility, military affairs, domestic economy, property, clothing, vehicles, tools, food, utensils, crafts, chess, Taoism, Buddhism, spirits, medicine, and natural history.'

[17] Sur Liu Chih, voir *MSOS* 34 (1931), 64–65, et la notice du Catalogue Impérial consacré au *T'ung-tien* (*Ssu-k'u*, ch. 81, II, 1695).

téristique que sa date: en effet, vers le même temps furent terminés le vaste Rituel de la période K'ai-yüan, *Ta T'ang k'ai-yüan li* (732, en 150 ch.) et les règlements administratifs de la dynastie, *T'ang liu-tien* (739, en 30 ch.). S'inspirant du *Cheng-tien* et faisant de copieux emprunts aux deux recueils administratifs, Tu Yu (735–812) écrivit la première histoire générale des institutions, le célèbre *T'ung-tien* (801, en 200 ch.), modèle de toutes les encyclopédies politiques à venir.[18]

Or, ce qui caractérise cet ouvrage, c'est l'accent mis sur les sciences politiques. L'ordre de présentation des neuf parties est le suivant: 1. Economie politique (à la première place), 2. Examens, 3. Fonctionnaires, 4. Rites, 5. Musique, 6. Armée, 7. Lois, 8. Géographie administrative de la Chine proprement dite et 9, des régions frontières. Autrement dit, Tu Yu renonce à traiter 'sciences' et bibliographie (classes II et IV de nos tableaux), et donne la priorité aux institutions gouvernementales, réléguant rites et coutumes à une place secondaire. C'est une véritable revolution si on pense aux monographies des histoires officielles.

Les petits résumés placés à la tête de chaque section témoignent d'un esprit historique intéressé à l'évolution des institutions. La méthode— ordre chronologique des citations à l'intérieur des sections—reste cependant inchangée. C'est presque inutile d'ajouter que la conception de cette forme encyclopédique des sciences politiques est née dans le cerveau d'un haut fonctionnaire (Tu Yu fut ministre).

Le *T'ung-tien* a créé un précédent et les imitateurs et successeurs de Tu Yu furent nombreux. Parmi ceux-ci il y a trois ou quatre auteurs dont le nom mérite d'être retenu. De Cheng Ch'iao, qu'il fut la mode depuis trente ans de porter aux nues, nous avons parlé en passant.[19] Esprit inventif, cet historien a pourtant laissé une oeuvre où les idées originales disparaissent sous le fatras des idées reçues. Li Hsin-ch'uan (1166–1243), de la lignée des grands historiens critiques, méticuleux et lucides des Sung, avait écrit la chronique très richement documentée du début des Sung Méridionaux.[20] Or, le volume compagnon, sous le titre filandreux de 'Notes diverses sur la cour et le peuple depuis la période

---

[18] Sur ces ouvrages, voir R. Des Rotours, *Le Traité des Examens* (Paris, 1932), 84, 99 et 149. La classification des encyclopédies politiques a donné du fil à retordre aux bibliographes chinois. Celle du Catalogue Impérial est assez logique. Toutes les encyclopédies générales y sont classées sous la rubrique *lei-shu* (*Ssu-k'u*, chapitres 135–9), tandis que les encyclopédies politiques du genre *T'ung-tien*, les recueils de documents administratifs (*hui-yao*) et les collections de statuts (*hui-tien*), forment la classe à part des 'livres de gouvernement' *cheng-shu* (ch. 81–84). Cependant le *T'ang liu-tien* est considéré comme appartenant à une troisième classe, celle des livres sur le 'système administratif', *chih-kuan* (ch. 79–80). Sans parler de nombreuses contradictions mineures, il est décidément faux de mélanger les manuels et les recueils de documents.

[19] Voir ci-dessus, note 10.

[20] Le *Chien-yen i lai hsi-nien yao-lu*, chronique de 36 ans (1127–62) en 200 chapitres. Cette grande chronique fait suite à celle des Sung du Nord, *Hsu Tzu-chih t'ung-chien ch'ang-pien* (1174, original en 1063 ch.) par Li Tao (1114–83), lui-même continuateur de Ssu-ma Kuang. Je suis convaincu que le renom de Li Tao et de Li Hsin-ch'uan ira en augmentant.

Chien-yen' (*Chien-yen i lai ch'ao-yeh tsa-chi*, 40 chapitres écrits en 1202 et 1216), se révèle comme un excellent tableau des institutions. Wang Ying-lin (1223–1296), polygraphe et auteur de la meilleure encyclopédie générale, le *Yü-hai* (en 200 ch.), fut sans doute le cerveau le plus encyclo-pédique dans la cohorte des compilateurs. Il mérite d'être mentionné ici, parce que son encyclopédie, destiné à être le viatique des candidats aux plus hauts examens, reflète bien les préoccupations de l'époque (voir le tableau ci-dessous).

Nous avons déjà parlé de Ma Tuan-lin, le continuateur le plus digne de l'oeuvre de Tu Yu, en tant qu'historien original. Il faut cependant ajouter que son encyclopédie, le *Wen-hsien t'ung-k'ao* (c. 1317, en 348 chapitres), fruit de l'immense labeur d'un seul homme, n'est pas seulement une histoire générale (*t'ung*) des institutions, mais aussi un examen critique (*k'ao*) des documents originaux (*wen*) et des textes et dissertations apparentés (*hsien*). Cette confrontation libre des anciens lettrés et des écrivains con-temporains, des opinions d'autrui, ce dialogue où percent toujours la voix lucide et la chaleur combative de l'auteur, font de Ma Tuan-lin un écrivain exceptionnel. Les vues perspicaces et les jugements pondérés abondent dans ses préfaces et ses commentaires.[21]

Il serait fastidieux d'énumérer tous les ouvrages qui font suite au *T'ung-tien*, au *T'ung-chih*, au *Wen-hsien t'ung-ka'o* et aux autres encyclopédies: leurs plan, dessein, méthode ne changent guere. Il faut cependant relever quelques tendances qui se font jour dès les Sung et qui favorisent la com-pilation des compendiums. L'invention de l'imprimerie assure aux con-naissances une diffusion jusqu'alors inconnue et permet aux bourses modestes l'achat de livres. L'accumulation des bibliothèques à son tour renforce les assises d'une éducation livresque, fige le caractère littéraire des examens, aide au Néo-Confucianisme d'inculquer le conservatisme tradi-tionaliste et de répandre le respect de l'antiquité et le goût de l'histoire. Autant de raisons pour la demande accrue de résumés et d'inventaires. C'est aussi l'explication de la place de plus en plus grande qu'occupe la bibliographie (par exemple, dans le *Yü-hai* et le *Wen-hsien t'ung-k'ao*).

Un autre fait à signaler est le recul de l'initiative privée. Il devient de plus en plus difficile à un seul auteur de maîtriser toutes les branches de la littérature et la compilation des grandes encyclopédies passe entre les mains des rédacteurs anonymes d'une commission impériale. Les oeuvres individuelles sont remplacées par des entreprises collectives et officielles, ce qui n'augmente pas nécessairement leur valeur.

C'est encore plus vrai pour les collections de documents et statuts officiels dont la rédaction demande l'accès aux archives de l'Etat. Avant de passer à ce groupe d'ouvrages, je voudrais consigner dans un deuxième tableau la place assignée aux différents sujets dans quelques encyclopédies

---

[21] Il est étonnant qu'il n'existe ni traduction, ni étude de sa contribution personnelle.

et un recueil de documents. La classification est faite selon les mêmes principes que dans le premier tableau, sauf que nous avons ajouté une rubrique pour les institutions politiques (comme féodalisme et généalogie impériale) qu'il était difficile de classer sous les autres rubriques. Le calcul des pourcentages reste approximatif pour le *Yü-hai* et le *Sung hui-yao* (d'après le nombre des chapitres), mais pouvait être précisé dans le cas du *T'ung-tien* et du *Wen-hsien t'ung-k'ao* (d'après le nombre des pages dans l'édition *Shih-t'ung*). On remarquera que la répartition des matériaux confirme amplement les tendances relevées lors de l'étude des monographies.

TABLEAU DES ENCYCLOPEDIES (pourcentages)

| | *T'ung-tien* (801) | *Wen-hsien t'ung-k'ao* (1317) | *Yü-hai* (1290) | *Sung hui-yao* (1044–1242) |
|---|---|---|---|---|
| I. Rituel, coutumes | 50·2 | 25·6 | 21·5 | 22·5 |
| II. 'Sciences' | | 9·7 | 9·5 | 1 |
| III. Institutions<br>1. Administration<br>2. Géographie<br>3. Economie<br>4. Lois<br>5. Politique | 22·8<br>16·8<br>5·9<br>4·1 | 17<br>9·7<br>8·5<br>3·5<br>8·7 | 36·5<br>6<br>5·5<br>2 | 41<br>6·5<br>21·5<br>4<br>3 |
| IV. Bibliographie | | 17·3 | 19 | |

### 4. *Les recueils de documents et collections de statuts*

Avec les collections de documents nous quittons le domaine de l'historiographie proprement dite. Il convient de faire en effet une nette distinction entre les encyclopédies, qui s'éloignent déjà de l'histoire, mais présentent leurs matériaux dans une perspective d'historien, et l'assemblage de textes originaux dans un état brut et sans autre lien que celui de la rubrique où ils sont classés. Il est facile à voir pourquoi on les confond quelquefois: les deux procèdent du même art de la citation et de la même classification (celle des monographies). Il est vrai aussi qu'il y a de rares ouvrages qui sont à la limite des deux genres (comme le *Ts'e-fu yüan-kuei* que je compterais néanmoins parmi les recueils de documents).

Ces compilations se définissent donc de la façon suivante: I. Ce sont les oeuvres impersonnelles de commissions officielles, en général, le produit des offices d'historiographie; 2. elles ne contiennent que des documents officiels provenant des archives de l'Etat: édits et décrets impériaux, lois, statuts, règlements, et surtout des rapports de fonctionnaires (fonctionnaires de tous les échelons, mais dans la plupart des cas, hauts fonctionnaires); 3. elles donnent ces documents tels quels, sans apprêt, sans changement de style, en principe *in extenso*. Voilà pourquoi ces ouvrages, sans être de l'histoire, sont la meilleure source de l'historien moderne de la Chine. On ne saurait assez insister sur leur valeur documentaire.

La première 'collection des documents importants' fut le *T'ang hui-yao* (100 chapitres). Oeuvre de trois compilateurs à des dates différentes (804, 852, 961), elle fut achevée par un rédacteur qui entreprit aussi de réunir les documents relatifs à la période des Cinq Dynasties, *Wu-tai hui-yao* (961, 30 chapitres). Les documents qu'on y trouve classés sous de nombreuses rubriques relèvent en général des institutions politiques, économiques et sociales. Pour ne donner qu'un seul exemple de son utilité, celui qui voudrait étudier l'usure sous les T'ang, trouvera tous les documents à ce sujet réunis dans un seul chapitre du *T'ang hui-yao*.

Bien que commodes, il n'y a pas de comparaison possible entre ces deux *hui-yao* et les imitations que des compilateurs ont entrepris à une époque tardive pour une dynastie précédente, en tirant leurs matériaux de sources déjà existantes comme les histoires officielles.[22] Juste le contraire est vrai pour le *Sung hui-yao*, source monumentale de la plus grande valeur et qui n'est devenue accessible qu'en 1936. Des commissions officielles de la dynastie Sung ont réuni de temps en temps les dossiers qui ont été déjà utilisés ou non dans les différents ouvrages commandés à l'office de l'historiographie. Les titres de dix recueils—on dirait mieux de dix états, puisque les éditions consécutives furent parfois refondues—sont connus; leur rédaction remonte à la période entre 1044 et 1242; le nombre total des chapitres était de 2442! Il n'en reste aujourd'hui que 460 chapitres elatifs à la période 960–1224.[23]

Après avoir montré la place qu'occupent dans ce recueil les institutions (voir le Tableau des encyclopédies), il suffira de dire que le *Sung hui-yao* est une mine de renseignements où on trouve, dans leur texte original, la plupart des documents tronqués des autres sources, outre les documents introuvables ailleurs.

Il ne nous reste qu'un mot à dire sur les vastes collections des statuts et règlements administratifs des deux dernières dynasties, comme le *Ta-Ming*

[22] C'est le cas du *Hsi-Han hui-yao* (1211, 70 ch.) et du *Tung-Han hui-yao* (1226, 40 ch.), compilés par un même auteur sous les Sung. De même, les *hui-yao* consacrés à la période des Trois Royaumes et des Ming n'ont été réunis qu'à la fin du XIXe siècle; cf. Teng-Biggerstaff, op. cit., 158 ss.

[23] Voir ibid., 162 et T'ang Chung, *Sung hui-yao yen-chiu* (Shanghai, 1932). Cf. aussi la table très commode des états successifs chez Wei Ying-ch'i, *Chung-kuo shih-hsüeh shih* (Shanghai, 1947), 176–7, et la table des matières de la section économique dressée par Konuma Tadashi dans *Shigaku Zasshi* 48 (1937), 886–901.

*hui-tien* et la *Ta-Ch'ing hui-tien*.[24] Source inépuisable pour le spécialiste du détail administratif, pour l'historien général ce sont des monuments massifs de l'Etat bureaucratique. De multiples éditions, chaque fois augmentées, de plus en plus minutieuses, donnent ici une image saisissante de la lourde, de la monstrueuse machinerie, avec sa paperasserie, ses heurts et, néanmoins, son roulement. Toutefois, les innombrables victimes du rouleau compresseur, il faut aller les chercher ailleurs. Ici n'est servi que celui qui voudrait écouter le bruit sourd d'un appareil précis et perfectionné, aboutissement et incarnation complète de ces fonctionnaires-lettrés qui ont dominé et écrit l'histoire de la Chine.

[24] Sur ces ouvrages, voir W. Franke, *Preliminary Notes on the Important Chinese Literary Sources for the History of the Ming Dynasty* (Chengtu, 1948), p. 42, et J. K. Fairbank, *Ch'ing Documents* (Cambridge, Mass., 1952), vol. 1, pp. 59–60 et 66–71.

# 7. CHINESE BIOGRAPHICAL WRITING

## D. C. TWITCHETT

*Professor of Chinese, University of London*

The writing of biography in any given society not only throws into relief the motives, preoccupations, and interests of its authors, but also illuminates the relationships existing between the individuals who provide its subjects and society as a whole. To the historian, biographical writings are most valuable source material, but in the use of this material he needs a clear understanding of these factors and of the effects which they have upon the finished work. For the western historian working in the field of Chinese history, the special outlook and ideology of the traditional scholar-bureaucrat class on the one hand, and the very different status of the individual in his social relationships on the other, make such an understanding particularly vital.

As in every field of historical writing, China is unusually well-supplied with biographical material. The Standard Histories alone contain thousands of biographical entries, while the collections of specialized biographies of various kinds and entries in Local Gazeteers bring the total to an enormous figure. If we take into account the works written for funerary or commemorative occasions, and for use in the family cults, the number can be almost indefinitely expanded. The remarks which follow do not, of course, hold good for every one of these items. However, until the beginning of western-style biography—a development which even today is still only in its infancy—this great corpus of writings extending over a period of two millenia shows a strong and unbroken tradition which demonstrates most forcibly the extraordinary continuity of Chinese literary culture. Although the following generalities refer in the first instance to the biographical entries in historical works, since the latter provided a model for less ambitious writings they have some relevance in a wider context.

In an officially compiled Standard (or Dynastic) History, or any work modelled on this form, biographical entries are included in the section entitled *chuan* or *lieh-chuan*. The use of this term, and indeed biographical writing as a whole, began with Ssu-ma Ch'ien's *Shih chi* (Records of the Historian).[1] Before his time we are faced with a complete blank. However, there is some reason to suppose that Ssu-ma Ch'ien did not simply invent

---

[1] Cf. the paper by A. F. P. Hulsewé, above, pp. 34–37.

the form. In the first century A.D., when the first extant independent biographical materials—the earliest indisputably authentic epitaphs inscribed on stone, and the *pieh-chuan* of which fragments have survived— begin, the form is already rigid and formalized. In the situation of the Han, it is too much to suppose that the *Shih chi*, compiled as it was within the Palace, had a wide circulation over a considerable area of China, even among the scholar class. The source of this widespread class of writings cannot have been the *Shih chi*, but must be sought elsewhere, possibly in writings connected with the clan cults. But whatever this type of writing may have been, it has not only vanished without a single trace, but it does not even figure in the bibliography of the History of the Former Han Dynasty (*Han shu*). I doubt whether this mystery is soluble in the light of the present state of our knowledge, but it is safe to say that some such form of biography must have been the source of Ssu-ma Ch'ien's *lieh-chuan* form and of that of the early epitaphs and separate biographies. The very name of the form, *chuan*, may also have been adopted from this common source.

The medieval historians, however, had a different explanation for the word *chuan*, linking it with the usage in which it forms part of the names of the oldest commentaries on the Spring and Autumn Annals (*Ch'un-ch'iu*).[2] In this connection the term originally means 'something handed down' and thus 'tradition', and its use for the commentaries on the Spring and Autumn Annals may derive from the fact that these commentaries are in fact the 'traditions' attached to the text of the classic in the various schools of Confucian learning. From an early period these 'traditions' were attached to the text of the canonical text itself, and, although they were held to be much less reliable than the text of the Classic itself, with its rigid chronological framework, they ranked above the apocrypha, and were accepted as a sort of secondary classic.

The 'tradition', especially that known as the *Tso chuan*, extend the field of history far from the dry chronicle of court ritual centred on the King which is presented by the Spring and Autumn Annals. On the one hand, by breaking away from the rigid straightjacket of chronology and the ritual calendar, these works were able to develop a coherent continuous narrative style in dealing with events. On the other hand, the divorce from court ritual enabled these 'traditions' to present episodes from the lives of ministers and nobles, and from events in the provinces. Their contents have a much more direct bearing on everyday policies and affairs than do those of the Classic itself. Moreover, the contents of the 'traditions' draw heavily on the body of semi-folklore and oral tradition rather than upon the documentary records of professional annalists which provided material for the court chronicles of which the Spring and Autumn Annals were only a single example. In this respect the 'traditions' had something in common

[2] Cf. the paper by P. van der Loon, above, pp. 26–27.

with such early compilations as the *Chan-kuo ts'ê* (Stratagems of the War-ring States) and *Kuo Yü* (Discourses of the States).

The category *lieh-chuan* in Ssu-ma Ch'ien's monumental history, what-ever the background of the word *chuan*, was a completely new departure in Chinese historical writing. These chapters deal not only with the bio-graphies of notable individuals, but with various foreign peoples—a tradi-tional arrangement which persisted in Chinese official historiography until this century. The characteristic which linked these apparently diverse types of material was that the entries were designed to develop and follow through a given topic from beginning to end, whether the theme was the career of an individual or the relationships of a foreign people with the Chinese court. They were thus quite distinct from the *pên-chi*, or Basic Annals, and from the chronicles on which these were modelled, which consisted of rigidly dated discreet facts, and deliberately avoided pointing out any lines of development or causal relationships except of the most superficial sort. Neither did they share the preoccupation of the Annals with matters of ritual significance.

Ssu-ma Ch'ien's *lieh-chuan* have more in common with the older 'tradi-tions' and anecdotal histories than the name *chuan* and the development of a theme unhampered by the restrictions of a chronological framework. His *lieh-chuan* also show the looser organization, the wider range of subject matter, the relaxation of the emphasis on Court affairs, and the ready acceptance of materials whose strict historicity was, to say the least, doubt-ful. With regard to this semi-fictional and folkloristic aspect of the *lieh-chuan* it is perhaps worth mentioning that many scholars see in the Records of the Historian (*Shih chi*) not only the beginning of the conventional form of dynastic history, but also the seeds of fiction writing.[3] The latter cer-tainly drew heavily on the polished technique of narrative prose writing perfected by Ssu-ma Ch'ien in his great history.[4]

On the basis of the materials in the *Shih chi* a reasonably good case may be made out for a parallelism between the Spring and Autumn Annals and the '*pên-chi*' (basic annals) sections on the one hand, and the three 'tradi-tions' and the *lieh-chuan* sections on the other. This assessment of the rela-tive roles of the two categories, with its implicit evaluation of their relia-bility, became an article of faith with the official historians of later cen-turies, although, as in so many other instances, orthodox theory and prac-tice often diverged widely. The theory can hardly be better expressed than in the following quotation from the first great work of Chinese historical criticism, the *Shih-t'ung* (Generalities on History) of Liu Chih-chi.[5]

[3] See Maspéro, 'Le roman historique dans la litterature chinoise de l'antiquité', *Mélanges posthumes sur les religions et l'histoire de la Chine* (1950), iii, 55–62.

[4] An interesting parallel suggests itself between the part played by the historians in the de-velopment of narrative prose in China and the West.

[5] See *Shih-t'ung t'ung-shih* 2 *lieh-chuan* 6 (Ssu-pu pei-yao edition, p. 13b). On Liu Chih-chi, see the paper by E. G. Pulleyblank, below, pp. 136–51.

The rise to prominence of annals and biographies began with the *Shih chi* and *Han shu*. The annals are in chronologically arranged form (*pien-nien*). The biographies take the form of connected events (*lieh-shih*). The chronological form (*pien-nien*) sets out in order the years and months of Emperors and Kings as does the Classic of Spring and Autumn. The form of connected events (*lieh-shih*) records the actions of subjects and ministers like the Traditions to the Spring and Autumn Annals. In the case of the Spring and Autumn Annals, they made Traditions to explain the Classic itself. In the case of the *Shih chi* and *Han shu* they provided biographies to explain the basic annals.

This theory of the relative roles and importance of the basic annals and biographies in the officially compiled histories and the assumption on this classical analogy that the latter category was the less reliable, became a matter of orthodox belief for historians, and is the assumption underlying many of the discussions of biography in the memorials of the History Office during T'ang and Wu-tai times.

However, between the time of Ssu-ma Ch'ien and the writing of the *Shih-t'ung* (710) a complete change had occurred in the circumstances under which official histories were written. These changes made the analogy with the Spring and Autumn Classic a very misleading one, and its preservation as an orthodox belief had unfortunate results upon the biographies which were thus foredoomed to an inferior status within the framework of a history.

The T'ang period saw the establishment of a system of history compilation which lasted, with modifications, until the end of the Manchu dynasty in 1911. After this official machinery had been set up, the historian had access to source material for writing his biographical entries equally voluminous and reliable as that which was used for the Annals. It would therefore be quite wrong to imagine that the *lieh-chuan* of the histories compiled under later dynasties contain the same imaginative elements which made the 'traditions' and Ssu-ma Ch'ien's *lieh-chuan* at once historically suspect and more lively. In this connection it is important to bear in mind that Ssu-ma Ch'ien had attempted a much more grandiose task than the compiler of a dynastic history. Dealing with the whole of Chinese history down to his own day, he was presented with a much longer and more sparsely documented period, and was forced to accept traditions of a suspicious nature where nothing else was available. It is both unrealistic and unfair to criticize him on this count, and it would be quite wrong to extend such criticism to his successors on the grounds that the *Shih chi* provided them with their model.

From the Han period onwards the semi-fictional and folklore element, which found no place in an official history compiled from adequate documentary sources, led a separate existence on the borderline between history and literature. The material which such works contain is often such as to interest a modern historian even when the Confucian scholar would have considered it trivial. But although there are superficial resemblances in form and style between some of these works and the *lieh-chuan* of official histories, resemblances which are not merely attempts to add an air of verisimilitude and authority to them, but which go back to their common origins, they are rarely cast in truly biographical form, but consist of fragmentary anecdotes.

During the four centuries between the decay of the Han and the reunification of the empire by the Sui, a great amount of non-official biographical writing went on. Among these writings were many collections of lives of local worthies under such titles as *Ch'i chiu chuan* (Biographies of Elders) and *Hsien-hsien chuan* (Biographies of Worthies), which represent the earliest form of those works of local antiquarian interest which developed later into the Local Gazeteer.[6] The details in such works were naturally somewhat more intimate than those in centrally compiled histories, and, since the intention of the author was normally to delineate character rather than to illuminate an official's career, their subject matter is nearer to that of western biography. But the divergence from the norm which these works display can easily be exaggerated.[7] The same is true of the individual biographies which appeared in the same period under such titles as *pieh-chuan*. Although these works show that contemporary writers were willing to regard an individual's career as a suitable subject for a separate work standing on its own interest outside the framework of a history, they appeared during a period when the state historiographical machine was in decay, and disappear when the T'ang reintroduced rigid rules for official compilation.[8]

We must now consider the method by which the *lieh-chuan* were compiled during this later period, and attempt to discover the motives of the historian in writing biography.

An official history was compiled by the History Office (*Shih kuan*), a government office staffed by members of the bureaucracy and supervised by a high-ranking minister.[9] The material which eventually became a

[6] Considerable numbers of these works are mentioned in the bibliographical chapters of the *Sui Shu* and *Chiu T'ang shu*. A number are still preserved, for example the *Ch'ên-liu ch'i-chiu chuan* of Su Lin, *Ju-nan hsien-hsien chuan* of Chou P'ei, *Hui-chi hsien-hsien chuan* of Hsieh Ch'êng, etc., but most of them were preserved in the *Shuo fu* and exist only in much abbreviated form.

[7] See for example the remarks of Shih-hsiang Chen in *FEQ* XIII I (1953), pp. 49–51.

[8] They also appear during a period when social organizations were loosened and when there were strong links with India and a society with a strong epic tradition through Buddhism. Again see Shih-hsiang Chen, loc. cit.

[9] On the official compilation of histories see *T'ang hui yao* 64–64, *Ts'ê-fu yüan-kuei* 554–60. Tamai Zehaku, *Tō no jitsuroku senshū ni kansuru ichi kōsatsu* in *Shina shakai keizai shi kenkyū* (1943). Pulleyblank, *The Tzyjyh Tongjiann Kaoyih and the sources for the history of the period 730–763, BSOS* 13 (1949–51). Cf. also the paper by Yang Lien-sheng, above, especially pp. 44–46, 53–57.

dynastic history went through a long and complicated process of preliminary drafting, and the first problem which faces us is at which stage in this
process the biographical entries became a part of the history.

The primary forms of the history, the Diaries of Activity and Repose
(*Ch'i-chü chu*), and the Records of Current Government (*Shih-chêng chi*)
were compiled by the Court Diarists and by a Great Minister respectively,
and were submitted to the History Office in strictly chronological form.[10]
This was inevitable, as they were composed day by day. The next stage
was the production of the Daily Records (*Jih-li*) which incorporated the
material from the diaries and certain reports from government departments.[11] The material from all these earlier works, together with reports
on a variety of matters the rendering of which was a duty of all officials,[12]
was selected, abbreviated, and edited into a Veritable Record (*Shih-lu*) for
each reign. This Veritable Record was organized in chronological form.
Biographical entries were appended, during some reigns at least, probably
at the end of the month or year of decease of their subject. The earliest
surviving work in this form, the *Shun-tsung shih-lu* preserved in the collected
works of Han Yü,[13] contains biographical entries of this type, but these
are not very complete, and account for by no means all of the persons
dying during the period who were later accorded biographies by the Old
T'ang History (*Chiu T'ang shu*). However, too much weight should not be
placed on this, since the recension we possess is undoubtedly an abbrevia-
tion of the full original. There is a good deal of further evidence that biographies had a place in the Veritable Records.[14]

[10] According to *Hsin T'ang shu* 47 the Diarists submitted these reports at the end of each
quarter. See R. des Rotours, *Traité des Fonctionnaires*, i, 151 ff. See also *T'ang liu tien* 8 (Konoe
edition, pp. 24b–25a). The Records of Current Government were compiled not by the Diarists
(*Ch'i-chü-lang*), but by one of the great ministers taking an actual part in the proceedings recorded.
They were sent to the History Office monthly. See *Ts'ê fu yüan kuei* 560, p. 9a, *T'ang hui yao* 56, etc.

[11] On these documents see Tamai loc. cit., and Chin Yü-fu, *T'ang Sung shih-tai shê kuan hsiu-shih
chih chih-tu k'ao* in *Kuo-shih-kuan kuan-k'an* 1/2 (1947), pp. 6–18, especially p. 15.

[12] On these reports see *T'ang hui yao* 63 (*Chu-ssu ying sung shih-kuan shih-li*); *Wu-tai hui-yao* 18
(same section); *T'ang liu-tien* 10 (Konoe edition, p. 26a) on reports of portents, etc.; and Chin
Yü-fu, op. cit., pp. 12–13. It seems, however, from *Hsin T'ang shu* 47 (des Rotours, op. cit., p. 160)
that at times the Diarists also incorporated documents which they 'corrected and revised a little,
to fill out the gaps in the National History'. An Edict of 817 (*Ts'ê fu yüan kuei* 560, pp. 8b–9b,
and *T'ang hui yao* 56) complains in fact that most of what the diarists composed followed the
Edicts and Rescripts rather than their own observations.

[13] See the text in *Han Ch'ang-li chi*: *Wai-chi* 6–8. See also Solomon, *The Veritable Record of the
T'ang Emperor Shun-tsung* (1955), an integral translation of the text. Solomon never questions the
authenticity of the text, and Ch'ên Yin-k'o also accepted it at its face value in his study 'The
Shun-tsung shih-lu and the Hsü hsüan-kuai lu', in *HJAS* 3 (1938), pp. 9–16. See Pulleyblank,
'The Shun-tsung shih-lu', *BSOAS* 19 (1957), pp. 336–44.

[14] There are a number of references in the *Tzu-chih t'ung-chien k'ao-i* to biographies (in all cases
of very high ranking ministers) in the Veritable Records, spreading over the eighth to tenth
centuries. An even clearer evidence for this is to be seen in *T'ang hui yao* 64 (*Shih-kuan tsa-lu*),
'In the sixth month 812 the Emperor was reading the Veritable Record of Su-tsung. He noticed
that in the Biographies of Great Officials there were many insubstantial phrases and flights of
empty style . . .' A surviving work written in this *Shih-lu* style with biographies added in the text
is the *Wu-yüeh pei shih*, which consciously imitates a Veritable Record.

Leaving this controversial point aside for a moment, the next stage in the compilation was the National History (*Kuo-shih*). This was a full-scale history on the *Shih-chi* and *Han shu* model, and comprised Basic Annals, Monographs, and Biographies. In fact the only difference between such a work and a Standard History was that it dealt with a reigning and not a defunct dynasty.[15]

It is clear then that the biographical entries which were eventually incorporated into the *lieh-chuan* of a completed history were composed at a relatively late stage in the process, either for the Veritable Record or for the National History. At this stage, the bulk of the historian's task was the selection and editing of material for eventual inclusion, rather than original composition. A vast mass of official documentation was available to the History Office, and it is clear that a high proportion of most dynastic histories consist of verbatim extracts (even if mutilated and torn out of context) from actual governmental papers. It is most important for us to understand first of all whose biographies the historians thought worthy of inclusion, and secondly where the materials were found for them.

The first problem was one which continually occupied the historian. On the one hand, the total omission of a person's life was a simple and effective form of criticism which was frequently resorted to. For example, the historians of late T'ang and Wu-tai times, who almost all belonged to the examination-bureaucrat class, used this method to criticize the rival group of professional finance experts.[16] Similar considerations have led, throughout history, to our being very ill-informed on the activities of another rival group, the eunuchs. But such omission could be easily justified by the political theory to which the historian subscribed. The official historian was above all compiling a corpus of precedent for future generations of Confucian bureaucrats, not attempting to provide a complete picture of his age. The intrusion into places of power of such rival groups was a matter which was of no interest unless they could be held up as a warning or example for the future. The following passage from a memorial by the early ninth-century historian Lu Sui shows clearly the theoretical standard by reference to which inclusion was justified:

> Wherever a man's meritorious achievements are not enough to warrant their being handed down to posterity, and where his goodness or wickedness are insufficient to serve as an example, even though he is a rich and powerful person [the Historian] should merely record his death in the appropriate place. [Various persons, listed by name] . . . were all

[15] On the National Histories see Pulleyblank, loc. cit., and *T'ang Hui-yao* 63–64 *passim*; cf. also the paper by Yang Lien-sheng, above, pp. 45, 56.

[16] This is clear from Wang Gung-wu, 'The *Chiu Wu-tai shih* and History Writing during the Five Dynasties', *Asia Major*, new series, vi, 1, pp. 1–22, and from my own study of professional finance experts in late T'ang times.

Great Ministers of the Han, who ranked in nobility with the Feudal Lords, yet the historian considered that they were just ordinary persons who had merely filled their office honestly and conscientiously and who had done nothing to achieve fame or reputation for meritorious deeds, and so he did not devote a biography to any of them. On the other hand in the case of [list of names] . . . all either remained commoners to the end of their days, or established their fame by resigning from their state, or cultivated their virtue and wrote books, or propounded marvels and resolved perplexities, or held fast to the Way and averted calamities. They were thus given biographies in the same category as the Duke of Chou, the Duke of Shao, Kuan tzu and Yen tzu. Thus among the rich and noble there are some who should be suppressed while among the poor and humble there are others who should be expanded upon. Confucius said 'Duke Ching of Ch'i had a thousand teams of horses, but on the day of his death the people could think of no good deed for which to praise him. Po I and Shu Ch'i starved at the foot of Mount Shou-yang and yet the people sing their praises down to this very day.' This being the case, why should the scholar whose purpose is set and who wishes to give illumination to posterity pay any attention to nobility and rank? When rich and powerful persons have accepted responsibilities and gained positions of power, and yet cannot hand down any example to posterity, this is because their virtue is not cultivated and they pay little attention to righteousness and much to temporal profit . . .[17]

Similar expressions of theory could very easily be multiplied for the following centuries, and it is clear that the biographies contained among the *lieh-chuan* were selected to provide precepts and examples for the reader. Such a didactic purpose theoretically motivated the compilers in their selection of material for the Basic Annals and Monographs, and, while the annals illustrated the conduct of Emperors and showed the interaction of their character and actions upon the rise and fall of their dynastic mandate, the biographies were to give examples of the conduct of ministers and subjects. In some cases the didactic aim is clear, as for instance in the categorized series of 'Loyal ministers', 'Oppressive officials', 'Literary figures', 'Recluses', etc., and in the frequent groupings of figures who shared some common office or interest. But the outright statement of the historian's view is reserved for his postscripts, and it is still possible to read the included biographies without the obvious intrusion of the historian's personal views.

The principle of selection for didactic purposes and of the omission of undistinguished persons of exalted rank was adhered to even during periods comparatively undistinguished in the historical field. The following passage comes from a memorial submitted by the History Office in 933:[18]

---

[17] See *T'ang hui-yao* 64.
[18] See *Wu-tai hui-yao* 18 (*Shih-kuan tsa-lu*).

. . . If they are such that the matters in them may be taken in connection with those contained in the *lieh-chuan* of the Dynastic Histories or Veritable Records then we request that they be included in the annals and biographies . . . But if there are those who have performed no service of merit to the state, nor any action of virtue to the people, but (whose biographies contain) only a record of their career and personal fame, or just give an account of their petty talents and insignificant abilities, if there is nothing which can be transmitted to posterity as an example, then in all cases I request that they shall not be held entitled to come within the scope of compilation.

Ever since there were histories written in the form of Annals and Biographies successive ages have all had writers of history and all have kept to a fixed system which may not be relaxed. . . .

The efficiency with which the process of selection was put into force varied from period to period. Fortunately for the modern historian the test by which a person was considered to have performed actions worthy to serve as an example to the future was not too rigorous, and many of the biographies which are preserved appear—at least to the eye of a non-Confucian reader—to be merely straightforward accounts of commonplace official careers. Moreover, it took considerable strength of mind on the part of a historian to exclude a person who had recently held high office, and whose relatives and partisans might still be in places of power. Thus high rank gave a person a more than even chance of selection, irrespective of his merits in the light of orthodox theory.[19]

This system of selection determined the personalities who would be included. Perhaps a more far-reaching effect was exercised on the final shape of the *lieh-chuan* by the method of compilation. Theoretically, the official historians writing the biography of a bureaucrat, with a special emphasis on his career in office, had access to an amazing mass of information about their subject. For his family background there were extensive officially compiled works of genealogy.[20] For his official career the Board of Civil Office (*Li-pu*) kept personal dossiers for all serving officials, which included not only their successive appointments, but the annual assessments of ability from their superiors. Moreover, the Department of Merit Assessments (*K'ao-kung-ssu*), a subordinate branch of the same board, had, as one of its responsibilities, the task of preparing on the death of a member of the bureaucracy a document called an Account of Conduct (*Hsing-chuang*), which was a sort of *curriculum vitae* of the individual. This is described as follows in the New T'ang History (*Hsin T'ang shu*) 46:[21]

---

[19] For the repercussions which could result from partisan writing of history, see the accounts in *Ts'e fu yüan kuei* and *T'ang hui-yao* 63–64 of the troubles relating to the *Chien-chung shih-lu*, written by Shên Chi-chi, the *Shun-tsung shih-lu* and the *Hsien-tsung Shih-lu*.

[20] See the material collected in *Ts'ê-fu yüan-kuei* 560, pp. 13b–22a.

[21] See Rotours, op. cit., p. 59.

The Secretary and Under-secretary of the Department of Merit Assessments are responsible for . . . Accounts of Conduct (*hsing-chuang*). When an official dies they send one to the historians. When a posthumous name is to be granted to an official by the Court of Sacrifices they use this Account of Conduct to decide whether or not it is suitable. When they wish to engrave a stele, they assemble the officials to discuss what is fitting to be written on it, and report the outcome to the family of the deceased. . . .

Two other sources, however, preserve what was possibly a ruling of the Statutes (*ling*) on this question, and suggest that the custom was more limited than this might imply.[22] They read:

In all cases where employed officials of the third rank or above, and titular officials of the second rank or above die, their Assistant Clerk (*Tso-shih*)[23] will write an Account of Conduct and transmit it to the Department of Merit Assessments. This department will be responsible for his successive employments and for checking. . . .

This suggests first of all that the Account of Conduct was not prepared for all officials, but only for those of very high rank.[24] A memorial from the Department of Merit Assessments submitted in 810 complains that this rule was being infringed and that other persons than the *Tso-shih* (Assistant Clerk) were submitting Accounts of Conduct.[25] It quotes as authorities an Edict dated 763 and the Regulations (*ko*) of 791 and it seems that this ruling with its limitation to the highest ranks of the hierarchy was more or less permanent. However, another memorial of 819[26] apparently envisages the submission of Accounts of Conduct with requests for posthumous titles even on behalf of '. . . persons without office and of lowly status . . .' A possible explanation is that whereas the rendering of an Account of

[22] See *T'ang hui-yao* 79, *T'ang liu-tien* 2.
[23] I translate *Tso-shih* deliberately in a vague fashion, as the correct reading here is doubtful. *T'ang hui-yao* 79 and the *Kuang-ya shu-chü* edition of *T'ang liu-tien* read *tso-shih* (Assistant Recorders), a term also occurring in the phrase *men-hsia tso-shih* in a Memorial of 801 quoted in *T'ang hui-yao* 80, which would suggest that it is a misreading for *tso-shih*, the Diarist of the Left, who was an employee of the Chancellery. But it is odd that he should be referred to under this title, which had lapsed in official use a century before. The correct reading of *T'ang liu-tien* 2, however, is that of the Sung and Konoe editions, *tso-li* (subordinate officials). Not only is *T'ang liu-tien* a less secondary source than the *T'ang hui-yao*, but its reading here is borne out by a quotation of the same passage of the statutes in *T'ung tien* 104 (Shih-t'ung edition, p. 551a). This section of *T'ung tien* is almost certainly quotation from the *K'ai-yüan li* and is thus roughly contemporaneous with the *T'ang liu-tien*.
I therefore take *tso-shih* as a general term for subordinates, synonymous with *tso-li*, and possibly a miswriting of the latter. The phrase *men-hsia tso-shih* thus becomes two separate terms, *men-hsia* (disciples) and *tso-shih* (official subordinates).
[24] The limits of rank laid down in *T'ang liu tien* 2 were extended downward by one degree during the Wu-tai period, but they still included only a fraction of the bureaucracy, even allowing for high-ranking posthumous titles.     [25] See *T'ang hui yao* 80.     [26] See *T'ang hui-yao* 80.

Conduct was an obligation on the *Tso-shih* in the case of high-ranking bureaucrats, other persons might have such an account rendered, as the 819 memorial says '. . . by sons or younger brothers of his family, by disciples or former subordinates . . .' or by local officials.

These documents also suggest that the Account of Conduct was by no means such an official and authoritative document as the New T'ang History might lead us to believe. The Board of Civil Office was merely responsible for the details of official employment and for checking, and for forwarding it to the Court of Sacrifices for considerations of posthumous ritual. The actual composition was the responsibility of persons who were closely linked with the deceased in some way.[27] A passage in the Comprehensive Statutes (*T'ung Tien*) throws further light on the Department of Merit Assessment's connection with other varieties of monumental writing which were more closely linked to the cult of the ancestral temple than to the requirements of the historian:[28]

> In 670 the old system was revived whereby the Chief Secretary of the Department of Merit Assessments was made responsible for matters concerned with the examination and inspection of Family biographies (*chia-chuan*), Epitaphs (*pei*), Funerary odes (*sung*), Eulogies (*lei*), Posthumous titles (*shih*) etc. . . .

Presumably the responsibilities of the department in such matters were limited to ensuring that no improper claims and pretensions were included in these private documents. But it is also clear that the department did not draw up an Account of Conduct from the records of the Board of Civil Office but merely corrected and supplemented with official data documents forwarded to them and destined not only for the historian, but also for ritual use. It is also apparent that, in their revision of an Account of Conduct, the department had access not only to official records, which were used sparingly, but to various funerary writings.

The admission of such unofficial material into the Accounts of Conduct, and the practice of having these documents drawn up by a former subordinate or associate of the deceased, meant a grave departure from the ideal of compilation from original documents. The memorial of 933 quoted above has some remarks on these sources which are worth quoting:[29]

[27] See the Edict of 5th month 737 cited in *T'ang ta-chao-ling chi* 81 (*Shih-yüan ts'ung-shu* edition, p. 8a) which orders that: 'In the case of those who are already deceased their sons and grandsons together should compile an account of their doings and send it to the History Office . . .' This shows that often family accounts were rendered direct to the History Office without the intermediation of the Board of Civil Office.

[28] See *T'ung tien* 23 (Shih-t'ung edition, p. 136a).

[29] See *Wu-tai hui-yao* 18 (*Shih-kuan tsa-lu*), Memorial of 933. The best criticism of the whole system is to be found in a Memorial of Li Ao submitted in 819 and quoted in *T'ang hui-yao* 64, *Ts'ê fu Yüan kuei* 559, pp. 11a–12a.

The great majority of the Accounts of Conduct are composed by disciples and former subordinates (of the deceased). They contain a great deal of meaningless ornament and literary flourishes. Now we request that Accounts of Conduct which are submitted in the future shall be in all cases straightforward accounts of achievements and should not be empty ornament and flowery style . . .

It is clear then that the material supplied to the History Office as drafts for official biographies was much less reliable than might appear on first sight, and that the full documentation on the subjects' careers which was preserved in the Board of Civil Office was rarely used. This additional source material would have provided the historians with much additional detail and also with the dates which are so conspicuously lacking in most *lieh-chuan*. There is some evidence that the History Office prepared biographies independent of the Veritable Records as early as the T'ang period. From the Wu-tai period onwards this became a regular practice, and collections of biographies were compiled as separate works.[30]

The reason why the historian was willing to make do with such second-rate material is closely bound up with the implications of the theoretical parallel with the Spring and Autumn Annals. Acceptance of this theory meant that the historian could relax the rigour of his critical methods in dealing with what were to him only illustrative examples throwing light on the main thread of history developed in the basic annals (*pên-chi*). Here again theory was much diluted in practice, and undoubtedly the *lieh-chuan* were the object of close criticism. But the theory allowed the acceptance of this system of personally compiled documents as drafts for biography, and the system was perpetuated by the fact that the same department who provided the Accounts of Conduct to the historians also had responsibility for the various types of 'biographical writings' designed for the ancestral cults of private families.[31]

Another consideration must also be remembered. We tend to assume an ideal situation in which the History Office had access to the vast bulk of state papers in the various ministries, and that editing was a process which began in the History Office. The official regulations on the forwarding of documents to the historians fell far short of this ideal, and actual practice fell shorter still. In fact, apart from the texts of actual edicts and memorials, the bulk of the material at the historians' disposal had *already* been processed in some other government department. Not only was this true of the obligatory returns made by the various offices of state, but the very Diaries which formed the skeleton for the annals were compiled by officers

---

[30] See Wang Gung-wu, op. cit., pp. 8–12.

[31] Li Ao's memorial shows that the historian took notice not only of the *hsing-chuang* submitted by the Department of Merit Assessments but also of the 'deliberations about posthumous titles'— that is the opinions expressed about the *hsing-chuang* by that department.

belonging to the Chancellery and Secretariat—offices whose heads were usually deeply involved in factional intrigue. The historian thus had to contend with a great deal of material which had been prepared with historical use in view, and also had continually to deal with inter-departmental obstructionism and slackness on the part of many offices in rendering reports.[32] This may have been another factor which inclined them to accept the material from the Accounts of Conduct without attempting to utilize the official dossiers more systematically.

It would be misleading, however, to put too great an emphasis on the character of the Accounts of Conduct as 'private' documents in contrast to state papers. In fact the intimate connections between the official Confucian ideology professed by the historians and the family cults in the great bureaucratic households ensured that documents written from either standpoint would have much in common. This is clearly shown by those fortunate cases where we have either Accounts of Conduct or Epitaphs of persons who have official biographies in the *lieh-chuan* of a Standard History. When the funerary writings are stripped of the religious elements proper for the occasion, the picture which they give of their subject is essentially the same as that given by the official historian, and if anything the account of his successive employments and his achievements in office is more complete.

A glance at the contents of such *lieh-chuan* and their predecessors will show the common interests which guided both the official historian and the writer for the family cult. To begin with the biography identifies the family branch to which the individual belonged by giving the traditional family seat. This information is often expanded by a brief account of his immediate forbears. Such information is of course given in greater detail in the non-official biographical writings, Epitaphs, etc. The private document in fact had much more adequate sources here than the Board of Civil Office could have provided, for in many cases the author could have access to a Family Chronicle (*Chia-chuan*). Such family chronicles were available outside the family itself, in some instances, and the *Ku-chin shu lu* catalogue of 720[33] lists no less than fifty-five such works totalling 1,611 chapters in the possession of the Imperial Library. Such works were also employed in the compilation of official genealogies, and, as we have seen above, were examined by the Department of Merit Assessments for accuracy.[34]

This preliminary section of a biography provided the reader with the information which enabled him to 'place' the subject in his relationship

---

[32] See the memorial of the History Office dated 708, 11th month, in *T'ang hui-yao* 63 (*Chu-ssu ying sung Shih-kuan shih-li*), which complains that although the schedule of matters to be reported is set out in the Regulations and Ordinances, for many years the rules have fallen into abeyance and nobody sends in reports. There are a number of similar complaints in *Wu-tai hui-yao* 18.

[33] Quoted in *Chiu T'ang shu* 46 (Po-na edition, pp. 17b–18b).

[34] See *T'ung tien* 23, loc. cit.

with his family. This relationship was of particular significance during the medieval period when the great aristocratic families had surrounded themselves with privilege. The *lieh-chuan* continues with the 'biography' itself. These sections are constructed around an outline career, presented in the form of the subject's successive official appointments, promotions, his titles, honours, enfeoffments, etc. These appointments are rarely dated systematically, and the total effect might be compared to a graph of which only one of the co-ordinates—that of rank—can be accurately determined, while the other—that of time—is known only at a few points. It is this outline of an official career which suffers most from the compilation of the *lieh-chuan* directly from the *hsing-chuang* (Account of Conduct).

The skeleton provided by this *curriculum vitae* is filled out by a variety of devices. The first of these, and one which is particularly widespread, is the use of formulaic passages and conventional episodes designed to demonstrate the individual's fitness for the category under which the historian wishes to include him. Professor Herbert Franke has already drawn attention to a number of these *topoi*, and his list might be considerably expanded.[35] Many of them are of considerable antiquity, and Ssu-ma Ch'ien in his *Shih chi* already uses a repertory of such formulae. The historian thus had a precedent of the highest authority for their use, and since most of them were designed to illustrate the Confucian virtues of their subject, they were readily accepted also in the writings of a ritual and memorial style. They are a feature against which the reader should be constantly on his guard, as they are as often attempts to link the subject with some paragon of Antiquity as they are descriptions, even in the most oblique and metaphorical sense, of his actual character or conduct.

These *topoi* were to a large extent introduced in the Epitaphs and Accounts of Conduct by their private compilers. The second device for filling out a *lieh-chuan* was perhaps more often used by the historian himself. This was the introduction of lengthy quotations of notable memorials submitted to the throne by the subject, and, in the case of literary figures, quotations of well-known poems and other writings. Such quotations often form practically the whole of a *lieh-chuan*, and often appear to have been selected as much from stylistic reasons, or from their exposition of the conventional orthodox viewpoint on a topic, as from their intrinsic interest.

[35] See Herbert Franke, 'Some remarks on the interpretation of Chinese dynastic histories', *Oriens* 3 (1950), pp. 113–22, and especially pp. 120–1. The insertion of such *topoi* into the *hsing chuang* is mentioned by Li Ao (loc. cit.): 'Those who write *hsing-chuang* today are former subordinates if they are not actual disciples of the deceased. There is none of them who does not falsely interpolate examples of benevolence, righteousness, correct ritual conduct, and wisdom, or tell lies about his loyalty, respectfulness, graciousness and kindness. They do this not only because they are not truthful in their intentions, but simply because they wish to give an empty reputation to him from whom they have received favours . . .'

The third type of material used to add body to the biography is the description of the actions of the individual in his official capacity. This material is of the greatest interest for the historian, as it is for the most part neither conventional nor to be found elsewhere. The incidents included are of course highly selective, and frequently a minor policy put into force by the subject whilst a Magistrate of some unimportant County will be described at length, while his decisions as a high officer of state will be passed over in silence. The selection for these sections was made with an eye to the orthodox virtues, of course, but they remain virtually the only source for provincial history in the era before the Local Gazeteers provide us with their more adequate picture.

The biography ends with the death of the subject and with the posthumous honours which were accorded him, and this is frequently followed by an eulogy and brief account of his descendants. This material is almost invariably quoted from one or other of the funerary compositions.

This description of the typical *lieh-chuan* entry is perhaps unfair to the occasional biography in which a happy turn of phrase or some vivid use of detail suddenly throws light on the individual. But the typical example is as dry and impersonal as the Annals themselves, and the modern reader in search of some clue to the personality of the subject will find it very difficult to form any picture of the man as an individual, even when he has mastered the cliché forms in which character is described. The difficulty of reconstructing a satisfactory picture without resource to large quantities of non-biographical materials is admirably illustrated by the recent biographies of Tu Fu and Po Chü-i by William Hung and Arthur Waley.[36]

When we lament the lack of personal information in the *lieh chuan* we are in a sense criticizing the historians for their failure to achieve something which probably never entered their minds. Viewed from their own standpoint the biographies are quite adequate, for they illuminate the actions of men as 'subjects and ministers' and present precepts and examples for future generations of Confucian officialdom. However, at first sight it may seem curious that they should be so consistently impersonal when we remember that the bulk of them were derived from the Accounts of Conduct drawn up by persons who had been closely associated with their subject during his lifetime.

To understand this we must understand first of all the conventional position assigned to the individual in an oriental society, and secondly the identity of interest between the historian, with his didactic purpose, and the Confucian clan for whose ritual cult the Accounts of Conduct and the closely related Epitaphs were designed.

[36] See William Hung, *Tu-Fu China's greatest poet* (1952) and Arthur Waley, *The Life and times of Po Chu-i* (1949). Both rely almost exclusively on non-biographical material, in spite of the existence of a number of biographical works on their subjects.

In China an individual's status was very different from that in western societies. The Chinese considered the individual not so much as the unit from which society was built, but as a single element in a complex of interlocking relationships with various larger groups. This social attitude had far-reaching effects on law and custom, for each of the relationships in which the individual was involved bound him in some measure of collective responsibility. It is perhaps permissible to contrast western society, where, since comparatively early times, the individual has had a status as such, with that of the Far East, where the individual has remained until very recent years bound legally in various external relationships, and for our purpose it is clear that this fact helped to direct the attention of the historian-biographer to his subject's performance of his duties and obligations within these relationships, and especially to his actions within his relationship as a member of the bureaucracy. The result has been that biography has remained the exploration of a man's actions in some special function, rather than the presentation of a fully articulated picture of the individual in the round.

A necessary pre-requisite for the production of a biography which will stand as an independent literary work is that the society for which it is composed should find an individual's character and its interaction with his milieu a subject of sufficiently absorbing interest to hold the attention of the reader and provide a focus for his work. In the west this interest in the individual *per se* is epitomized in the hero epic, a literary form of popular origin which became an accepted vehicle for fine writing. Though the hero poem is of course far removed from biography, it is significant of the altogether different approach to the individual in China that the heroic poem and the epic are literary forms which have never taken strong roots there.[37]

Another interesting divergence in literature between China and the West is the absence in China of anything to parallel the Classical conception of tragedy—the most extreme artistic expression of the predicament of the individual *vis-a-vis* his environment. This has some bearing on biography, for tragedy and the tragic tradition have exercised a deep and lasting effect on Western biography, and helped to crystallize the interest of the Western reader around the individual *per se* by providing an attitude from which to view his relations with the forces of circumstance. The tragic tradition has, again, been responsible to a considerable degree for the high value placed by the Western reader on form, continuity, and pattern in biographical writings. This trend, which has remained instinct with writers in the European tradition, has no echo in China, where the disconnected and episodic character of all narrative writing, both in fiction and in history, is a most striking difference for the western reader.

[37] On this lack see M. Bowra, *Heroic Poetry* (1953). His views can be criticized in detail, but his general thesis on the lack of an epic literature in China is undoubtedly correct.

Biography viewed essentially as the account of the individual, rather than as the description of the individual seen as a member of a social or hierarchical group, flourished only during one period, the post-Han period of regional autonomy and division. This period was marked by a breaking up and loosening of ties within traditional society, meaning that the individual was somewhat less hemmed in by the conventional restraints. This attitude is exemplified by the flourishing of the individual-centred religion of Taoism at the expense of group-centred Confucian orthodoxy, and by the cult of individual tastes in literature. At the same time it was a period when Buddhism introduced into China a vast and highly developed literature produced by a civilization with a strong epic tradition and a distinct taste for individual characters. The church, in fact, maintained a tradition of biographical writing which was responsible for some of the finest work in the form in Chinese. These two factors, the relaxation of social ties and the introduction of Buddhism, combined to reorient the interest of the biographer away from the 'functional' approach to the individual. But the establishment of the T'ang dynasty, and the re-establishment of Confucian orthodoxy as the accepted ideology of the scholar, led to the re-imposition of the old restraints.

The historians were for the most part members of the class amongst whom the consciousness of the multiple relationships and responsibilities of the individual was most strong, the upper gentry. In this stratum of society not only were the formal signs of such relationships, such as the large patrilinear clan, most strongly evident, but the social and economic status of the clan was intimately dependent upon another of the relationships, that of the clan members as members of the bureaucracy. Since success in office brought credit and prosperity to the family as a whole, the accounts of meritorious performance of official duties would provide satisfying and significant reading for the spirits of the deceased ancestors of the clan to whom the funerary biographies were addressed, and give valuable precepts to future generations within the family. The almost complete concentration of orthodox Confucianism on various social relationships also meant that biographical material written for the family cult would concentrate on these aspects.

The entries devoted to individual family members in the family chronicles and genealogies are extremely formalized. The type pattern consists of (*a*) Details of parentage, (*b*) Date of birth, (*c*) Where applicable, details of entry into government service and official career, (*d*) Details of service in the administration of the family cult, (*e*) Notice of death, burial, posthumous honours bestowed by the court, and details of the appropriate rites to be celebrated in respect of him by the clan, (*f*) Details of marriages, (*g*) Descendants. Here again the purely functional note reappears. The sole difference is that two functions are admitted as of interest, the official career, and benefactions or service to the clan—i.e. noteworthy actions within the clan-relationship. As in the official biographies, material which is of great interest is deliberately omitted if it does not conform with the ideal of the scholar-bureaucrat; for example, even predominantly mercantile clans rarely mention trade in the entries concerning their members.

It is also worth noting that by no means all family members were given extended epitaphs. These were confined to the meritorious examples in the clan, in just the same way as biographies were confined to the meritorious examples in the public service. Lastly, it is quite certain that, whatever the close connection between epitaph-memorial writing and official biography, the status of the latter was eventually so unassailable that the rules of compilation of at least one clan chronicle advise the compilers that where a biography exists, it should have precedence and be quoted *in extenso*.[38]

The terms of reference of the official historian and the writer of an epitaph were thus virtually identical. Both were interested in the individual seen as the combination of his multiple relationships in the Confucian sense. Both were interested above all in his career as an official, for this was the end to which all orthodox education shaped the individual, and he fulfilled his purpose in the relationship of minister and ruler. Both were written with the design of providing an example to the future generations of scholar-gentry. Thus the writer of an Epitaph or Account of Conduct had in practice done all that the historian was presumed to do in theory, and there was no strong argument against the historian taking over these ready-composed documents save their lack of chronology and their generally unofficial nature. The traditional theory of the parallel with the Spring and Autumn Annals overruled the first objection, and the supervision exercised by the Department of Merit Assessments acted as a check on their contents.

Thus official biography became in practice the imitation of eulogistic memorial writings. The immense authority of the Standard Histories meant that departure from this norm became unthinkable. The same type of 'functional approach' characterizes to a lesser but nevertheless perceptible degree the collections of specialized biography which were compiled in considerable numbers during later dynasties. Whether the subject is a monk or an artist, his biography will very seldom give any hint of the personality spreading beyond his professional function. This type of biographical writing, although generally disappointing when read as biography, is nevertheless a rich source of material, for it presents us with an unrivalled picture of the workings of a bureaucratic machine through a period of two millenia. It is one of the basic causes, also, for modern his-

[38] *Fan-shih chia-shêng* 1 (*Fan-li*).

torians' preoccupation with institutional matters to the exclusion of the approach to historical problems through biography which has proved of such value in the West.

In only one respect do the Chinese literati appear to have found this convention unsatisfactory, and this has nothing to do with the shortcomings which I have mentioned. One conspicuous lack in the *lieh-chuan* type biography is an adequate chronological framework. During Sung times and later a type of biography called *nien-p'u* arose. This attempted to fit the events of an individual's life into a chronological pattern after the examples of the annalistic form. It has most frequently been employed as a skeleton framework to which could be fitted the literary productions of poets, and at its best provides the reader with such copious material that it places its subject in his historical context in the manner of a western 'Life and Times'. However, the number of *nien-p'u* is very small when compared with the immense bulk of biographies written in *lieh-chuan* form, and, since it seems never to have occurred to the official historians that accuracy of dating would have been a desirable refinement of the traditional form, it exercised no influence on their productions. The *nien-p'u* continued down to the present day as a parallel but separate medium in which one might deal with a career, but what it gained in precision, it lost by abandoning the 'connected narrative of events' of the *lieh-chuan*. The *nien-p'u* is not so much a biography as a collection of notes for a biography.

The literati never felt the lack of any personal element in the *lieh-chuan*, but this does not mean that they had no interest in personal idiosyncrasies of character and more private aspects of life. These interests were 'compartmentalized' into another literary medium, the miscellaneous notes or notebooks (*pi-chi*). Here, however, there was seldom any attempt to present any extended picture of a whole life, but only short jottings on character rather in the manner of the fragmentary entries in such works as Aubrey's *Brief lives*. Although not primarily biographical, these works are a valuable complement to the organized *lieh-chuan* with its lack of personal interest. But their contents are by no means always reliable. Incorporating much tradition and hearsay, they merge by infinite gradations into the world of fictionalized history and historical romance which has always been a strong literary tradition in China.

In short, Chinese traditional historians have provided us with a wealth of biographical material. But this is less accurately dated and subjected to less scrupulous criticism than the other sections of historical works. It is, moreover, biography in a strictly limited sense, derived from the eulogistic writings of family cults, and concerned with only one aspect of the subject's life. Lastly, it is concerned almost exclusively with members of the same social group as its authors. Within these self-imposed limitations, and viewed from the strictly circumscribed intentions of the authors, the results are perfectly adequate, but for the modern scholar these limitations present a serious problem and account for much of the impersonal atmosphere which makes such a forcible impression on one beginning the study of Chinese history.

# 8. SOME ASPECTS OF CHINESE PRIVATE HISTORIOGRAPHY IN THE THIRTEENTH AND FOURTEENTH CENTURIES

## HERBERT FRANKE

*Professor of Far Eastern Studies, University of Munich*

One of the major differences between European and Chinese historiography in the past has been the predominance of official historiography in China. The standard dynastic histories concentrate on the institutional and administrative aspects of persons and events to such a degree that we may safely say they report for the most part only what was known to the metropolitan bureaucracies. The picture of the past as given by these sources is, therefore, in a way one-sided. Only occasionally can we check their accuracy against independent sources, usually in periods when there was a multistate system in China or when we have documents from foreign states which had diplomatic (or belligerent) relations with China. Many events, for example the various rebellions of the peasantry, are known to us only from the official records, and almost no documents of the rebels, if they ever existed, have survived to present us their aims and ideology. A notable exception is the Taiping rebellion. The onesidedness of historical outlook which results from these circumstances can best be understood if we were to suppose, as a comparison, that we had only the *res gestae* of the medieval emperors in Europe to be our major source for European history in that period, that we did not have those numerous private (in the broadest sense) chronicles and records which supplement the documents of the chanceries.

If we look for similar sources in medieval China we have to define first what is meant by *private* historiography. Perhaps a suitable definition might be that the concept of 'private' should be measured according to the degree of independence from bureaucracy, particularly from the historical offices in the capital. By this definition the ideal private historian would be a writer who never held any office. But even in this case it is doubtful whether the fundamental concepts of private historiography would be very different from those of official historiography. A certain element of Confucian ideology was almost invariably common to both. This is why the Buddhist chronicles deserve special attention, because they not only correspond to the definition of private historiography given above, but also have a different ideological background. A clear distinction between private and official historiography is, in many cases, impossible. Many gradations exist between what are unquestionably clear extremes on either side. The result is a certain difficulty in outlining the characteristics of private historical writing as a category. One might perhaps venture to say that private historians did not always try to cover a whole dynasty, but tended to concentrate on a certain segment, in time, space, or subject. Moreover, it is clear that a local history of a certain district or town would usually reflect local loyalties and the ideas of provincial gentry members, though local historians almost invariably used the forms developed by official historiographers (annals, biographies, topical monographs, etc.).

In addition to this concentration of subject matter, there were also attempts to compile comprehensive histories, dealing with all Chinese history from the earliest times on. In these cases the writers mostly relied on published sources. The purpose of such compilations and historical encyclopaedias was, in most cases, to provide examination candidates with the knowledge they needed.

Another point which must be clarified is the concept of *historiography* itself. Only a part of the sources which scholarship may use for historical research are to be classified primarily as historiography from the point of view of Chinese traditional bibliography or of classification according to contents. The 'notebooks' (*pi-chi*), for example, have a high value as historical sources because they give so many details of a colourful nature. The bibliographies usually classify these works under class three, *tzu* (non-canonical writers), either under the heading 'Miscellaneous' (*tsa-chia*) or even under 'Fiction' (*hsiao-shuo*). An excellent characterization of the *pi-chi* has been given by Lin Yu-tang:[1] 'Memoirs or notebooks are the laziest form of literature, requiring no organisation of material, and therefore the most popular literary occupation of Chinese scholars. Such notebooks vary from serious and sometimes highly important records of historical events and documents, written to supplement official histories, to the most disorderly jumble of tales of ghosts, fox spirits, and reincarnations, all these sometimes co-existing in the same volume. In general, the notebooks come well under the general classification of "scholars gossip"'. The purpose of the authors was in most cases the desire to supply materials for learned and witty conversations, an aim which was often expressed in the prefaces to such works. But often the authors hoped to supplement the official histories by writing down their own experiences and information. Another purpose was to illustrate traditional ethics by giving examples of behaviour both laudable and blamable. Finally there was a motive which usually accompanied the other motives, namely, entertainment. It is clear that their details on cultural history have particularly high value. It is equally clear that, written by and for scholars, they also reflect the ideology of the literate class with all their traditional concepts. Very seldom do we learn

[1] *The Gay Genius* (London, 1948), p. 352.

about the lower classes; most events are reported from among the class of learned officials.

In the following pages a short and necessarily incomplete survey of non-official historical writings of the thirteenth and fourteenth centuries A.D. will be given. Since this period is characterized by an abundance of private historiography, in which almost every form of historical literature is amply represented, the limitation of the survey to these two centuries may be justified. The works will be reviewed in the following order:

1. Works to be regarded primarily as historiography.
    (a) General histories.
    (b) Special or local historical writings.
2. Works of a miscellaneous nature.
3. Buddhist historical writings.

In every case the edition used has been indicated; this does not mean, however, that it is always the best or most reliable edition, because I have had to confine myself to those editions that were easily available.

## 1. *Historical writing*

### (a) *General histories*

In the thirteenth and fourteenth centuries conditions for private historio-graphy were, in some respects, not unfavourable. These years saw the collapse of three empires (Chin, Sung, Yüan). However atrocious the cir-cumstances of the downfall of those dynasties may have been, one thing seems to be certain: with the collapse of a dynasty considerations of taboos, fear of omnipotent court officials, and censorship ceased to exist and a freer expression of opinion was *a priori* possible. Even loyalty to the old regime might find veiled or open expression. This applies particularly to Sung loyalty, which must have been strong for almost a whole generation after the downfall of the dynasty in 1275–80. There is a whole literature centred around nostalgic reminiscences of the Sung and praise for those who supported the lost cause. The astonishing thing is that literary activi-ties which implicitly tended to disregard the new state of affairs and to praise the old one could develop under the new rulers. Not a few of these works were printed under the Yüan, and many more were circulated as manuscripts. If we consider the parallel situation after the fall of Ming in the seventeenth and eighteenth centuries, with its strict censorship and many cases of literary persecution,[2] or even the rigorous insistence on cer-tain taboos under the Ming,[3] the absence of similar campaigns seems to be a striking feature of Mongol rule. One almost gets the impression that the Mongols simply did not care what the former subjects of the Sung wrote,

[2] Cf. L. C. Goodrich, *The Literary Inquisition of Ch'ien-lung* (Washington, 1935).
[3] Cf. Ku Chieh-kang, translated by L. C. Goodrich, 'A Study of Literary Persecution under the Ming', *HJAS* (1938), iii, 254–311.

at least as long as no open rebellion against the new rulers was advocated. Perhaps there was so little possibility of a revival of Sung that the Mongols could afford to disregard purely literary expressions of Sung loyalism. A striking example of the relative freedom of historical discussion is afforded by Yang Wei-chen (1296–1370) and his 'Dissertation on legitimate succession' (*Cheng-t'ung-pien*) to be found in the *Cho-keng lu*.[4] This long essay, dated 1343, severely criticized the compilers of the three Standard Histories of Sung (covering the period 960–1280), Liao (907–1125), and Chin (1122–1234) for recognizing the Liao and Chin as legitimate dynasties. According to Yang the transfer of power from Sung to Yüan should be dated in 1276 so that the Yüan reign titles (*nien-hao*) should from that year on succeed those of Sung; Liao and Chin should be treated as foreign barbarians with no right to dynastic prerogatives of their own. Yang underlines his position by using the personal names of Liao and Chin rulers instead of their posthumous names throughout his essay. Yang's advice was not followed by the compilers (who were partly Chinese), but it remains remarkable that a Yüan subject like Yang could express himself in this way, implying that the Yüan rule over North China prior to the fall of the Sung capital was somehow illegitimate. Equally remarkable is the fact that in 1366, although the empire was already tottering, this essay was printed in the *Cho-keng lu*, a book which, in addition, contained many other entries showing unrestricted pro-Sung tendencies.

Another factor should be mentioned here, although I do not feel qualified to interpret its importance for the historiography of the Sung dynasty. There are indications that there existed under the Sung an official ban on private historical writing. This problem deserves special investigation, which would be beyond the scope of this paper. Perhaps a closer study of Sung history can show how far this ban on private historiography was actually effective and whether the surprisingly great number of early Yüan works on Southern history may have been a consequence of the annihilation of the Sung empire.

Official historiography under the Yüan has not met with great approval from the Chinese bibliographers. The three dynastic histories of Sung, Liao, and Chin were regarded as full of omissions, hastily compiled and stylistically inferior. It remains to be investigated whether that verdict would also apply to those historical writings which, though published under individual authors' names, are in fact more or less official historiography. We would in passing draw attention to some of the better-known works of this semi-official type. Apart from such works as the *Huang-yüan sheng-wu ch'in-cheng-lu* (Record of the sacred wars of the August Yüan

---

[4] Ch. 3, No. 1 (pp. 1a ff.). For Yang, see H. A. Giles, *Biographical Dictionary*, No. 2415; *Ming-shih*, ch. 285; *Hsin-Yüan-shih*, ch. 238; *Chung-kuo jen-ming ta-tz'u-tien* (Chinese Biographical Dictionary, Commercial Press, Shanghai, 1933), p. 1281 III. On the *Cho-keng lu*, see below, pp. 128–9.

Emperor) which goes back to a Mongol court chronicle (Altan Debter)[5] we should mention in the first rank the *Kuo-ch'ao ming-ch'en shih-lüeh* by Su T'ien-chüeh (1294–1352).[6] This work was one of the sources for the biographies (*lieh-chuan*) of the Yüan History (*Yüan-shih*); it contains biographies of forty-seven famous statesmen and generals of early Yüan. But it would certainly be wrong to describe it as private historiography. The author was a high-ranking official, at one time Minister of the Interior (*li-pu shang-shu*) and a member of the Central Chancery (*chung-shu-sheng*). He also edited the *Kuo-ch'ao wen-lei* (Classified anthology of the present dynasty) which, too, is by no means a private effort but an official enterprise with all the resulting limitations. This work preserved some historical texts of importance which were later published separately, e.g. the *Cheng-mien-lu* (Record of the campaigns against Burma).[7] Another instance of official texts appearing in this Yüan anthology is the *Chao-pu tsung-lu* (General account of police actions)[8] describing military actions against rebellions of aboriginal tribes in South-west China and of various local rebel leaders in other provinces. Again, the work by Liu Min-chung, the 'Conquest of Sung' (*P'ing-Sung lu*) in three chapters, belongs to the category of official histories.[9] Liu was a Yüan Han-lin academician, and an abstract of his book is to be found in the *Kuo-ch'ao wen-lei*, ch. 41, 14b–20b.

It does not seem that there were many attempts in the thirteenth and fourteenth centuries to re-write Chinese history as a whole or to present a historical synopsis on new lines. One work, however, must be mentioned here because it is indeed a 'private' history, although its success in China was not very great.

*Shih-pa-shih-lüeh*.[10] This 'Abstract from the 18 Histories' had in Japan, unlike China, a considerable success—which is not at all flattering to the Japanese, because the *Ssu-k'u* editors thought the book far too summary

---

[5] Pelliot-Hambis, *Les Campagnes de Gengis Khan* (Leiden, 1951), pp. xi–xv. The *Ssu-k'u* rejects this work because of factual errors, omissions, and lack of order in the arrangement of facts: *Ssu-k'u ch'üan-shu tsung-mu t'i-yao* (Catalogue to the Complete Library in Four Sections; 4 vols., Commercial Press, Shanghai, 1934), p. 1156. This work is hereafter cited simply as *Ssu-k'u.*

[6] Ed. *Wu-ying-tien ch'ü p'an shu; Ssu-k'u*, p. 1277; Pelliot, *BEFEO* 9 (1909), p. 434; A. Wylie, *Notes on Chinese Literature* (Peking re-edition, 1939), p. 28.

[7] Re-ed. in *Shou-shan-ko ts'ung-shu*, translated by E. Huber in *BEFEO* 9 (1909). The *Shou-shan-ko* editor apparently did not notice that the text occurs word for word in *Kuo-ch'ao wen-lei*, ch.41, 27b–33a: *Ssu-pu ts'ung-k'an* (Collection of facsimile reprints of Chinese texts), Commercial Press, Shanghai (hereafter cited as *SPTK*).

[8] Re-ed. in *Shou-shan-ko t.s.* The text corresponds to *Kuo-ch'ao wen-lei*, ch. 41, 38b–58b, a fact not mentioned by the *Shou-shan-ko* editor.

[9] Re-ed. *Shou-shan-ko t.s.* For Liu, see *Yüan-shih*, ch. 178. *Ssu-k'u*, p. 1137 lists the book under *tsa-shih* 'Miscellaneous Histories'. The preface, incidentally, is interesting as a specimen of the attitude of early Yüan scholars towards the Sung. Chia Ssu-tao, Sung chancellor from 1259–75, is regarded as responsible for the defeat of Sung.

[10] Ed. *Kambun Taikei*, vol. 5, in 7 ch. *Ssu-k'u*, p. 1107; *Shina Gakugei Daijii* (ed. 1944), p. 517, gives a survey of its sources and the transmission of the text.

and condensed, fit only for a village preparatory school. (The Japanese editor in *Kambun Taikei*, Dr. Shigeno, also stressed its value for beginners in Chinese history; see his preface dated 1910.) Although I have not been able to subject the whole work to thorough analysis, it seems to me clear that the *Shih-pa-shih-lüeh* cannot be regarded as a very original achievement. Practically nothing is known about its author, Tseng Hsien-chih, which confirms the private character of his work. It begins with remotest antiquity and ends with the overthrow of the Sung in 1275–6. As in so many other works of the Yüan period, traces of Sung loyalism can be found here and there. Thus it gives the Sung reign titles right up to 1276, although the Yüan already had their own from 1260 on. Some emphasis is laid on Confucian doctrine and its development in Sung times. The book not only mentions the death of Chu Hsi in 1200 but gives also a succinct account of the discussion of the 'wrong doctrines' about that time, i.e. the struggle against the Neo-Confucians.

Among those who in the thirteenth and fourteenth centuries wrote glosses and commentaries on the existing histories, Hu San-hsing (1230–1302) should be mentioned. It would, of course, be an impossible task to go through the whole of Hu's Commentary to Ssu-ma Kuang's Comprehensive Mirror for Aid in Government (*Tzu-chih t'ung-chien*) and try to find out where he expresses new ideas on history or shows independent judgement on issues of general importance. His commentary is usually regarded as particularly informative on questions of historical geography, but improvements on earlier identifications of place names or other questions of dispute are certainly not what we would regard as evidence of a significant approach to history in general, however great the amount of scholarship shown in these notes may be. In his preface, Hu, like his basic author Ssu-ma Kuang, regards the Comprehensive Mirror as a work from which posterity may draw lessons on questions of political behaviour. Praise and blame are for him, as for indeed almost all Chinese historians, essential elements of historiography. History is regarded as a mirror of political ethics, to be judged according to Confucian standards. He shares the view of those who maintain that the *Tao* manifests itself not only in the classical books but also in history (preface, p. 2a in the 1917 Commercial Press edition). Hu was a former Sung official who did not accept a post after the overthrow of the Sung, and certainly had no sympathy for the new rulers. If his political views did find any expression in his commentary at all, we would have to seek them first in his remarks on the barbarian neighbours of China.

### (b) *Special or local histories*

Whereas the thirteenth and fourteenth centuries did not add much to the general histories, whether private or official, there is a wealth of works dealing with single periods and events. Only a small part of them can be mentioned here. In some cases it is doubtful how far these works really come under the definition of private historiography in a strict sense. They might be based on official records, and where the authors are not known they may well have been active or former officials. This official character is, for example, evident in the *Chung-hsing yü-wu lu* (Records of defence against the insults [of barbarians] in the Renaissance Period).[11] This short book in two chapters is a chronological account of the wars and diplomatic relations between the Southern Sung and the Jurčen up to 1165. It is compiled from official sources; which ones could perhaps be ascertained by a comparison with the annals that existed before 1275. The *Ssu-k'u* editors did not think it worthy of inclusion in the imperial library: they considered the presentation of facts erroneous and too much based on hearsay. The real reason for this rejection would rather seem to be that the book presents the Jurčen, the ancestors of the Manchus, in a rather unfavourable light. Some of the works mentioned below might also be regarded as official histories in so far as they draw on official documents and records which happened to be accessible to the author.

*Sung-chi san-ch'ao cheng-yao* (Important events under the last three Sung emperors).[12] This anonymous work in five chapters contains the annals of Li-tsung, Tu-tsung, and the 'young ruler' Kung-tsung, thus covering the period from 1228 to 1276. An annex contains the annals of the Sung pretenders who tried to continue their resistance against the Mongols after the fall of Hang-chou. This supplement is written by Ch'en Chung-wei (fl. 1280) and has a separate entry in *Ssu-k'u*, p. 1153. The *Sung-chi san-ch'ao cheng-yao* was written under the Yüan, whom it calls Ta-Yüan, the 'Great Yüan'. But this is about the only concession made to the new regime. The *Ssu-k'u* editors, who listed the book under the heading *pien-nien*, 'annals', stated that the ideological basis of the book is correct (*cheng*) and included it among the books to be copied for the emperor. It was printed under the Yüan. The short preface, however, does not tell us where and when; the author says he wrote the book in order to supply later official historians with material—a phrase which one meets with very often among 'private' historiographers.

Another book which deals with the last phases of the Sung is *Hsien-ch'un i-shih* (Events from the Hsien-ch'un period).[13] It is anonymous, but it may be assumed that the author was a former Sung official who had access to official documents, an opinion also suggested by the *Ssu-k'u* editors who regard the work as *tsa-shih* 'Miscellaneous History'. It covers the period from 1265 to 1272, ninth month, and contains a great number

---

[11] Ed. *Pi-chi hsiao-shuo ta-kuan*. *Ssu-k'u*, p. 1150.
[12] Ed. *Pi-chi hsiao-shuo ta-kuan*. *Ssu-k'u*, p. 1046.
[13] Ed. *Shou-shan-ko t.s.* in 2 ch. *Ssu-k'u*, p. 1135.

of official documents, edicts and memorials. Chia Ssu-tao plays a prominent part, but it seems that there is no attempt made to make him appear as the abominable creature he was supposed to be by other contemporary authors. The *Hsien-ch'un i-shih* is incomplete; the last two years of the Hsien-ch'un period (1273 and 1274) are not dealt with, whereas the title seems to indicate that the book originally covered the whole period.

There are many books on the fate, works, and deeds of Sung gentry members that were written after 1276. One of the most extensive works of this kind of patriotic literature falls outside the time limit set for this paper because it is a Ming work. It should, however, be included in this survey as it is a major source on Sung loyalism:

*Sung i-min lu* (Records of Sung loyalists) by Ch'eng Min-cheng.[14] The author was a doctor (*chin-shih*) of 1466 (see his biography in *Ming-shih*, ch. 286) who collected all the available writings of famous Sung loyalists and poems in their praise, so that the book is rather more an anthology of Sung loyalism than a purely historical work. In ch. 15 the fantastic story that the last Mongol emperor Shun-ti (r. 1332–68) was a son of the last Sung ruler, enfeoffed as Ying-kuo-kung by Qubilai, is repeated. This was regarded as ridiculous by the *Ssu-k'u* editors, who therefore relegated the book to the *ts'un-mu* category (books which were not copied for the emperor).

If the work listed above is more literary than historical, the following collection belongs certainly to the category of history:

(*Sung-chi*) *Chao-chung lu* (Records of eminent patriots at the end of Sung), anonymous.[15] It contains biographies of some 130 persons who distinguished themselves as patriots under the last reigns of the Sung dynasty. The events related range from 1235 to 1289 (death of Hsieh Fang-tê). The biographical data given are rather full and some of the battles between Sung and Yüan are reported in great detail, for example the siege of Hsiang-yang (1268–73). The atrocities committed by Mongol troops are also described, which perhaps accounts for the fact that no printed edition of the Yüan period is known. According to the *Ssu-k'u* editors it is more reliable than the corresponding biographies of Sung loyalists in the official Sung History; they recommended its use to supplement the Standard History.

Turning to private historical writing of the Yüan we have to mention a work which even in its title proclaims that it is a private production:

*Keng-shen wai-shih* (Unofficial history of the emperor born in 1320), by Ch'üan Heng.[16] This is an annalistic history of the last Mongol emperor, throwing much light on details of history which are more or less neglected

---

14 Ed. *Pi-chi hsiao-shuo ta-kuan* in 15 ch. *Ssu-k'u*, p. 1341. A. Wylie, *Notes*, p. 29.
15 Ed. *Shou-shan-ko ts'ung-shu* in 1 ch. *Ssu-k'u*, p. 1274.
16 Ed. *Ts'ung-shu chi-ch'eng. Ssu-k'u*, p. 1157.

in the official dynastic history (*Yüan-shih*). As the author lived in the northern part of Central China there is quite a lot of information on those parts. Some of the rebellions of the 1350s and 1360s are described vividly, and the last phases of Yüan rule in Ta-tu (Peking) are recorded with details which we do not find in the *Yüan-shih* itself. The emperor Shun-ti appears as a basically good ruler who had but the fault of trusting bad ministers too much. The *Keng-shen wai-shih* is a good example of how far a private history may deviate from the official ones. This does not mean that the work is more scholarly or more neutral in its treatment than the *Yüan-shih*, for example, but because the accent (or tendency) is a different one, we are given details differing from the standard official sources. For Ch'üan Heng believed in the interrelationship of the ruler's power (*tê*) and his dealings with women in the 'inner palace', which gives him an opportunity to write down some delightful (and some gruesome) stories of harem life in the capital. How far court gossip is responsible for these stories we shall never know, but are we justified in regarding the sober, dry-as-dust biographies in the standard histories as more reliable only because they emanate from an official bureau and tell us nothing on marital life? We have to remind ourselves, from time to time, that the biographies (*lieh-chuan*) are mostly based on official documents and that even when we can trace the source of a biography to the literary collection of an individual author we have mostly to do with outlines of career, necrologues, etc., which are perhaps as uninformative for the personality of a man as, say, a questionnaire filled in by an applicant for a readership in a university. We should be grateful for any source which, although based on very traditional and even magical concepts, gives us a different picture of a period or a person. In the case of Shun-ti it is quite clear that the picture of him given by Chinese historians is influenced by the age-old cliché of what Granet used to call 'roi débauché'.

Whereas the historians mentioned above wrote down what they read or heard somewhere, we have also some sources where the author describes what he has seen and witnessed for himself. To this category belong diaries, memoirs, and similar writings. It is unfortunate that we have so very few writings of this kind from the earlier periods of Chinese history and from outstanding persons. Nevertheless, there are some texts to which we must concede a particularly high value as sources because they acquaint us with the immediate impressions of a man who has been 'on the spot'. Such diaries might well come under the definition of 'private historical writing' even if they come from the pen of a high official. Best known to the Western public is, perhaps, the diary of the Taoist Ch'ang-ch'un's travels through Asia and his audience at Chinggis Khan's residence. As we have an excellent translation[17] together with many relevant details on the religious life

[17] Arthur Waley, *The Travels of an Alchemist* (London, 1931).

of the early thirteenth century we need not go into more detail. Nor will it be necessary to mention other travelogues of the thirteenth century; we refer instead to E. Bretschneider's *Mediaeval Researches*. But there are some other texts based on personal experiences which have been less studied by Western sinology.

*Hsiang-yang shou ch'eng lu* (Record of the defence of Hsiang-yang), by Chao Wan-nien.[18] This work is a record of the siege of Hsiang-yang in 1206 by the Jurčen troops (not by the Mongols, as the *Ssu-k'u* mistakenly states). Its author was a staff secretary to the commanding officer and thus an eyewitness of the siege. Of special interest is the appendix, where a detailed description of various kinds of defence and assault weapons or instruments is given. The purpose of the author, as he states in his colophon (p. 12a), was to contribute reliable material for future historians who would have to praise the achievement of the successful defenders of the town. The *Ssu-k'u* editors had a low opinion of the work and relegated it to the *ts'un-mu* category (not to be copied for the emperor) because of its 'fragmentary and incomplete statements', which made it, as they say, partly incomprehensible. In reality the reason for this attitude of the Manchu bibliographers may have been the fact that Chao Wan-nien speaks of the Jurčen usually as *lu* 'slaves' and in other uncomplimentary terms. The book was written soon after the event (1207) and is therefore a source of considerable value. A similar diary is the *Pao-Yüeh lu* (Record of the defence of Yüeh), by Hsü Mien-chih.[19] It records the siege of Shao-hsing by the Ming troops in 1359 and was written immediately after the event; the preface is dated 1359, tenth month. Like the preceding work it is a first-hand source written by an eyewitness who lived in the beleaguered town during the crucial months of 1359. The author states in his preface that he wishes to praise the merits of the successful defender of the town, Lü Chen, and to prevent the sufferings of the population from being forgotten in future times.

There is a certain number of texts dealing with events of the early Ming years which, too, may be regarded as private historical writing, but which we shall leave out of account here because all the necessary data may be found in W. Franke's excellent survey of sources for Ming history.[20] Instead we shall mention some works of predominantly historical character which, however, might as well be included among the miscellaneous writings of *pi-chi*.

*San-ch'ao yeh-shih* (Unofficial history of three reigns), anonymous.[21] This

---

[18] Ed. *Pi-chi hsiao-shuo ta-kuan*. *Ssu-k'u*, p. 1151.

[19] Ed. *Shih-wan-chüan lou ts'ung-shu*. *Ssu-k'u*, p. 1293. Pelliot, in *BEFEO* 9 (1909), p. 223; A. Wylie, *Notes*, p. 159.

[20] *Bulletin of Chinese Studies*, 7 (1947), pp. 107–224; *Studia Serica*, 9, 1 (1950), pp. 33–41.

[21] Ed. *Ku-chin shuo-hai*. *Ssu-k'u*, p. 1154. There is another entry in the Imperial Catalogue on a *San-ch'ao yeh-shih* 'Unofficial History of Three Reigns', p. 2970, among the *ts'un-mu* of *hsiao-shuo*, 'fiction'. It seems that this is the same book as that on p. 1154; moreover, the text reprinted in the *Ku-chin shuo-hai* is certainly incomplete.

is a short work of ten folios only, which contains anecdotes of the reigns of the last Sung emperor. Chia Ssu-tao appears here in a very unfavourable light; he is the subject of several satirical poems. The book must have been written after 1279, the last year mentioned. Although it calls the Mongols Ta-Yüan, 'The Great Yüan', its author was certainly a former Sung official. The *Ssu-k'u* editors condemned its style and rejected it to the *ts'un-mu* category of *tsa-shih* 'Miscellaneous histories'.

*Chin-yü lu* (Records left over from destruction), by Hsü Ta-cho.[22] The author, a man from Suchou, must have written this collection of historical anecdotes after 1276. Chapter 1 contains stories about famous persons of Sung from the tenth century on. The author was a loyalist who did not even try to conform with Yüan chronology or phraseology. Chapter 2 is chiefly concerned with stories from Su-chou, both ancient and contemporary. He describes in some detail the atrocities committed by the Jurčen when they invaded the Su-chou region in 1130; and also, apparently from personal experience, the conquest, or rather occupation, of that town by the Mongols in 1275.

### 2. *Works of a miscellaneous nature*

Some of the characteristics of the *pi-chi* (notebooks) have been mentioned above. As they are often of a highly literary or artistic nature we are told stories and anecdotes which show us a person from a less formal side than do the official biographies. Some biographical accounts in *pi-chi* works again could well figure in a Standard History. In still other cases highly important documents and records have been preserved in a *pi-chi* work, e.g. some travelogues of the thirteenth century. The first work we mention is a source of major importance, although the *Ssu-k'u* editors classify it as 'fiction' (*hsiao-shuo*):

*Kuei-ch'ien-chih* (Memoirs from retirement), by Liu Ch'i.[23] The author was a Chin official who finished his work, according to the preface, in 1235, one year after the overthrow of his state. He complains of the decadence of his time and thinks that his notes will serve as a warning to future generations. In a way this work may be compared to the writings of Sung loyalists after 1280; like them, it served as a source for the compilation of the official history. Chapters 1 to 6 contain mostly biographies of prominent Chin statesmen and literati, ch. 7 to 10 are of a more anecdotal nature, whereas 11 and 12 are interesting as the account by an eyewitness of the fall of K'ai-feng in 1234. This part of the book has been utilized by Haenisch[24] in a long study of an episode from the last days and weeks of

---

[22] Ed. *Wang-ch'ui lou ts'ung-shu* in 2 chapters.
[23] Ed. *Pi-chi hsiao-shuo ta-kuan* in 14 ch. *Ssu-k'u*, p. 2932; A. Wylie, *Notes*, p. 159.
[24] 'Die Ehreninschrift für den Rebellengeneral Ts'ui Lih', *Abhandlungen der Preussischen Akademie der Wissenschaften* (1944), H.4.

Chin. Chapter 13 contains more or less general reflections on philosophy and history, ch. 14 literary productions from the pen of Liu Ch'i and his friends.

*Ch'ien-t'ang i-shih* (Events from Ch'ien-t'ang), by Liu I-ch'ing.[25] I fail to understand why the *Ssu-k'u* bibliographers regarded the *Ch'ien-t'ang i-shih* as 'miscellaneous history' (*tsa-shih*), whereas they classified the *Kuei-ch'ien chih* as 'fiction'. Both works are very similar in nature; the *Ch'ien-t'ang i-shih* contains even more 'unhistorical' entries (e.g. on local folklore of the former Sung capital, etc.) than Liu Ch'i's work. The political tendency of the book is Sung-loyalist. The diary of the abduction of the Sung imperial family to Shang-tu (ch. 9 of the book) has been translated by A. C. Moule,[26] a text by Yen Kuang-ta where no great sympathy for the Mongols can be found—again evidence for the comparative freedom of literary expression under the Yüan. Liu I-ch'ing seems to have been strongly critical of Chia Ssu-tao. On the other hand the heroic Sung official Wen T'ien-hsiang (1236–82) is praised for his patriotism, as are other loyalists.

Another work by a Sung loyalist is *Tung-nan chi-wen* (Information on the South East), anonymous.[27] It is classified as 'fiction' and contains anecdotes of the Southern Sung period as early as Hui-tsung (r. 1101–26), mostly from court circles, high officials and literati, in addition to some stories of the supernatural and some ethnological observations. Its value as a historical source is inferior to that of the *Ch'ien-t'ang i-shih*.

To the better-known works of a miscellaneous character belongs *Kuei-hsin tsa-chih* (Miscellaneous notes from the Kuei-hsin quarter) by Chou Mi.[28] The author lived 1232–1308 and held office until 1276. After the fall of the Sung he declined to serve the new regime and lived in retirement in the Kuei-hsin quarter of Hang-chou. His *Kuei-hsin tsa-chih* is a loose collection, in which may be found not a few data on political and intellectual life in the former Sung capital. The span of time covered by the work is from the middle of the thirteenth century to 1305. Biographical data on literati are, of course, numerous, but there are also some anecdotes concerning Chia Ssu-tao and reports on contemporary events, e.g. the all too famous (or infamous) looting of the graves of the Sung emperors (pieh 1, 46b–49a, hsü 1, 37b–38b), or the siege of Hsiang-yang (pieh 2, 37a–48a, one of the most important texts on the siege of this famous fortress).

A much smaller work where literary matters figure prominently is *Shan-fang sui-pi* (Notes from the mountain house), by Chiang Tzu-cheng.[29]

[25] Ed. *Wu-lin chang-ku ts'ung-pien* in 10 ch. *Ssu-k'u*, p. 1136.

[26] Hang-chou to Shang-tu A.D. 1276, *TP* 16 (1915), pp. 393–419.

[27] Ed. *Shou-shan-ko ts'ung-shu* in 3 ch. *Ssu-k'u*, p. 2931; A. Wylie, *Notes*, p. 159.

[28] Ed. *Chin-tai pi-shu* in altogether 6 ch. *Ssu-k'u*, p. 2930; A. Wylie, *Notes*, p. 159; R. des Rotours, *Traité des Fonctionnaires* (Leiden, 1947), pp. cxii–cxiii.

[29] Ed. *Chih-pu-tsu chai ts'ung-shu* in 1 ch. *Ssu-k'u*, p. 2933; A. Wylie, *Notes*, p. 159.

Next to nothing is known about the author, who must have lived *c.* 1280 (he mentions the years 1278 and 1279, p. 10b). He records a number of occasional poems, some of them with a distinct political pro-Sung flavour. There are some on Chia Ssu-tao (pp. 14b–17b), in which he is severely criticized for ruining the state of Sung and betraying his country. On the other hand, a loyalist is praised for his bravery (3a–b). The Mongols are called *pei-ch'ao*, 'the Northern Dynasty', although Chiang Tzu-cheng must have lived under the Yüan.

Turning to the Yüan proper, one should perhaps mention *Yü-t'ang chia-hua* (Refined conversations held in the Academy), by Wang Yün.[30] The author, who lived 1227–1304, held high offices under Qubilai. In his notebook he deals not only with antiquarian subjects and events from ancient history and literature, but also with contemporary affairs, which justifies its inclusion in a survey of sources. The 'Notes of an Embassy to the West' (*Hsi-shih chi*), by Liu Yu, a travelogue on Central Asia, is to be found ch. 94, 4b–9a.

Another similar work is *Sui-ch'ang tsa-lu* (Miscellaneous notes from Sui-ch'ang), by Cheng Yüan-yu.[31] It is not dated; its author lived 1292–1364, and, as he reports the death of Tu Pen, must have written the book after 1350. There are many stories and anecdotes about Sung loyalists, a remarkable fact for so late a time, and narratives of events from 1275–6. Contemporary stories concern rather the local worthies and literati of Chekiang than the leading figures of the author's time. Interesting is the account of the desecration of the Sung emperors' tumuli near Shao-hsing (pp. 9a–9b), which disagrees with the sources assembled in *Cho-keng lu*, ch. 4, No. 1. This violation of the imperial tombs by lamaist clerics about 1285 must have caused an uproar of patriotic sentiment in Southern China. We find it mentioned in quite a number of different sources with more or less revolting details.[32]

The amount of contemporary material is likewise small in *Jih-wen lu* (Diary notes), by Li Chung.[33] This short work was finished between 1364 and 1368 (it mentions the date of 1364, but calls the Yüan still 'our national dynasty'). Apart from the usual entries on strange phenomena and portents it contains a few contemporary stories such as the description of illiteracy among non-Chinese officials (cf. *Asia Major*, 3, 1 (1952), p. 28). A strong anti-Buddhist feeling is evident in this collection.

To the same period belongs *Chih-cheng chih-chi* (Unprejudiced notes from the Chih-cheng period [1341–67]), by K'ung Ch'i.[34] Its author was a

[30] Ed. *SPTK* in 8 ch. (= Coll. Works of W., ch. 93–100); *Ssu-k'u*, p. 2558; A. Wylie, *Notes*, p. 134.     [31] Ed. *Pi-chi hsiao-shuo ta-kuan. Ssu-k'u*, p. 2935; A. Wylie, *Notes*, p. 159.
[32] There is a thorough study of the subject by P. Demiéville, 'Les tombeaux des Song Méridionaux', *BEFEO* 25 (1925), 458–67.
[33] Ed. *Shou-shan-ko ts'ung-shu. Ssu-k'u*, p. 2557; A. Wylie, *Notes*, p. 134.
[34] Ed. *Yüeh-ya t'ang ts'ung-shu* in 4 ch. *Ssu-k'u*, p. 2970.

descendant of Confucius, who lived in retirement in Ssu-ming (Chekiang); the preface is dated 1360 (although the date of 1363 is mentioned, ch. 4, 35b). The chief merit of the book lies perhaps in the numerous stories of local folklore (mostly from the Ssu-ming and Li-yang districts, in Chekiang and Kiangsu respectively), but there are also many anecdotes about prominent contemporaries, such as the Mongol chancellor Toqto, the poet Sa'dullā (b. 1308), the historian Ou-yang Hsüan (1283–1357), and emperor Wen-tsung (r. 1330–2). Attention should be drawn to the fact that sometimes dialogues are recorded in the colloquial language. Apparently the author had very uncompromising ideas about the seclusion of women from the outer world: he gives some deterrent examples of what may happen if a woman leaves the 'inner apartments' and ventures to attend a party outside. But in view of his ancestry we should not expect a more easygoing attitude. As a historical source the book certainly has some value.

The most comprehensive work of this category in the thirteenth and fourteenth centuries is *Cho-keng lu* (Notes taken during breaks in farm work) by T'ao Tsung-i.[35] We can be brief here because there exists an excellent study of its author and the book itself by F. W. Mote, as well as an index.[36] Some remarks will suffice to give an impression of this work. It is a source of the highest value, because it has preserved not only data on contemporary events witnessed by the author or his friends, but also extracts from earlier works which are either lost or not easily accessible. It seems that T'ao never held any office during his long life (*c.* 1320–after 1402), but this does not mean, as Mote has pointed out, that he was disinterested in what was happening around him. He seems to have had personal contacts with many of his prominent contemporaries, and the scope of his reading as evidenced by his quotations from other works is very extensive. In 1366 a printed edition of the *Cho-keng lu* appeared, still under the Yüan, who, again, apparently did not object to a book which contains many pro-Sung stories and anecdotes. It is encyclopaedic insofar as it contains entries on almost every conceivable subject, from literary and artistic topics to historical notes such as the genealogy of the Yüan dynasty and the highly informative list of Mongol and Inner Asiatic tribes in ch. 1. Even if there are some stories which are certainly pro-Sung, we would be mistaken in regarding the work as anti-Mongol. For each story which could be interpreted as Sung-loyalist, we could point to one which praises Mongol rulers, statesmen, and officials. We must be grateful that this important source for the political and cultural history of the thirteenth and fourteenth

[35] Ed. *Kuang-wen t'ang* in 30 ch. *Ssu-k'u*, p. 2935. A. Wylie, *Notes*, p. 159.
[36] 'Notes on the Life of T'ao Tsung-i', in *Silver Jubilee Volume of the Zinbun Kagaku Kenkyusyo* (Kyoto, 1954), pp. 279–93. *Index du Tcho Keng Lou*, (Centre d'Etudes Sinologiques de Pékin, 1950).

centuries can now be used easily by means of the Index of the Centre Franco-Chinois.

As the *Cho-keng lu* is essentially a compilation, one is tempted to try to discover the primary sources which formed its basis. Among those primary sources we find *Shan-chü hsin-hua* (Recent conversations in the mountain dwelling), by Yang Yü,[37] printed a few years earlier than the *Cho-keng lu* (1360). Here too we may be brief, as a short study of the book and an integral translation have been published recently.[38] This translation will perhaps permit us to judge the value of a typical *pi-chi* (notebook) for the historian. Yang Yü (1285–1361) for some time held metropolitan offices in the 1330s and therefore may take credit for the notes which relate personal experiences at the court. It should be noted that here, as well as in the appendix to the *Keng-shen wai-shih*, the last Mongol emperor Shun-ti appears in a rather favourable light and not at all as the typical 'roi débauché'. On the contrary, Yang relates on several occasions the frugality of Shun-ti, who opposed unnecessary luxury. It could perhaps be objected that these stories might have been invented by the author. But then why did he invent stories? If Yang Yü had really witnessed recklessness and debauchery on the part of the emperor, he might perhaps have been silent, if he was trying to whitewash the ruler. It is not very probable that almost twenty-five years later he should go to the length of concocting stories, when he himself was an old and retired man who had no more worldly aspirations of promotion, even assuming there was a chance that his book might become known in the distant capital.

### 3. *Buddhist historical writings*

We shall not be concerned here with Buddhist historical literature relating chiefly to members of the Buddhist clergy, like the *T'ien-t'ai chiu-tsu chuan* (Biographies of the Nine T'ien-t'ai Patriarchs) (pref. dated 1228) or other collections of biographies which concentrate on monastic life. What interests the historian is the attempt of Buddhist writers to compile *general* or world histories in imitation of the 'secular' (or Confucian) prototypes. This kind of historiography could certainly be called private and unofficial, even if such a work were later presented to the emperor or prefaced by some prominent literati of the time. If there should really exist histories at all which might contain data or concepts different from orthodox official ideology, we would have to look among the Buddhist works to find them (or perhaps Taoist ones; I do not know whether the Taoist Canon contains any works attempting to interpret history in

[37] Ed. *Chih-pu-tsu chai ts'ung-shu. Ssu-k'u*, p. 2934. A. Wylie, *Notes*, p. 159.
[38] H. Franke, in *Journal of Oriental Studies Hongkong*, 2, 2 (1955); the translation ('Beiträge zur Kulturgeschichte Chinas unter der Mongolenherrschaft') is vol. xxx, pt. 2 of *Abhandlungen für die Kunde des Morgenlandes* (Wiesbaden, 1956).

terms of Taoist religion and philosophy). There are, of course, quite a number of Buddhist works dealing with events or tendencies about which we may also find details in other 'laic' works or which are as such interesting for the intellectual history of a period.[39] For our purpose these are not as important as those which try to give a complete summary of history, where the interplay of traditional Confucian and Buddhist ideology can be seen. One of the earliest attempts to write a Buddhist history (or should we rather call it encyclopaedia?) seems to have been the *Li-tai san-pao chi* (Record of the Three Jewels under successive dynasties) finished by Fei Ch'ang-fang in A.D. 597.[40] The three first chapters give a history of Buddhism which is very Chinese (and un-Indian) insofar as the author tries to fit everything into an exact chronology and applies the sexagenary cycle throughout his book, which is arranged according to Chinese rulers. Buddha himself is said to be born in the ninth year of Chuang wang, in a *kuei-ssu* year (688 B.C.)—a chronological accuracy which would have bewildered an Indian *bhikṣu*.

From the period which concerns us here we should mention as a general history written from a Buddhist point of view *Fo-tsu t'ung chi* (General chronology of Buddha and his patriarchs) by Chih-p'an.[41] The work was printed about 1271. The author shows evidence of considerable scholarship in this extensive history. A list of works consulted is given (pp. 131 III–132 II). He also mentions the models from which he took his general plan: for the basic annals (*pen chi*), biographies (*lieh-chuan*), and hereditary houses (*shih-chia*) he followed Ssu-ma Ch'ien's Records of the Historian (*Shih chi*); for the account of the expansion and vicissitudes of Buddhism (*t'ung-sai chih*) Ssu-ma Kuang's Comprehensive Mirror (*Tzu-chih t'ung-chien*) (p. 129 III). In other words, he did not try to develop a new pattern but imitated the standard forms of 'secular' history. This could not be done without some inconsistencies; it was not possible to combine church history with a pattern developed on entirely different material. A short survey of the general plan of the work will perhaps show its degree of dependence on the standard dynastic histories. Altogether the work tries to imitate their division into the five groups of basic annals (*pen chi*, ch. 1–8), hereditary houses (*shih-chia*, ch. 9–10), individual biographies (*lieh-chuan*, ch. 11–22), tables (*piao*, ch. 23–24), and monographs (*chih*, ch. 25–54). In spite of this imitation of the Records of the Historian, the author has to treat this general plan rather freely to apply it to the history of Buddhism. Thus he first expounds Buddhist doctrine in the *pen-chi* before entering into a chronological account of history. Ch. 2–4 contain

---

[39] E.g. the *Pien-wei-lu* in 5 ch., by Hsiang-mai, dated 1291, where we find discussions in the colloquial language of the thirteenth century; *Taishō Tripitaka*, vol. 52, No. 2116.

[40] Ed. *Taishō Tripitaka*, vol. 49, No. 2044, pp. 22–127.

[41] Ed. *Taishō Tripitaka*, vol. 49, No. 2035, pp. 129–475 in 54 ch. *Ssu-k'u*, p. 3025; Nanyo Catalogue No. 1661; A. Wylie, *Notes*, p. 168.

a life of Buddha, whose birth is recorded for the year 1027 B.C. Ch. 5 attempts to take the twenty-four Indian patriarchs as *points d'appui* for the *pen-chi*, with the consequence that almost no dates could be given. Ch. 6–8 are based on Chinese patriarchs (altogether seventeen).

The *shih-chia*, ch. 9–10, give a history of sects, chiefly the T'ien-t'ai (to which the author belonged), in the form of a filiation of patriarchs and biographies, including biographies of pious laymen. Other sects are dealt with in the *lieh-chuan* (biographies) section, ch. 11–22. The tables (*piao*) give in ch. 23 a list of Chinese rulers from Liang Wu-ti (502) to 1233, with some short entries on events affecting Buddhism. The most extensive part of the work is formed by the monographs (*chih*) which are in turn subdivided. Ch. 25 is a bibliography (*i-wen-chih*), a catalogue of Chinese Buddhist works classified according to schools; ch. 26 ff. are more or less biographical again, whereas ch. 31 and 32 try to imitate the geographical chapters of Standard Histories (*ti-li-chih*). Ch. 31 is cosmological and mythical, 32 gives real geography with maps of China and the western regions in Han times and of India. Ch. 33 seems to be modelled on the calendar monographs, as it contains a list of annual feasts with a detailed description of each. Ch. 34 to 48 give an account of the successful or unsuccessful propagation of the Law (*fa-yün t'ung-sai*) from the Chou to the emperor Li-tsung of the Sung (1236). There is also an appendix on the Yüan up to 1368, a later addition drawn from the dynastic history of the Yüan. As mentioned above, this part is an imitation of Ssu-ma Kuang's Comprehensive Mirror, using the Chinese rulers and their reigns as chronological framework. Ch. 49 and 50 are a kind of anthology of famous pro-Buddhist writings. Even Chih-p'an, the author, is represented, and one wonders whether he himself included his own production in the work. Finally ch. 51 to 54 are a *li-tai hui-yao* (important events from successive dynasties), with classified excerpts from the Standard Histories concerning Buddhism, such as a list of embassies which presented holy scriptures to the court, titles conferred upon monks, heterodox religions (Manichaeism and Zoroastrianism) or such *causes célèbres* as that produced by the *Hua-hu ching*, a Taoist book pretending that Lao-tzu had been reborn as Buddha in India.

It will be seen that the work is a mine of information, but one in which it is extremely difficult to locate the person or event one is looking for. The external framework of a dynastic history is present, but the author had to modify it according to his purpose. There is no attempt at introducing a purely Buddhist chronology, e.g. from the death of Buddha on. Chinese standard chronology is observed throughout, as indeed are the proper designations of Chinese rulers, even if they were known to be fervent anti-Buddhists. It seems that the pattern set by the dynastic histories and Ssu-ma Kuang's Comprehensive Mirror was too powerful to allow an independent method. In spite of this conformity with existing Confucian histories, the *Ssu-k'u* bibliographers relegated the work to the *ts'un-mu* category. They considered this close imitation of the official histories, particularly with regard to the basic annals, where Buddha and the patriarchs provide the chronological basis, as objectionable plagiarism and an insult to dynastic histories and their principles.

A more handy work to use is *Fo-tsu li-tai t'ung-tsai* (Encyclopaedia of Buddha and his patriarchs under successive dynasties), by Nien-ch'ang.[42] It was finished about 1333 or 1334; two prefaces are dated 1341 and 1344. The pattern is that of an annalistic history from the earliest times to 1333.[43] Ch. 1 deals with the various Buddhas and Buddhist cosmogony; 'real' history begins in ch. 2 with the mythical Chinese emperor P'an-ku. The sequence is that of Chinese rulers, though with some significant differences in comparison with *Fo-tsu t'ung-chi*. Nien-ch'ang notes Chinggis Khan's enthronement in 1206 and from that year on faithfully records not only the Sung (and Chin up to 1234) but also the Yüan reign titles. He even goes to the length of finishing his entries in 1333 by wishing the August Emperor ten thousand times ten thousand years (*wan-wan sui*)—an exhibition of loyalty which none of the monks writing under the Sung apparently thought necessary. Nien-ch'ang himself belonged to the Dhyāna sect. One would rather expect this pro-Mongol attitude from a Lamaist. Otherwise he seems to treat the warring states of the twelfth and thirteenth centuries more or less equally. He notes first the year according to the Sung reign title, but gives those of Chin, Hsi-hsia and later of Yüan as well, including the dates of accession and death of rulers in the various countries. I fail to see why the *Ssu-k'u* bibliographers thought the *Fo-tsu t'ung-tsai* worthy to be copied into the emperor's library but not the *Fo-tzu t'ung-chi*. Perhaps it was because Nien-ch'ang quotes so extensively from Confucian authors. Whereas Chih-p'an tells us almost nothing about Buddhism in the northern states of Chin, Yüan, and Hsi-hsia, Nien-ch'ang sometimes gives a lengthy account. A comparison of the entries in both works for the same year is interesting, but would lead too far. We might sum up by saying that the 'secular' content in Nien-ch'ang's chronicle is much fuller than in Chih-p'an's and that it is more a general history with special reference to Buddhism, whereas Chih-p'an tried to write an encyclopaedia of Buddhism in the formal framework of a dynastic history.

We should be grateful to Professor Takakusu that he reprinted in the same volume as the other two works, *Shih-shih chi-ku lüeh* (Abstract of

---

[42] Ed. *Taishō Tripitaka* in 22 ch., vol. 49, No. 2036, pp. 477 I–735 II. Nanyo Catalogue No. 6137. A. Wylie, *Notes*, p. 169; *Ssu-k'u*, p. 3024.

[43] For a connection between Buddhist chronicles of the thirteenth century and Rasīd ad-Dīn, see *Oriens* (1951), iv, 21–26.

historical researches on Buddhism), by Chüeh-an.[44] The work must have been finished in 1354. It covers the whole of Chinese history from remote antiquity (the mythical emperors San-huang and Wu-ti, with an additional diagram of still more legendary figures such as Hun-tun and P'an-ku) to 1276, the final overthrow of the Sung. The pattern is that of an annalistic chronicle adopting the reigns of Chinese rulers for chronology. The author, in contrast to Nien-ch'ang, did not show any particular deference to the Yüan. For example, he calls Qubilai *Ta-tan-kuo hsieh-ch'an huang-ti* 'the emperor Seĉen of the Tatar state', thus using his personal name (tabooed in theory) and not giving his dynastic titles as most 'secular' writings of that period do. The 'secular' element is still stronger than in Nien-ch'ang's chronicle; if we were to leave out everything concerning Buddhism there would still remain a rather detailed abstract of Chinese history with no essential data missing. Buddha does not make his appearance before the reign of king Chao of Chou; from then on we find stories of the Indian patriarchs inserted from time to time. Chinese Buddhism is dealt with, as one would expect, from the famous dream of emperor Ming of Han (r. A.D. 58–76) on. The *Ssu-k'u* editors criticized the *Shih-shih chi-ku lüeh* on some points, for example because the author listed rulers in his annals which according to the Ch'ien-lung bibliographers had no right to appear with a reign title of their own; but on the whole they had a rather favourable opinion of it. It might be added that the three Buddhist works we have dealt with show one distinct advantage over the standard dynastic histories, in that they usually mention their sources.

Trying to sum up, it might be said that there are disappointingly few historical sources in the period under review which present us an individual, personal, and first-hand account. For most of the crucial events we have no realistic eyewitness accounts. This applies to a certain extent to the numerous letters contained in the works of authors. Such letters usually deal with theoretical or ethical problems, even where they concern contemporary affairs. We note a certain lack of individual expression, if we compare China with medieval Europe. But it may be unfair to ask for individuality where the medium is an idiom as highly stylized and conventional as the Chinese literary language. European sources in Latin are much more individual and personal, and can reflect a personality, even if it be through faulty grammar or orthography. The 'individual element' in history is not easily accessible in China; we can only try to turn to such sources where we may reasonably hope to learn something more about a person or an event than we know from the official accounts, in other words to the *pi-chi* (notebooks) and similar works of a miscellaneous character, or to the few texts where somebody records his personal experiences.

[44] Ed. *Taishō Tripitaka* in 4 ch., vol. 49, No. 2037, pp. 737–902; *Ssu-k'u*, p. 3023; A. Wylie, *Notes*, p. 168.

# 9. CHINESE HISTORICAL CRITICISM: LIU CHIH-CHI AND SSU-MA KUANG

E. G. PULLEYBLANK

*Professor of Chinese, University of Cambridge*

It is a truism, at least among sinologists,[1] that China possesses a wealth of historical writing unequalled by any other country before modern times. It would not, however, be true to say that Chinese methods of history writing and canons of historical criticism would always receive correspondingly high praise.[2] We are commonly told that the method was simply one of mechanical scissors-and-paste compilation with only a primitive exercise of criticism in the choice of rejection of material. Yet, while there is a measure of truth in this judgement as it applies to much run-of-the-mill official and other history writing in China, it hardly does justice to the quality of scholarly acumen and historical thought displayed by the great Chinese historians.

Certainly the introduction of western methods at the end of the nineteenth century meant a very great revolution in Chinese historical studies, as in the field of natural science, but it must strike an observer as remarkable the extent to which twentieth-century Chinese historians have been able to draw on their own tradition while enlarging their conceptions and introducing greater rigour through influences from outside. This has no doubt been partly due to nationalist conservatism and has not always been wholly beneficial but it is also a tribute to the resources available in Chinese tradition.

Moreover, quite apart from its continuing vigour and permanent value, which will have to be proved in years to come, the Chinese attitude to history and critical thought on the subject are clearly matters of fundamental importance for the understanding of the past of this most historically minded of all peoples.

Taken in its widest sense the topic, Chinese historical criticism, is

[1] Many western historians are apparently unaware that the Chinese wrote history at all. See, for instance, J. W. Thompson, *A History of historical writing* (2 vols., New York, 1942), which devotes a chapter to Arabic, Persian, and Mongol historians in the Middle Ages but which confines its references to China to the astonishing statement, 'This book [the Mongol chronicle of Sanang Setsen] supplemented by some information gleaned from Chinese annals is the sum total of our knowledge of the history of the Mongols in Far Asia, especially in China' (p. 354). If he had taken the trouble to find out something about these 'Chinese annals' which he dismisses so contemptuously, the author might have been forced to revise his remarks in the introduction about the pre-eminent historical-mindedness of Christian Europe.

[2] See, for example, C. S. Gardner, *Traditional Chinese historiography* (1938), p. 64.

nothing less than the whole history of Chinese historiography studied from the point of view of its purposes, concepts and guiding rules, whether formulated or not; every paper in this symposium will contribute to it. What I shall attempt here is the much more limited task of dealing with one or two examples of Chinese thinking about historical method and of the application of critical techniques. In so doing I shall be disregarding altogether the bulk of works that fall into the traditional category of Historical Criticism (*shih-p'ing*), namely those known as Historical Discussion (*shih-lun*). These works consist largely of comments on historical events or historical writings from a moralistic standpoint, and though of interest as revealing Chinese political and ethical interpretations of history, are not of primary concern for my purpose.

## The Shih-t'ung (Generalities on History)[3]

Comments by historians on their own or each other's work can be found from the time of Ssu-ma Ch'ien (*c.* 100 B.C.). Evidence that history had become recognized as a separate branch of learning is provided by the appearance of the four-category book classification system in the third century A.D., history being one of the categories, and by the establishment of History Schools in both Northern and Southern dynasties in the following century.[4] The first actual treatise on the writing of history in Chinese (or, as far as I can discover, in any language) was the *Shih-t'ung* (Generalities on History)[5] of Liu Chih-chi (A.D. 661–721, also known as Liu Tzu-hsüan),[6] completed in 710.

Liu Chih-chi claimed descent from the imperial house of the Han

---

[3] Since this article was written Byongik Koh has published an extensive article, 'Zur Werttheorie in der chinesischen Historiographie auf Grund des Shih-t'ung des Liu Chih-chi (661–721)', *Oriens Extremus* (1957), iv, 5–51, 125–81. (The first part was also published in *Chintan hakpo* (Seoul, 1957), xviii, 87–130.) I have used it to correct some matters of detail. Professor William Hung has been engaged for many years on a translation and commentary to the *Shih-t'ung* which will no doubt be a definitive work on the subject.

[4] The first works to use the four category system were Cheng Mo's *Chung-ching* (*c.* A.D. 250) and Hsün Hsü's *Hsin-pu* (A.D. 264) in which the order was classics, philosophers, history, and belles-lettres. The first to use the now standard order which places history before philosophers was Li Ch'ung, between 317 and 322.

After Shih Lo established the state of Chao in 319 he appointed Directors for four schools, the third being the History School (*Chin-shu* 105.1a). In the southern dynasties of Sung and Ch'i there were four schools corresponding to the fourfold book classification—Classics (Ching-hsüeh), Esoterics (Hsüan-hsüeh), History (Shih-hsüeh) and Literature (Wen-hsüeh) (*Sung-shu* 93, biography of Lei Tz'u-tsung; *Nan-ch'i shu* 16, Pai-kuan chih; Chin Yü-fu, *Chung-kuo shih-hsüeh Shih* (1944), p. 223.

[5] In his preface Liu Chih-chi justifies the name *Shih-t'ung* (1) by comparing it to the *Po-hu t'ung*—the *Shih-t'ung* proceeded from the History Office just as the *Po-hu t'ung* proceeded from discussion in the White Tiger Hall, (2) by reference to the title Shih-t'ung-tzu bestowed on Ssu-ma Ch'ien's descendants in the time of Wang Mang (*Han-shu* 62, biography of Ssu-ma Ch'ien).

[6] Biographies in *Chiu T'ang-shu* 102; *Hsin T'ang-shu* 132. See also *Shih-t'ung*, sections 36 'Tzu-hsü' and 49 'Wu-shih'; Fu Chen-lun, *Liu Chih-chi nien-p'u* (1934).

dynasty and his ancestors had served under the Northern Wei dynasty in the early sixth century. A 'great-uncle' (actually a cousin of his grand-father), Liu Yu-chih,[7] had been a well-known scholar in the early years of the T'ang and had been engaged on the composition of the National History. This may possibly indicate a family interest in historical studies. Chih-chi's father, Ts'ang-ch'i had some fame as a littérateur and served as a mandarin, though he did not rise very high.

Liu Chih-chi tells us something of his upbringing and introduction to historical studies in the autobiographical section of the *Shih-t'ung*:

> When I was a child I received instruction from my father and early began to make excursions into the field of letters. When I was still of an age to wear an embroidered jacket and white silk trousers I was given the Book of Documents in Ancient Characters (*Ku-wen shang-shu*) to read but I always had trouble with its difficult phrases and found it hard to recite. Though I was frequently beaten I did not master it. When I used to hear my father expounding for my brothers the Spring and Autumn Annals with the Tradition of Tso (*Tso chuan*), I would put aside my own book and listen. After the lesson was over I would explain it to my brothers. I sighed to myself and said, 'If all books were like this I would not be lazy any more.' My father thought this unusual and thereupon began to teach me the Tso Tradition. In a year he had ex-pounded it all and I could recite it. At the time I was just 12 years old [eleven by our reckoning]. Although I had no deep understanding of it, yet I could roughly give the main sense. My father and brothers wished me to study all the subcommentaries and explanations and become perfect in the words of this one classic. I declined because I had not learned of matters later than the Capture of the Unicorn [the end of the Spring and Autumn Annals] and I begged to be allowed to read the other books of this category in order to broaden my knowledge. Next I read the Records of the Historian (*Shih-chi*), the History of the Former Han Dynasty (*Han-shu*) and the History of the Three Kingdoms (*San-kuo chih*). Then, since I wished to know the continuities and changes and how successive events had followed one another from ancient times to the present, I attacked the whole class [of historical writing] and without instruction from a teacher read from the Han restoration down to the Veritable Records of the Present Dynasty. By the time I was 17 [16 by our reckoning] my reading was fairly comprehensive. The books I read were largely borrowed or hired. Though some of the rolls were imperfect and there were missing portions, I knew fairly well the main course of events and the outline of the words.[8]

[7] *Chiu T'ang-shu* 190A; *Shih-t'ung t'-ung-shih* 12.30b (Ssu-pu pei-yao).
[8] *Shih-t'ung t'ung-shih* 10.11a. b. On the histories referred to in this passage see the papers by P. van der Loon and A. F. P. Hulsewé, above, pp. 24–30, 31–43.

Liu Chih-chi's historical studies were interrupted at this point while he prepared himself for the literary examinations by which he hoped to seek entrance into official life. He was successful in passing the Chin-shih examination in 680 and was appointed Registrar of Huo-chia County in Huai Prefecture. He remained in this post for a considerable number of years, certainly until 695 and probably until 699. [9] From time to time he submitted memorials to the throne on topics of the day, no doubt hoping to attract attention to himself and gain advancement, but although his name gradually became known he remained in his lowly provincial post. It was, however, not far from the Eastern Capital, Loyang, at which the court stayed during most of this period, and his duties were evidently not very pressing, for he tells us that he had leisure to pursue his interest in history and to travel to Loyang and borrow the books he needed for his studies.

During these years he had the ambition to write a major work of history covering the whole period from the restoration of the Han Dynasty (A.D. 23) to his own day, collating and correcting the numerous works that already existed as Confucius was reputed to have done for the Classics. However, as he says:

> I feared that if I were rashly to carry out the example of Confucius without having Confucius' reputation I would startle vulgar opinion and be blamed by my contemporaries, receiving no thanks for my trouble. Whenever I took my writing brush in hand I would sigh irresolutely, and so it went on. It was not that I wanted to do something beyond my powers. I was really within my powers but I did not dare to do it. [10]

It is quite likely that this represents in part at least his reasons for not writing his major work. He speaks of the isolation in which he found himself as a result of his interest in history, especially because of his sceptical attitude towards revered texts. Purely literary pursuits were more popular and the atmosphere was not favourable for independent historical scholarship. Meanwhile his growing reputation as a scholar was finally recognized in 699 when he was given a sinecure in the household of a prince and ordered to assist in compiling the *San-chiao chu-ying* (Gems and Blossoms of the Three Doctrines), an encyclopaedia or anthology of Buddhism, Taoism and Confucianism sponsored by the Empress Wu. [11]

After the completion of this work in 701 Liu Chih-chi was appointed Assistant Secretary of the Writing Office (*Chu-tso tso-lang*) and in addition attached to the History Office. Except for short intervals, he was engaged

---

[9] In 695, still holding the same office, he sent two memorials which are recorded in *T'ang Hui-yao* 40 and 81. See Fu Chen-lun, op. cit., pp. 64–68.

[10] *Shih-t'ung t'ung-shih* 10.12b.　　　　　　　　[11] Fu Chen-lun, op. cit., pp. 69–74.

on writing official history for most of the rest of his career. Having come out of his provincial isolation to live in the capital, Liu Chih-chi now at last found friends who shared the same interests and among whom he could express more freely his original ideas. His first and closest associate was Hsü Chien who collaborated with him on the encyclopaedia. Somewhat later he met Wu Ching who worked on the National History for many years and also wrote the Important Deliberations on Government of the Chen-kuan period (627–49) (*Chen-kuan cheng-yao*), which is still extant; and there were a number of others who are less well known. It was at this time that Liu Chih-chi wrote his Family History of the Liu Clan (*Liu Shih chia-shih*) and Study of the Genealogy of the Liu Clan (*Liu Shih p'u k'ao*) in which he boldly rejected the tradition that the Han imperial house, from which he himself claimed descent, had been descended from the Emperor Yao.[12]

The last years of the Empress Wu's reign and the reign of Chung-tsung (705–10) were troubled by unsettled and corrupt political conditions and were not propitious for the writing of detached and impartial history. This was especially true after 705 when numerous Chief Ministers and other highly placed persons were jointly in charge of the History Office. Immediately after Chung-tsung's accession and the old Empress's death Liu Chih-chi was ordered to take part in writing the Veritable Records of the Empress Wu which was hastily compiled in a few months. He felt very dissatisfied at the way in which his work was interfered with and frustrated and when the court moved to Ch'ang-an towards the end of 706 he stayed behind in Loyang at his own request.

In 708 he was specially summoned to Ch'ang-an to join the History Office. After a time he found the situation intolerable and sent an outspoken letter of resignation to Hsiao Chih-chung, one of the Chief Ministers who were jointly supervising the writing of the National History. His complaints, under five headings, throw an interesting light on the difficulties which a conscientious historian was likely to meet in trying to write official history in China. Some of his points are reminiscent of complaints that have been made about official history in our own day. They may be summarized as follows:

1. Whereas the great histories of former times were written by one man, now the practice of collective compilation has grown up. Everything has to be scrutinized and passed back and forth and nothing is ever decided.

2. In the Former Han Dynasty all documents from provincial authorities went first to the archivist before being sent to the Chief

---

[12] Liu Chih-chi's biographies say that he wrote these works after his letter of resignation to Hsiao Chih-chung in 708 but this is an error. See Fu Chen-lun, op. cit., pp. 84–85.

Minister; but nowadays it is very difficult for historians to get access to any government documents.

3. In ancient times historians made their words public and were not afraid to risk the displeasure of the mighty. More recently it has been customary to write histories in secret within the palace in order to avoid importuning by interested persons; but in fact, with the large number of those engaged on history, this has meant that it has become impossible to write anything critical of a person in authority without his immediately knowing and objecting.

4. In ancient times historians writing privately had a free hand in establishing their own working standards. Now high-placed officials jointly supervise and give contradictory instructions.

5. If there must be overseers their proper function should be to divide up and allocate tasks; but not even this is being done and the historians are left to idle away their time doing nothing.

Liu went on to complain bitterly of the disappointment and frustration to which he personally had been subjected and to beg to be allowed to return to his former retirement in Loyang. In spite of the strong terms in which he expressed his grievances, however, his request was refused. If we are to believe him, his remarks greatly offended certain of the Chief Ministers and he was for a time in danger of their vengeance; but they were all overthrown in 710 when the Empress Wei's bid for supreme power was defeated, and he escaped. Just about this time he completed his *Shih-t'ung*.[13]

In the years that followed, under the Emperors Jui-tsung and Hsüan-tsung, Liu Chih-chi continued to work in the History Office. It is not recorded whether he found things more to his satisfaction but at any rate he collaborated in the production of three Veritable Records, those of Ching-tsung and Jui-tsung and a revised version of the Empress Wu's. By this time he held the high ranking but largely honorific post of Left Grand Councillor (*Tso san-ch'i ch'ang-shih*), and on the presentation of the three Veritable Records to the throne in 715 he was created Viscount of Chü-ch'ao County.[14] In 719 we find him engaged in a public controversy about the texts of certain classical works. It is sad that after attaining a certain degree of recognition he should have ended his career under a cloud. In

[13] The preface to the *Shih-t'ung* is dated in the spring of Ching-lung 4 (710) and there is a reference to Chung-tsung as the present emperor. The final section ('Wu- shih'), however, refers to the downfall of Hsiao Chih-chung and the other Chief Ministers in the sixth month of that year, after the death of Chung-tsung, so it may have been added or added to after the completion of the rest of the work. The letter to Hsiao Chih-chung is contained in this section. See also the biographies in *Chiu* and *Hsin T'ang-shu* and *T'ang Hui-yao* 64. The letter is also referred to in the paper by Yang Lien-sheng, above, pp. 53–54.

[14] In his study of the genealogy of the Liu clan Chi-chi had concluded that his branch of the family were descended from the Marquises of Chü-ch'ao and not from a more senior branch of the Han royal family.

721 he attempted to intervene when his son was accused of a crime. For this he was sent into exile as Vice-Prefect of An Chou (now Lu-an Hsien in Jy-pei), and he died soon afterwards.

The works of official history on which Liu Chih-chi collaborated have long since disappeared except in so far as they were incorporated into the Old T'ang History (*Chiu T'ang shu*) or preserved in brief quotations elsewhere. It is perhaps even more regrettable that his works on the genealogy of his own clan have perished. The *Shih-t'ung* was, however, the work by which he chiefly wished to be remembered by posterity and we may be thankful that it at least has survived.

Concerning the composition of this work Liu says in his autobiography:

> [During my period in the History Office] in all that I wrote I wished to carry out my long-cherished principles but my fellow workers and the high officials in charge of the work were completely out of sympathy with this. All that I wrote and edited was vulgar and of low standard. Although in my own eyes I felt that I was bending and conforming, I still incurred much ill-will from the History Officers. Alas, though I was well-fitted for my task, yet my principles were not put into practice; though I received employment in my generation, yet my good intentions were not fulfilled. I was filled with gloomy discontent and solitary resentment. If indeed I should have nowhere to confide my feelings but keep them to myself unexpressed, I was afraid that after my death I would be unknown. So I withdrew and privately wrote the *Shih-t'ung* to make known my mind.[15]

The Generalities on History falls into a class of critical and philosophical treatises which it is difficult to define precisely. Liu Chih-chi himself mentions the *Huai-nan-tzu*, Yang Hsiung's *Fa-yen*, Wang Ch'ung's *Lun-heng*, Ying Shao's *Feng-su t'ung-i*, Liu Shao's *Jen-wu chih*, Lu Ching's *Tien-yü*, and Liu Hsieh's *Wen-hsin tiao-lung* as having furnished him with models.[16] The

---

[15] *Shih-t'ung t'ung-shih* 10.13a.

[16] *Huai-nan-tzu*, 'The Book of the Prince of Huai-nan', is an eclectic philosophical work, Taoist in tendency, compiled under the auspices of Liu An, Prince of Huai-nan, who died in 122 B.C. *Fa-yen*, 'Model Sayings', was written by Yang Hsiung (53 B.C.–A.D. 18), a Confucian of the Old Text School, in imitation of the Analects of Confucius. Translation by E. von Zach, 'Yang Hsiung's Fa Yen', *Sinologische Beiträge* iv (Batavia, 1939). *Lun Heng*, 'Critical Essays', probably completed in A.D. 82 or 83, was the work of the rationalistic and satirical Confucian philosopher Wang Ch'ung. English translation by A. Forke, *Lun Heng, MSOS* Beibände 10 and 14 (1906–11). *Feng-su t'ung-i*, 'Popular Traditions and Customs', is a compendium of folklore written in the second century A.D. by Ying Shao who also wrote on Han governmental institutions. *Jen-wu chih*, 'The Study of Human Abilities', by Liu Shao, was completed around A.D. 235. Translation by J. K. Shryock, *The Study of Human Abilities; the 'Jen Wu Chih' of Liu Shao* (American Oriental Series, No. 11, American Oriental Society, New Haven, 1937). *Tien-yü*, 'Exemplary Discourses', by Lu Ching of the state of Wu in the period of the Three Kingdoms (third century A.D.) exists only in a few fragmentary quotations found in encyclopaedias. These have been collected both by Yen K'o-chün and by Ma Kuo-han. *Wen-hsin tiao-lung* is an immensely influential work of literary criticism written at the beginning of the sixth century; see Vincent Yu-chung Shih, *The Literary Mind and the Carving of Dragons*, 1959.

last mentioned provides a particularly close parallel and may well have exerted considerable direct influence on him. It is a book of literary criticism on historical lines in which various literary forms are discussed in succession. The chapter on history,[17] though considered superficial by Chi Yün,[18] has some quite sensible remarks to make, and there are echoes and even verbal parallels in the *Shih-t'ung*. Liu Chih-chi's treatise on history follows a similar pattern to Liu Hsieh's on literature. There is also a resemblance in style since both use the same antithetical rhythmic prose. This is not surprising, however, since it was the normal prose style for practically all purposes until the *ku-wen* or free-prose movement of the middle and late T'ang.

The *Shih-t'ung* is divided into 35 Inner Sections (ch. 1–10) and 13 Outer Sections (ch. 11–20). Speaking loosely one can say that the Inner Sections constitute the theoretical development of the subject while the Outer Sections provide supplementary material. In the Inner Sections Liu Chih-chi deals first with the classification of historical works—the Six Schools (*Shu-ching, Ch'un-ch'iu, Tso-chuan, Kuo-yü, Shih-chi,* and *Han-shu*)[19] and the Two Types (annals-biography and chronicle). He then has a number of sections devoted to the different parts of the standard annals-biography type of history—Book of Documents, Basic Annals, Hereditary Families, Biographies, Tables, Monographs, Discussions and Criticisms, Prefaces and Rules of Procedure, Titles and Headings—including one, Section 3, *tsai-yen,* dealing with a suggested new division for dynastic histories which was never adopted. Then follow sections on Setting of Limits, Arrangement and Order, Nomenclature, Selection of Material, Recording of Literary Pieces, Supplements and Commentaries, Taking Over (on the dangers of mechanically incorporating earlier texts into later compilations), Localities (of family origin), Words, Excessive Verbiage, Narration, Classification (of people)—treating of various technical problems faced by historians, especially Chinese official historians. Section 24 (Honest Writing, *chih-su*) and 25 (Crooked Brush, *ch'ü-pi*) deal with the difficulties of writing truthfully and the dangers of deliberate distortions of the record. Sections 26 and 27 are concerned respectively with judgements

[17] First there is a rapid survey of the principal histories written up to Hsieh's time with, in each case, a summary criticism of their merits and demerits. Then certain general points are picked out for brief discussion—the respective advantages and disadvantages of the annals-biography form of the Standard Histories and the chronicle form; the danger that in histories of early times the brief records of antiquity will be filled out by later unsubstantiated legends; the danger in contemporary history that real worth will be neglected when it lacks power and worthless men with powerful connections will be unjustly praised; the gravity of the historian's social function as the arbiter of praise and blame.

[18] Chi Yün, 'P'ing Wen-hsin tiao-lung' incorporated as marginal notes to Huang Shu-lin's edition of the *Wen-hsin tiao-lung* (Ssu-pu pei-yao), 4.1a.

[19] i.e. the Book of Documents, Spring and Autumn Annals, Tso Tradition, Discourses of the States, Records of the Historian, and History of the Former Han Dynasty: see generally the papers by P. van der Loon and A. F. P. Hulsewé, above, pp. 24–30, 31–43.

made on various historians by other historians and on mistakes that have
been made through seeing non-existent ulterior motives and hidden mean-
ings behind the statements of historians. The remaining Inner Sections deal
with imitations (good and bad) of former models, things that should and
should not be recorded, people who do or do not deserve to have biographies, the difference between literary and historical talents, autobiographical prefaces, prolixity and concision, miscellaneous minor writings
of a historical character, the qualities needed for a History Official. The
method in general in all the Inner Sections is to enunciate principles and
then to give a historical survey with examples of how the principles have
been observed or (more often) violated. Finally there is appended an
autobiographical section, from which quotations have already been
made.[20]

The first two Outer Sections give the history respectively of the History
Offices and of the Standard Histories in successive ages. Then come the
sections 'Suspicions about Antiquity' and 'Doubts about the Classics'
which have made Liu Chih-chi notorious for his scandalous boldness in
daring to call into question even Confucius himself. The section 'Shen-tso'
seeks to demonstrate the superiority of the *Tso-chuan* over the other commentaries to the Spring and Autumn Annals. The remaining sections
consist mainly of miscellaneous notes which supplement material already
contained in the Inner Sections (occasionally showing glaring inconsistencies with what has been said there). The last section 'Against the
Times' consists mainly of Liu Chih-chi's letter of resignation to Hsiao
Chih-chung cited above and corresponds to the autobiographical section
which ends the first half of the book.

The modern western historian is likely to feel disappointment at Liu
Chih-chi's emphasis on the purely formal aspects of official Chinese historiography. Nevertheless, it is important to recognize in this a salient
aspect of the Chinese attitude to history which, in degree if in no absolute
sense, distinguishes it from the attitudes of other peoples. History was to
the Chinese (1) official and (2) normative. To make a just and definitive
record of the past was a function of government just as it was a function of
government to bestow titles and honours on the dead as well as on the
living. Moreover, this record served an essential moral purpose by holding
up good and bad examples through which virtues could be encouraged
and vice deterred. It was natural that considerations of ritual and decorum

---

[20] The table of contents lists three additional sections after Section 36 'Tzu-hsü', making a total
of 52 sections. These have now disappeared.   The biography of Liu Chih-chi in the *Hsin T'ang-shu*
already gives the total as 49, so they must have been lost very early. According to P'u Ch'i-lung,
the Sung encyclopaedia *Ch'ün-shu k'ao-so* placed one of these sections after Section 33 and gave the
total as 'over 50 sections'. I have not been able to confirm this but if it is correct it means that
the three lost sections were probably all within the Nei-p'ien and not at the end of it. (See
*Shih-t'ung t'ung-shih* 10.19a.)

should always play a large part in thinking about history. Moreover, the official character of history was bound to be to the fore at the time of Liu Chih-chi in view of the great activity there had been in the newly organized History Office of the T'ang Dynasty during the preceding half century or more, and he was bound to direct his remarks towards it.

This attitude to history, rationalized by an appeal to psychology of a more individualistic kind, is well illustrated by the following passage from the introduction to the section on the history of history officials of successive dynasties. At the same time we can see in it Liu's passion for the past for its own sake.

When man takes form between heaven and earth his life is brief as a mayfly in the world, as the white colt crossing the gap [i.e. the sun crossing the sky—a single day].[21] Yet he is ashamed not to achieve meritorious deeds during his lifetime and hates to perish without leaving a name. From emperors and kings down to poor commoners, from courtiers near the throne to distant wayfarers in the mountains and forests, there is none that does not work and strive for merit and fame. Why is this? It is that they think to create an imperishable thing. And what is it that can be called imperishable? It is only to have one's name recorded on bamboo and silk. If formerly the world had been without bamboo and silk, if there had been no history officers at the time, then whether it was a question of sages such as Yao and Shun, Yin I and Chou Kung, or of villains such as Chieh, Chou, Wang Mang and Tung Cho, whether virtuous men like Po-i and Liu-hsia Hui or bandits such as Tao Chih and Chuang Ch'iao, whether parricides such as Shang Ch'en and Mao Tun[22] or filial sons such as Tseng Shen and Min Sun, once they had followed the mutability of things, even before the earth had dried on their grave mounds, good and bad would have been indistinguishable, beautiful and ugly would have perished forever. But if history officers are not lacking, if bamboo and silk survive, then though the man himself has perished, vanished into the void, his deeds are as if present, bright as the Milky Way. So scholars who come after can open the wrappers and boxes [which hold the books] and meet in spirit the men of antiquity, without leaving their own houses they can exhaust a thousand ages. When they see a worthy example they think of emulation, when they see an unworthy one, they examine themselves within—just as unruly sons were afraid when the Spring and Autumn Annals were completed, and the deeds of rebellious subjects were recorded when Nan-shih came. Such is the way in which deeds and words are recorded, such is the way in which they encourage good and reprove evil. From this we

---

[21] The 'white colt' appears in *Chuang-tsu* 22. See *Tz'u-hai*.
[22] For Shang Ch'en, later Mu Wang of Ch'u, see *Tso-chuan*, Duke Wen, 1st year, and *Shih-chi* 40.

see that the advantages of history are very great. For that which living men strive for marks out the vital path for the state. Can those who have the governance of states neglect it?[23]

With such high and solemn ends in view, questions of order and wording which may seem petty to us, naturally assumed great importance— though it must be confessed that Liu Chih-chi's criticisms of minor points sometimes seem merely captious. Yet Liu was a man with a real feeling for history and there is often a valid point behind an idea which seems perverse in its application.

On his suggestions for reforming the content and arrangement of the Standard Histories the most interesting concern the monographs (*chih*). Three of the traditional monographs could, he felt, either be eliminated altogether or drastically curtailed, namely those on astronomy, bibliography, and portents. He felt that it was all right to record the appearance of comets, eclipses, and similar extraordinary phenomena which occurred during a dynasty, but general astronomical matters were timeless and therefore unsuitable for inclusion in a historical work. Similarly it was proper to record the composition of notable works during a dynasty but it was otiose and violated the proper limits of a dynastic history to include a catalogue of all books, past and present, that existed. (We may be thankful that historians from Pan Ku onwards were not such purists.) It would be pleasant to be able to record that in criticizing the monographs on portents Liu Chih-chi rejected omens and portents altogether but this is not so. He accepted as a fact that there had been omens which had been proved by the event. His attitude was, however, comparatively rationalistic, for he objected to the elaborate 'five-elements' theories of the Han, the deliberate search for past omens after the event and the multiplication of records of supposedly good and bad signs that were often indulged in by official historians. Whenever possible he preferred to use human explanations for human events. Thus he blamed Ssu-ma Ch'ien for attributing the fall of Wei to the decree of Heaven that Ch'in should unite the empire: 'When one discusses the rise and fall of states one ought certainly to take human affairs as the essential; if one must bring fate into one's discourse then reason is outraged.'[24]

Also of great interest are Liu Chih-chi's suggestions for new monographs. He again mentions three, one on cities, one on clans, and one on exotic plants and animals presented as tribute. The first two subjects at least are matters of historical importance which could usefully have been dealt with in monographs in the dynastic histories. The third seems more trivial. Although later dynastic histories did not add them to the number of

[23] *Shih-t'ung t'ung-shih* 11.1a, b.
[24] *Shih-t'ung t'ung-shih* 16.9b. Cf. the historian's comment at the end of the 'Wei shih-chia' in the *Shih-chi*. (*Shiki kaishū kōshō* 44, p. 50.)

standard monographs, Liu Chih-chi's suggestions probably had some influence, as we shall see.

Another suggestion of Liu Chih-chi's was that instead of scattering decrees, memorials, and similar documents through the basic annals, monographs, and biographies, one should gather them together in a special section. The idea for this was based on the supposed old distinction between histories of words and histories of deeds and as such is perhaps rather pedantic. Nevertheless, it would certainly have been convenient for the reader to have been able to find such texts all in one place and properly classified rather than having to hunt for them. This idea was not adopted in later dynastic histories although the intention of such separate works as the *T'ang ta chao-ling chi* (Collected major decrees and ordinances of T'ang)[25] to some extent corresponded to it. Chang Hsüeh-ch'eng had a similar plan for writing local histories. He wished to divide them into three books, a gazetteer proper, a book called *Chang-ku* containing administrative matters, and a book called *Wen-hsüan* containing literary pieces.[26]

Throughout the *Shih-t'ung* there is an emphasis on the omission of what is not essential or is unworthy of being recorded and on concision of expression, which represents a very typical Chinese attitude to literary composition of every kind but which one feels was often of rather dubious value in its effects on historical writings. It may have made for *gravitas* and better literary style but one is likely nowadays to be more conscious of the concomitant obscurity or, at least, loss of vividness. Yet we usually find that Liu Chih-chi himself was really more concerned for the restriction of the record to what was of genuine historical interest than for ritual or stylistic proprieties for their own sake.

Thus he insisted that the documents to be recorded should be ones which had genuine information in them and he objected to the inclusion at length of high-flown but empty and hypocritical texts such as those connected with the supposed 'abdication' of the last emperor of a dynasty in favour of the first emperor of the next. In general he objected to the use of euphuistic fine writing in histories (though his own style is still very much in that tradition). He believed in concision and the elimination of literary flourishes but not in the changing of colloquial speech into more archaic literary language. He pours scorn on those historians who made barbarian rulers speak in high-flown phrases full of classical allusions and praises those who retained vulgar expressions at the expense of elegance. 'If things are all to be recorded without error the words must be close to the actual ones,

---

[25] The compiler of this work, Sung Min-ch'iu, was also responsible for the *Ch'ang-an chih* and a *Ho-nan chih*, works on the T'ang capitals. This suggests that he may have been influenced by Liu Chih-chi.

[26] *Wen-shih t'ung-i* 6, 'Fang-chih li san shu i'. On Chang Hsüeh-ch'ang, see the paper by P. Demiéville, below, pp. 167–85.

so that one may almost dwell with the men of the past. Why should one be content with their chaff and husks?'[27]

Liu's feeling for historical realities is also revealed in his attitude to the effects of geography on people. It was customary in putting a man's place of origin at the beginning of his biography to refer not to his actual birthplace but to the reputed place from which the family had originally come, perhaps several centuries before. But, protests Liu Chih-chi, 'people have no fixed substance, they change according to the locality'.[28] A southerner is still a southerner even if he is from illustrious northern stock. Moreover, claims to illustrious ancestors are often fraudulent. (We are reminded of Liu's debunking of the claim of the Han royal family, from which he himself was descended, to be descended from the Emperor Yao.)

He had a realistic appreciation of the fact that different conditions obtained in earlier ages. Thus whereas Sun Sheng[29] had alleged that the Tso Tradition ignored the outlying states of Wu and Yüeh because they were barbarian, Liu pointed out that in those days China had been divided into many separate states and communications were difficult so that information about remote areas like Wu and Yüeh would have been hard to obtain.[30] Similarly, it was not a matter of superiority (as some alleged) that records of high antiquity were much briefer than those of later times. There was a constant tendency for fuller records to be available for the recent past than for remote times.[31]

Liu Chih-chi's notoriety in China was traditionally due to his boldness in finding fault with previous historians, even with canonical works such as the Spring and Autumn Annals. To us his criticism, mostly confined as it is to *ad hoc* objections to particular, often very minor, details, may seem rather superficial. He is still far from any fundamental questioning of Confucian tradition. Yet, as with his Han dynasty predecessor Wang Ch'ung, whose example he cites, his willingness to question sacred texts and so reduce them to the level of ordinary books undoubtedly contributed to the sceptical stream in Chinese philosophical tradition and was not altogether lost. Liu Chih-chi comes before the great advances in textual criticism of Sung and Ch'ing times and naively accepts spurious texts which later scholars rejected, but his example must have helped to stimulate critical studies.

The reason for untruth in historical records on which Liu laid most stress was deliberate twisting or concealment (*ch'ü-pi*). Historians ought stubbornly to record the truth in spite of pressure from the powerful, but examples of such courageous conduct were rare and usually led to a bad end for the historian. On the other hand examples of deliberate suppression or

---

[27] *Shih-t'ung t'ung-shih* 6.4a.     [28] Ibid., 5.20a.
[29] The author of the *Wei Shih Ch'un-ch'iu* (on San-kuo Wei) and the *Chin yang-ch'iu*; biography in *Chin-shu* 82.     [30] *Shih-t'ung t'ung shih* 7.17b.     [31] Ibid., 9, Section 33.

distortion were legion. Some might be excusable on the grounds of filial piety. A son ought to speak only good of his father. Confucius had extended the same principle in concealing faults in his own state of Lu. Even if this were an excusable fault, the danger it held for the existence of a 'true record' ought to be recognized by those who came after. It was better to record the ill and good impartially. Far worse were the distortions introduced for corrupt reasons out of a desire to flatter one's superiors or to pay off scores. As an example of the subservience of historians to the powers that be, he points out that those who loyally resist at the end of a dynasty are commonly termed 'rebels' by the historians of the new regime. One could show examples of people being executed for recording the truth but never of people being punished for telling lies.[32]

Though Liu Chih-chi went farther than most, he was by no means the first to express generalized scepticism about records of the past. Even Mencius had said, 'It would be better to be without the Book of Documents than to give entire credit to it.'[33] More important is the attempt to use criteria to distinguish true from false. In general Liu's criteria for rejecting passages in texts can be classified under three headings: (1) internal inconsistency, (2) inconsistency with other, more reliable sources, (3) inherent impossibility. These are sound principles. If Liu's application of them often seems disproportionately trivial, it was no doubt because of the lack of systematic text-critical techniques and inadequate conceptions of what was inherently possible. Thus he rejected a story about a murder by means of poisoned wine on the grounds that the poison would have dissipated after six days![34] Liu's criticism also suffered from the almost universal failing of Chinese critical scholarship of concentrating on isolated points instead of seeing things as connected wholes. Nevertheless, he should be given full credit for his ruthless willingness to doubt accepted authorities and for his firm sense of reality.

Liu Chih-chi has been blamed as a historian for preferring histories limited to one dynasty on the model of the Former Han History (*Han shu*) to general histories that overstepped dynastic boundaries such as the Records of the Historian (*Shih-chi*). It is true that he insists on respect for the 'limits', chronological and otherwise, of any given work to a perverse degree. It is part of his general emphasis on order and decorum. Yet in his own work, which is as much a history of Chinese historiography as a theoretical manual, he has really written 'general history' (*t'ung shih*). It is interesting to note that he uses quite consistently periods which are not dynastic but cover larger units of time: 'high antiquity' (*shang-ku*) down to early Chou; 'antiquity' (*ku*) roughly the Spring-and-Autumn Warring States periods; 'middle antiquity' (*chung-ku*) Former and Later Han; and 'recent antiquity' (*chin-ku*) or 'recent age' (*chin-tai*) from the Three King-

[32] Ibid., 7, Sections 24 and 25.   [33] Mencius VII.2.iii (Legge).   [34] *Shih-t'ung t'ung-shih* 20.1a.

doms to his own day. In general he is at one with the prevailing Chinese tendency to see history as a decline from the pristine excellence of earlier times; in particular he regards the 'recent antiquity' as a period of decadence. There is, however, nothing doctrinaire in his attitude and just as he is ready to see flaws in antiquity, he is willing to recognize merit in the recent past. One of the historians for whom he has the highest praise is a 'modern', Wang Shao, the author of a now lost *Sui shu* (Sui History) in 80 *chüan*. Even his *bête noire* Wei Shou, the author of the Wei History (*Wei shu*), against whom he inveighs on every possible occasion, is allowed the merit of having placed his monographs *after* the biographies instead of between the basic annals and biographies as was normally done. As his modern biographer says, Liu Chih-chi's aim was to see impartially the flaws in what he admired and the good points in what he disliked.[35]

Liu Chih-chi was a man of independent ideas with a lifelong enthusiasm for historical studies and inspired by a rare historical insight, the most important of the three qualities which he regarded as essential for a historian, the others being 'talent' (*ts'ai*) and 'learning' (*hsüeh*).[36] It is a pity that the strong conservative tradition of Chinese official historiography which inhibited the free development of his own talents (as well, no doubt, as feeding and sustaining them) was so little influenced by his spirit. In spite of Hsüan-tsung's praise and the eulogies of his friend Hsü Chien, who said that every historian ought to have the *Shih-t'ung* constantly by his side,[37] the common run of scholars was scandalized by the freedom of criticism displayed in it.

In the ninth century Liu Ts'an wrote a work in ten *chüan* entitled the *Shih-t'ung hsi-wei* (Analysis of the Shih-t'ung), now no longer extant, to refute Liu Chih-chi's attacks on canonical works.[38] Sung Ch'i, one of the authors of the New T'ang History (*Hsin T'ang shu*), commented slightingly at the end of the chapter containing Liu Chih-chi's biography along with those of some of the historians of his circle, 'From Chih-chi onwards how clever they were at scoffing at the ancients but stupid in what they did themselves!'[39] Nevertheless, as the eighteenth-century scholar, Ch'ien Ta-hsin, showed, many of Liu Chih-chi's ideas had an influence on the composition of the New T'ang History. Thus, while there were no monographs on clans or exotic products, the Genealogical Tables of Chief Ministers fulfilled much the same object as the first and the inclusion in the Geographical Monograph of notes on tribute articles received from various localities was based on a similar idea to the second. The New T'ang

---

[35] Ibid., 4.16b. Cf. Fu Chen-lun, *Liu Chih-chi nien-p'u*, pp. 109–10.
[36] The occasion in 703 on which he spoke of this is recorded in *T'ang Hui-yao* 63 and also in his biographies. Cf. *Shih-t'ung t'ung-shih* 10, Section 35 'Pien-chih'.
[37] *Chiu T'ang-shu* 102.5b (po-na-pen).
[38] *Chun-chai tu-shu chih, hou-chih* 1.22a (Ssu-pu ts'ung-k'an).
[39] *Hsin T'ang-shu* 132 (end).

History, moreover, often suppressed references at the beginnings of bio-graphies to the places where a man's family claimed ultimately to come from, did not include decrees relating to fictitious 'abdications', omitted rhyming Criticisms after each chapter, and so on—all ideas suggested by the *Shih-t'ung*.[40] The elimination of balanced prose (*p'ien-li wen*) in the New T'ang History was perhaps due more to the *ku-wen* movement associ-ated with Han Yü than to Liu Chih-chi's strictures against excessive ornamentation—he would not have approved the way in which colloquial speech was improved into good literary style in the New T'ang History.

Other examples of the influence of the *Shih-t'ung* in the Sung dynasty could be found[41] but perhaps the most important one to mention is that of Cheng Ch'iao, the author of the *T'ung-chih* (General Treatise). Cheng Ch'iao's ideas on history as expressed in the General Preface to his major work, while influenced by Liu Chih-chi, also differ in certain points. Be-cause of Chang Hsüeh-ch'eng's praise of him Cheng Ch'iao has come to be looked upon as a historical thinker on a par with Liu Chih-chi and Chang Hsüeh-ch'eng themselves.[42] This, however, seems unjustified.[43] Cheng Ch'iao was really a bibliographer and encyclopaedist. The point that appealed to Chang Hsüeh-ch'eng was his advocacy of 'general history' (*t'ung-shih*), or history that was not limited to a single period, rather than the standard dynastic form of history. Cheng argues this point forcefully—to the point of condemning Pan Ku, the author of the first history restricted to a single dynasty, in most intemperate language. Yet his own *T'ung-chih* is a mere stringing together of basic annals and biographies from existing dynastic histories and has suffered almost the same neglect that befell the *T'ung-shih* (General History) in 620 *chüan* composed in the Liang Dynasty. As Liu Chih-chi remarked about the latter and similar books, scholars preferred to go to the smaller and more convenient original works.[44]

The portion of the work which Cheng Ch'iao valued most and the only portion which is now used is the 20 monographs (*lüeh*), several of which constitute innovations. Yet in general these monographs are encyclopaedic rather than historical in character. A monograph on clans is included but is merely a sort of etymological dictionary of surnames and does not give actual clan histories as suggested by Liu Chih-chi. Cheng Ch'iao also follows Liu Chih-chi in including monographs on cities (*Tu-i-lüeh*) and on insects and plants (*K'un-ch'un ts'ao-mu lüeh*) but the former is hardly more than a list and the latter is also purely encyclopaedic and not historical in character. In his Geographical Monograph Cheng Ch'iao's classification by

[40] Ch'ien Ta-hsin, *Shih-chia-chai yang-hsin lu* ch. 13, p. 303 (Basic Sinological Series).
[41] See note 25, above.                                                     [42] *Wen-shih t'ung-i* 5, 'Shen Cheng'.
[43] This is the opinion of Chin Yü-fu. See his *Chung-kuo shih-hsüeh shih*, pp. 252-3.
[44] *Shih-t'ung t'ung-shih* 1.13a, b.

means of natural features rather than political boundaries has been praised, but is it not really another illustration of the timeless, non-historical character of his thought? One is led to think that his emphasis on 'general history' came not so much from a sense of the continuity of change between successive dynasties as from looking on the world as fundamentally constant and changeless with only a surface flux. Without wishing to denigrate Cheng Ch'iao's immense achievements as a polymath and the down-to-earth realism of his scholarship, one hesitates to give him the title of historian—at least in the same breath as Liu Chih-chi and Chang Hsüeh-ch'eng.

Some eminent scholars evidently knew and valued the *Shih-t'ung* in the Sung dynasty and there is evidence that it was printed, but on the whole it was neglected. It circulated in manuscript until the beginning of the sixteenth century, and as a result considerable corruption crept into the text. With the renewed interest in historical scholarship in the Ch'ing dynasty the *Shih-t'ung* attracted the attention of several scholars and critical editions and commentaries were prepared. The standard edition is the *Shih-t'ung t'ung-shih* (Comprehensive commentary of the *Shih-t'ung*) of P'u Ch'i-lung (1752). It should be compared with the Ming edition reproduced with text-critical notes in the *Ssu-pu ts'ung-k'an*.[45]

## Ssu-ma Kuang and the Tzu-chih t'ung-chien

Although we owe a great debt to Chinese official historiography for the amplitude and continuity of the records it has preserved for us, we can see from Liu Chih-chi's bitter remarks that in its institutionalized form it tended towards a cramping and uniform mediocrity that was very frustrating for a man of any originality of mind. It is not surprising therefore that such men tended to express their individual views of history in works not in the pattern of the official dynastic histories and written outside the History Office. It often happened that the new forms thus created were then given official sanction and imitated or continued.

Thus Liu Chih-chi's son, Liu Chih, in the *Cheng-tien* (Governmental Institutes), and Tu Yu, who enlarged and completed this work to form his *T'ung-tien* (Comprehensive Statutes), both working privately, invented the form of encyclopaedic institutional history.[46] Tu Yu's prefaces to the

[45] On the transmission of the text, see Byongik Koh, op. cit., i, 21–28. I have not seen the *Shih-t'ung t'ung hsün-ku pu* of Huang Shu-lin, the other principal commentary current in the Ch'ing dynasty. Chi Yün made a popular abridged edition of P'u Ch'i-lung's text and commentary, known as the *Shih-t'ung hsiao-fan* (4 *chüan*). There have been several commentaries more recently. Of these I have seen that of Ts'ao Ch'ü-jen (1926), to which Ho Ping-sung contributed an essay. and the abridged text with commentary by Liu Hu-ju in the Hsüeh-sheng kuo-hsüeh ts'ung-shu, I have not seen the *Shih-t'ung p'ing* of Lü Ssu-mien. Among other writers on Liu Chih-chi should be noted Kanai Yukitada, *Tōdai no shigaku shisō* (1940).

[46] See the paper by E. Balazs, above, pp. 90–92.

various sections and some of his scattered comments show a mind actively trying to understand the processes of history, especially the mistakes which had led to the disaster of the An Lu-shan rebellion. The same is true of Su Mien's *Hui-yao* (Collection of Important Documents), later enlarged into the *T'ang Hui-yao*, though such of Su Mien's comments as are preserved do not show quite the same penetration as those of his more illustrious contemporary. Both these works provided models for later continuations under official auspices.

Undoubtedly the most ambitious and most productive of all such individual works was the *Tzu-chih t'ung-chien* (Comprehensive Mirror for Aid in Government) of Ssu-ma Kuang.[47] This great work in 294 *chüan*, covering in chronicle form the whole history of the period 403 B.C. to A.D. 959, must rank along with Ssu-ma Ch'ien's Records of the Historian as one of the highest achievements of traditional Chinese history writing. Ssu-ma Kuang, who lived during the eleventh century A.D., was one of the leading conservative statesmen of the Northern Sung dynasty, the foremost opponent of the reformer Wang An-shih. The annalistic (*pien-nien*) form which he adopted for his history was not new and might even be thought retrograde in comparison to the topical arrangement of the Standard Histories—basic annals, monographs, tables, biographies. In practice, however, the mechanical way in which material is split up into the various sections of the standard histories without cross references of any kind means that to get a complete picture even of a man's biography or of a topic treated in a monograph one must not only look at the immediately relevant chapter but also hunt laboriously through other parts as well. This is even more true if one is interested in seeing the course of events as a whole. By comparison it is easier to follow a sequence of events from day to day and year to year, even though it is often tedious to wade through irrelevant material at the same time. Moreover Ssu-ma Kuang does to a limited extent provide connecting links—though he was far from binding events together in a causal nexus and treating them as connected wholes, something never fully achieved by traditional Chinese historians.

I do not wish to deal here with all aspects of Ssu-ma Kuang as a historian but merely with his methods and critical standards, about which we happen to be particularly well informed. They mark a major advance in the history of Chinese historiography; and whereas in Liu Chih-chi we find reflections on history writing which are sometimes penetrating but which often suffer from being too much governed by theory divorced from practice, in Ssu-ma Kuang we find strict critical standards consciously applied in the construction of a 'possession for the ages'.

---

[47] Otto Franke made a study of Ssu-ma Kuang's work and Chu Hsi's abridgement of it in 'Das Tse Tschi T'ung Kien und das T'ung Kien Kang Mu', *Sitz. d. preuss. Ak. d. Wiss.: phil. hist. kl.* (1930), pp. 103–56.

Like Liu Chih-chi, Ssu-ma Kuang was inspired by an early acquaintance with the Tso Tradition to a lifelong passion for historical studies.[48] More-over, his austere, realistic nature which expressed itself in politics by a staunch and unbending conservatism, expressed itself in scholarship by emphasis on actuality and practicality. He was not concerned merely to acquire a vast erudition, he wished to organize knowledge into convenient and manageable form. He thought that the chronicle form was better suited to his purpose than the annals-biography form, so he conceived the idea of writing a continuation of the Tso Tradition down to the beginning of the Sung dynasty in which the diverse and scattered records found in other works would be combined into a single chronicle.

His first step was to set out in the form of a chronological table the main events from the Warring States to the end of the Five Dynasties, the same period later covered by his main work. This he presented to the throne in 1064 as the *Li-nien t'u* (Chart [or Table] of Successive Years) in 5 *chüan*.[49] Two years later in 1066 he presented to the throne under the title *T'ung-chih* (Comprehensive Record) a chronicle of the history of the Warring States period in 8 *chüan* which were ultimately revised to form the first eight chapters of the Comprehensive Mirror. As a result of this he received the mandate of the Emperor Yang-tsung to 'compile the records of events of rulers and ministers in successive ages'.[50] In reply Ssu-ma Kuang memorialized the throne:

Since I was a child I have ranged through all the histories. It has appeared to me that in the annal-biography form the words are diffuse and numerous so that even an erudite specialist who reads them again and again cannot comprehend and sort them out; how much the more, though a prince amid his ten thousand daily concerns must wish to know comprehensively the merits and demerits of former ages, will it be difficult for him to accomplish his desire. Disregarding my inade-quacy I have constantly wished to write a chronological history roughly in accordance with the form of the Tso Tradition, starting with the Warring States and going down to the Five Dynasties, drawing on other books besides the Official Histories and taking in all that a prince ought

[48] *Sung-shih* 336. Another historical work which Ssu-ma Kuang read as a child and which helped to stimulate his interest both in historical studies as such and in providing helps to readers was the *Hsiao shih*, 'Small history', of the T'ang dynasty writer Kao Chün. It was a series of excerpts from Standard Histories from the *Shih chi* down to the Veritable Records of the T'ang dynasty, presumably made for the use of students. It was no doubt of only minor value as a work of history and has long since perished. Arnold Toynbee gives similar examples in volume x of his *Study of History* of future historians being stimulated by minor, as well as major, historical works. Cf. *Chih-chai shu-lu chieh-t'i* 4, p. 103 (Basic Sinological Series); *Wen-kuo Wen-cheng Ssu-ma Kung chi* 62, 'Yü Liu Tao-yüan shu' (Ssu-pu ts'ung-k'an).

[49] This was later incorporated into the *Ch'i-ku lu* of Ssu-ma Kuang, of which it forms ch. 11–15. See *Ch'i-ku lu* 16, 'Li-nien t'u hsü', and 'Chin Li-nien t'u piao' prefaced to the *Ch'i-ku lu*.

[50] *Hsü tzu-chih t'ung-chien ch'ang-pien* 208.2b.

to know—everything pertaining to the rise and fall of dynasties and the good and ill fortune of the common people, all good and bad examples that can furnish models and warnings.[51]

He asked that he should be allowed to continue the work under the same title, *T'ung-chih*, and requested that two scholars Liu Shu and Chao Chün-hsi, who had specialized in history, should be appointed to assist him. This request was granted. Chao Chün-hsi had to retire into mourning because of his father's death and his place was taken by Liu Pin.

The following year (1067) Ssu-ma Kuang was commanded to read his *T'ung-chih* in the emperor's presence. In recognition of the work the Emperor Shen-tsung bestowed on it the name *Tzu-chih t'ung-chien* (Comprehensive Mirror for Aid in Government), wrote for it an imperial preface and gave Ssu-ma Kuang 2402 *chüan* of old books from the library of his former residence as Prince Ying.[52] With this official support the work continued, but it was not of course official history in the sense of history written in the History Office. Ssu-ma Kuang had his own office for the purpose of compiling it, over which he had sole control.

Not long after the work started Wang An-shih came to power and began introducing his reform measures. Ssu-ma Kuang was the leader of the opposition and the differences between the two became increasingly pronounced. In 1070 Ssu-ma Kuang was sent away from the capital to the region of Ch'ang-an and in the following year he asked to retire with a sinecure to Lo-yang. He was allowed to take his library and the office for writing the *T'ung-chien* with him and it was no doubt this period of enforced political inactivity that enabled him to bring his grand scheme to such a successful conclusion. Liu Shu had retired to look after his aged parents in Nan-k'ang (Kiangsi) already in 1070.[53] Liu Pin remained at K'ai-feng but soon fell foul of Wang An-shih and was sent to a provincial post. Although they continued to work on the project by correspondence the effectiveness of their collaboration must have been greatly hampered.[54]

---

[51] Ibid.　　　[52] *Sung-shih* 336 and *Hsü tzu-chih t'ung-chien* 64, Chih-p'ing 4/10/*chia-yin*.

[53] See 'Liu Tao-yüan Shih-kuo chi-nien hsü' in *Wen-kuo Wen-cheng Ssu-ma Kung chi* 65, Ssu-ma Kuang's preface to a work on the Five Dynasties period by Liu Shu. Liu Shu remained at his home in Nan-k'ang for several years before obtaining permission to make the long journey to Loyang to visit Ssu-ma Kuang. He remained there several months. On his return journey he learned of his mother's death, his already weak health gave way and he suffered a stroke. He died at the age of forty-seven (Chinese style) in 1078. Ssu-ma Kuang seems to have had a very special regard and affection for him. See also 'Ch'i kuan Liu Shu i tzu cha-tzu', op. cit., 53.

[54] The letter to Fan Tsu-yü translated in Appendix I makes it clear that at that time (1070) Liu Pin was working on the Liu-ch'ao period and Liu Shu on the Five Dynasties. According to Ssu-ma K'ang, Ssu-ma Kuang's son, as quoted in *Wen-hsien t'ung k'ao* 193, however, Liu Pin's portion of the work was confined to the Former and Later Han (completed before Ssu-ma went to Loyang), Liu Shu was responsible for the San-kuo and Liu-ch'ao periods and Fan Tsu-yü did the Five Dynasties as well as T'ang. (This information is also given, without indication of the source, in Hu San-hsing's preface to his commentary to the *Tzu-chih t'ung-chien*. According to the

Another collaborator, Fan Tsu-yü, had now been added to the group, however, and he soon joined Ssu-ma Kuang in Loyang. It would seem that he had begun work in 1070 at K'ai-feng while Ssu-ma Kuang was at Ch'ang-an and Ssu-ma Kuang wrote him a letter (see Appendix, below, pp. 160–4) giving detailed instructions on how to proceed. From this we learn exactly how the work was organized and what rules were laid down by Ssu-ma Kuang for his assistants.[55]

The first step was to compile a skeleton General Outline (*ts'ung-mu*) in chronological order. In the case of the T'ang period, which was assigned to Fan Tsu-yü, the basis of this was the successive Veritable Records. Then all sorts of additional works—Standard Histories, miscellaneous histories, collections of anecdotes, collected literary works, etc.—were combed for relevant matter and references to book and chapter were entered in the skeleton in the appropriate places, new heading being added if necessary. After this task had been accomplished, work began on making the Long Draft (*ch'ang-pien*). The outline was gone through heading by heading. Under each all the references noted were looked up. If the various accounts agreed, the fullest was to be copied into the draft. If no one account contained all the information provided by the various sources, they were to be conflated with connections provided by the compiler. If the sources disagreed, the most probably correct account was to be chosen on the basis of the evidence, or, if that failed, on rational considerations. In such cases a note was to be inserted in the draft setting out the differing accounts and giving the grounds for accepting the one selected. Various principles were laid down as to what should or should not be included but in general it was better that the Draft should contain too much rather than too little. (It may be of interest to note that Ssu-ma Kuang actually uses the expression 'scissors-and-paste' in describing the way in which the Long Draft was to be compiled. When it was necessary to insert material in the Draft, the long manuscript roll was cut with scissors and the inserted portion was pasted in.) It is said that the Long Draft when completed occupied two

*Ssu-k'u t'i-yao* 88, under *T'ung-chien wen-i*, it appeared in Shao Po-wen's *Wen-chien lu* but I have not been able to find it there.) Presumably Liu Pin's political involvements at the capital and subsequent provincial exile prevented him from carrying on and the uncompleted portion of the Liu-ch'ao period was taken over by Liu Shu in retirement. Liu Shu died in 1078, six years before the completion of the work. From a letter which Ssu-ma Kuan wrote to Sung Min'ch'iu just about this time we know that the work was then only down as far as the middle of T'ang, which must have left the completion of the Five Dynasties period to Fan Tsu-yü. (The letter to Sung Min-ch'iu is not in Ssu-ma Kuang's collected works but is quoted by Kao Ssu-sun in *Wei-lüeh* 12.10b (Shou-shan ko ts'ung-shu); cf. also *Wen-hsien t'ung-k'ao* 193.) That Liu Shu was concerned with the Nan-pei ch'ao is confirmed by the *T'ung-chien wen-i* which records discussions between him and Ssu-ma Kuang on points of Liu-ch'ao history. That he also worked on the Five Dynasties is shown by his authorship of the *Shih-kuo chi-nien* (see previous note). See Chang Hsü, *T'ung-chien hsüeh* (1945), pp. 40–42.

[55] The stages in the work are also briefly described in the letter from Ssu-ma Kuang to Sung Min-ch'iu cited in the preceding note.

rooms in Ssu-ma Kuang's house in Loyang.[56] The part belonging to the T'ang dynasty contained some 600 *chüan*.[57]

When the Long Draft had been completed by his assistants Ssu-ma Kuang's own part began. He worked through the Long Draft, abridging the text and selecting the most essential points to be included. In this way he reduced the length to the present size of 294 *chüan*. The 600 *chüan* belonging to T'ang were reduced to 80. Although this was the only part of the work exclusively done by Ssu-ma Kuang himself, it seems clear from the way in which he laid down exact instructions for the preparatory stages that he exercised a close supervision the whole time.

The work was completed in stages and each part was presented to the throne as it became ready.[58] Before Ssu-ma Kuang went to Lo-yang it had been completed down to the end of the period of the Three Kingdoms. The work on the later portions, especially T'ang and the Five Dynasties for which there were a large number of sources, took up the most time. The whole was completed and presented to the throne in 1084.

Along with the *Tzu-chih t'ung-chien* itself in 294 *chüan* Ssu-ma Kuang presented to the throne an Outline (*mu-lu*) in 30 *chüan*, no doubt based on the original General Outline, and an Examination of Differences (*K'ao-i*) also in 30 *chüan*, consisting of notes on divergencies between the sources for various passages in the *T'ung-chien*. It must have been based on the notes prepared for the Long Draft by Fan Tsu-yü and the other collaborators. Its publication along with the Comprehensive Mirror was an innovation of the greatest significance. Ssu-ma Kuang was not content merely to choose among his sources according to his subjective judgement (or to allow his assistants to do so) and then to publish his narrative in oracular fashion. He wished to have the choices made on explicit objective grounds and then to expose them to public judgement. It says much for the diffusion of learning and general high level of scholarship in the Northern Sung, the age of the first use of printing for secular purposes, but it says even more for his own scientific attitude.

According to Kao Ssu-sun, writing in the twelfth century, 322 works were used as source material for the *Tzu-chih t'ung-chien*.[59] It is not clear where he got this figure. In another work he gives the titles of 228 of them.[60]

---

[56] See the quotation from Li Tao's collected works (now lost) contained in *Wen-hsien t'ung-k'ao* 193 under 'Tzu-chih t'ung-chien'. Li Tao reported that his father had said that a certain Chang Hsin-sou, whom I have not been able to identify further, had told him that the drafts for the *Tzu-chih t'ung-chien* filled two rooms in the house in Loyang. The poet Huang T'ing-chien had also examined the draft and had been amazed to find it all written so carefully. In the Yüan dynasty a single sheet of what must have been the General Outline, for the year Yung-ch'ang 1 (322) was preserved in the library of a Mr. Hsü of Yü-yao and comments were written on it by Liu Kuan and Huang Chin (*Liu Tai-chih wen-chi* 18.18b, and *Huang Hsüeh-shih wen-chi* 21.9a, both Ssu-pu ts'ung-k'an).   [57] See Li Tao's preface to the *Hsü tzu-chih t'ung-chien ch'ang pien.*
[58] *Sung-ch'ao shih-shih* 3, pp. 40–41 (Basic Sinological Series).   [59] *Wei-lüeh*, loc. cit.
[60] *Shih-lüeh* 4.11b ff. (Ku-i ts'ung-shu).

Chang Hsü has more recently searched through the *K'ao-i* (Examination of Differences) and listed 301 titles, classified under a number of headings, of works that are mentioned there.[61] This list is, however, not complete even for the *K'ao-i* and there were undoubtedly other works besides which were used but which do not happen to be mentioned in the *K'ao-i*.[62] The exact number is of no importance but it is interesting to note the great variety of the works consulted—official histories, Veritable Records, chronicles, miscellaneous histories of various kinds, private biographies, geographical works, collected literary works, inscriptions, poems, anecdotes, etc.

Ssu-ma Kuang believed in casting his net widely but not in accepting indiscriminately anything he happened to find in it. In his letter to Fan Tsu-yü he said, 'Veritable Records and Official Histories are not necessarily always to be relied upon and anecdotes are not necessarily without foundation. Make your choice by your own scrutiny.' So, whereas the editors of the New T'ang History are rightly criticized for including many stories of doubtful authenticity for the sake of embellishing their text, Ssu-ma Kuang's work, which used an even wider variety of sources, escapes this censure.

In his instructions to Fan Tsu-yü Ssu-ma Kuang said, 'If the accounts contain discrepancies as to dating or statements about the facts then I request you to choose one version for which the evidence is clear or which in the nature of the case seems to be closest to the truth.' Thus we see that he had two main criteria for distinguishing false from true, (*a*) positive evidence—chiefly in the form of contradictions with known facts such as the calendar, and (*b*) inherent probability. If we compare this with actual examples in the *K'ao-i* we find that there has indeed been meticulous care in examining the sources for discrepancies, especially in the matter of dating but also in other particulars. Apart from this we find judgements based on what is considered inherently unlikely. Stories are rejected because they are contrary to a man's character or probable motivation, because they are considered to be the slanders of his enemies or the inflated praises of his friends or kinsmen, or simply because they are regarded as frivolous anecdotes. There is of course a large element of the subjective in this but it is an element which is inevitably present in the judgements of historians, for which they must depend on their general knowledge of men and affairs. The scientific historian tries to reduce the field of such subjective judgement by rigorous techniques of textual analysis and the confrontation of each question with all available evidence, but he can never entirely get rid of it. On this basis Ssu-ma Kuang was

---

[61] *T'ung-chien hsüeh*, pp. 45 ff. See also Ts'ui Wan-ch'iu, *T'ung-chien yen-chiu* (1934), pp. 38–62.

[62] For example the *Kao Li-shih wai-chuan* (Unofficial Biography of Kao Li-shih) was certainly used but is not mentioned in the *K'ao-i*.

certainly a scientific historian, since he first tried to establish the truth on objective grounds. The most impressive thing, of course, is that he insisted on reasons being explicitly given.

From our modern point of view one of the most serious limitations of Ssu-ma Kuang's method—an often-mentioned limitation of almost all traditional Chinese historians—was the restriction of attention to one isolated event at a time, with a certain amount of backward and forward glancing, generalizing about a man's character, etc., but without the attempt to see each event interwoven into a complex mesh of inter-relationships with other events. What resulted from the enormous labours of Ssu-ma Kuang and his team was a superb chronicle, but still a chronicle and not a history in our modern sense.

Another serious limitation from the technical standpoint was the failure to study sources as such. This was not an absolute failure—one does find remarks here and there in the *K'ao-i* about the bearing of the facts about the authorship of a text on its reliability either as a whole or as applied to a particular case. Still, in general, texts were treated as ultimate data and no attempt was made to analyse further their origins or interrelationships. Text B, partially based on text A, was treated as if it were independent and worthy of equal consideration. This again was not a limitation peculiar to Ssu-ma Kuang alone but common to most Chinese scholarship —though advances were made in the seventeenth and eighteenth centuries.

At any rate, a better understanding of Ssu-ma Kuang's methods should dispel certain myths such as the idea that it was impossible to exercise sophisticated historical criticism within the framework of scissors-and-paste compilation or that Chinese historians had no conception of probability but only of certainty.

After Ssu-ma Kuang there were many continuations and imitations of the Comprehensive Mirror which frequently copied the practice of including a *K'ao-i*. The practice remained, however, almost entirely confined to this genre and in general historians went on compiling their texts without any consciousness of a need to quote or discuss their evidence.

An important offshoot of the Comprehensive Mirror was the *Tzu-chih t'ung-chien pen-mo* (Narratives from Beginning to End from the Comprehensive Mirror for Aid in Government) of Yüan Shu. As the name indicates the aim of the work was to set forth 'the beginnings and endings of events recorded in the *Tzu-chih t'ung-chien*' (together with what came in between). Yüan Shu felt the difficulty alluded to above of wading through irrelevant material while trying to follow a given sequence of events in the chronicle so he hit on the simple plan of extracting all the material relevant to such major sequences of events and putting it together under one heading. His work deals with 239 topics in this way. The text itself consists merely of unaltered extracts from the *Tzu-chih t'ung-chien* and there is no effort beyond this to work over the material and treat each sequence of events as a whole. Nevertheless, it was a step towards getting away from the restriction to isolated particulars. Later works of this category, like their prototype, were mainly limited to the rearrangement of material from a previous work but the *Ming-shih chi-shih pen-mo* (Narratives from beginning to end from Ming history) was written before the *Ming-shih* itself.[63]

*Later developments*

In the main the story of advances in historical criticism after Ssu-ma Kuang is concerned with commentaries on existing histories rather than with works of synthesis. As such it is bound up with the history of scholarship in general, especially the study of the classics, and also with philosophy. I should be exceedingly rash to attempt to give an outline of this development stretching over seven or eight centuries, but in order to round out my story I shall mention the names of one or two leading figures.

After achieving a very considerable development in Sung times culminating in the work of such scholars as Wang Ying-lin (1223–96) and Hu San-hsing (1230–87), 'investigation of evidence' (*k'ao-cheng*) studies suffered a decline in the Ming dynasty, owing, it is generally held, to the dominance of neo-Confucian philosophy, whether of the school of Chu Hsi (1130–1200) or of Wang Yang-ming (1472–1529), with its emphasis on 'general meaning' (*ta-i*). A revival began in the seventeenth century with the school of Han learning tracing its origins to Ku Yen-wu (1613–82). From then on through the eighteenth century and into the nineteenth critical studies of the classics flourished and the same influence was felt in the field of history. Ku Yen-wu himself made important contributions to historical studies as well as to other branches of learning.

The best-known names in the field of history are those of Wang Mingsheng (1722–98), Ch'ien Ta-hsin (1728–1804), and Chao I (1727–1814). The first two were mainly concerned with *k'ao-cheng* studies in the narrow sense. Thus they examine individual passages in the histories and correct or supplement them with additional material.

Chao I, though more restricted in his scholarship, is perhaps the most interesting of the three because of the advance he shows towards overcoming those traditional limitations of Chinese historiography mentioned above in connection with Ssu-ma Kuang. The circumstances of his life gave him comparatively few opportunities for studying rare and out-of-the-way sources. Making a virtue of necessity he emphasized the importance of the official histories as opposed to all the variety of subsidiary material drawn on by the *k'ao-cheng* scholars. He read and re-read the Standard

[63] For an account of all the works of this class, see Chin Yü-fu, *Chung-kuo shih-hsüeh shih* pp. 196–201.

Histories but instead of drawing on vast erudition to comment on minute points of detail he noted down general remarks about the various books or the events they described that struck him as of interest. He discussed the way in which the various dynastic histories had been compiled and from what sources, and he compared those works which covered the same period. He wrote on such topics as the use of eunuchs as provincial officials in Northern Wei, the great clans in the southern dynasties, the way in which the Empress Wu listened to criticism, the shift of the seat of the capital from the north-west in Han and T'ang to the north-east in Ming and Ch'ing. Some of his points are mere curiosities but in many cases he has hit on problems which are of real interest to modern historians and his work can certainly be read with profit by them.

Of the Ch'ing dynasty scholars who turned their attention to historiographical problems the greatest of all was, however, Chang Hsüeh-ch'eng. He is the subject of a separate paper by Professor Demiéville.[64]

*Appendix*

Letter from Ssu-ma Kuang to Fan Tsu-yü giving instructions on preparing the Long Draft for the T'ang period.

When I previously sent a confidential memorial I thought that those giving instructions in the palace changed their office after two years. I did not know that under the new regulations they must wait five years. Will this mean a delay? I am fearful and ashamed.

The General Outline (*ts'ung-mu*) that you have been making up to now has consisted in taking out and tabulating the items in the Veritable Records. Those items in the Veritable Records that have to be moved forward or back, you will already have noted underneath the items they belong to.

For instance in the Veritable Records under the 23rd year of Chenkuan Li Ching died. Under this heading Ching's biography appears for the first time. The affair of his fettering himself and reporting rebellion should be noted under the first year of I-ning of Sui (617) at the time when the Duke of T'ang was taking up arms. The defeat of Hsiao Hsien should be noted in the fourth year of Wu-te (621) when Hsien was destroyed. The beheading of Fu Kung-shih should be noted in the 7th year (624) at the time of the pacification of Chiang-nan. The capture of Hsieh-li should be noted in the 4th year of Chen-kuan (630) at the time of the defeat of the Turks. The rest should be treated similarly.

How can one proceed forthwith to make the Long Draft while (items from) the Old T'ang History and the rest have not yet been noted in?

[64] See below, pp. 167–85.

I request that you take all items from the basic annals, monographs, and biographies of the New and Old T'ang Histories and the comprehensive chronicles, and also items having a bearing on historical events from supplementary records, family biographies, records, anecdotes—including also the collected literary works of the various writers—and according to date note the section or chapter from which they come underneath the items (in the Outline) to which they belong. Those items that do not appear in the Veritable Records should also be added under year, month and day. If there is no indication of day, append the item to the month and say, 'This month'. If there is no indication of month, append the item to the year and say, 'This year'. If there is no indication of the year append it to the beginning or the end of the affair (to which it belongs) . . . [Here a number of examples are given from the *Tso-chuan*. E.G.P.]

. . . If there are items which cannot be attached in this way, then you should estimate the approximate date and attach it under a certain year.

Such things as Tzu-han's declining of the jade in the *Tso-chuan* cannot be given a certain date. If for instance in the case of Chief Ministers there are examples of loyalty and probity or of viciousness and corruption which have no place to which they can be attached then put them under the date when they were appointed as ministers; in the case of officials, under the time when they came to office. This rule will not apply if it is appropriate to attach the item under the time when they were dismissed or died.

Even if an item only slightly impinges on the affair [to which it is attached] there will be no harm in noting too much.

For instance, in the case of all the biographies which have one or two sentences touching on the taking up of arms by the Duke of T'ang, you should just note the names underneath the item in the Outline. Even if at times there are no additional details that can be drawn upon, the reference can be used to check points where there is disagreement or to prove dates.

When I saw Tao-yüan [i.e. Liu Shu] he said, 'Even this amounts to over 1000 *chüan* [to be gone through]. If one read one or two *chüan* per day it would require two or three years' labour.'

After you have finished adding all these notes in this way I request that you compile a Long Draft starting with the Taking up of Arms (617) and going down to the abdication of Ai-ti (907). As for items that you find in the books you read from now on which refer to matters before the Taking up of Arms and after the Abdication, I request that you have the scribes copy them out separately on rough paper, leaving a line or more of empty space between each item (to allow for cutting with scissors and pasting) and give the ones that relate to Sui and before to Kung-fu [Liu Pin] and the ones that relate to Liang and after to Tao-yüan [Liu Shu] so that they can each enter them into the Long Draft.

When compiling the Long Draft I request that on the basis of the references under each heading of the General Outline to the basic annals, monographs and biographies of the Old and New T'ang Histories, the miscellaneous histories, anecdotes, literary works, etc., you look up and extract [the passages] and examine them together. When among the various accounts the same matter is recorded in different words, I request that you choose one account which is clear and detailed and record it. If one version is at the same time both fuller and less detailed in various respects than another, then I request that you select something from both and combine and fit the parts together, using your own words to compose a proper account according to the style of narration used in the *Tso-chuan*. This should all be written in large characters.

If the accounts contain discrepancies as to dating or facts, then I request that you choose one version for which the evidence is clear or which in the nature of the case seems to be closest to the truth and write it into the main text. The result should be placed below in a note and in addition you should set forth there the reasons for accepting one version and rejecting the others.

> First note the rejected versions thus, 'Such and such a book says . . . such and such a book says . . .' Comment, 'Such and such a book has such and such evidence', or if there is no such evidence, then reason it according to the circumstances of the case . . . [Then say] 'Now we follow such and such a book as established.' If there is no means of deciding between true and false, then say, 'Now we retain both versions.' Veritable Records and Official Histories are not necessarily always to be relied upon, miscellaneous histories and anecdotes are not necessarily without foundation. Make your choice by your own scrutiny.

In the matter of the year-periods adopt the later. For instance in the first year of Wu-te (618), from the first day of the first month refer to it as the first year of Wu-te of T'ang Kao-tsu and do not refer to the second year of I-ning of Sui. After the first day of the first month of Hsien-t'ien of Hsüan-tsung (712) do not refer to the third year of Ching-yün. After the first day of the first of K'ai-p'ing of Liang (907) do not refer to the fourth year of T'ien-yu of T'ang.

I request that such *fu* (prose poems) and the like as are merely literary pieces, such decrees as do no more than make appointments, such strange and uncanny happenings as are no more than an occasion for wonder and gossip, such humorous stories as do no more than raise a laugh should all be excluded. This should not prevent you from recording such poems and *fu* as express satire:

> For example, in the time of Chung-tsung, the words of (Li Ching-po's) 'Returning Waves' poem, 'I fear that the clamour is indecorous'; and in the time of Su-tsung Li Pi's 'Praise of the Melon of the Yellow Dais';

decrees which admonish or persuade:

> For example the decree of Te-tsung at Feng-t'ien taking blame on himself, the decree persuading the three warlords of Ho-pei when Li Te-yü was attacking Tse Chou and Lu Chou. You should also retain decrees proclaiming matters of major political importance to the four quarters of the empire or those which promote officials because of merit or degrade them because of crimes. Even if the words used are untrue it is important to know what was the pretended merit or false accusation at the time. If the verbiage is excessive it is permissible to extract what is essential;

strange and uncanny happenings which give warnings:

> All national disasters recorded in basic annals should be retained, but it is not necessary to do so in the case of matters in the relevant monograph which are forcibly made to fit events of the time. Prophecies such as Li Chun's rumour about the Wu family which gave rise to slaughter and rebellion should be retained. Ones which wantonly try to show coincidences such as the idea that a 'tree' entering a 'peck measure' would make the surname Chu need not be recorded. Cases of physiognomizing where it is said, 'This [man] should be avoided by men', 'This (man) should be joined by other men'; cases of auspicious objects where the ruler is fond of such things and flatterers have made them fraudulently, or where there have really been credible examples—these should be retained. The rest need not be. If uncanny occurrences give warnings such as the spirit writing on Wu San-ssu's door, or if as a result of them something is started, as when Yang Shen-ch'in's tomb shed blood, they should be retained. The rest need not be;

humorous stories which are edifying:

> For example, when Huang Fan-cho said that his own son was the most pitiable, or when Shih Yeh-chu said that all the ministers were of inauspicious physiognomy—these should be retained. The rest need not be.

Please retain all these. In general the Long Draft should err on the side of including too much rather than too little. A thousand myriad earnest prayers!

I now send you two rolls of the Extended Copy (*kuang-pen*) prepared by Tao-yüan [Liu Shu],

> This is what is extracted from the Long Draft. I have already returned the Long Draft to Tao-yüan.

because I think you might like to see a sample. I very much wish that I could see you and that we could discuss everything together fully but there is no means of arranging it. I eagerly thirst for it. You will have already copied out the eight *chüan* of the Chronicle of the Chin dynasty which I previously sent for you to make a fair copy. Please hand over the original to my son K'ang to bring back. Even if you have not finished please hand it over, for on the post road to the Nan-k'ang Army this summer three *chüan* were lost. If I again lose these, then there will be no copy left. After the fair copy has been made, send it right back. There is no objection to sending the Chronicle of Wei that you recently requested. I am now having Li Yung-ho bring it to you. If there are any alterations tell the Commander to write it out separately and change it into square characters.

My eyes are hurting as I write this letter beneath the lamp. Pardon its lack of care.

Kuang

[P.S.] Whenever a man first appears in the Long Draft, you should note underneath, 'A man of such and such a place', or if his father or grandfather have already appeared above, then make a note, 'Son of so and so' or 'Grandson of so and so'. I now also send one *ts'e* of the Long Draft made by Kung-fu [Liu Pin]. I think you might like to see a sample. Please keep it as well as the two *chüan* of Tao-yüan's Extended Copy. There will be no need to return them afterwards.

*Commentary*

This letter was known and used by eighteenth-century scholars but has since largely dropped out of sight. The only modern scholar who seems to have looked at it at all is Katō Shigeshi who alludes to it briefly in his introduction to his translation of the *Tzu-chih t'ung-chien* in the *Zoku koku-yaku kambun taisei*. It did not appear in the first Sung edition of Ssu-ma Kuang's works in 80 *chüan* (preface by Liu Ch'iao dated 1132), but it was included in *chüan* 63 of the second, enlarged edition of the works, known as the *Ssu-ma T'ai-shih Wen-kuo Wen-cheng kung ch'uan-chia-chi* (or more briefly as *Ch'uan-chia-chi*) also in 80 *chüan*, prepared, it would seem, by Ssu-ma Kuang's descendants in the second half of the twelfth century. There is a modern reprint of this edition in the *Wan-yu wen-k'u*.

The letter was also appended to a work known as the *T'ung-chien ch'ien-li* compiled by Ssu-ma Kuang's great-grandnephew Chi who gathered together a number of notes found among Ssu-ma Kuang's papers concerned with the rules to be followed in writing history, divided them up under thirty-six headings, made four illustrative tables and appended two letters to Fan Tau-yü and eleven to Liu Shu. Chi's postface is dated 1166. The work is no longer extant in its original form. An abridged version with eleven headings instead of thirty-six and no tables, and omitting the letters to Liu Shu was placed at the beginning of Ch'en Jen-hsi's Ming edition of the *Tzu-chih t'ung-chien*. Ch'en also changed the name to *T'ung-chien shih-li*. This text included the above letter to Fan Tsu-yü in a slightly abbreviated form, without the beginning and ending but with the postscript as if it were a separate document. This *T'ung-chien shih-li* was copied into the *Ssu-k'u ch'üan-shu* and is also reprinted by Hu Yüan-ch'ang in the *Chiao-k'an Tzu-chih t'ung-chien ch'üan-shu* with a postface dated 1869. It is also an uncommon work and I have only been able to see it through the kindness of Professor Hiraoka of the Jimbun Kagaku Kenkyusho in Kyoto who supplied me with a microfilm by airmail. A complete text of the *Ch'ien-li* proper, with all thirty-six headings but without the tables or appended letters, existed in the collection of Chang Chin-wu at the beginning of the nineteenth century (see the postface of Hu Yüan-ch'ang and *Ai-jih ching-lu ts'ang-shu chih*, 9.2.b ff.)

The *Shih-li* itself deals mainly with questions of nomenclature and terminology and is only of minor interest. The letters of Liu Shu were omitted in the abridged version, perhaps as the *Ssu-k'u t'i-yao* suggests, because of the existence of the *T'ung-chien wen-i* compiled by Liu Shu's son, which may have duplicated the material. According to Hu San-hsing, who discussed the work in the preface to the *T'ung-chien shih-wen pien-wu* (and expressed doubts about the genuineness of the material in the work itself, though not about the letters) the *Ch'ien-li* originally contained two letters to Fan Tsu-yü. The editors of the *Ssu-k'u t'i-yao* say that two letters were contained in the abridged *Shih-li* but they may have supposed that the postscript to the first was the second letter. That there was once a second letter which is contained neither in the *Ch'uan-chia chi* nor the abridged text of the *Shih-li* is indicated by an allusion by Li Tao in a passage quoted in *Wen-hsien t'ung-k'ao* 193. Hu San-hsing also states that Ssu-ma Chi got the two letters to Fan Tsu-yü from the School at San-Chü (Chü Hsien in Chekiang).

I first came across this letter in Ku Tung-kao's *Ssu-ma Wen Kung nien-p'u* (preface dated 1733) 5.35.a (Chiu-shu chai ts'ung-shu). It is here evidently copied from the abridged text of the *Shih-li* omitting the postscript. An excerpt from the letter was quoted by Ch'üan Tsu-wang in 'T'ung-chien fen-hsiu chu-tzo k'ao', *Chi-ch'i t'ingchi*, *wai-p'ien* 40.20.a

## 10. CHANG HSÜEH-CH'ENG AND HIS HISTORIOGRAPHY

P. DEMIÉVILLE

*Professor of Chinese Language and Literature, Collège de France*

During the Ch'ing period (1644–1911) Chinese culture reached one of its apogees; in many ways, even in philosophy, the era of Ch'ien-lung (1736–96) may be said to hold its own with our Siècle des Lumières. In the field of historiography, this period is characterized mainly by the trend towards erudition, philology, and textual criticism which prevailed, especially under Ch'ien-lung, in the studies concerning the Confucian Canon and its exegesis.[1] In the early years of the dynasty the forerunners of the reaction against Neo-Confucian scholasticism, Ku Yen-wu (1613–82) and Huang Tsung-hsi (1610–95), were both interested in history. A large part of Ku Yen-wu's Notes on Daily Learning (*Jih-chih lu*), a repository of wide and varied scholarship, deal with historical matters, including historiographical theory, and he was an active promoter of such auxiliary sciences of history as historical geography, historical linguistics, epigraphy, and archaeology. Huang Tsung-hsi initiated the history of philosophical schools with his Studies of Ming Confucian Scholars (*Ming-ju hsüeh-an*), and he took part in the preparation of the Ming History (*Ming shih*), though indirectly through his disciple Wan Ssu-t'ung (1638–1702), as he did not want to co-operate personally in an official undertaking of the Manchu conquerors.

The compilation of the Ming History (*Ming shih*) was the chief historical achievement in the first part of the dynasty.[2] Unlike the Standard Histories compiled under the Yüan and Ming dynasties, the *Ming shih* was prepared with great care and the best scholars of the time took part in the work, either officially or indirectly, over a period of sixty years (1679–1739). The reports and discussions concerning its plan, its form and other debatable points, were collected and edited for reference when the Draft for a Ch'ing History (*Ch'ing shih kao*) was commenced shortly after the fall of the dynasty.[3] They evince an interest in history which remains somewhat ex-

---

[1] The best account I know of Ch'ing historiography is that by Naitō Torajirō in *Shina shigaku shi* (History of Chinese Historiography) (Tōkyō, 1949, second edition 1953, pp. 375–584). It is compiled from notes taken by students at his lectures at Kyōto University in 1919–21 and 1925 and edited after his death by his son with the help of Kanda Kiichirō and others. Unfortunately the notes concerning Chang Hsüeh-ch'eng were incomplete and only some of them could be included (see pp. 467 and 584–5).

[2] Naitō, op. cit., pp. 375–80. I have not been able to consult Li Chin-hua, 'A History of the Compilation of the Ming Dynasty History', *YCHP Monograph* 3 (Peking, 1933).

[3] Liu Ch'eng-kan, *Ming-shih li-an* (Wu-hsing, 1915).

traneous to strictly historiographical questions. The main discussions seem to have been connected with the doctrinal conflict around Neo-Confucianism: was the Ming History to be written in the annalistic and moralizing form of Chu Hsi's Outlines and Details based on the Comprehensive Mirror (*T'ung-chien kang-mu*)? Was there to be a special section for the biographies of Neo-Confucianists (*tao-hsüeh chuan*)? Should this section be divided into separate sub-sections for the Neo-Confucianists of the school of Chu Hsi and those of the school of Wang Shou-jen? Or again, was the documentation to be restricted to official documents (the Veritable Records, *shih-lu*, in particular), or were private records and stories (*yeh-shih*) to be taken into account, especially concerning the reign of Hui-ti (1399–1402), whose final fate and legitimacy were controverted? Finally, the traditional plan of the Standard Histories was adopted, no separate biographies were devoted to Neo-Confucianists, and private documents were not used. The Neo-Confucianist conservatives, above all the T'ung-ch'eng school, criticized the anti-Chu Hsi attitude which had eventually prevailed.

The Ming History marks no new departure in Chinese historiography, but though an official and collective work it was a far less bureaucratic affair than most of the Standard Histories compiled from the T'ang onwards and testifies to the interest taken in history by the early Ch'ing scholars. For obvious reasons little is known about the main discussions, those that must have raged around the fall of Ming and the advent of Ch'ing. The Chekiang region, in which historiography was to have its main centre in Ch'ing times, had also been a centre of obdurate resistance to the Manchus. Huang Tsung-hsi, a native of Yü-yao, between Ning-po and Shao-hsing, had taken an active part in the armed local resistance in the years 1644–9, and refused to the end to serve the Manchus. Yet his writings on Ming history were placed at the disposal of the board of compilers of the *Ming shih*, and the preliminary draft (*Ming shih kao*) is said to have been written by his disciple Wan Ssu-t'ung, who is also said to have made use of a Documentation for the Ming History (*Ming shih an*) compiled by Huang Tsung-hsi himself. In the first half of the eighteenth century, another figure of the Chekiang school of historiography, Ch'üan Tsu-wang (1705–55), a native of Ning-po who was considered the best historian of his generation, wrote many biographies and epitaphs of the last Ming loyalists in his home region; they were published long after his death in duly expurgated form.[4]

With the Ch'ien-lung era, when critical philology (*k'ao-cheng*) reigned supreme in Confucian studies, historical studies took a similar turn. In the

---

[4] Hummel, *Eminent Chinese*, pp. 204–5. Ch'üan Tsu-wang's 'Questions and Answers on the Canon and History' (*Ching-shih wen-ta*, in *Huang-Ch'ing ching-chieh*, cccii–cccix) have little theoretical interest.

first half of the era, the fashion was rather in favour of collecting new material to complement ancient histories, as in the Complementary Annotations (*Pu-chu*) to the Tso Tradition (*Tso-chuan*) and the History of the Later Han (*Hou Han shu*) by Hui Tung (1697–1758) and other similar works; in the second half, textual criticism was predominant, for example in the Discussions on the Seventeen Histories (*Shih-ch'i-shih shang-ch'üeh*) by Wang Ming-sheng (1722–98), the Investigations into Discrepancies in the Twenty-two Histories (*Nien-erl-shih k'ao-i*) by Ch'ien Ta-hsin(1728–1800), the Notes on the Twenty-two Histories (*Nien-erl-shih cha-chi*) by Chao I (1727–1814), the Critical Researches on the Bibliographical Treatise of the Sui History (*Sui-shu ching-chi-chih k'ao-cheng*) by Chang Tsung-yüan (1752–1800), and many others. The auxiliary disciplines of history—epigraphy, archaeology, bibliography, textual criticism, historical geography—were cultivated and had eventually far-reaching effects on the development of historiography; but no large and original works of history were undertaken or, if they were, they came to nothing, as in the case of the new histories of the Sung and Yüan dynasties which were undertaken or projected by Shao Chin-han (1743–96) and his friend Chang Hsüeh-ch'eng (see below) and by Ch'ien Ta-hsin. Pi Yüan's Continuation of the Comprehensive Mirror for Aid in Government (*Hsü Tzu-chih t'ung-chien*) was not published before the beginning of the nineteenth century (1801), nor did the New Redaction of the Yüan History (*Yüan shih hsin-pien*) of Wei Yüan (1794–1856) come out before the present century (1905).

It was at the height of this remarkable tide of philological criticism, which was to have sweeping and devastating effects on the future of the Confucian tradition, that there appeared in China a historical genius of the first magnitude, ranking with Ibn Khaldun or with the greatest historiographers of Europe. Chang Hsüeh-ch'eng (styled Shih-chai; 1738–1801) used to say that he had received from Heaven the gift of history;[5] scarcely was he out of his teens when he expressly styled himself a historical genius.[6] In the perspective of Chinese historiography his main achievement was his critical reaction against the excess of criticism which was rampant in his day. But the permanent and universal value of his work lies in his profound reflection on the theory of history, its methods, its ideological background. On the eve of the greatest upheaval of Chinese culture since the revolution of Ch'in Shih-huang-ti, it was his lot to proceed to a review and reappraisal of the ideas concerning history which had been part and parcel of the Confucian tradition since its origins.

Chang Hsüeh-ch'eng was born in 1738 in Shao-hsing (Chekiang), the home of several famous writers of modern China, not far from Yü-yao which had been the home of Wang Shou-jen (Wang Yang-ming, 1472–

---

[5] Family Letter (1765), *I-shu*, ix, 68b.      [6] *Shih-ts'ai.* Yao Ming-ta, 7.

1528) and Huang Tsung-hsi, and Ning-po which was the home of two prominent Ch'ing historians, Wan Ssu-t'ung, a disciple of Huang Tsung-hsi, and Ch'üan Tsu-wang, an elder contemporary of Chang. He thus belonged to the so-called school of the East of the Che (Che-tung), the Che being the Ch'ien-t'ang River or river of Hang-chou which gives its name to Chekiang province and divides its south-eastern part, with Shao-hsing, Yü-yao and Ning-po, from its north-western part. Chang Hsüeh-ch'eng had a strong regional feeling and made some fuss about the opposition of this school to the school of the West of the Che (Che-hsi), a name geographically inaccurate as it also covered the southern part of Kiangsu province, well to the north-east of the Che River, with the homes of Ku Yen-wu (K'un-shan) and of Ch'ien Ta-hsin (Chia-ting), both in the vicinity of Shanghai.[7] Doctrinally the Che-tung school inclined towards the Neo-Confucianism of Wang Shou-jen with its stress on synthetic intuition, while the Che-hsi school remained more faithful to the tradition of Chu Hsi with its 'gradualist' methods and its insistence on study and erudition. The outstanding representatives of these two schools in the latter half of the eighteenth century were Chang Hsüeh-ch'eng and Ch'ien Ta-hsin.

Chang Hsüeh-ch'eng's father was a petty official, but the peasant extraction of the family was not far back. The Chang clan, whose origins were in Fukien, had settled during the twelfth century in the hills near the city of Shao-hsing, where it numbered as many as 10,000 persons at the beginning of the eighteenth century. The agricultural resources of the land being no longer sufficient to ensure their living, some of them became urbanized and gradually rose on the social ladder. Chang Hsüeh-ch'eng's grandfather had joined the administration as a clerk: he was something of a scholar, for his grandson reports that he spent his old age reading Ssu-ma Kuang's Comprehensive Mirror.[8] His son, the father of Chang Hsüeh-ch'eng, managed to become a doctor (*chin-shih*), but he had a mediocre career. After living on lessons given at Shao-hsing, he was appointed district magistrate in Hupeh for five years (1751–6), after which he had to resign on a charge of misappropriation of funds. Being too poor to return to his native province, he stayed teaching in Hupeh until his death in 1768. His widow then remained in the care of Chang Hsüeh-ch'eng, with the whole family making up a household of about twenty mouths, and all these people for many years followed Chang Hsüeh-ch'eng

[7] As far as erudition goes Ch'ien Ta-hsin (1728–1804) seems to have been the greatest scholar of his time, greater than both Chang Hsüeh-ch'eng and Tai Chen. The names Che-tung and Che-hsi had been in use in T'ang and Sung administrative geography, but the territories so designated never included, it seems, any part of the present province of Kiangsu. An important essay was devoted by Chang Hsüeh-ch'eng to the Che-tung school, *I-shu*, ii, 23a–25a.

[8] Postface of 1785, *I-shu*, xxix, 11b. On Ssu-ma Kuang, see the paper by E. G. Pulleyblank, above, pp. 151–66.

through his wandering life, including the dead bodies, which, for lack of money, could not be sent back to the clan cemetery in Chekiang.[9]

Chang Hsüeh-ch'eng seems to have been an only son, and something of a spoilt child. He was a puny lad and his health was poor. In his old age he is described as deaf, stammering, with a red nose, his face covered with warts, and constantly subject to headaches. He was slow and obdurate as a boy, and schoolwork did not please him. But he soon took to devouring the Philosophers and above all the Historians, who were not included in the school curriculum and were even forbidden. Between his fifteenth and his eighteenth years, when his father was district officer, Chang Hsüeh-ch'eng sold the hairpins and ear-rings which made up the dowry of his wife (he had been married when thirteen years old) in order to buy paper and writing-brushes and bribe his father's clerks to make them copy all sorts of texts of the Chou period, which he wanted to arrange according to the plan of the Standard Histories to form an 'Eastern Chou History'. The head of the clerical staff found him out, he was punished, and the 'Eastern Chou History' remained unfinished.[10] It was then that he used to style himself a 'historical genius' and to boast immoderately before his father's visitors who, out of respect for the magistrate, did not dare to set him down. This crisis of adolescence ended suddenly when he entered his twentieth year. In a letter written later,[11] he recalls that his mind then opened, and he began to understand texts without the help of commentaries; the books of history, in particular, became so familiar to him that he imagined, as if by paramnesia, that he had previously studied all those he happened to open.

At the age of twenty-two (1760), he left his people in Hupeh to go to Peking and try his luck at the competitive examinations. After staying with some members of his clan from Chekiang who had settled at the capital, he was admitted to the State Seminary (*Kuo-tzu chien*) as a boarding student. He went up three times for his second degree (*chü-jen*) before succeeding in his thirtieth year; and only ten years later (1778) did he obtain the doctorate (*chin-shih*). Meanwhile he met in Peking some high-placed scholars who became interested in him. His first patron was Chu Yün (1729–81), that learned academician who first suggested to Emperor Ch'ien-lung the idea of undertaking the monumental collection of Chinese literature known as the Complete Library in Four Sections (*Ssu-k'u ch'üan-shu*), with its critical catalogue, the elaboration of which occupied all the Chinese intelligentzia at the end of the eighteenth century.[12] In

---

[9] Autobiographical poem (1797), *I-shu*, xxviii, 51a: 'In four years I had to move house five times, with all the household including the sick and the dead. In the midst of all the luggage, with the hens and the dogs, the drawings and the books, we had to carry the coffins, chased through the waves of the rivers, through the dust of the roads . . .'

[10] Yao Ming-ta, 7.                                              [11] Family letter, *I-shu*, ix, 73a.

[12] Chang Hsüeh-ch'eng does not seem to have had anything to do with the *Ssu-k'u ch'üan-shu*. He was too much of an outsider in official circles.

1771 Chu Yün took him to Anhwei, where he had been appointed Commissioner for Education. It was at that time that Chang Hsüeh-ch'eng began the nomadic life he was to lead almost to his death, and which hindered him greatly in his work. He describes it in a letter of this period:[13] 'I am compelled to beg from door to door like a cheap vagrant; I don't know where to find the money I need for my perpetual shiftings. I try my hand at little business deals, running after 10 per cent profits. To make matters worse, I have an impediment in my speech, nor am I clever at talking or at writing calling-cards to ask for interviews. I only sit there from day to day, muttering unintelligible words . . . I have had an inborn taste for history ever since I was a boy: and yet lucky if, by pawning my clothes and blankets, I managed to buy some of the Standard Histories. Besides, my eyesight is weak; I loose the thread of my ideas; I forget a great deal . . .'[14]

In 1773 Chu Yün was called back to Peking to collaborate on the *Ssu-k'u ch'üan-shu*, whose bureau had just been opened. Chang Hsüeh-ch'eng followed him back to the capital. He then started chasing about the environs of Peking, presenting himself to local officers he had known in town and who got him sundry jobs, such as the revision of local gazetteers (*fang-chih*), the temporary presidency of local academies (*shu-yüan*), some work in correcting examination copies, in amending genealogical registers (*tsung-p'u*), and so on. Yet he found time to write some essays on historiography. But historiography was not the fashion then in learned circles, and Chang Hsüeh-ch'eng feared to estrange the scholars who could help and protect him. Therefore he only sent round his manuscripts to a restricted and chosen circle of friends, insisting that they were not to be shown to everyone. 'Please', he once wrote to Ch'ien Ta-hsin,[15] 'take care not to speak of my poor essays to outsiders . . . The work of a writer who would not come forward to reform the abuses of his time, would be valueless. But whoever wants to reform abuses must go against fashion. Now fashion is more formidable than the laws and ordinances of the Office of Criminal Law.' In another letter,[16] we find him reproaching the scholars of his time for attaching too much importance to concrete and analytic research on texts, instead of working out their material in a spirit of synthesis: they were like silkworms which only ate the mulberry leaves without unreeling their silk-thread. He himself, he added, had been led to develop

---

[13] To a grand-nephew, concerning study (1766), *I-shu*, xxii, 39a.

[14] His poor memory may explain why he speculated so much on history instead of practising it.

[15] In 1798, *I-shu*, xxix, 58b–59a. Yao Ming-ta, 25, seems to be wrong in assigning this letter to 1772.

[16] Written in 1796 to Wang Hui-tsu, *I-shu*, ix, 25b–26a. Wang Hui-tsu (1731–1807) is well known as the author of the *Shih-hsing yün-pien* and the *San-shih t'ung hsing-ming lu*, both of which were prefaced by Chang Hsüeh-ch'eng (*I-shu*, viii, 1a–4b), who was a promoter of the indexing of Chinese books (see on this point *I-shu*, x, 15a–16a).

personal views that opened a new path in historiography. He was conscious of the novelty of his views in this field, a field that had lain fallow for a long time. But his ideas were so unusual that he dreaded the consequences: he was going to be misunderstood, he was going to frighten the world, he was going to be covered with insults and outrages. Elsewhere,[17] he declared it was going to take one hundred years for his work to be recognized and appreciated, as had occurred to the poetry of Tu Fu in T'ang times. He was convinced he had opened a new path for the future in historiography.[18] Some people would compare him to Liu Chih-chi (661–721), the famous author of the Generalities on History (*Shih-t'ung*); but Liu Chih-chi had only dealt with the methodology of history (*shih-fa*), while he himself dealt with its 'idea', its meaning (*shih-i*). No one today was interested in these questions. The concern of scholars was with erudition and philology; they thought only of patching up the texts of the Confucian Canon. The value of this kind of research did not escape him, though he did not excel in it; he loved and respected it, but he knew his limits. His own work was directed in a quite different way, towards history, its principles, its methodology, its bibliography. And there he found no predecessor, no model, no understanding. He stood alone, rejected by his peers, abandoned by all, without even some disciples around him to comfort him . . .

Chang Hsüeh-ch'eng probably exaggerated his misfortunes. There was in him some degree of persecution mania, as often happens to men not in harmony with their time. All he had to do, after all, was to accept a post in the provincial administration, to which his degrees entitled him. But when such a post was offered him, in 1787, he refused outright.[19] In the independence he had chosen, however, he did not lack support, at least not to the extent of which he complained. After Chu Yün, who had helped him for seven years (1766–73), he found a new patron in the person of Pi Yüan (1730–97), a great administrator and a great scholar. Pi Yüan was interested in history and we owe to him a continuation of Ssu-ma Kuang's general history of China, the *Tzu-chih t'ung-chien*, which stopped at the tenth century. The *Hsü Tzu-chih t'ung chien*, or Continuation of the Comprehensive Mirror for Aid in Government, is not unworthy of the masterpiece which it completed for the Sung and Yüan periods. It is difficult to determine the part taken by Chang Hsüeh-ch'eng in the writing of it, but we know that it was thanks to his advice that Pi Yüan succeeded in obviating by various correctives the defects of the annalistic form, a form which Pi Yüan, like Ssu-ma Kuang, had inherited from the primitive

[17] Letter to Chu Hsi-keng, a son of Chu Yün, quoted by Ch'ien Mu, 427, from a manuscript belonging to the University of Peking.

[18] This and what follows is freely abridged from a family letter written in 1790, *I-shu*, ix, 68b–69a. On Liu Chih-chi, see the paper by E. G. Pulleyblank, above, pp. 136–51.

[19] Yao Ming-ta, 61.

chronicles of the *Ch'un-ch'iu* (Spring and Autumn Annals) type and whose perpetuation from age to age has been a plague on Chinese historiography.

Another work with which Chang Hsüeh-ch'eng was entrusted by Pi Yüan was a monumental bibliography of Chinese historiography entitled An Investigation into Historical Documents (*Shih-chi k'ao*). This work was intended to represent for the historical literature of China what the *Ching-i k'ao*, or Investigation into the Confucian Canon and its Exegesis, published in 1701 by Chu I-tsun, represented for the canonical literature. Nothing has been preserved of the *Shih-chi k'ao* on which Chang Hsüeh-ch'eng worked ceaselessly from 1787 until shortly before his death in 1801, except some plans and tables showing that he had applied in this work some of his most cherished historiographical theories.[20] One of these theories was a sort of pan-historicism according to which all documents, no matter what they were, were worth mentioning in a bibliography of history. 'In my opinion', Chang Hsüeh-ch'eng wrote in this connection,[21] 'the whole forest of works that fill the universe between Heaven and Earth belong to history. The six books of the Confucian Canon have only been called a Canon (*ching*) because the Saint (Confucius) resorted to these six books of history in order to enlighten posterity. As for Philosophy (*tzu*) and Literature (*chi*), they also proceed entirely from History (*shih*). Only tardily (in T'ang times), when this appurtenance was forgotten, did there arise the distinction between four different sections of documents (Canon, History, Philosophy, Literature) . . .' Consequently, Chang Hsüeh-ch'eng had included in his *Shih-chi k'ao* canonical as well as philosophical and literary works; in fact, the works usually classified as history took up only one third of his bibliography of Chinese history.[22]

Pi Yüan, while he was governor-general of Hupeh and Hunan, entrusted Chang Hsüeh-ch'eng with still another task: the preparation of a new edition of the General Gazetteer of Hupeh (*Hu-pei t'ung-chih*). This interested Chang Hsüeh-ch'eng deeply, as he also had his ideas on local gazetteers (*fang-chih*). Either because, due to his unstable life, he often found himself (like many other scholars of his time) led by circumstances to be busy with gazetteers, or because gazetteers were then in general favour owing to the current interest in 'concrete' learning (*p'u-hsüeh*), or for other less contingent reasons, Chang Hsüeh-ch'eng assigned an extreme importance to the *fang-chih*. They ought, he thought, to have been drawn up and composed with as much care and thoroughness as the Standard Histories, for which they should become an important source of

[20] *I-shu*, xiii, 34a–38b, and Complement (*pu-i*), 59b–60b; Yao Ming-ta, 132–7.
[21] Letter to Sun Hsing-yen (1753–1818) concerning the *Shih-chi k'ao*, *I shu*, ix, 42a–b. It seems that this enormous compilation was actually finished in 1798, but the death of Pi Yüan (1797), under whose name it was to come out, prevented its publication.
[22] Yao Ming-ta, 136, quoting a manuscript belonging to Ma Hsü-lun (lately Minister of Education at Peking).

materials. He proposed that the authorities be ordered to have them revised officially every thirty or at least every hundred years,[23] and that they should establish to this end local archives, to be regularly kept up to date and looked after by a special staff.[24] He himself took infinite care to obtain first-hand documentation on the various regions whose gazetteers were revised by him in the course of his wandering life. He would spend months making investigations on the spot, gathering information on local persons of note, on the chief families and their genealogy, calling personally on widows and virtuous women whose biographies were to be included in the *fang-chih*. He used to go about the country in a cart with rolls of paper and a jar of wine (no doubt Shao-hsing wine!), collecting manuscripts, inscriptions, local traditions, and so on.[25] Then, after he had collected his documents, he proceeded to arrange them according to highly systematic plans, which he worked out at great pains. In his gazetteers Chang Hsüeh-ch'eng illustrated, or at least intended to illustrate, his theories concerning the difference between mere collection and compilation of documents (*chi-chu*) and their elaboration into real personal 'works' (*chu-shu*, *chuan-shu*).[26] It is necessary, he said, to begin by documentation and inquiry, which is not too easy in itself. But then one should proceed to make a selection, to choose what should be left out and what should be taken in; the materials should not be presented pell-mell.[27] In reply to a correspondent who wondered why he did not write books instead of arguing about how books should be written, he boasted that his gazetteers were real 'works' which deserved to be ranked with the best Standard Histories and would gain him immortal glory.[28]

In spite of such over-statements it is indeed to be regretted that only some scraps remain of these actual examples of Chang Hsüen-ch'eng's methodology. His General Gazetteer of Hupeh was never published, because just as he was about to finish it, in 1794, Pi Yüan who had commissioned it, had to leave Hupeh. The authorities who succeeded him appreciated neither the peculiar ideas of Chang Hsüeh-ch'eng about his work, nor probably his person; the cantankerous old scholar must have been a nuisance to everybody. The manuscripts of his General Gazetteer were

[23] 'Record of a discussion on gazetteers with Tai Chen' (1773), *I-shu*, xiv, 39b.

[24] Letter on gazetteers, in answer to the bachelor Chen, *I-shu*, xv, 11b. See also Fu Chen-lun, 'Chang Shih-chai's Historiography', *Yenching Annual of Historical Studies*, I, v (August, 1933), 130.

[25] Yao Ming-ta, 43, 76.

[26] More exactly *chi-chu* means the writing down, the notation of historical facts, and *chuan-shu* their record in a composed form. The distinction between documents and history was already made, clearly though far less forcibly, by Liu Chih-chi and Cheng Ch'iao; see the texts quoted in Ho Ping-sung's Introduction to Yao Ming-ta, 9–11.

[27] Letter to Ch'en Shih (1794), *I-shu*, xiv, 23b–24a.

[28] Letter to Chou Chen-jung (1789), *I-shu*, ix, 43a–43b. Chou Chen-jung was a local official who in 1777 had commissioned Chang Hsüeh-ch'eng with the compilation of the gazetteer of his sub-prefecture, Yung-ch'ing in Chihli. This is one of Chang Hsüeh-ch'eng's gazetteers of which rare copies are known to exist (there is one in the Library of Congress).

so completely lost and forgotten that in the last edition I have seen of the *Hu-pei t'ung-chih* (1921) Chang Hsüeh-ch'eng is not even mentioned among the former scholars who dealt with the history of the province. If the Chinese authorities had been wise enough to carry into effect the project he worked out at the end of the eighteenth century for the establishment of a methodical corpus of local archives and local gazetteers, China today would dispose of an incomparable documentation on her modern history and we should not have to be content with the archives of the central government and the imperial court.

After 1794, when he lost the support of Pi Yüan, Chang Hsüeh-ch'eng went back to his native province of Chekiang and there, after some more or less miserable years, his eyesight gravely affected, he died in 1801, aged sixty-three. In his lifetime he had only printed a small number of his essays on historiography and the philosophy of history, and of these only a few copies, wilfully limited for reasons explained above. More than thirty years after his death, in 1832–3, some more essays, fragments, and letters were published in K'ai-feng by one of his sons under the double title of General Meaning of Historiography (*Wen-shih t'ung-i*)[29] and General Meaning of Bibliography (*Chiao-ch'ou t'ung-i*).[30] This edition was reprinted by a grandson of Chang Hsüeh-ch'eng at Kuei-yang in 1878, and there were several later reprints. It was from this poor edition, in five fascicles (*ts'e*), that Chang Hsüeh-ch'eng was to be known throughout the nineteenth century. In 1920, thirteen fascicles of 'Derelicta' (*Chang-shih i-shu*) were published in Hangchow by care of the Provincial Library of Chekiang. Finally a much larger edition, in thirty fascicles, critically established by a group of Chekiang scholars, was published with the same title in 1922 at Wu-hsing (northern Chekiang).[31] Some more materials have been recovered since, and in 1937 the National University of Peking undertook their publication under the direction of Professor Ch'ien Mu, but this publication came to nothing.[32]

The first to revive interest in his work was the Japanese sinologist, Naitō Torajirō, who in 1920 sketched his biography from a manuscript

[29] *Wen-shih*, a term used in the Bibliographical Treatise of the *T'ang-shu*, il, as the title of a section of books dealing with historiography and literary history and criticism, has also been translated as Literature and History, Cultural History, etc.

[30] Literally 'collating'.

[31] All references to the (*Chang-shih*) *I-shu* in the present paper are to this xylographic edition of 1922. A typographic reprint of it, in eight volumes of smaller size, summarily punctuated, has been published by the Commercial Press in 1936.

[32] Some unpublished manuscripts are edited or quoted in Ch'ien Mu's History of Chinese Scholarship in the Last Three Hundred Years (*Chung-kuo chin san-po-nien hsüeh-shu shih*), Commercial Press, 1937 (here referred to as 'Ch'ien Mu'). I have heard from a Chinese friend of Professor Ch'ien Mu that the latter, who is now teaching in Hongkong, published during the war a paper on 'The unpublished manuscripts of Chang Hsüeh-ch'eng' in the Bulletin of the Provincial Library of Szechwan (*Ssu-ch'uan sheng-li t'u-shu-kuan kuan-k'an*); I have not been able to see this paper, a reprint of which is said to have been published in Peking without Ch'ien Mu's name.

copy of some of his writings he had obtained from China.[33] This was followed in 1922 by a more elaborate book by Hu Shih, in which the protagonist of the Literary Revolution expressed his regret that a foreigner had been needed to rescue this great Chinese figure from oblivion and proceeded to expose the life and thought of Chang Hsüeh-ch'eng in annalistic form (*nien-p'u*, a form contrary to all the theories of Chang Hsüeh-ch'eng).[34] A revised and much enlarged edition of Hu Shih's book was published in 1931 by Yao Ming-ta;[35] and since then there have been many studies in China (and also in Japan and elsewhere).[36] It is, in short, the Western impact which made China turn her attention to Chang Hsüeh-ch'eng. Faced with the necessity of renovating the principles and procedures of her historiography, China had to vindicate in this field, as in others, the spirit of objective generalization which is proper to science. She then remembered that long ago, towards the end of the eighteenth century, such a spirit had been heralded by an obscure scholar of Chekiang whose whimsical ideas had been ignored in his own time, but provided valid food for modern thought.

What remains of his work is but a jumble of bits and fragments, as chopped up as was his life. There are a few finished essays, mostly philosophical, many drafts and plans, and a great deal of letters affording a most vivid and intimate insight into Chang Hsüeh-ch'eng's personal story and the intellectual life in Ch'ien-lung's China. But, *more sinico*, a systematic exposition of his thought is scarcely to be found in his writings.

The historiographical thought of Chang Hsüeh-ch'eng can only be understood in the light of, or more exactly as a reaction to, his time. The fashion among his contemporaries was the critical study of the Confucian Canon. Born with a taste for history, Chang Hsüeh-ch'eng bade defiance to the exclusive primacy of these studies—Biblical studies, we would say— and the excess of philological erudition which they entailed. He nursed a grudge against Han Yü because, when he initiated a renaissance of

[33] *Shinagaku*, I, iii–iv (Kyōto, 1920); reprinted in *Kenki shōroku* (Kyōto, 1928), 113–36, and in *Shina shigakushi* (Tōkyō, second edition, 1953), 612 sq.

[34] *Chang Shih-chai hsien-sheng nien-p'u* (Commercial Press); review in *BEFEO* (1923), xxiii, 478–89.

[35] *Chang Shih-chai nien-p'u* (Commercial Press), with a valuable Introduction by Ho Ping-song, a well-known Chekiang scholar.

[36] Two unpublished doctorate theses have recently been devoted to Chang Hsüeh-ch'eng in the U.S.A.: David S. Nivison, *The Literary and Historical Thought of Chang Hsüeh-ch'eng: a Study of his Life and Writings, with Translations of Six Essays from the Wen-shih t'ung-i* (Harvard University, 1953); Chu Shih-chia, on Chang's work concerning local gazetteers (Columbia University, about 1950). An excellent summary and appreciation of Chang Hsüeh-ch'eng's thought is given in D. S. Nivison, 'The Philosophy of Chang Hsüeh-ch'eng', *Occasional Papers*, 3 (Kansai Asiatic Society, Kyōto, 1955), 22–34; see also, by the same author, 'The Problem of "Knowledge" and "Action" in Chinese Thought since Wang Yang-ming', *Studies in Chinese Thought, The American Anthropologist* (1953), vol. 55, No. 5, pt. 2, 126–34, and a short paper in Japanese concerning Ch'ang's attitude towards Buddhism in *Journal of Indian and Buddhist Studies*, 8 (Tokyo, March, 1957), 102–5.

antique letters prior to Buddhism, the famous forerunner of Neo-Confucianism had directed this renaissance towards the Confucian Canon, instead of directing it towards history.[37] During the Ch'ing period, in part for political reasons, historical studies had fallen into some disfavour and Chang Hsüeh-ch'eng, who had his theories on education, wished that they should reappear in the curriculum of the schools and examinations, and even that they should be placed in the first position.[38] Never, as a matter of fact, had history occupied the first position in Chinese tradition, not since, with the rise of the Confucianist school (*ju-chia*) under the Han dynasty, the earliest documents of Chinese literature had been set up as a Canon (*ching*), a corpus of normative scriptures fixing a 'rule' of life[39] and which came to be placed before History (*shih*) in the fourfold classification of literature in use since the T'ang dynasty. It is quite true, Chang Hsüeh-ch'eng contended, that these scriptures contain a rule of life; but the title of Canon was given them tardily and only because Confucius had handed them down for the instruction and edification of posterity. In themselves they were nothing but historical documents: and so they had been considered by Confucius himself.

This is one of the senses, if I am not mistaken, in which may be construed the memorable phrase that opens the works of Chang Hsüeh-ch'eng: 'The sixfold Canon is all history.'[40] There is in that phrase an element of polemic, of personal apology. Chang Hsüeh-ch'eng himself explained that he wanted to forestall the specialists of the Canon who might have reproved him, a historian, for meddling in their affairs when he wrote on the Canon.[41] But that is just the point, he said: the books of the Confucian Canon quite definitely fall into the province of history, and the Confucianist school was wrong in classifying them apart from history. In a deeper sense, this phrase is connected with all his philosophy of history. Its ambivalence should be well understood. Chang Hsüeh-ch'eng asserts that the Canon, the Confucian Bible, is history. Turn the proposition around, and inversely history will also constitute a Canon, history will have a canonical value, a value as a rule and norm. And that is precisely what Chang Hsüeh-ch'eng believed. The Bible is history, because history is a Bible. Chang Hsüeh-ch'eng's purpose, I believe, was not to profanize the Canon, but rather to canonize history, to sacralize it just as Hegel divinized it.[42]

---

[37] Letter to Wang Hui-tsu (1796), *I-shu*, ix, 26a.      [38] Yao Ming-ta, 60, 143.

[39] The word 'canon', meaning originally a carpenter's rule, is similar to *ching*, the warp of a tissue. The Western metaphor points to a milieu of builders and geometers, the Chinese term to a vocabulary of sericulturists and weavers.

[40] *Liu ching chieh shih yeh*, 'Doctrine of the Canon of Changes', *I-shu*, i, 1a; also 'Answering a guest', *I-shu*, iv, 44b; and elsewhere.

[41] Letter to Chu Kuei (1796), *I-shu*, xxviii, 44a–b; cf. Yao Ming-ta, 123, and Ch'ien Mu, 426. Chu Kuei (1731–1807) was a brother of Chu Yün.

[42] 'Gott regiert die Welt; der Inhalt seiner Regierung, die Vollführung seines Planes ist die Weltgeschichte' (*Vorlesungen über die Philosophie der Geschichte*, ed. Reclam, 74).

We have on this point one of Chang Hsüeh-ch'eng's most elaborate and significant writings, if not one of the clearest, his essay of 1789 entitled, after Han Yü and others, 'Tracing the Tao to its source' (*Yüan-tao*).[43] In it the Tao is defined, in the spirit of the Canon of Changes, as the Way in which nature proceeds in its perpetual becoming. On the Heavenly plane (*t'ien-tao*), this Way consists in the alternance of Yin and Yang which structures the cosmic energy. But that Way of Heaven is invisible to Man; in the wording of the Canon of Changes, it is metaphysical, 'above physical forms'.[44] Its manifestations on Earth, alone visible to Man, are described by Chang Hsüeh-ch'eng in social terms. His reasoning, characteristically Chinese, goes as follows. The Tao, he says, gets its principle from Heaven, but Heaven's workings are not manifest; they elude Man's understanding. Man can only know the Tao by its manifestations on Earth, as they are revealed in Man himself. For the Tao to take shape, to appear visibly in bodily forms (*hsing*), it is necessary to have 'three men in a house' (*san-jen chü-shih*). 'Three men in a house' will necessarily distribute among themselves the tasks of daily life, cooking, bringing in the wood, getting the water from the well, and so forth; they are the prototype of human society, with its division of work. When differentiated and organized, human society is an equilibrium of social categories, a sort of terrestrial hypostasis of the celestial equilibrium of Yin and Yang. Thus human history—social history—has its origin in Heaven; and the Saints (*sheng-jen*), the great demiurges who established social order here below, who founded civilization with its institutions, its social laws, its moral values, did nothing but realize on Earth the Way of Heaven, the metaphysical Tao. The Saints moreover were but disciples of ordinary men, of the people, for the people remained more spontaneous, less selfconscious, closer to nature—which is to say closer to Heaven—and it is in the people that the Tao manifests itself in the most immediate and authentic fashion: 'The Saints have to learn from the people.'[45]

It was in high antiquity, during the Three Dynasties, that this manifestation of the Tao reached its perfection; the zenith was attained with the Western Chou, at the time of the Duke of Chou. Later, with the Eastern Chou, in Confucius' time, decadence set in; Chang Hsüeh-ch'eng remains faithful to the old Chinese perspective of a 'reverse progress', a regression, a devolution from antiquity onwards: the ideal of the future is to be sought in a revival of the golden age of ancient times. Confucius, he says, was still a Saint but, unlike the Saints of yore, he was no longer a King; he did not possess effective power to make the Tao reign on Earth: he could not

---

[43] *I-shu*, ii, 1a–14a. The title is borrowed from Han Yü, and also from the *Huai-nan-tzu* and from Liu Hsieh; cf. *I-shu*, ix, 40a.

[44] *Hsing-erl-shang che wei chih tao*, *I ching*, Hsi-tz'u, I, 12 (Legge, 377).

[45] *I-shu*, ii, 2b–3a, 8b.

enact it, only learn it (*hsüeh*) and teach it (*chiao*). Knowledge was divorced from action, teaching from governing; education ceased to be in the hands of officials; private doctrines appeared, the Philosophers began their gratuitous speculations, and the hallowed *étatisme* of yore was wrecked.

For teaching the true Way, Confucius had at his disposal written documents, texts in which the actual facts of ancient times were recorded. These texts now form the Confucian Canon. They were the archives of antiquity, the written testimonies of the early Saints and of the institutions and regulations which they had created (*tso*).[46] At the same time they also form a normative code, a Canon, since the facts recorded in them were the realization on Earth of the Heavenly Tao. And that is why, according to Chang Hsüeh-ch'eng, Confucius restricted himself to the transmission (*shu*) of these documents without adding to them anything of his own invention (*shu erl pu tso*). Rather than decree theoretical prescriptions of his own, which he could not translate into reality since the Saints, in his time, had lost all real power, he preferred to let the facts speak for themselves: the objective facts of history, those that are set forth in the Canon. Therefore he abstained from any explicit commentary on the *Ch'un-ch'iu*, though implying judgements of value in his revision of the text.[47] According to a saying of Confucius which was current in Han times and which Chang Hsüeh-ch'eng often quotes: 'There is more pungency and clarity in showing the Tao in action, in the facts themselves, than in expressing the Tao with empty words.'[48] The Tao is inherent in facts, in the concrete reality of history; it should not be looked for outside of the world. It is immanent in that concrete world which the Canon of Changes calls the world of 'vessels',[49] a world informed by the Tao as vessels are filled by water:[50] hence the variant 'The sixfold Canon is all vessel' for 'The sixfold Canon is all history'.[51] There are no transcendent principles (such as *i-li*, justice and reason; *hsing-ming*, human nature and destiny; and so on) beyond the human plane, the plane of facts; abstract ideals are but 'empty words'.[52]

There is nothing very original in most of these views. They conform with the immanentist tendency of all Ch'ing thought and, more generally,

---

[46] This point is developed in another essay, also entitled *Yüan-tao*, which is included in the *Chiao-ch'ou t'ung-i, I-shu*, x, 1a sq.

[47] 'Explaining *t'ung*', *I-shu*, iv, 43b. In this respect Chang Hsüeh-ch'eng stuck to the tradition of Ssu-ma Ch'ien, *Shih-chi*, ed. Takikawa, xlvii, 83 (Chavannes, v, 422–3): *pi tse pi, hsüe tse hsüe*, etc.

[48] *Shih-chi*, ed. Takikawa, cxxx, 21. The commentary notes that this saying was taken from a 'woof' (*wei*) of the *Ch'un-ch'iu*. It is also quoted in the *Ch'un-ch'iu fan-lu* of Tung Chung-shu (ed. *Ssu-pu ts'ung-k'an*, vi, 3b), from whom Ssu-ma Ch'ien may have heard it (cf. Kang Woo, *Les théories politiques du Tch'ouen-ts'ieou*, Paris, 1932, 177).

[49] *Hsing-erl-hsia che wei chih ch'i, I-ching*, Hsi-tz'u, i, 12 (Legge, 377).

[50] 'The Che-tung school', *I-shu*, ii, 25a (applied to the *li*).

[51] *Liu ching chieh ch'i yeh*, '*Yüan-tao*', *I-shu*, ii, 7b.　　　　　　[52] *I-shu*, ii, 23b–24a.

with the congenital abhorrence of abstraction and of 'empty words' which is a fundamental feature of Chinese thought.[53] As early as the eleventh century Su Hsün (1009–1066), the father of Su Shih (Su Tung-p'o), in his Discussion of History (*Shih-lun*), maintained that history had the same purpose as the Canon and that they completed each other;[54] in 1285 Hu San-hsing (1230–1307), in the preface to his commentary on Ssu-ma Kuang's Comprehensive Mirror,[55] set forth the notion of history as mirroring the Tao in the facts and events it relates and as being thereby coequal to the Canon; and the very phrase about the sixfold Canon being history is borrowed from or at least inspired by Wang Shou-jen (1472–1528), the fellow-countryman of Chang Hsüeh-ch'eng, revered by him as a patriarch of the Che-tung school.[56] Chang Hsüeh-ch'eng drew on ideas which were common in his time. These may appear to us strange and archaic; but substitute Weltgeist for Tao, and Hegel is not so far removed. His originality lies in the historiographical theories which he elaborated against this philosophical background. Some of these theories have quite a modern tinge.

History deals with facts; in Chinese the words *shih*[3], 'history', and *shih*[4], 'fact', 'event', are etymologically related.[57] 'The Ancients never strayed from facts (*shih*),' Chang Hsüeh-ch'eng says, 'in order to indulge in theories (*li*).'[58] *Li* and *shih* formed an old dichotomy which had been current throughout the medieval period of Chinese thought until Sung Neo-Confucianism replaced it by the pair *li* and *ch'i*. One of the practical conclusions drawn by Chang Hsüeh-ch'eng was that the historian should refrain from gratuitous theories and stick to facts; he should therefore respect documents, for these are the expression of facts. He should never, for instance, modify one word of a text he quotes or uses or, if he does change the wording, he should duly inform the reader of it and should put the original text before him in his notes.[59] As Chang Hsüeh-ch'eng says, he should take care not to let the Human in him (the 'all too human')

---

[53] 'Was nun die Wissenschaft selbst angeht, so begreift die Geschichte der Chinesen nur die ganz bestimmten Fakta in sich, ohne alles Urteil und Räsonnement' (Hegel, *Vorlesungen* . . ., 192). Little did Hegel suspect that this very 'factualism' had been conceptualized into a national philosophy.

[54] *Chia-tung chi*, ed. *Ssu-pu ts'ung-k'an*, viii, 1a–b. Cf. Joseph L. Levenson, 'Redefinition of Ideas in Time: the Chinese Classics and History', *FEQ* (May, 1956), xv, 3, 401.

[55] P. 28 of the Prolegomena to the new Peking edition of the *Tzu-chih t'ung-chien* (1956).

[56] *Wang Wen-cheng-kung ch'üan-shu*, ed. *Ssu-pu ts'ung-k'an*, i, 16b–17a (Henke, *The Philosophy of Wang Yang-ming*, 69–70); cf. Nivison, 'The Problem . . .' (above, n. 36), 121.

[57] Wang Kuo-wei thinks that they were originally one and the same word (*Shuo-wen chieh-tzu ku-lin*, 1262–4). See also Lao Kan in *Ta-lu tsa-chih*, XIV, iii (Taipei, 15 February 1957), 66. Compare the ambiguousness of the words for history in the European languages, which led to such clumsy distinctions as Kant's and Nietzsche's *Geschichte* and *Historie*, Hegel's *res gestae* and *historia rerum gestarum*, Croce's *storia* and *storiografia*, etc.

[58] 'Doctrine of the Canon of Changes', *I-shu*, i, 1a.

[59] Letter in answer to Shao Chin-han, *I-shu*, ix, 15a–b.

encroach upon the Heavenly:[60] in other words, his subjective opinions should never distort historical data, as these are manifestations of the Heavenly Tao.

The respect for documents does not imply, however, that the historian should exclude any intervention of his personality into his work. He will refrain, of course, from cheap literary effects, and also from hackneyed judgements such as praising Yao and Shun or censuring Chieh and Chou, approving the Kingly Way and disapproving tyranny.[61] But Chang Hsüeh-ch'eng denounced with all his energy the traditional methods of mechanical compilation which Liu Chih-chi far back in the seventh century had vainly tried to check and with which the West rightly reproaches Chinese historiography. He distinguished with perfect clarity on the one hand the task of collecting, collating and criticizing the documents, and on the other that which in history must be choice, interpretation, evaluation, and all that he included in the term synthesis (*yüan-t'ung*).[62] To be a historian worthy of the name, it is not enough to collect facts diligently and to arrange them at random, according to chronology or by any other arbitrary principle. He must organize them, bring out the essential points, and this implies individual judgement (*tu-tuan*) as opposed to mere compilation (*pi-tz'u*) and research (*k'ao-so*).[63] Only thus will he become a real author (*ch'eng-chia*), a composer of personal works (*chuan-shu*). The 'compiler' is like general Hsiao Ho who catered for supplies in Liu Pang's wars against Hsiang Yü, the 'author' like general Han Hsin who was in charge of strategy.[64] Both are necessary, but Chang Hsüeh-ch'eng does not conceal the superiority of the latter. No one, he thinks, is a true historian without temperament (*ch'i*) and passion (*ch'ing*), though these should be duly controlled by reason (*li*).[65] Impartiality (*kung*) is essential, but it should not be the mere effacement of the historian's personality.[66]

The historian should be free to apply the historiographical forms which best suit his temperament and his subject. Chang Hsüeh-ch'eng proceeds to a thorough review, discussion and re-evaluation of the various forms used in the Chinese historiography of the past. He himself favours neither the annalistic form, whose continuous use has been so harmful to Chinese history, nor the form of the Standard Histories with its restriction to a single dynasty and its mixture of annals, tables, treatises and biographies. This latter form, he thought, had had its hour of vitality with the individual

---

[60] *I-shu*, v, 2a; iv, 19a.                                    [61] 'Historian's virtue', *I-shu*, v, 2a.

[62] These views are developed in the essays 'Doctrine of the Canon of History', *I-shu*, i, 8b–21a, and 'Answering a guest', iv, 42b–50a. 'Synthesis' is a free translation, but, I think, not incorrect, for *yüan-t'ung*, a term heavy with traditional associations.

[63] 'Answering a guest', *I-shu*, iv, 42b–50a.

[64] Letter in answer to Huang Ta-yü, *I-shu*, ix, 1b.

[65] 'Historian's virtue', *I-shu*, v, 2b.

[66] The theory of *kung*, impartiality, objectivity, as opposed to *ssu*, subjectivity, prepossession, is developed in three essays of the *Wen-shih t'ung-i*, *I-shu*, iv, 3a–19a.

authors of the first Standard Histories, Ssu-ma Ch'ien, Pan Ku, Ch'en Shou, Fan Yeh, etc.; but since the T'ang, who had bureaucratized history, it had become a lifeless framework, just as had happened with the programmes for public examinations.[67] His own ideal was the type known as General History (*t'ung-shih*); hence his admiration for the General Treatise (*T'ung-chih*) of Cheng Ch'iao (1104–62), though he well knew of its imperfections.[68] Chang Hsüeh-ch'eng planned to write a Sung History (*Sung shih*), but as usual he did not go beyond plans and drafts. These he discussed in a letter addressed in 1792 to his friend Shao Chin-han, who was also engaged in writing a Sung History.[69] The ideas set forth in this letter are highly nonconformist and show an astonishing freedom in conception and imagination. His *Sung shih*, had he completed it, would have marked a new departure in Chinese historiography.

History is not a mere compilation by bureaucrats, nor is it an amusement for scholars. It should aim at reforming the world, at restoring the Heavenly Tao on Earth; its ultimate purpose is pragmatic and moral. In this respect Chang Hsüeh-ch'eng, who was a pious Confucianist, shared in the moralizing tendency with which Chinese historians have also been reproached (but on that score they are in good company everywhere even today).[70] His notion of the high moral import of history was the main incentive for his diatribes against the philological school of his time. Chang Hsüeh-ch'eng was not blind to the merits of philology; he himself knew how to apply to historical texts the methods of exact research that scholars like Tai Chen or Ch'ien Ta-hsin had perfected for the study of the Confucian Canon. But he refused to admit that scholarship be reduced to a jumble of 'petty studies' (*hsiao-hsüeh*), as philology is called in Chinese—'embroidered girdle-toys, conundrum games', as he called them.[71] He could not jeer enough at those scholars of his day who spent their lives studying a little corner of a single one of the books of the Canon, hoping to attach their name to some minute discovery that would make their colleagues jealous.[72] What ignorance of the Tao, he said, of that Great Tao that the Ancients lived, that they saw and heard in their everyday experience, that was 'their food and their clothing'![73] Neo-Confucianism had tried in vain to react against textual pedantry, against the letter that kills the spirit; it had only succeeded in losing sight of the texts, the very expression of the Tao: it had acted like a physician who, wishing to treat a patient

---

[67] 'Answering a guest', *I-shu*, iv, 43a sq. On Ssu-ma Ch'ien and Pan Ku see the paper by A. F. P. Hulsewé, above, pp. 34–43. On 'bureaucratized history' see also the papers by Yang Lien-sheng and E. Balazs.

[68] Ibid. Chang Hsüeh-ch'eng enumerates eight advantages and three disadvantages of the *t'ung-shih* form in his essay 'Explaining *t'ung*', *I-shu*, iv, 37a–39b.    [69] *I-shu*, ix, 19b–21b.

[70] From 1760 down to 1892 the chair of history at the Collège de France (occupied by Michelet from 1838 to 1851) was called 'chaire d'histoire et de morale'.

[71] 'Explaining History', *I-shu*, v, 6a.    [72] '*Yüan-tao*', *I-shu*, ii, 10a.    [73] Ibid.

for a disease of the viscera, can find no better way than to pull them out.[74]

Chang Hsüeh-ch'eng fought for history on two fronts: on the one hand against too much philosophy on the part of Neo-Confucianism, on the other against too much philology on the part of the Ch'ing critics of Neo-Confucianism. He also rose against his contemporaries for concerning themselves exclusively with the past, with ancient books. History, he maintained, cannot ignore the present. The documents of the past come to life in the light of the present; and their study may also shape the present.[75] History is no mere matter of the past; it should serve to reform the present and foresee the future. We have a truly prophetic letter on the decay of the Ch'ing dynasty addressed by Chang Hsüeh-ch'eng to the executive government on the occasion of Ch'ien-lung's death in 1799.[76] The supreme virtue of the historian is inspiration (*shen*), which enables him, as it is said in the Canon of Changes,[77] to foretell the future, whereas knowledge (*chih*) only serves the purpose of storing up the past. But the one should not be without the other.[78] It is the union of inspiration and knowledge that makes the complete historian, the historian whose science, in Chang Hsüeh-ch'eng's words, 'commands Heaven and Man and glorifies the Great Tao'.[79]

Were we to look for a counterpart of Chang Hsüeh-ch'eng in our own social and cultural background, a name obtrudes itself so forcibly that one might almost be tempted to embark upon an exercise in *bioi paralleloi* such as we used to practise at school. A few hints offered without any claim to serious comparison (which of course would have to stress the differences) may help the reader not familiar with China to form an idea of what Chang Hsüeh-ch'eng means in Chinese culture. Giambattista Vico was almost his contemporary, since he died at Naples in 1744, six years after the birth of his Chinese colleague far away near the coast of the Yellow Sea. Both were infatuated with history and spent their lives reflecting on its import and its philosophical foundations. They had the same ardent and impatient natures; the same independence of mind, the same difficulties in their material careers; the same flashes of genius that shot through peculiar obscurities due to the queer form both gave to their writings and to the restraints of a terminology ill adapted to their thought, for both were original thinkers who exploded the traditional categories of their

---

[74] '*Yüan-tao*', *I-shu*, ii, 12b–13a.

[75] '*Shuo-lin*', *I-shu*, iv, 24b; '*Shih-te*', *I-shu*, v, 6b. In this latter essay, 'Historian's virtue', Chang Hsüeh-ch'eng sings the praises of the Ch'in dynasty, that brushed away the past and restored the state control over education as in the golden age. The Ch'in are also eulogized in '*Yüan-tao*', *I-shu*, ii, 8b. On the authoritarian or totalitarian elements in Chang Hsüeh-ch'eng's thought, see Nivison, 'The Problem . . .', p. 133.

[76] *I-shu*, xxix, 35a–42a; cf. *BEFEO*, xxiii, 487–8. I am not sure who is meant by *chih-cheng* in this letter.     [77] *I-ching*, Hi-tz'u, i, 11 (Legge, 371–2).

[78] *I-shu*, i, 14b–15a; ii, 11b.     [79] 'Answering a guest', *I-shu*, iv, 43b.

day. Vico battled both against Cartesian rationalism and abstraction and against the narrow erudition of the learned compilers and text-critics of his time, who in the wake of the Benedictines, the Bollandists, etc., were preparing the renovation of history in Europe, but whose philology was still divorced from real history and from philosophy; his express aim was to break the bulkhead between philology and philosophy, to fecundate them mutually, to convert the 'certainty' of historical *facts*, as established by philology, into *truths* of reason which were the object of philosophy (*verum ipsum factum*).[80] Vico's conservatism in matters of religion and morality has its parallel in the strict Confucian orthodoxy of Chang Hsüeh-ch'eng, who was resolutely opposed to any sort of scepticism or libertinism. 'There are two things', he wrote, 'all writers should beware of: discussion of the Saints and disrespect for ruler and father.'[81] Some of his contemporaries, such as Wang Chung (1745–94) who dared dethrone Confucius from his supreme position, placing him on the same footing as Mo-tzu,[82] or Yüan Mei (1716–98) with his unconventional ethics, his feminism, his erotic interpretation of the *Kuo-feng*,[83] were his *bêtes noires* and provoked him to outbursts of fury. Vico safeguarded his catholicism by deliberately excluding the *storia sagra*, Biblical history, from his researches. As to Chang Hsüeh-ch'eng, it was certainly against all his intents and purposes that some of his theories were to be invoked later on by the precursors of the Chinese Revolution.[84] And yet there is no doubt that, just as Vico foreboded many trends of modern historiography in Europe, Chang Hsüeh-ch'eng was in advance of his time and heralded a turning-point in the long history of Chinese historiography.

[80] *De antiquissima Italorum sapientia* . . . (1710), I, i; *Scienza nuova seconda* (1744), I, ii, 9–10.
[81] Letter to Ch'ien Ta-hsin (1798), *I-shu*, xxix, 58b.            [82] Yao Ming-ta, 114–16.
[83] Yao Ming-ta, 129–31; also a letter to Sun Hsing-yen (1796), from a manuscript acquired in 1937 by the National Library of Peking and published by Ch'ien Mu, 451–2. The text translated in *BEFEO*, xxiii, 487, is from *I-shu*, v, 24a–25a.
[84] Chang Hsüeh-ch'eng's ambiguous doctrine about the Canon as history was diversely utilized by the pre-reformist writers of the nineteenth century; it was dragged into the quarrel between the *ku-wen* and *chin-wen* schools (cf. Levenson, *FEQ*, xv, 3, 400–2). In his History of Chinese Thought and Scholarship in Modern Times (*Chin-tai Chung-kuo ssu-hsiang hsüeh-shu shih*, Shanghai, 1947), ii, 475–6, Hou Wai-lu presents Chang Hsüeh-ch'eng as an outright assailant of feudalism and a forerunner of democracy. Similar differences of interpretation have arisen in Italy concerning Vico.

# 11. HISTORICAL WRITING IN TWENTIETH-CENTURY CHINA: NOTES ON ITS BACKGROUND AND DEVELOPMENT

J. GRAY

*Lecturer in the History of the Far East,*
*School of Oriental and African Studies, University of London*

The preceding papers have made it clear that the limitations of traditional Chinese historiography were related to the theory of government and society, and of the position of China in the world, which the theory involved. As China was believed to be the only civilized nation, there was no external standard of comparison. As the internal standard was a legendary golden age to which all succeeding regimes were by definition inferior, there could be no concept of progress or development. The monopoly of political authority by the imperially-appointed scholar-officials led to indifference among historians to institutions and groups which did not share this sole source of prestige and power, and led also to a scheme of cause and effect which magnified the role of the bureaucracy almost to the exclusion of other factors. Within this scheme, the essentially moral training of the bureaucracy led to an undue emphasis on moral causes of historical events.

The virtues as well as the vices of traditional historical writing sprang from the same sources. The habit of keeping full and accurate records of events and institutions and of compiling statistics, and the interest in the working of fiscal and political organs, sprang from that very bureaucratic bias which was a limiting factor in other respects. The need to do justice to the career of individual office-holders and scholars produced the unrivalled wealth of biography which survives, and without which, for all its faults, our knowledge of China's past would be considerably poorer. The absence of rival nations and civilizations gave China a sense of continuity: events could usually be interpreted without too much strain on probability, in terms of the recovery or the decline of good government, throughout ages when European history was limited by having nothing to record but the lack of government. If a search for causation was inhibited by, among other factors, the fact that Chinese society was overwhelmingly agrarian, at the same time the fact that imperial and provincial revenues were so closely tied to the prosperity of peasant proprietors, and therefore to their position *vis-à-vis* the locally powerful, to their productivity, and to the state of water control, gave Chinese history a bias towards the recording of social and economic conditions in the countryside which was absent from history in the west.

When the West broke in in the nineteenth century and forced China to accept that her traditional interpretation of her position in the world no longer fitted the facts of the distribution of power, inventiveness and organized political and social life, the revolution which then began was one in which the re-interpretation of China's past inevitably played a key part. Consequently, the writing of history in twentieth-century China was conditioned by the demands and the emotions of the attempted reforms of the late nineteenth century and of the revolution which succeeded them. Reform or revolution could only be justified if the traditional views of China's past were destroyed, and if the appropriate comparisons with the development of other countries were made. Also, the threat of partition in the late nineteenth century, the disunity of the warlord period and consequent helplessness before Japan during the First World War, the results in the Far East of the Versailles Treaty, the conquest of Manchuria by Japan, and western indifference to the event, the final Japanese invasion of 1937, and throughout the whole period perpetual small humiliations, all kept the urgent necessity of a resurgence of nationalism before the eyes of Chinese thinkers, so that the history of modern Chinese historiography is in one aspect part of the history of modern Chinese nationalism. It was also related to the introduction of modern western culture as a whole to China. The effective diffusion of western knowledge in China was packed very largely into a short period before and after 1920, although this intellectual revolution had a much longer pre-history; but in this decade or so of intellectual ferment historians were readily responsive to the swift changes of fashion in science and philosophy, and in sociological theories and methods. The interpretation of China's past was also closely tied up with the embittered political controversies between the Nationalist and Communist parties and within the Marxist group, between Stalinists and Trotskyists. Finally, the economic insecurity of centres of study and of individual historians, and the political chaos of a divided and invaded land made the formation of stable, continuous, and co-ordinated research difficult, although it did not prevent (indeed may even have encouraged) a formidable output of historical writing.

In these circumstances, the writing of a history of the development of modern Chinese historiography must wait on fuller knowledge of the whole political and intellectual revolution, and this in turn must wait on the production of a large number of monographs. There are other obstacles to the production of even the most modest and tentative attempt. The first is the sheer bulk of historical writing: not one per cent of it could be read for the purpose of writing this paper. The second is that most of the best work appeared in scattered, often short-lived, periodicals, of which European holdings are only fragmentary.

Consequently this paper will do no more than sum up briefly the background of development where knowledge of it is at present readily accessible. It does not pretend to offer any but the most tentative conclusions, on what was one of the most prodigious intellectual efforts of modern times.

Three main factors operated in the modernization of Chinese historiography. The first consists of the situation which made a changed interpretation of the national past essential. The second was the means of change available in Chinese historiographic tradition itself. The third was the influence through precept and example of modern western historical scholarship and its vigorous Japanese offshoot. The national situation and its demands on the historian went through changes which will be referred to throughout the rest of the paper.

The limitations of the national tradition are clear. Nevertheless, it had a considerable contribution to make. In the first place, the first essential in many fields of research was the handling and criticism of texts, and here traditional scholars had provided techniques and standards which were a valuable basis for further advance. In the second place, China had had her own critics in the past—so much so that Liang Ch'i-ch'ao was able to criticize traditional historiography in acceptable modern terms largely by quoting the writings of such Chinese historical theorists as Liu Chih-chi and Cheng Ch'iao.[1] In the third place, considerable advances had been made during the Ch'ing dynasty in historiography, advances to which the reluctance of Ch'ing scholars to write works of full historical synthesis should not blind us.

It was in the study of the sources of the history of the classical age that traditional historians could most assist, and from the point of view of revaluating China's past this ancient and supposedly formative period was the key. There had been a long minority tradition of scepticism towards and criticism of the Classical texts, and several of the most prominent early sceptics were historians rather than classical scholars. Liu Chih-chi devoted a chapter to his doubts on the authenticity of several revered texts. Ouyang Hsiu did not accept the commentaries on the Spring and Autumn Annals and refused to believe that Confucius had anything to do with the Book of Changes. Ssu-ma Kuang pointed out inaccuracies in Mencius' references to the ancient period.[2] From the early eighth century onwards there was an almost continuous line of doubters, and if all the doubts had been brought together and examined, it would have been found that very little of the canon and its ancillary texts had been left free of suspicion. The ancient text of the Book of Documents (*Shu Ching*) was the subject of con-

---

[1] See Liang Ch'i-ch'ao, *Yin-p'ing Shih Ho-chi*, chuan 16, pp. 7 ff. On Liu Chih-chi see the paper by E. G. Pulleyblank, above, pp. 136–51.

[2] On Ssu-ma Kuang see the paper by E. G. Pulleyblank, above, pp. 151–66.

tinuous controversy. Confucius' editing of it and of the Odes had been doubted, the *Chou Li* had been proved not to have been written by the Duke of Chou, and Cheng Ch'iao had dismissed the Odes as mere folk-poetry. Doubt had been made respectable to some extent by the example of Chu Hsi, the patriarch of Neo-Confucianism, but when that philosophy became the official orthodoxy Chu Hsi's scepticism was ignored. To the vast majority of scholars the Classics and a great deal of more obviously spurious literature attached to them remained unshaken.

What was missing up to this point was systematic method. With the exception of the Modern Script school, who refused to accept the Ancient Script texts,[3] the early sceptics were isolated individuals who had been struck by isolated anomalies. Only in the Ming dynasty were attempts made to bring all the doubts together into one publication and so lay the basis for organized study.[4]

The controversy over the authenticity of the Ancient Script produced more sustained and detailed arguments, but it was ineffective because the supporters of the Modern Script were at least as credulous as their rivals towards the texts which they favoured. Nevertheless, an examination of the controversy shows that all the same types of criticism as were employed in modern times to attack the classics as a whole were used at one time or another to attack parts of the Ancient or Modern scripts. For example, the checking of texts for corruptions by means of checking rhymes in the ancient pronunciation, the comparison of current texts with passages in other books purporting to be quoted from the original work, even the use of archaeological data for a comparison of style, and many other techniques of later importance, are all to be found in works on the Ancient and Modern Scripts controversy between the Sung and Ming dynasties. One is forced to the conclusion that the need was not so much for new methods as for a change in the intellectual climate which would stimulate the systematic development of the means already available.

Such a change of intellectual climate had to some extent been provided by the fall of the Chinese Ming dynasty and the conquest of China by the Manchus. This event produced a profound effect on many men who lived through it. The nationalist reaction, especially of men associated with the Tunglin opposition group, and the need they felt for a profound examination of why the Ming dynasty had collapsed, were not unlike the situation

[3] The controversy over Ancient and Modern Scripts centred on problems concerning the Book of Documents (*Shu Ching*). The extant version of this work can be divided into two parts: (*a*) chapters deriving from a so-called *ku wen* (ancient style characters) text; (*b*) chapters deriving from a so-called *chin wen* (new style characters) text. It is generally accepted that (*a*) were forged after Han times, but this still leaves the earlier problem of the authenticity of a *ku wen* text which was current in Han times. See P. Pelliot, 'Le Chou King en caractères anciens et le Chang chou che wen' (*Mémoires concernant l'Asie Orientale*, ii, Paris, 1916) and B. Karlgren, *Philology and ancient China* (Oslo, 1926), pp. 95–100.

[4] In the General Study of Forgeries (*Ssu-pu Cheng Wei*), published in 1568.

produced by the nineteenth century defeats of China by the Western powers, and provided one of the most stimulating intellectual shocks in Chinese history.

The results in the field of history proper will be considered below. In classical studies the effect was to produce an attempt to sweep aside the exegesis which had accumulated round the Classics since the T'ang dynasty, to get back to the originals, and to restore the texts as far as possible, mainly by philological methods.

This group of men, closely bound in loyalty to the defeated Ming and in a common attitude to classical studies derived from their concern at the decay of Chinese society, were able to found for the first time a co-operative, organized, and continuous group of studies associated with textual criticism. Co-operation made inductive studies possible; something like an inductive science of the study of the phonetics of ancient Chinese was founded and maintained through the eighteenth and nineteenth centuries.[5] However, the faith in the Classics which was a fundamental factor in the motivation of the school at the same time set limits to their criticisms. As Kaizuka Shigeki writes,[6] their work was based 'on the supposition that the Classics were the surviving and accurate records of the rule of the ancient sage kings, forming a unitary body of facts, all records of events within which were of equal historical value, their contradictions being capable of resolution by the correction of the texts'. Consequently the school, for all its historical acumen in other fields and its normal bias towards historical rather than philosophical solutions, failed to take a historical view of the classics, and failed in particular to use its unprecedentedly exact knowledge of the texts to study their historical interrelations. The school remained, in fact, as far as its classicist aspect is concerned, essentially conservative.

Others not directly associated with the school, however, used the new techniques in a more critical manner, and in the course of the mid-Ch'ing dynasty several classical texts were proved to be forgeries. The Ancient Script version of the Book of History finally succumbed to three independently written attacks of which the most influential was that of Yen Jo-chü.[7] The 'River Diagrams' which were an important part of the basis of the cosmology of the orthodox Neo-Confucian school were proved by

[5] The degree to which the methods of Ch'ing classical scholarship were analogous to those of contemporary European science was discussed in an influential essay by Hu Shih. See *Hu Shih Wen Ts'un*, ii, 539.

[6] See Kaizuka Shigeki's Introduction to Chinese History (*Chūgoku Rekishi Nyūmon*), p. 31, for a brief account of the development of the study of the history of the classical age.

[7] Yen Jo-chü (1636–1704), *Shang Shu Ku-wen Shu-cheng*, first printed in 1745. The other major attack on the authenticity of the Ancient Script version of the Book of Documents was by Hui Tung in his *Ku-wen Shang Shu K'ao* (1774). Ts'ui Shu (see below, p. 191, n. 9), or more probably his brother Ts'ui Mai, came to similar conclusions.

Hu Wei to be forgeries of late date.[8] The *K'ao Hsin Lü* of Ts'ui Shu,[9] a general examination of the authenticity of ancient works, carried scepticism to a new height. The conscious objectivity of Ts'ui Shu's writing is comparable with that of the eighteenth-century sceptics of Europe.

In the field of history proper, Chinese precedents also offered a basis—and more important, an acceptable, because Chinese, rationale—for modernization. In his Methodology for the Study of Chinese History, Liang Ch'i-ch'ao built up his case against traditional concepts of history by a series of quotations from China's own critics of the old ideas.[10] He quotes Liu Chih-chi, Cheng Ch'iao and Chang Hsüeh-ch'eng on the limitations of dynastic history, of the composite annals-biography (*chi-chuan*) form, and of compilation by official committees in place of private individuals. He quotes Liu Chih-chi again on the inconvenience of the chronicle form. The Sung scholar Yang Wan-li is quoted on arrangement by topics (the *chi-shih pen-mo* form) and Liang's comments imply that Yang favoured it because it made possible a proper exposition of cause and effect.[11] The ideas of the men thus quoted have been touched on in earlier papers. It is sufficient to point out here that Liang, in this most influential of all essays on historiography in this formative period, is able to lean so heavily for support on Chinese historical theorists in building up a case against Chinese traditional writing.

If there were some helpful Chinese precepts, there were apparently fewer Chinese examples which were relevant to Liang's conception of history. In his account of Ch'ing dynasty historiography he singles out for praise only four works: The Topographical Essentials for the Study of History by Ku Tsu-yu;[12] the Exposition of Events in the Spring and Autumn Annals by Ku Tung-kao;[13] the Studies of Ming Confucian Scholars by Huang Tsung-hsi;[14] and the Notes on the Twenty-two His-

[8] See Hu Wei, *I-t'u Ming Pien* (1706), which completed the work of Huang Tsung-yen, brother of Huang Tsung-hsi (see below, pp. 192–3) and of Mao Ch'i-ling.

[9] Ts'ui Shu, *K'ao-hsin Lü* (Record of Enquiry into Beliefs), was written between 1783 and 1814. It was printed in 1824–5 but almost completely neglected until it was reprinted in Japan by Naka Michiyo in 1903–4. Interest in Ts'ui Shu was revived in China by Hu Shih and Ku Chieh-kang (see below, pp. 202–4) and his influence on the modernization of Chinese thought was very great. A definitive edition of his few surviving works was edited by Ku Chieh-kang and printed in 1936.

[10] See *Yin-p'ing Shih Ho-chi*, chuan 16, pp. 7 ff.

[11] Ibid., p. 20, where Liang gives his own favourable opinion of the *chi-shih pen-mo* form as a gloss on his quotation of Yang which reads: 'The completion of an affair is recorded after its origins have been described, and the details of its development precede the account of how it is finally resolved. Thus circumstance which would otherwise remains hidden are revealed, and the minute and scattered causes of the event are brought together.'

[12] Ku Tsu-yü (1631–92), *Tu Shih Fang-yü Chi-yao*, first printed between 1796 and 1821 in a combined edition with the *T'ien-hsia Chün-kuo Li-ping Shu* of Ku Yen-wu (see below, pp. 192–4).

[13] Ku Tung-kao (1679–1759), *Ch'un-ch'iu Ta-shih Piao*, printed about 1748.

[14] Huang Tsung-hsi (1610–95), *Ming-ju Hsüeh-an*, completed in 1676. Later, Huang began a similar work on the philosophers of Sung and Yüan, which was completed by his pupil Ch'üan Tsu-wang.

tories of Chao I.[15] These, says Liang, were the only creative historical works of the period. The first he singles out for having reached a new level in the organization of historical materials, the second for the methods used to reorganize the material of the Ts'o Commentary. The third he regards as being 'the true beginning of Chinese historiography'; the fourth had transcended the narrow *k'ao-cheng* methods of the Ch'ien Lung period to 'teach us how to search for vivid and significant historical materials'.

Liang was concerned here to use Chinese examples to fortify ideas drawn from the modern west; he was not attempting to evaluate Ch'ing dynasty historiography as a whole. As a whole, indeed, it was more useful in providing bad examples than good, and the absence of attempts at the writing of full syntheses made it uninteresting to a generation to which the task of history was to provide broad reinterpretations. Nevertheless, although modern Chinese historians might affect to despise Ch'ing historical writing, they were obliged to make use of it. The west could provide a deeper consciousness of historical ends and means, but even for those Chinese historians who had the opportunity to study thoroughly the actual historical writing of the west, as opposed to translations of theoretical textbooks of historiography (usually indifferent and out of date), the only possible practical training in the study of Chinese history was based on Ch'ing writing. The west might provide the ideals, but Ch'ing scholarship provided the day-to-day habits of research.

The value as well as the influence of the heritage of Ch'ing dynasty historiography has perhaps been underestimated. There has been a tendency both in China and abroad to condemn the Ch'ing tradition as one of pedantry, to accept in fact the opinions of the Neo-Confucian opposition, who contrasted their own broad views with the hair-splitting criticism of the Han-hsüeh tradition. In accepting this condemnation we forget, first, that the Neo-Confucian point of view was essentially unhistorical, and that their criticisms applied to almost everything which could be called history. Second, we forget that the Ch'ing tradition of historiography, although it may have become narrow and pointless, was not founded by pedants. It was begun by men whom a national disaster had forced to reconsider the past in the hope of preventing a repetition of disaster. Its first motivation was essentially practical. A summary of the background of some of the leading figures of the movement will illustrate this. Huang Tsung-hsi was the son of a Tunglin martyr and himself a member of the Fu-she group which was the spearhead of the Tunglin opposition to the eunuch rule of late Ming. When North China was lost to the Ch'ing armies, he organized the defence of his native city with his own resources and the assistance of other local volunteers. When the Ch'ing completed their conquest, he refused to serve them. Ku Yen-wu had already begun in the last years of

15 Chao I (1727–1814), *Nien-erh shih cha-chi*, completed in 1796 and printed in 1799.

Ming to turn his studies to more practical matters in opposition to contemporary policies and scholarship. He too organized local defence in his native area and after defeat refused to serve the conquerors. Wang Fuchih retreated south with the Ming princes but left them in disgust at the continued faction struggles in the southern courts and went into retirement.

Although their philosophical opinions differed, their common patriotism and their common experience of the paralysis of late Ming China produced political theories closely similar, which amounted, briefly, to the condemnation of autocracy and over-centralization. This was combined with condemnation of Sung philosophy and scholarship, the impracticality of which they regarded as having been a fundamental cause of the decay of China under the Ming. In contrast, they turned to a historical view of events. Wang Fu-chih's historical writing[16] was in fact an attempt at inductive proof of a historical hypothesis: that China had been strongest and best able to repel barbarians when her provinces had been strongest, even and perhaps especially when this had meant a corresponding weakening of the central government. Ku Yen-wu was inclined to similar views; and although he did not express them so precisely, the nature of his major historical work (*T'ien-hsia Chün-kuo Li-ping Shu*) implies them: it was an encyclopaedic compilation of historical material on the topography, defence, water conservancy, taxation, and social conditions of China, significantly arranged locality by locality.[17] Huang Tsung-hsi cast his anti-autocratic opinions in a historical form in a book entitled *Ming I Tai Fang Lu*.[18] His greatest historical work, however, was his history of Ming scholarship (*Ming-ju hsüeh-an*) which, in pursuit of the idea of the connection between Sung philosophy and the decay of Ming, traced carefully the rise, development, and decline of the different schools and documented their interrelations, maintaining throughout, in spite of the polemical origins of the work, a scrupulous impartiality.

Other aspects of early Ch'ing historical studies fill out this picture. The historical geographies of the period were almost all inspired, not like those in later times by an academic interest in the identification of ancient place-names (although the problem could not be avoided), but by a practical interest in the defence of China. Each local section of Ku Yen-wu's

[16] Wang Fu-chih (1619–92). His chief historical works were his *Tu T'ung Chien Lun* and *Sung Lun*, which consist mainly of comments from the point of view of his political principles, but also partly of critical comments of considerable value. He also wrote two short works of political theory, his *Huang Shu* and *E Meng*. Very little of his work was printed before the twentieth century and consequently it escaped the Manchu censorship which distorted the work of his contemporaries, among whom similar opinions may have been very common.

[17] Ku Yen-wu (1613–82), *T'ien-hsia Chün-kuo Li-ping Shu*, compiled between 1639 and 1662 and first printed 1796 and 1821. His *Jih-chih Lu* (Notes on Daily Learning) has sections of historical comment which were the basis of his very great influence on subsequent historians.

[18] *Ming I Tai Fang Lu*, written in 1662, had little influence until interest in it was revived by the revolutionaries of the twentieth century.

*T'ien-hsia Chün-kuo Li-ping Shu* begins with a consideration of local topography, the siting of garrisons, and the military history of the area. In his
Daily Learning (*Jih-chih Lu*) the section on Historical Method is headed by
a note which also shows his interest in military history: it consists of a
number of quotations showing that both Ssu-ma Ch'ien and Ssu-ma
Kuang always described military campaigns in as much detail as possible,
whereas Chu Hsi's abridgement of the Comprehensive Mirror cuts out all
such detail as unimportant, thus showing, Ku comments, that 'Chu Hsi
missed Ssu-ma Kuang's point'. It was Ku Yen-wu's relative Ku Tsu-yu,
however, who carried out the most systematic study of historical geography
from the strategic point of view.[19] The son of a scholar of late Ming
interested in the same subject, Tsu-yu fought against the Manchus with
the Cheng rebels in Formosa. In method, his work shows great critical
acumen in the selection of materials. In conception, 'it takes geography as
the warp and historical events as the woof', as Liang Ch'i-chao wrote of it.
His discussions of the location of the capital and of what he calls 'strategic
points', 'areas of logistic weakness', 'trouble spots' and 'basic areas', have
for the first time in Chinese historiography something of the Machiavellian
quality in them. He argues objectively from the nature of the locality and
from inductively demonstrated tendencies for it to be militarily vital or
politically troublesome, and so the simple orthodox concept of interior
versus borders is broken down by this close and intelligent historical
analysis.

The interest in technology which produced the *T'ien Kung K'ai Wu* and
Hsü Kuang-ch'i's *Nung-cheng ch'üan-shu*[20] is not irrelevant. Personal connections between the technologists and the historians were close, and the
two forms of study overlapped in some cases. Ku Yen-wu's historical
studies of local water conservancy were clearly related to his own practical
ventures in land reclamation; to complement this, Liu Hsien-t'ing[21] regarded the production of a good edition of the Classic of Waterways as an
essential step in his practical scheme for the extension of irrigation in the
North West.

There is no doubt in fact that the founders of the Ch'ing tradition of
historiography were not mere pious and pedantic exegesists, but included
men most conspicuous for their concern with practical problems of administration, defence, and technology, and most emotionally involved in

[19] i.e. *Tu Shih Fang-yü Chi-yao*; see above, p. 191, n. 12.
[20] The *T'ien-Kung K'ai-Wu* of Sung Ying-hsing, published in 1637, a treatise on technology,
survived only in Japan, where it was reprinted several times from 1771 onwards. It was reprinted
in China in 1927. The *Nung-cheng ch'üan-shu* of Hsü Kuang-ch'i (1552–1623), was the most elaborate compilation up to that time on Chinese agricultural technology. The author was a convert of
Ricci.
[21] Liu Hsien-t'ing (1648–95). His technological interests were probably inspired by the Jesuit
missionaries, like those of Hsü Kuan-ch'i (see preceding note). See Naitō Torajiro, *Shina Shigaku
Shi*, p. 413, and A. W. Hummel, *Eminent Chinese of the Ch'ing Dynasty*, p. 521.

the supreme political problem of their age. Even their absorption in classical studies sprang from these practical roots: Neo-Confucianism, they believed, was an impractical view of life and must be replaced; its replacement demanded first of all an attack on its view of the classics; and this could best be done by sweeping aside the Sung commentaries and penetrating to the original texts, first to restore them, then to re-interpret them.

It may be argued that all this was no more than the traditional attitude to history in its relation to contemporary government. It was no longer, however, merely the study of past administration in order to improve present-day administration. Perplexity over the fall of Ming produced new schemes of cause and effect in the work of Wang Fu-chih and Huang Tsung-hsi; and if Ku Yen-wu and his school were suspicious of easy hypothecation, nevertheless the *Li-ping Shu* collection implies a causal nexus richer than any which had preceded it in Chinese historiography. A new subtlety also appears in Wang Fu-chih's discussion of 'praise and blame', in his insistence that no individual is entirely good or bad, and that how a man behaves in a crisis depends as much on circumstances as on his character. The implication clearly is that the character of the individual is usually only one factor in a complex of causes.

In the early years of the dynasty, the centres of historical research were thus largely anti-Manchu—the loyalist groups themselves, the Ming History Compilation Board in which through their pupils and associates the loyalists were influential, and the island on the T'ai Hu lake where other loyalists infiltrated the compilation board of the Imperial Gazetteer. By the reign of Ch'ien Lung, the Ming survivors were long dead, the compilation of the Ming History had dragged on into a new generation of compilers, the Imperial Gazetteer had been steered away from contemporary political purposes by Yen Jo-chü, and the compilation of the Complete Library in Four Sections (*Ssu-k'u ch'üan-shu*) had brought the most prominent scholars in China under the patronage—and the censorship—of the Manchu government. The original motivation of the historical schools had largely faded, while the Ch'ien Lung inquisition harried the remnants of opposition with a severity out of all proportion to their importance. If any historians of the period were still interested in the problems which had obsessed the founders of the Liang Che schools, they apparently thought it safer to keep their attention elsewhere. Historians as a whole contented themselves with the leisurely pursuit of *k'ao-cheng* textual studies which tended to become an end in themselves. Typically, the historical geographers of the school of Ku Tsu-yu were ridiculed by Hung Liang-ch'i, Tai Chen, and Chang Hsüeh-ch'eng, and historical geography was put in its place as a branch of *k'ao-cheng*.[22]

[22] On *k'ao-cheng* studies generally and Chang Hsüeh-ch'eng in particular, see the paper by P. Demiéville, above, pp. 167–85.

On the other hand, there were gains. In an atmosphere (pace Chang Hsüeh-cheng's complaints) of encouragement, economic security, and academic calm, *k'ao-cheng* history began to develop towards an organized co-operative enterprise, as *k'ao-cheng* classical studies had already done. Phonetic studies, the use of epigraphy, and chronological and geographical ancillary studies, which had all been pioneered in early Ch'ing, now became normal tools of historical research, used with confidence and discipline by numerous scholars.

Other tenets of the Liang Che founders were taken up and developed. Ku Yen-wu's belief that the historian has a primary duty to make use of all surviving relevant sources was taken up and widely applied. The *I Shih* of Ma Su[23] was the most monumental effort of this kind, incorporating all surviving literary material, including lost texts reconstructed for the purpose from later quotations, to make up a topically arranged compilation (*chi-shih pen-mo*) of China's ancient history; but although as a feat of scholarly endurance it does justice to Ku Yen-wu's idea, it is wholly uncritical and indiscriminate in its use of the materials. With this exception, attempts to use existing material to the full did not take the form of new synthesis, but of commentaries on existing texts. Many of these, however, were so full and elaborate that we must recognize in them the first tentative steps towards the production of new historical works. Of special significance among these were works in which the separate dynastic histories of periods of political division in China were collated into single, though not yet fully synthesized, wholes.[24] The climax of the use of the widest possible range of materials came with the *Shih-ch'i shih shang-chüeh* of Wang Ming-sheng (1722–98), printed in 1787, which used not only conventional materials and private histories, but epigraphy, local gazetteers, novels, belles lettres, family archives, and Buddhist and Taoist works.

The most distinguished figure in Ch'ien Lung scholarship was the prolific historian and classicist, Ch'ien Ta-hsin.[25] His work, and the choice of subjects for his many biographies, show his close adherence to the ideals and methods of Ku Yen-wu, although he did not express his theoretical views at length. His greatest quality was, as Naitō Torajiro puts it, 'an unrivalled exact knowledge of what could usefully be used as historical material for a given subject', a knowledge which he applied in exacting and comprehensive critical studies. His most influential work was his Investigations into Discrepancies in the Twenty-two Histories (*Nien-erh shih k'ao-i*), completed in 1782. It was typical of the scholarship of his age

[23] Ma Su (1621–1673), *I Shih*, printed in 1670.

[24] Of these the most important was the collation of the histories of the Five Dynasties by P'eng Yüan-sui in his *Wu Tai Shih Chi-chu*. Of this work Naitō Torajiro writes (op. cit., p. 421): 'From a modern point of view his method is entirely scientific.'

[25] See Hummel, op. cit., p. 152, for a brief biography of Ch'ien Ta-hsin by Tu Lien-che; also Naitō Torajiro, op. cit., p. 438.

that while on occasions he held official appointments, for most of his life he was employed as a teacher in the great privately-endowed academies of the time.

Although the attitudes of Ku Yen-wu, Wang Fu-chih, and Huang Tsung-hsi had disappeared, they had secured one important negative victory in the complete ousting of the praise-and-blame school. Moreover, their attitudes were not so completely rejected as is often supposed. Even Ch'ien Ta-hsin, the most accomplished and prolific of the textual *k'ao-cheng* school of the Ch'ien Lung period, still insisted that the purpose of history was to study 'institutional change'. Perhaps, in fact, concentration on *k'ao-cheng*, on the recovery of lost texts and the use of hitherto neglected sources, and on the production of research aids, and the reluctance actually to compose new history, was, in the state of the subject, more scholarly than we now tend to assume. At any rate, the strictures of Chang Hsüeh-ch'eng, written as they were from the lonely heights of a new metaphysical view of the nature and importance of history, tended to be somewhat exaggerated.

Summing up what Ch'ing historiography passed on to its revolutionary successors, we can point to several significant factors. First, an example was provided of the work of a group of impassioned patriots in circumstances not altogether dissimilar from those of late nineteenth- and twentieth-century China. If Ku Yen-wu, Wang Fu-chih, and Huang Tsung-hsi were regarded as nationalist political theorists rather than as historians, their influence on historical writing was none the less (and may actually have been the greater) for that. Second, a large number of works were produced in which contradictions and omissions of the Standard Histories had been pointed out, resolved or amended. Third, a mass of necessary ancillary studies of all kinds were provided, many of which have still not been superseded. Fourth, a critical discipline was developed, already applied in detail to many problems of, for example, the authenticity of texts, or the determination of dates, which might certainly have been developed from foreign examples, but only at a great expenditure of training, ingenuity, and drudgery which the circumstances of revolutionary China might have made both difficult to organize and intellectually distasteful. Fifth, there was a significant expansion of the source material available, and precedents for the use of a wider range of types of material. Sixth, an appreciation was shown of the necessity of studies at the local as well as the national level, expressed as a political conviction by Wang Fu-chih and Ku Yen-wu, elaborated in theory by Chang Hsüeh-ch'eng, and put into practice by a large number of historians, in however unsatisfactory a way.

Foreign influences entered China from the Opium War onwards, but on the intellectual level they were insignificant until the last decade of the nineteenth century. In strong contrast to the situation in Japan, conservatives opposed to westernization controlled the government of China and the first study and translation of foreign works was carried on only surreptitiously, under cover of the diplomatic Language School founded in 1861 after the occupation of Peking by Anglo-French forces. Further translation work was done in the 'seventies and 'eighties by the Kianguan Arsenal. It was, however, only under the leadership of K'ang Yu-wei in the 'nineties, that the first significant beginning was made in the study of western thought and western society; and it was in the newspapers and journals of his Society for National Rejuvenation (Ch'iang Hsüeh Hui) and in associated reforming publications that some of the first and most important translations and discussions took place. The influence of the west spread from its centres in Canton and Shanghai to small but vigorous groups in the inland provinces.

The first major step towards the re-interpretation of Chinese history was taken in the context of K'ang's reform movement. K'ang had passed the metropolitan examination with distinction and therefore had a claim on the attention of Chinese scholars. He was in a position to appeal to them for support on their own grounds, and in two works he put forward a new view of the classical age and of the meaning of Confucianism. He rejected the view that Confucius was the conservative transmitter of the actual records of a golden age. Instead, he argued, Confucius had invented these records in order to support his own revolutionary ideas on society and government; he had in fact 'twisted the past in favour of present changes'. This was an abuse of learning of which many Chinese scholars in the past had been accused, but in the case of Confucius it was presumably justified by the transcendent value of his ideas. Confucius, in fact, referred not to the past but to the future of mankind. From the Li Yün section of the Book of Rites, K'ang took the theory of three ages of human society—the age of chaos, the age of recovery, and the final age of the Great Harmony —and made this very uninfluential and obscure speculation the centre of his interpretation of Confucian thought, supporting his ideas by a strained interpretation of the bare and factual chronological entries of the Spring and Autumn Annals. The highest possible credentials were thus to be bestowed on the reformers.

This theory was a mixture of Chinese and western elements. From the west came the rejection of the Golden Age idea and its replacement by an evolutionary concept, as well as the whole system of anti-autocratic political theory and the advocacy of civil liberties and the rule of law which was now fathered on Confucius. From Chinese scholarship came, first, the technique by which those among the revered texts which were inconvenient from the point of view of this interpretation were demonstrated to be forgeries of the period of the Wang Mang usurpation (a less excusable 'twisting of the past in favour of present changes'). Second, the strained interpretation of the laconic Spring and Autumn Annals, made possible by the use of the Kung Yang in place of the Tso commentary, was derived from the same Modern Script party.[26]

K'ang's historical conclusions were too naive to make converts among the conservatives and made only very temporary conquests among the radical party; but many of his arguments were good and his critical methods were so arresting that the first chapter of his book Confucius as a Reformer (*K'ung-tzu Kai-chih K'ao*) may be said without too much exaggeration to be the effective starting point of modern Chinese historiography.

K'ang's reform movement failed and he and his followers were scattered in exile. Liang Ch'i-ch'ao escaped in a Japanese warship; K'ang escaped with the connivance of a British consul. K'ang's subsequent career in both politics and scholarship was unimportant; but Liang Ch'i-ch'ao continued to develop and in his exile in Japan and his travels during the same period was able to build up a then unrivalled knowledge of western learning which made him the most influential figure in journalism and scholarship for the first twenty years of the new century.

K'ang Yu-wei, a member of the gentry and a graduate steeped in traditional ways of thought, had sought to reconcile reform with traditional beliefs and loyalties. Liang Ch'i-ch'ao until his exile in Japan and his foreign travels accepted Kang's point of view, but wider reading of foreign history and first-hand acquaintance with modern western life soon made the maintenance of K'ang's attitudes impossible. Levenson's study of Liang[27] shows that the basis of this thought was a conflict between his emotional need to be loyal to Chinese traditions and his acceptance of the necessity of reforms based on European examples. In a flood of comment on the history of East and West (spread mainly over the years 1899–1912, that is, between his having outgrown K'ang's ideas and his return to China and to active politics), Liang tried one expedient after another to reconcile this contradiction. He started from the belief that the Classics if purified and understood aright provided a revelation which not only contained the desirable western values but expressed them at a more universal level. Greater experience of the west, however, forced him towards the unpleasant conclusion that the classics were really irrelevant to China's

[26] See K'ang Yu-wei, *Hsin-süeh Wei-ching K'ao* (1891) and *K'ung-tzu Kai-chih K'ao* (1897). In the form used by K'ang this interpretation of the Kung Yang Commentary is traceable to Wei Yuan and Kung Tzu-chen, who had revived the Modern Script point of view in the early nineteenth century; and it is interesting that in the hands of his predecessors, as well as of K'ang Yu-wei himself, the Modern Script theories were identified with reforming tendencies, especially in the case of Chuang Ts'un-yü (1719–88) and Kuang Tzu-chen (1792–1841), the founder and chief popularizer respectively of the Modern Script school. K'ang's strength as a scholar came, however, from his having enjoyed the eclectic teaching, exceptionally liberal and tolerant for its time, of the Cantonese Neo-Confucian scholar Chu Tz'u-ch'i.

[27] J. R. Levenson, *Liang Ch'i-ch'ao and the mind of Modern China* (1953).

modern problems. Another rationalization had to be found for continued loyalty, so reverence for Chinese culture is replaced by loyalty to the nation—his traditional culturalism becomes something more like modern nationalism. At the same time, the oppressive sense of the superiority of the west is soothed by a number of devices of historical explanation. His 'Great Harmony' idea of progress derived from K'ang's Confucius as a Reformer gives way to a form of social Darwinism which reduces history to a war of each against all and splits the conception of the west into the conception of separate nations unequal in power and creativity and all more or less flawed; China is thus not so exceptional. At the same time, he attempts to put the credit for European progress on individual genius rather than regional, racial, or social characteristics. Finally, he begins to take comfort in the fact that what is to be admired in the west—democracy, the rule of law, technology, and scientific creativity—are extremely modern in origin as well as incomplete. Chinese history can be rationalized against this background in a less uncomfortably humiliating way. The conclusion which issues from these speculations is that China's ancient adjustments being better than those of the west, with a real but limited self-government in the family and the absence (after the Chou dynasty) of an aristocracy, there was not the same stimulus to struggle for freedom, so the Chinese system gradually hardened into an autocracy which was actually contrary to the spirit of Chinese tradition. More generally speaking, it was the fact that China's society was classless that made it superior to that of pre-modern Europe while giving it less incentive to develop.

In this phase of Liang's thought, we are already halfway to the final phase in which western culture is rejected as materialistic and Liang returns to belief in the superiority of Chinese society and culture in its suppositious stressing of non-materialist ends. His rejection of the west, already implicit in his writings, came after China's 'betrayal' at the Versailles Peace Conference, but it also reflected (and constantly quoted) European self-disgust after the First World War.

Thus Liang's view of Chinese tradition goes through several phases: first, it contains all human wisdom if read aright; next, it is expendable if necessary for China's survival as a nation; third, this uncomfortable possibility is softened by whittling the concept of 'western culture' down to the great and unique Anglo-Saxons and the others who are not much better than China and who have not been at all better for very long; fourth, however slight the comparative claims of Chinese tradition, they must be emphasized as a basis for national pride and revived national feeling; fifth, western culture is inferior in that it cannot control the power it has created.

This is the background and the motivation of Liang's most influential period, as analysed by Levenson. The analysis, however, leaves some aspects of the question almost untouched. Liang's opposition to Sun Yat-sen's party probably had more influence on his thinking than is suggested. The western materialism which he rejected may well have been in fact the anti-landlord social programme of Sun Yat-sen's Three Principles and the pragmatism which he was reluctant to accept may well have been the pragmatism of Sun Yat-sen—the peasant brought up not on Confucian scholarship but amid Taiping legends; educated not in the traditional academies but in a western medical college; residing abroad in the first place not as an exiled intellectual but as a member of a westernized Chinese business community; wholly indifferent to Confucianism and hostile to the privileges it sanctioned; advocating a nationalism based not on the educated gentry minority to whom Liang appealed and whom he continued to regard as the inevitable leaders of Chinese society, but on the rousing of the peasant masses to a sense of common purpose in the creation of a new world.

Also, Levenson's contrast of tradition versus innovation is too simple. Chinese tradition did not even for Liang have to be rejected as a whole or preserved as a whole; and the weakness of Levenson's argument lies in the assumption of this unnecessarily rigid dichotomy.

Although the period 1900 to 1919 is that of Liang Ch'i-ch'ao's greatest influence, the period thereafter is that of his best historical writing. With journalism and politics behind him, he turned to academic life, and with the advantages which his broad studies of world history had brought him, continued research in Chinese intellectual history, free at last from the necessity of constant attempts at value comparisons. In this period, his contributions to the history of Chinese Buddhism were his most important work.

In this period also he produced in his Methodology for the Study of Chinese History[28] and its Continuation, his maturest thoughts on historical theory. He argued that history was potentially a positive science, although one hampered by dependence on incomplete data, and advocated an empirical attitude, but in spite of this he could not wholly shake himself free of the idea that history should be the servant of nationalism. Indeed he maintained a sort of 'praise and blame' attitude, although the objects of censure or adulation now included groups as well as persons, and on occasion the whole nation.

Although his theory was influential, his insistence that the duty of the historian was, essentially, the feeding and guiding of national feeling, was already somewhat anachronistic; the development of the revolution had already begun to provide more complex problems to stimulate historians. But Liang's own work had provided in the first place a much richer store of possible approaches to China's past. Moreover, he had introduced a generation of Chinese students in Japan, as well as a larger public in China, to modern Japanese historical writing, and therefore to modern

[28] See above, p. 191 and n. 10, n. 11.

Japanese studies of Chinese history. The first modern attempt at a general history of China was directly inspired by the work of the Japanese historians Naka Michiyō and Kuwabara Jitsuzō, and was written by Liang's fellow-pupil of K'ang Yu-wei, Hsia Tseng-yu.[29]

A considerable part of the importance of Liang's book, and of so much more of his writing, was semantic: his real genius lay in his ability to invent Chinese equivalents for European ideas out of a vocabulary encrusted with three thousand years' accumulation of unique associations. Japanese usage helped Liang and others in this respect. Nevertheless, later theorists and translators of European theory were largely dependent on the results of Liang's almost poetic gifts.

Finally, Liang had widened the definition of Chinese culture in his search for new elements of value outside the Classics. Chinese Buddhist philosophy was a part of the curriculum of the Wan Mu Ts'ao College of K'ang Yu-wei, and provided essential elements in the Great Harmony utopian scheme. Liang's work also revived interest in the non-Confucian thinkers of the Warring States period.

His influence in this respect, however (in spite of Hu Shih's tribute)[30] was the least of several. New aspects of the Chinese past were becoming of interest and consequently new kinds of materials were assuming the dignity of historical sources. The emergence of modern Chinese nationalism and the study of other cultures brought about an interest in Chinese popular culture in its forms of drama, folk-song, and folk-tales, and the traditional novels and short stories. Societies were formed for their study, and three scholars independently began to work on their history. Wang Kuo-wei published his first studies of the history of Chinese drama,[31] which have never been wholly superseded. Hu Shih returned from America in 1917 and produced in 1918 his influential preface to a new edition of the Dream of the Red Chamber, in which he justified the writing of the history of popular literature and outlined a method of approach. Similar studies were pursued by Ku Chieh-kang.[32] These studies were not only

[29] For a brief study of this work and its background, see Chou Yü-t'ung, 'Wu-shih nien lai Chung-kuo chih Hsin Shih-hsüeh' (China's new historiography in the last fifty years), in *Hsüeh Lin*, iv, 1. The great influence of Japanese thought and scholarship on developments in China still remains a neglected subject in the west, although most western influence in China came via Japan. This subject, however, would need a separate and lengthy study.

[30] Hu Shih, *Ssu-shih Tzŭ-hsü*, p. 108, writes that Liang's essay 'Chung-kuo hsüeh-an ssu-hsiang pien-ch'ien chih ta-shih' (Changing trends in Chinese scholarship and thought) 'opened up a new world for me; it made me know that outside the Four Books and the Five Classics China yet had learning and thought.' Quoted in Levenson, op. cit., p. 83.

[31] See his history of Sung and Yüan drama (*Sung Yüan Hsi-ch'ü Shih*), the most influential of Wang's many works on popular literature.

[32] The autobiographical preface which Ku wrote for the first volume of the symposium Discussions on Ancient History was translated by A. W. Hummel and published (Leyden, 1931) as *The Autobiography of a Chinese Historian*. It provides a good, though one-sided, picture of the historiographical aspects of the modern Chinese revolution.

intrinsically interesting. They also supplied, through Ku Chieh-kang, a new and initially devastating approach to the classical texts. Ku was born into a scholarly family and received a thorough training in classical studies from his grandfather, a student of Han-hsüeh philology. He was then sent to a western-type school and received an education which gave him some elementary idea of scientific method. In common with his schoolmates, he became an ardent supporter of Sun Yat-sen and the revolution; but partly because of his impatience with the 'empty talk' of his fellow conspirators, and partly from a feeling that he was not by nature a leader of men and could have little to contribute to politics, he turned his revolutionary iconoclasm to the field he knew best, the field of classical scholarship. He entered Peking University and studied under Chang Ping-lin. Chang was a supporter of the Republican revolution, but of Liang's generation. He was the most distinguished philologist of his time, but just as Liang Ch'i-ch'ao was unable throughout his life to shake off the Modern Script School influences on his thinking, Chang Ping-lin on the other hand (perhaps because he had seen what had happened to Chinese tradition in the hands of the Modern Script School as represented by the Reform party) preserved an unreasoning bias towards the Ancient Script classics. Ku Chieh-kang was disappointed with his teacher. He did not on that account favour the Modern Script interpretation, which was distorted by willingness to 'twist the past in favour of present changes'; but the courageous questioning and the brilliant argument of the first chapter of K'ang Yu-wei's Confucius as a Reformer (*K'ung-tzu Kai-chih K'ao*) influenced him profoundly. While at Peking University, Ku became a keen theatregoer. His interest in the theatre quickly passed over into the methodical accumulation of material on its history and on comparison of the divergent versions of each play as performed by different companies. His interest spread to the history of the familiar folk-tales of his youth and to folk-music. Transmission by word of mouth was common to all these forms of popular art, and Ku began to build up a feeling for the processes of such transmission. In the early nineteenth century, the iconoclastic scholar Ts'ui Shu in his Record of Enquiry into Beliefs[33] had given his opinion that the supposed records of the early kings of China appeared to have been built up in successive distinguishable layers. In Japan, Naitō Torajirō had developed the idea that much of the material of the classics was developed from oral tradition. Ku Chieh-kang, according to his own account, arrived at similar conclusions independently by finding that his experience of the accretion of material round a theme in drama or in the traditional novel fitted the history of the classical stories of the emperors Yao, Shun, Yü, and their legendary predecessors. The testing of hypotheses based on this analogy became his life's work. Until 1917 he worked in

[33] See above, p. 191, n. 9.

isolation, but in that year Hu Shih on his return from America began to lecture in Peking University on the history of Chinese literature and philosophy; and in Hu Shih, Ku Chieh-kang found a mind which worked like his own. The two, teacher and student, although only two years apart in age, formed the nucleus of a group of like-minded scholars. Their essays and correspondence on the subject of the classical texts and the techniques of criticism were published from 1926 onwards in the periodical series, Discussions of Ancient History.[34]

This group, of which Hu Shih is usually considered the leader, formed a new factor in the development of Chinese scholarship. In reaction against the painful weighing of East and West which had inspired and muddled the work of Liang Ch'i-ch'ao and his generation, Hu Shih proclaimed his freedom from devotion to either and his adherence to a completely pragmatic approach to the problems of China, and incidentally to the study of the past. He brought the philosophy of Dewey to China (followed by Dewey himself and by Bertrand Russell also). In politics, Hu Shih became the leader of the liberal centre; in scholarship, the advocate of a mature scientific method and the principle of 'boldness in hypothesis, caution in proof'. He provided a rationale for the impartial academic study of the past, and the small and scattered band of Chinese historians who were more interested in history than in political pamphleteering or nationalist exhortation owe a great deal to his eloquent pen, although his own actual historical output was small.

The historical work of the school was weakened, however, by its quite remarkable neglect of the results of recent developments in archaeology. Ku Chieh-kang professed to have known nothing of the work of Wang Kuo-wei up until the very eve of the publication of the first number of the Discussions of Ancient History, and noted the existence of the new archaeological materials only as something he must study in future.

The most important of these new finds were made in Honan from 1888 onwards. The erosion of the bank of the Yüan river near Anyang exposed inscribed fragments of bone and tortoiseshell which the local people sold as 'dragons' bones' for use in medicines. These came to the notice of scholars who began to collect them[35] and by 1906 there were three or four thousand fragments extant. In that year, Lo Chen-yü, an indefatigable collector of historical materials, began to take an interest in the finds. By 1911, he had collected about twenty or thirty thousand and about the

---

[34] *Ku Shih Pien*, 1926–41. This publication was the focus of discussions on ancient history and especially on criticisms of ancient texts. Ku Chieh-kang's other work consisted mainly of the editing and reprinting of the work of earlier and neglected sceptics. See especially his *Ku Chi K'ao Pien Ts'ung K'an*, and the periodicals *Shih-hsüeh Nien-pao*, *Yü Kung*, and *Ch'ing-hua Hsüeh-pao*.

[35] The pioneers were Wang I-jung and Liu E. Wang's collection of oracle bones, amounting to about 1,000 pieces, passed into the hands of Liu E after Wang's suicide in 1900. Liu published the first collection of oracle bone inscriptions in 1903.

same number existed in other collections. In 1928, the Institute of History and Philology of the Academia Sinica sent the first organized expedition to the site. By then a considerable literature existed on the subject and deciphering and analysis had begun, mainly by Wang Kuo-wei and Lo Chen-yü. The archaeologists Li Chi and Tung Tso-pin made important advances in the study of the bones in the years immediately succeeding the first expedition. The finds proved to be the records of divination in the Shang-Yin dynasty and proved by their mere existence that that dynasty was not entirely legendary, but work on them soon produced more dramatic results. Wang Kuo-wei demonstrated that information could be deduced from them which confirmed many statements in ancient texts which had come to be neglected as completely untrustworthy if not actually forged. Tung Tso-pin showed that the relative chronology yielded by the Oracle Bones confirmed in general the account of the Shang Yin given by Ssu-ma Ch'ien, whose work until then wholly lacked corroborative evidence; and Wang Kuo-wei showed that the list of Yin kings given by the Bamboo Books was generally accurate. It was in addition possible to deduce a great deal concerning the political and social system of early China. The deciphering of the inscribed characters was, as Creel writes, one of the greatest achievements of twentieth-century world scholarship,[36] but the analytical study of the bones is still in its infancy.

These discoveries were the first in point of time of a series which enriched the materials of Chinese history, so rich in printed records and until then so poor in all else. Of almost equal interest to historians but at the other end of Chinese history was the huge archival depository discovered in Peking towards the end of the century in the course of repairing one of the buildings of the imperial palace. These proved to be the records of the Nei K'o, which was the cabinet during the early Ch'ing period until its replacement as the centre of policy-making by the Chün-chi ch'u during the Yung Cheng reign (1723–36). Thus an archive unique in Chinese history was offered to the historian. It was neglected in the chaos of the last years of the Empire, several tons even being sold for waste paper, but eventually, once more through the efforts of Lo Chen-yü, arrangements were made for its safe keeping and eventually it was put in the charge of the Academia Sinica. Scholars of Peking University began the work of classification. Documents of special intrinsic interest were published in three periodical series,[37] but by the outbreak of the Sino-Japanese War only a small part had even been catalogued. In the last three or four years, however, references to the archive have become so frequent in Chinese historical writing that we can conclude that historians are at least making systematic use of it.

[36] H. G. Creel, *Studies in Early Chinese Culture* (1930), p. xiii.
[37] *Ming-Ch'ing Shih Liao*; *Ch'ang-ku Wen-hsien*; and *Shih-liao Hsün-k'an*.

In 1930 Sven Hedin and the Sino-Swedish expedition returned to the Great Wall, where in the ruins of a strong-point at Etsingol they found ten thousand wooden strips of the Han period. This was by far the largest of a number of such finds. The first publication of the strips was delayed by the Sino-Japanese War, but in 1943 Lao Kan produced four mimeographed volumes of texts and comments and work began on them at the conclusion of the war. They did not therefore add much to Chinese historical studies before 1949 and their study is not yet far advanced. Naturally, the frontier organization of the Han dynasty is the subject on which they throw the most direct light and they have been fully studied in this connection. They throw light also on many aspects of economic organization, agriculture and irrigation. Japanese and European scholars have made considerable contributions to their analysis.[38] The finds confirm at several places information in the History of the Later Han Dynasty (*Hou Han shu*) and it is also interesting that several emendations of the Han Histories suggested by the Ch'ing dynasty *k'ao-cheng* scholars have been confirmed by the wooden strips.

In 1894 a storehouse of literature, manuscripts, wooden strips, and Buddhist works of art was discovered at Tun Huang in the extreme northwest of Kansu, when a wall in a Taoist shrine, formerly a Buddhist monastery, collapsed. The Chinese local authorities did not report the finds and it was not until the visit of Sir Aurel Stein thirteen years later that they became publicly known. Subsequent work provided further finds at Tun Huang, and similar materials were discovered further west at Turfan and elsewhere by von de Coq, Grünwedel, and the Japanese scholar Otani. The materials discovered varied in value. The classical texts provided in general only confirmation of existing texts, but the works of popular fiction and poetry put the early history of Chinese colloquial literature on a new and firm foundation. Other documents provided for the first time the means of reconstructing local administrative law and practice, at least for this small area. Most important of all, the 'equal allotment' system, the actual application of which had come to be generally doubted, was proved to have been an effective reality.

In China the first scholars to pay serious attention to these finds were Lo Chen-yü and Wang Kuo-wei. But it is remarkable that thereafter Chinese studies were few and most of the work done has been by Japanese or western scholars.[39]

Of the new archaeological material, only the Anyang finds were studied early enough to contribute new conclusions before 1920. Their tendency,

[38] For an account of research so far on the Han wooden strips, see Hulsewé, 'Han-time documents', *T'oung Pao* (1957), xlv, 1.
[39] For a brief account in English of the Tun Huang finds and in particular of the Stein collection in the British Museum, see L. Giles, *Six Centuries at Tunhuang* (London, 1944), which gives a bibliography of western, Chinese, and Japanese studies.

as we have seen, was to confirm that some of the early texts which had
been rejected as untrustworthy or at least beyond corroboration contained
at least some historical matter among the accretion of legend. The principal figures in their decipherment and analysis were Lo Chen-Yü and
Wang Kuo-wei, and their connection with material which provided results
satisfactory to more conservative minds was not entirely accidental. Wang
Kuo-wei had begun his career by receiving a western education in Japan,
had studied and translated nineteenth-century European philosophers and
published outlines of psychology and of jurisprudence. Like Liang Ch'i-
ch'ao, however, he found a synthesis of western ideas and old loyalties
impossible and under the influence of his conservative friend Lo Chen-yü
(who still took the attitude that the modern thinkers of Europe had
nothing to say that the discredited non-Confucian thinkers of the Warring
States period had not said better), he relinquished his western studies,
denounced western materialism in the approved terms, and gave himself
up to the study of ancient China and the classics, on the basis of a study of
Ch'ing dynasty *k'ao-cheng* methods. Having already distinguished himself
as the pioneer in the study of the history of the Chinese drama, he now
proved himself in the field of ancient history to be the most brilliant Chinese
scholar of the twentieth century. Students of China of whatever persuasion
turn constantly to Wang's work, which has the classical quality that it can
become out of date without ever becoming expendable. His importance
from the point of view of method is that he brought the techniques of his
chosen Ch'ing dynasty masters Ku Yen-wu, Tai Chen, and Tuan Yü-ts'ai
to bear on the Classics in a twentieth-century context of new archaeological evidence on the one hand and of a far greater scope for historical
hypothecation on the other.

Thus, by 1920, a wider context of ideas had been provided, mainly in
the first instance by the comparisons between China and abroad elaborated by Liang Ch'i-ch'ao; the methods of Ch'ing dynasty classical studies
had been modernized by Wang Kuo-wei; and a philosophical justification for empirical history-writing had been provided by Hu Shih. The
new Universities acted as active centres of research and disseminated the
new points of view, in spite of political chaos and of financial difficulties
which often prevented even the regular payment of salaries. Translations
of foreign works had by then brought China's educated minority into full
relations with world thought and scholarship and a steady flow of returning
students provided a constant enrichment of background and of methods.

Events in 1920 provided a stimulus which brought the accumulated
experience of these preceding twenty years into sharp focus and began a
movement which has earned the name of a Chinese renaissance. When the
news of the handing over of German rights in Shantung to Japan by the
peacemakers of Versailles reached China, three thousand students in

Peking National University demonstrated and set fire to the residence of the warlord prime minister Tuan Ch'i-jui. Protest spread all over China, led by students and teachers of the universities. Merchants and workers in the coastal cities joined in boycotts and strikes and all classes were for the moment united against foreign bestowal of Chinese territory and against the warlords and their venal government in Peking. The immediate result was the fall of the ministers who had acquiesced in Japanese demands in return for assistance in maintaining their power. The long-term political result was the creation at last of a Chinese public opinion which, if it could not immediately bring warlordism to an end, at least became an important new factor in the struggle, bringing about a shift in warlord alliances and the eventual victory of the Kuomintang, then hemmed in and helpless in Kwangtung. In the intellectual field, it brought to maturity certain movements of thought already apparent. The change-over from the classical written style understood only by scholars to a colloquial style based on the spoken tongue, not only in political discussions but also in academic and creative writing, was hastened by the breath of democracy which had been felt for a moment after May 4th. The universities, through the new National Union of Students, which became a vital sector of Chinese politics, gained immensely in influence. The nationalist urgency of the Reform period, which had faded somewhat in the international breathing-space of the early part of the century, now returned, but with a significant new content. The repudiation of Tsarist rights in Manchuria by the Soviet Union, set against the apparent cynicism of Versailles, brought about an interest in Communism. At first this interest sprang mainly from nationalist feeling and had little relation to Communism as such, but Comintern representatives quickly weeded out the mere nationalists from the new Communist Party of China.

A vigorous debate began, mainly in the pages of the magazine *New Youth*, which resolved itself into a struggle between Hu Shih's pragmatism and the Marxists, the latter represented by two Peking University teachers who had been active in the May 4th protest, Li Ta-chao and Ch'en Tu-hsiu.[40] Hu Shih and pragmatism lost heavily. The cosmopolitan detachment expressed by some of Hu Shih's followers was bitterly resented at a time when even illiterate labourers in Shanghai and Canton were rushing to patriotic martyrdom. The empirical politics of the group, advocating 'progress drip by drip and drop by drop', seemed fantastically inadequate to China's desperate situation, so much so that their advocacy seemed to many a deliberate attempt at obstruction.

In history, the debate swung inevitably to the classical age, and its first result was a controversy over whether or not the 'well-field system' of

[40] For a brief account of the arrival of Marxist influence in China, see B. Schwarz, *Chinese Communism and the Rise of Mao* (1952), ch. 1.

equal allotment of agricultural land had ever really existed.[41] Hu Shih argued that the documentary proof of its existence was negligible and demonstrated this by a brilliant analysis of the texts on which belief in the system was based. His opponents replied with arguments drawn from the early history of land ownership all over the world, quoting Maine, Seebohm, Vinogradoff and a cloud of sociological witnesses to show the inherent probability of the existence of some such system at some early stage in Chinese history. The two sides in fact never found common ground on which to join battle; and unfortunately the no-man's-land between them embraced what most historians would call history.

The Marxism which dominated Chinese historical writing after 1920 was not, in general, of a narrow and stultifying kind. In the first place, in the early years, dogmas of the Stalinist kind were not important; in the second place, after 1927 the Chinese Communist Party was driven underground, so that its relations with Chinese intellectual life were remote, while within the Party academic intellectuals were a luxury which the hunted conspirators in Shanghai and the beleaguered Robin Hoods of Chinkang Mountain could not afford. Marxism in academic circles took the form of free and fruitful experiment with economic determinism, the political implications of which, in a country in which all important political groups accepted the necessity of a socialist revolution, in theory at least, were not very cramping.

The chief effect associated with the predominance of economic determinist presuppositions arose less from the presuppositions themselves than from the state of Chinese society that encouraged them. The effects of the breakdown of traditional government and the prevalence of unscrupulous military rule were complicated locally by disastrous effects on the peasant economy of China's new participation, in conditions of impaired sovereignty, in world markets. The old society broke down completely over large areas. Traditional relations between owners of land and tenants and between rural lenders and borrowers disappeared in the anarchy of civil war and were replaced by cruder forms, backed by savage political repression. A bastard feudalism not unworthy of fifteenth-century England grew up rapidly, and in response to it a wave of rural revolt which terrified the landowners into committing themselves further and further to blind resistance. It was in these circumstances that the study of Chinese economic and social history began, and there was inevitably a strong tendency to read back the conditions of the twentieth century into earlier times.[42]

After 1927, when Chiang K'ai-shek by his Shanghai *coup d'état* drove the

---

[41] See *Hu Shih Wen Ts'un*, ii, 587 ff.

[42] The principal studies associated with the debate on the nature of Chinese society on the eve of revolution were brought together in a symposium, *Chung-kuo she-hui shih ti lun-chan* (3 vols., 1932).

Communists and the socialist left wing of the Nationalist Party into the wilderness and delivered his peasant auxiliaries over to the tender mercies of the local conservatives, Chinese politics became abruptly and as it proved irremediably polarized. This did not have a proportionate effect in intellectual life, because on the whole China's intellectuals were inclined to moderation and indeed they alone provided what little centre remained between the two warring political extremes. Nevertheless, among historians there remained a broad difference of method and approach which was not unrelated to political attitudes, even discounting the strictly Communist historians on the one hand (caught up in the Stalin-Trotsky struggle) and the historical apologists for Chiang Kai-shek's pseudo-Confucian 'New Life' Fascism on the other. In 1946, Ch'i Ssu-ho distinguished two groups, describing them as the 'antiquarians' and the 'sociologists'.[43] The gulf had already been revealed in the 'well-field controversy'; and one might with some show of reason go back to an older vocabulary and label them *k'ao-cheng* and *ching-shih* respectively, the first implying a kind of scholasticism detached from everyday affairs, the second a concern with the contemporary—usually political—relevance of historical matter.[44]

The *k'ao-cheng* or 'antiquarian' group was partly composed of scholars who had somehow contrived to ignore all that had happened in the preceding hundred years and partly of certain empiricists of the Hu Shih persuasion who found it easier in practice to be cautious in proof than to be bold in hypothesis: to some extent it was the result of understandable disorientation in a perplexing and swiftly changing world. The other group was partly composed of sociologists feeling their way cautiously along the time dimension of the institutions they studied, partly of honest patriots intent on quick answers, and partly of scholars of wholly modern or wholly foreign education who were not really competent to deal with Chinese historical records. The distinction is one which to some extent we always have with us: the historians with too little or too much imagination are not unknown elsewhere. But in China the complementary tasks of hypothecation and verification were too seldom brought together. The explanation is partly a political one. The flight of Liang Ch'i-ch'ao, Lo Chen-yü, and Wang Kuo-wei to the safety of *k'ao-cheng* studies was rationalized by the profession of a sudden enlightenment on the nature of western materialism; but the phrase they use is almost invariably 'western materialism and its class-struggles'. Fear of sociological hypothecation was related to fear of the social implications of such theorizing; while, on the other hand,

---

[43] Ch'i Ssu-ho, 'Hsien-tai Chung-kuo shih-hsüeh P'ing-lun', in *Ta Chung* (1946), vol. i, No. 1.

[44] On this second aspect of traditional Chinese historiography, see especially the paper by E. Balazs, above, pp. 78–94. A similar divergence appears in twentieth-century Japanese historical writing.

distaste for the necessity of providing evidence for sociological hypotheses which were emotively related to political convictions was much commoner on the left than on the right. In this way, the polarization of Chinese politics limited the effectiveness of historical work as a whole and delayed its maturity.

The period from 1930 to 1937 provided a measure of stability and peace and a more relaxed and hopeful atmosphere. The study of history began to lose its cruder forms of dependence on the current problems of nationalism and revolution, although these inevitably and naturally continued to provide the background of the historian's efforts. In several of the Chinese universities distinguished history schools developed, and historical writing was more and more published in academic and specialized periodicals instead of in the general political or intellectual journals. A small body of research which was both careful in method and significant in subject began to be built up.[45] The obsession with ancient history passed away and effort was spread more evenly over the whole field. Attempts were made to work out more useful schemes for the periodization of Chinese history. At first the western scheme of ancient, medieval, and modern divisions of history was influential, although this bore no obvious relation to Chinese history, and it was even exaggerated into a scheme consisting of the 'ancient-fruitful' period, the 'middle-stagnant' period (covering everything from about the beginning of the Christian era to the Opium War), and the 'modern-revolutionary' period. A more significant variation of this scheme defined the ages before the fall of the Chou dynasty as feudal, using the word feudal in a narrow sense justified by the nature of Chou institutions; but this meaning of feudal was quickly overlaid by the adoption of its wider, Marxist, use. In the hands of Marxist historians, who applied it to the whole traditional and partly landlord-dominated society, the feudal period came to cover the whole of Chinese history until the Opium War. All such schemes involved immense sweeps of time within one period or were based upon assumptions about the general development of Chinese society too dubious to be useful. In practice, the traditional dynastic division was difficult to avoid and remained dominant until its replacement in theory (but not wholly in practice) by a particular Marxist scheme favoured by the Chinese Communist Party.

New schemes of periodization were the basis of the many general histories of China which were written at this time and during the Sino-Japanese war.[46] These as a whole were by no means merely textbooks.

[45] For translations of some of the most valuable periodical articles of this period, see E-tu Zen Sun and John de Francis, *Chinese Social History* (1956). The selection of articles for inclusion, however, is not one with which everyone would agree.

[46] The most influential of these were the *Chung Kuo T'ung Shih* of Chou Ku-ch'eng; the *Kuo Shih Ta Kang* of Ch'ien Mou; Fan Wen-lan's *Chung Kuo T'ung Shih Chien Pien*; and the unfinished *Chung Kuo Shih Pien* of Ch'ien Po-tsan.

They were consciously experimental, concerned more to define questions than to answer them, and were a most useful form of writing, providing a place for licensed speculation of a kind not encouraged in western historical scholarship—perhaps to our cost. They were charcoal sketches for the general history of China which Chang Hsüeh-ch'eng had demanded more than a century before.

Another characteristic of the historical writing of the period was that few of the leading scholars were historians by training. Most of them came to history from the study of the law, of economics, or of philosophy. The effects were not all bad. While, as a result, most Chinese historians had no direct experience of western or Japanese historical research through actual participation in it, nevertheless the special competence of such men was invaluable at that time, as that of Maitland, for example, had been in late nineteenth-century England.

Finally, most of the writers involved in these developments were young men. They are still alive and active today, mainly in the People's Republic, but also in Formosa, Hong Kong, and outside China. The pre-war work of these men can almost be said to have been their juvenalia, in fact though not in value.

The outbreak of the Sino-Japanese war and the retreat of the Chinese universities with the Nationalist armies into the south-west brought historical research almost to a standstill, though the movement towards the production of experimental general histories was strengthened by the very impossibility of research. The conditions of the immediate post-war period were even less conducive to sustained research. Inflation destroyed the incomes of Chinese intellectuals and it was not until the victory of the Communists that organized study was again possible on a national scale. Since then there has been an immense development of historical writing and of the collection and publication of historical materials. Yet although the history now being written preserves many links with the pre-war period the circumstances of its production are so different (although the producers are partly the same) that its study demands separate treatment.[47]

[47] For a brief account of part of the developments since 1949, see Jean Chesneaux, 'Les travaux d'historie moderne et contemporaine en Chine populaire', *Revue Historique* (1956), pp. 274–82.

# 12. EARLY JAPANESE CHRONICLES: THE SIX NATIONAL HISTORIES

## G. W. ROBINSON

*Formerly Lecturer in the History of the Far East,*
*School of Oriental and African Studies, University of London*

From China, Japan derived both her first impulse towards historical writing and the medium for its expression. Consequently, the chronicles, with which this paper is concerned, are not only all written in Chinese, but betray in a variety of ways the dominance of Chinese cultural influence in the Japanese court at the time of their composition. They form a series of annals, compiled by official committees at intervals during the eighth and ninth centuries, which purport to relate the history of Japan from the creation of the world to the year A.D. 888.

The first, most famous, and most splendid of these, the *Nihon Shoki* (Chronicles of Japan),[1] carries the narrative down to A.D. 697 and thus covers a far greater tract of time than all the remainder together. It was not compiled until the beginning of the eighth century; and it is only in that part of the narrative which extends from the first half of the sixth century that the element of fact may be said to equal and, ultimately, to oust that of fiction. With the exception of a briefer and cruder work, the *Kojiki* (Records of Ancient Matters),[2] written in a hybrid of Chinese and Japanese, the *Nihon Shoki* is generally accepted as the earliest extant historical work produced in Japan.

Second is the *Shoku Nihongi* (Chronicle of Japan, continued).[3] It was presented to the throne at the end of the eighth century and continues the chronicle to the year 791, thus constituting a record of the so-called Nara period.

---

[1] *Nihon Shoki*. This name is almost universally used by Japanese writers on the subject. The original name was *Nihon-gi*, this being almost universally used by western writers. An English translation of the work by W. G. Aston appeared in 1896, as Supplement 1 to the *Transactions and Proceedings of the Japan Society, London*, entitled *Nihongi, Chronicles of Japan from the Earliest Times to A.D. 697*, in 2 vols. (reprinted and published in one volume, London, 1956).

[2] *Kojiki*. Translated into English by B. H. Chamberlain, entitled '*Ko-ji-ki*' or '*Records of Ancient Matters*'. This originally appeared in 1882 as a supplement to vol. x of *Transactions of the Asiatic Society of Japan*. The more easily available second edition was published at Kobe in 1932, and has some annotations by W. G. Aston. Doubts about the date of the *Kojiki* have been expressed both in the last and the present centuries. The general opinion, however, is that the *Kojiki* is an authentic product of the early eighth century.

[3] J. B. Snellen's translation of the first six of the forty 'books' or chapters of the *Shoku Nihongi* appeared as follows: Books I–III in *T.A.S.J.*, Second Series, vol. xi (December 1934); Books IV–VI, in same, vol. xiv (June 1937).

The remaining four chronicles, which together cover only the next century, are: the *Nihon Kōki* (Later Chronicle of Japan); the *Shoku Nihon Kōki* (Later Chronicle of Japan, continued); the *Montoku Tennō Jitsuroku* or, as generally though too elaborately rendered, 'The Veritable Records of the Emperor Montoku'; and, finally, the *Nihon San Dai Jitsuroku* (The Veritable Records of Three Reigns of Japan).[4] We now have only ten scattered chapters of the original forty chapters of the *Nihon Kōki*; the remaining works, with the exception of some genealogical tables originally attached to the *Nihon Shoki*, have come down to us complete. This body of official chronicles is known collectively as the *Rikkokushi* or Six National Histories.[5]

The difference in scope between the *Nihon Shoki* and the other five works naturally involved the compilers in quite different problems. If, in this paper, the *Nihon Shoki* receives a disproportionate amount of attention, the reason is that, considered as historiography, it presents more features, of greater interest, than do its five successors.

The inception of this series of official chronicles about the turn of the seventh to the eighth century was only one among many activities, in which, in a crescendo of energy, the Japanese were not only imitating but striving to emulate the Chinese. They had substituted for their loose tribal organization a bureaucratic administration, modelled on that of contemporary T'ang China, and had promulgated legal codes so imitative that they have even helped modern scholars to reconstruct the lost or mutilated codes of the T'ang; they were writing Chinese poems, not wholly devoid of literary merit, and they had, for more than a century, been producing, under continental influence, works of sculpture of a quality which they never afterwards surpassed; and they appointed a committee, headed by a prince, to write the history of their country. By the end of the eighth century, the compilation of a chronicle, firmly based on court archives (and, to some extent, on living memory), had become something of a routine activity in a largely sinicized court; but the production of the first of the series involved a considerable imaginative and creative effort. While the aridity of the subsequent chronicles is such that Snellen prefaced his translation of a few chapters of them with the remark that 'all but the most hardened readers are earnestly advised to skip them altogether', the first, the *Nihon Shoki*, presents an elaborate and not inartistic answer to the problem of making history where none was before.

---

[4] None of these last four works is available in translation. The term *jitsuroku* (Chinese: *shih-lu*) was used in imitation of the Chinese, who applied the term to the official record of each reign compiled at the end of each reign (cf. the paper by W. Franke, above, pp. 60 ff); its meaning is little more than archives, or a compilation thereof, and the word has no weighty overtones.

[5] A seventh official compilation, the *Shin Koku-shi* (New National History), probably continued the story as far as 930, but, with the exception of fragments cited in other works, it no longer survives.

The resultant work has inevitably incurred a charge of fraud. Yet, though the result may be fraudulent, the intention may have been otherwise. Justly to deny the veracity of the narrative does not necessarily carry with it the right to impugn the integrity of the compilers, as has been done in recent years by most critics, both Japanese and foreign. More detailed consideration is given to this important question below; but, at this point, the general observation may be made that many of the contradictions, inconsistencies and anachronisms, which the critics justifiably brandish as evidence of historical unreliability, afford correspondingly poor evidence of editorial ingenuity and disingenuousness. The *Nihon Shoki* should, perhaps, be seen not as a cynical hand-out, foisted on a gullible readership, but as the product of patriotic pride and prejudice, feelings shared both by its authors and by the small number of their contemporaries who could read it.

The nature and even the existence of historiography in Japan before the end of the seventh century are matters rather of conjecture than of knowledge. There is, at least, little indication that the introduction of writing led immediately, in Japan, as it appears to have done in southern Korea, to the maintenance of historical records. There is some ground for supposing that the technique of writing (in Chinese) did not attract the attention of the Japanese until as late as the beginning of the fifth century, although Japan had been in active contact with China, as well as with Korea, since the middle of the third century, and in some sort of formal contact since the first century b.c. Even then, the technique probably remained for a century or more confined to foreign immigrants, who were employed by the natives to maintain registers of the foreign population and to inscribe memorial articles. Perhaps in the latter half of the sixth century, Japanese themselves began to read and write, and they may have taken the first steps towards historical recording at about this time by compiling genealogies, which survived to provide material for the compilers of the late seventh century. It is certain that the arrival of Buddhism in the sixth century gave impetus to the production of memorial inscriptions, some of which were actually composed by Japanese; these also were used as source material by the chroniclers a century later. But no attempt seems to have been made to write any sort of a history of Japan until the beginning of the seventh century. At that time, under the leadership of Prince Shōtoku, one of the heroic figures of Japanese history, whose true stature it is now scarcely possible to distinguish from the legendary, the Japanese imperial clan embarked consciously on the course of emulating China, politically and culturally. By the despatch of Japanese students, both Buddhists and lay, to work in China, the Japanese court was taking positive measures to drink Chinese culture at its source rather than persist in obtaining it by way of Korea or from foreign immigrants. Whatever the mixture of motives in these emulous activities, ranging perhaps from un-critical admiration to realistic political vision, it seems likely that China's voluminous records of her past, and even the written annals of the king-doms of Korea, would have impressed the Prince as being one of the essential trappings of a civilized state, if not as a useful aid to the establish-ment of dynastic claims. There is, therefore, at least strong inherent probability in the record of the *Nihon Shoki*, when it states that, in 620, Prince Shōtoku and the head of the most powerful clan at the time, the Soga, drew up some sort of a national history, although in some quarters this statement has been dismissed as a baseless fiction. It is further recorded that the bulk of this first historical work perished in the course of the *coup d'état* of 645, and it would thus not have been available to those who set to work on a similar project some decades later.[6]

The circumstances in which this latter project was set in motion by an imperial order of 681 were not altogether dissimilar from those of 620: some of the aspirations of 620 had been realized, but the advance towards a fully sinicized polity and culture was still proceeding, and a written national history still lay ahead as one of the necessary stages along that advance. The position of the Imperial clan, had, as a result of the political and administrative innovations of mid-century, become, by 681, unassail-able in practice, though the present occupant of the throne owed his posi-tion to the successful issue of a war against his brother; but the claims of the Imperial clan to supremacy and those of the other leading clans to their new 'ministerial' positions still required clarification, if not fabrica-tion.

The *Nihon Shoki* records that, in 681, the tenth year of his reign, the Emperor Temmu gave orders to six princes and six other noblemen to draw up a chronicle (or, possibly, only a genealogy) of the emperors and to record matters of antiquity. This bare statement is considerably ampli-fied in the preface to the *Kojiki*, dated 712: in the words of Chamberlain's translation, '. . . the Heavenly Sovereign (i.e. Temmu) commanded, saying: "I hear that the chronicles of the emperors and likewise the original words in the possession of the various families deviate from the exact truth, and are mostly amplified by empty falsehoods. If, at the present time, these imperfections be not amended, ere many years shall have elapsed, the purport of this, the great basis of the monarchy, will be destroyed. So now I desire to have the chronicles of the emperors selected and recorded; and the old words examined and ascertained, falsehoods being erased and truth determined in order to transmit the latter to after ages." ' This passage, highly controversial though it is in regard to the significance of

---

[6] It is a typical irony of the nature of the evidence surrounding this topic that the only portion of this history alleged to have been rescued from the conflagration is called *Kokki*, a term of quite obscure meaning.

certain phrases,[7] generally confirms the motives, adumbrated above, for the inception of historical work.

The specific project, so initiated, was never completed, and there is evidence that other similar projects were also abortive. It is clear that the task of producing a national history, which should satisfy all interested parties, proved long and difficult. Though the cynic may suggest that much of this time was occupied in fabricating and distorting, it is also clear that much time was consumed in gathering material and in something resembling genuine historical research. Various noble families were ordered to submit their genealogies and the provinces were ordered to produce provincial histories or gazetteers. Some of these latter were submitted before 720; and it appears, from those which have survived, that they were consulted by the compilers of the *Nihon Shoki*, who sometimes quoted from them almost verbatim.[8] In addition, Korean chronicles were gathered, consulted and quoted, as well as the written reports of members of embassies to China.

Although work began in 681, the *Kojiki* (Records of Ancient Matters) did not appear until 712. In this work, the story ends with the Empress Suiko, who had reigned a century earlier; and the latter part of the book consists only of bare genealogical statements about the successive rulers. Although it may have served to establish as facts some dynastic and clan claims, the crudity of the hybrid language in which it is written, together with its lack of a chronology, may be supposed to have made it, in the eyes of the aspiring Japanese court, too shoddy a document to stand comparison with the polished pages of Chinese history. Finally, in 720, the Chronicles of Japan (*Nihon Shoki*) was presented to the throne, and with this work the task was at last deemed complete.[9] The crudely written *Kojiki* was almost forgotten and the *Nihon Shoki* soon gained great prestige. In it, we find the Imperial house glorified, well beyond the confines of possible reality, in terms and in stories which had for centuries been associated with the rulers of China. Dates, precise to the day, are given for alleged events, allegedly as early as 668 B.C. And the whole seems instantly to have been accepted as the truth. Yet, in spite of the incredible nature of

[7] The foci of controversy are the phrases 'chronicles of the emperors' (*teiki*) and 'original words' (*honji*) or 'old words' (*kyūji*). Does *teiki* mean 'chronicles of the emperors', as Chamberlain, following traditional opinion, translates? Or does it merely mean imperial genealogies? There are strong but inconclusive arguments for both views. Again, does *ji* (in *honji* and *kyūji*) mean literally no more than 'words', or does it mean 'stories'? On this point turns the question whether the *Kojiki* is a compilation of material dictated orally by a man of exceptional memory, or whether it is a redaction of existing written material. Chamberlain takes the former view, but there is now weighty evidence and opinion of the other side.

[8] There exists the view, not widely held, that identity or close similarity of text between the *Nihon Shoki* and the local gazetteers (*Fudoki*) is attributable to copying *from* the former and not vice versa.

[9] The view exists that even the present work is only a draft, of which no final version was ever made. But the evidence for this view is slight.

much of the work, it bears many signs that the compilers had some notion of objectivity and of comparing conflicting versions of a story. These signs, already alluded to, will be further discussed elsewhere below.

While it may be taken for granted that early historical writing in Japan was dominated by that of China, it is important to consider which features and aspects of Chinese historiography were most closely imitated by the Japanese, and, if possible, to establish which of them contributed most to that particular form of untruth which was the first product of the Japanese chroniclers. In so far as form and content can be differentiated, we naturally find that the major effects of copying Chinese methods and models manifest themselves in form, though content did not by any means escape these influences.

By the time Japan embarked on historical writing, her earliest form of literature, China already had a long history of history, in the course of which historiography had passed through several stages of development, and ideas about the *raison d'être* of historical works had been conceived and expressed. The skill and rapidity which the Japanese notably display in the imitation, if not mimicry, of foreign techniques or activities, sometimes obscures the difficulties they inevitably encounter in apprehending the idea underlying what they are copying. This seems to have been so in the matter of historical writing. There is no indication that, when they undertook their first compilations, they had appreciated the Chinese notion of the function of history as a guide for sovereigns, in which the sins and errors of the past were displayed for caution, and the virtues and wisdom for emulation. Thus they neither indulged in moral innuendo or interpretation, nor consciously valued objectivity, despite certain appearances to the contrary. Their propagandist idea of the use of history, as implied in the *Kojiki* preface, cannot be found explicitly replaced by the Chinese notion until the preface to the Later Chronicle of Japan (*Nihon Kōki*), dated 840, in which the compilers say, 'We know that it is the function of history to ensure that no fault be concealed, which might serve as a warning, and that every excellence be published, which might illuminate the path of virtue.' In the three subsequent chronicles, these sentiments are repeated with a marked, almost mechanical similarity of wording. Though such prefaces may often advertise the very virtue most deficient in their wares, these later chronicles tend, on the whole, to support the claims to objectivity rhetorically made by their editors. Neither the *Nihon Shoki* nor the *Shoku Nihongi* has a preface; but it seems that the latter was the first chronicle to be compiled by men conversant with Chinese views of history.

The prefaces to the *Nihon Kōki* and subsequent chronicles explicitly connect the Chinese view of history with the institution of the official historian in China, which, under various names, had already existed for more than a thousand years. It is sometimes suggested that the absence of the official historian from the Japanese bureaucracy, otherwise so closely modelled on the Chinese, implies a major difference between the two countries in their attitudes to history. But this implication can be over-estimated. All the first historical works written in Japan were, in practice, compiled by official, if *ad hoc*, committees, appointed by the throne, at whose disposal all government archives, diaries, etc., were placed. More-over, in China, the head of a committee, entrusted with the task of com-piling a dynastic history, was not by any means always a professional or official historian, though his colleagues and subordinates would have been. In Japan, the chief editorial posts were in the hands of leading statesmen, progressively concentrated in one powerful family, but, in the case of each chronicle, it is possible to point to at least one member of the editorial board, who was simply a professional scholar, if not historian.

If there was little practical difference in the official status of the his-torians of the two countries, there was in the nature of things a vast difference between the compilers of a Chinese dynastic history and the Japanese historians in their relation to their subject matter. Into the Chinese dynastic histories, compiled by men working under a later dynasty, some tendentiousness, whether laudatory or denigratory, is generally admitted to have found its way. The T'ang historians of the Sui, writing soon after the overthrow of a detested regime, perhaps withheld some credit for some of its material achievements, while the Sung historians of the more remote T'ang are generally supposed to have shown indulgence towards a dynasty which they admired and a corresponding hostility towards its enemies. The Japanese, with their continuing dynasty, were never exposed to temptations of this particular kind. Not even in the *Nihon Shoki* do they provide a panegyric; and, once that had been produced, their work was always concerned with comparatively recent events, and their position *vis-à-vis* their subject matter became similar to that of the Chinese com-pilers of the *Shih-lu* or chronicles of individual reigns (Veritable Records).

For the form of their histories, the Japanese had two principal Chinese models from which to choose. (Were it not, of course, for the many other elements in the *Nihon Shoki* which betray the desire to imitate a Chinese work, it would be pointless to seek a specific Chinese exemplar for a work which, as pure chronicle, must inevitably resemble the primitive histories of n .merous other peoples.) The available alternatives were: the form initiated by Ssu-ma Ch'ien in his *Shih chi* (Records of the Historian) and used in the standard dynastic histories, in which a comparatively brief, chronologically arranged record is supplemented with much additional material in biographies and monographs; or the purely chronological record, exemplified by the Spring and Autumn Annals or by the *Han-chi* (Chronicles of the Han Dynasty), compiled by Hsün Yüeh (A.D. 148–209), and *Hou Han chi* (Chronicles of the Later Han Dynasty), compiled by Yüan Hung (A.D. 328–76). We cannot now tell what considerations led them to choose the latter. It is just possible that a political motive was at work; that is to say, it may have been felt that the dignity of the emperors would be best served by a work in which no separate section was specifically devoted to other persons. But such an explanation assumes, perhaps, too high a degree of sophistication. Instead, it seems more likely that they were driven, against their original intention, to adopt the purely chronological form by the paucity of their material. The description of the historical work, allegedly compiled by Prince Shōtoku in 620, suggests something on the lines of a Chinese dynastic history: it reads, in Aston's translation, 'a history of the Emperors, a history of the country, and the original record of the Omi, the Muraji, the Tomo no Miyakko, the Kuni no Miyakko, the 180 *be* and the free subjects'.[10] There is, moreover, some slight evidence that, for at least one of the above categories, the *be*, a separate monograph was prepared, and that its contents were ultimately incorporated into the chronological scheme of the *Nihon Shoki*. There is no doubt that the original title of the *Nihon Shoki* was *Nihon-gi*; and this name is exactly parallel to those of the two *Han-chi* mentioned above, the final character being the same in each case. Moreover, the two *Han-chi* and the *Nihon Shoki* each consist of thirty chapters, a slight formal resemblance which may well have been intentional. Although the pure chronicle form is more primitive than that devised by Ssu-ma Ch'ien,[11] it should be remembered that both *Han-chi* are, in fact, rearrangements of the respective dynastic histories, and it may be that the *Nihon Shoki*, also, is a rearrangement of material originally prepared in chronicle-cum-monograph form. If it is true that, in the case of the *Nihon Shoki*, there was simply not enough material out of which to fashion a convincing replica of a Chinese dynastic history, we may suppose that inertia or, possibly, conscious conservatism would have restrained subsequent editorial committees, though abundantly supplied with material, from departure from what they would have regarded as an illustrious example. At the same time, the use of the term *jitsuroku* (Chinese, *shih-lu*) in the titles of the last two of the series suggests that the Japanese eventually decided to imitate the *Shih-lu* (Veritable Records) which in China first became a regular production under the T'ang. There is certainly in the later chronicles a tendency, which gradually becomes more pronounced as the series progresses, to reproduce a certain feature of the *Shih-lu*, whereby to the entry recording the death of a notable person is appended a brief summary of his life. In

---

[10] The Omi, Muraji, etc., were various kinds of chieftain; the *be* were a kind of social organization or group, the exact nature of which is a matter of some dispute.

[11] On the structure adopted by Ssu-ma Ch'ien for his Records of the Historian, see the paper by A. F. P. Hulsewé, above, pp. 35-36.

addition, we occasionally find discursive digressions or comments on certain topics, which, together with the brief lives, serve to mitigate the severe disadvantages of the purely chronological scheme.

Perhaps the most flagrantly pernicious result of imitation of China is to be found in the chronological framework of the *Nihon Shoki*, whereby events of the remote and unrecorded past are dated with seeming precision according to the Chinese lunar calendar. Events assigned by the chroniclers to the seventh century B.C.—which, if they occurred at all, would have done so a millennium later—are dated with year, month and day, in just the same way as are those of the seventh century A.D., although knowledge of the calendar was, on the admission of the *Nihon Shoki*, only introduced to the court at the beginning of the seventh century. There are, moreover, indications that Chinese models originally induced the Japanese historians to ascribe at least one event to every year of a sovereign's reign, a course which inevitably would have led to fabrications. Whether these indications are reliable or not, it is certain that the contents of the *Nihon Shoki* were subjected to a Procrustean process, equally damaging to accurate narration, whereby the reigns of an inadequate number of sovereigns were stretched back to 660 B.C.

It is just these chronological antics which have given rise to the charge that the *Nihon Shoki* involves 'one of the greatest literary frauds ever perpetrated'.[12] Yet it is at least doubtful whether the intention was as fraudulent as this censorious phrase suggests. It is uncertain precisely how or when the Japanese decided on the year 660 B.C. as the date of accession of Jimmu, their first emperor, but scholars are agreed that a certain Chinese system of arithmetical magic or divination provided the method of calculation.[13] Since those who use magical methods or divination tend to believe in their results, we may be confident that this date commanded genuine credence. Although, as was remarked above, the number of sovereigns, legendary and historical, was inadequate plausibly to span so long a period as was thus involved, the implausible length attributed to many reigns is probably not solely due to this cause. Many peoples attribute exceptional longevity to the rulers and other heroes of their past; and the *Kojiki*, which does not employ a precise calendar, also attributes long

[12] W. Bramsen, *Japanese Chronology and Calendars* (*T.A.S.J.*, vol. xxxvii, Tokyo, 1910).

[13] According to the system of computation known as *Ch'an-wei* (Japanese, *Shin-i*), the 58th year of the sexagenary cycle is a year of revolution, major revolutions occurring in 58th years, 21 cycles (i.e. 1,260 years) apart. Now, the reign of Suiko (A.D. 593–628) was, generally speaking, a revolutionary period; the year 601, the 9th of the reign, was the 58th of the cycle, separated by precisely 1,260 years from the year of the alleged accession of Jimmu. It is therefore generally supposed that the year 660 B.C. was arrived at by counting backwards from 601. It should not be forgotten, however, that the only evidence that a calculation along these lines was made is such as we may hold to be implicit in the fact that Jimmu's accession is assigned to the 58th year of a cycle. There is no general agreement as to when the calculation was made. Disagreement is further widened by a few scholars who hold that a major cycle was 1,320 or even 1,380 years.

lives and reigns to many emperors, though the figures differ from those given by the *Nihon Shoki*. It may be noted that no attempt was made to show the earliest date of Japanese history as antedating that of China. Indeed, since neither the Chinese nor the Japanese employed, until modern times, an endless serial chronology, but used, instead, reigns and era-names, questions of relative antiquity tended to be obscured.

A sincere belief in the significance of New Year's Day, 660 B.C. cannot, however, excuse the deception involved in the precise dating of the events of the ensuing one thousand years. This, it will be admitted, must have been introduced simply for the sake of appearance; a series of events, of which the relative order was supposedly 'known', was arbitrarily assigned to specific days. Yet it is noticeable that even this process was not carried through with consistency. Many events are assigned only to a month, many are dated in the form 'this month' or even 'this year', while items relating to Korea are hardly ever assigned to a day. This latter feature signifies that the compilers faithfully followed their Korean sources. Thus the deception is not total.

Less flagrant, but more insidiously misleading, is the embellishment of the text of the *Nihon Shoki* with quotations from Chinese classical literature. Because no satisfactory method had yet been devised of writing Japanese, the compilers of the *Nihon Shoki*, equipped with some first-hand acquaintance with Chinese literature and with the normal aids to composition used by Chinese writers, set out to compose their history in Chinese prose. The resultant style, where stylishness is evident, is reminiscent of the Six Dynasties style, which persisted in China during the first century of T'ang rule among all writers except those of marked originality. This is a somewhat dreary vehicle of expression, except in the hands of a few masters, and only the eye of patriotism will find much to relish in the prose of the *Nihon Shoki*. There are, moreover, passages where some violence is done to the Chinese idiom, and others where the language can scarcely be called Chinese at all. Such passages are sufficiently numerous to confirm, what we learn from external sources, that not only the matter but also the language was supplied by Japanese and not by foreigners— which constitutes no mean feat, as any foreigner who has attempted to compose in Chinese will acknowledge. There are long passages, which simply constitute a cento of classical quotations, a series of elegant extracts, taken, it appears, as often from Chinese phrase books, thesauri or encyclopaedias, as from the original works. The most notorious example of this feature is provided by the ascription to a Japanese emperor of the late fifth century, of an edict of a Chinese (Sui) emperor of the late seventh century.

Nevertheless, we cannot simply dismiss as fiction all passages suffused with Chinese phrases and ideas, convenient though such a course might be for the modern critical historian. In spite of the worthlessness of much, or most, of this chinoiserie, there are still fairly numerous instances where it seems that historical facts have been clothed in such Chinese dress. It should be remembered by those who incline to think of the *Nihon Shoki* as a 'jackdaw tricked out in its frippery of peacock's feathers', or who make much of 'the desire of the compilers to display their learning', that the inclusion of elegant phrases from past writers, unacknowledged, is a normal feature of Chinese prose of nearly all periods, and that this is not necessarily 'disastrous to the interests of sober veracity', either in Chinese or in Japanese hands. It is important, as in the matter of the chronology, to form some idea, not only of how much deception or distortion was involved in the seemingly indiscriminate use of Chinese quotations, but also, if possible, of how much was either conscious or deliberate. In the first place, the use of Chinese terminology alone automatically involved falsifications, of which the compilers were almost certainly unaware. Like nearly all primitive historians, they saw the past in terms of the present, and applied to matters of remote antiquity terms which had only lately begun to have real significance, describing, for example, petty chieftains as emperors, and the rude shacks which they inhabited as palaces. For the modern reader, in search of facts, it is usually easy enough to make allowances for such errors as these; but if he is interested in discovering the viewpoint of the ancient chroniclers, he has to try to determine to what extent a grandiose vocabulary was, unthinkingly accepted, itself an obstacle to objective statement, rather than an instrument consciously adopted to eke out a bald, though not necessarily untrue, narrative. The problem is complicated, in this instance, by the peculiar linguistic situation. A Chinese word or phrase, which to the eye is heavy with implications of political or cultural advancement, may be read in Japanese as a flat, non-committal word, equally applicable to a primitive or an advanced society. Thus we are confronted with the highly technical and difficult question of the extent to which such phrases were 'read' by their users, and by the small circle of readers, in a Chinese or in a Japanese way. We may at least be certain that some mental confusion and consequent historical obfuscation, chiefly in the form of involuntary anachronisms, resulted from this situation.

The use of Chinese embellishment varied, as has been indicated, from the obscure but elegant two-character phrase to long passages, in which irreproachable Confucian sentiments are attributed to emperors and other heroes who can have been no more than illiterate tribal chieftains or priests. It is likely that the latter are due less to deliberate falsification or glorification than to an unconscious projection by the compilers of their own ideas into the past, a reflection in the intellectual mirror of their time. Though it is true that they made much use of thesauri, it is also certain that by the beginning of the eighth century, if not considerably earlier, many Chinese works, *in toto*, had been brought over to Japan and studied there. The list includes, among the orthodox Confucian texts, the Classics of Poetry, History, and Filial Piety, the Analects, the Spring and Autumn Annals, the Rites and Mencius; Mo Tzu, Kuan Tzu and Han Fei Tzu, among the works of the other schools; the *Shih chi* and the official histories of the Han and Sui dynasties, among the histories. This list, which cannot nearly be exhaustive, and which omits the numerous Chinese translations of the Buddhist canon, represents a considerable body of literature. Since such material would have constituted almost the sole intellectual diet of those qualified, by their literacy, to write a national history, it would have been surprising if Confucian ideas, as well as phraseology, had not saturated their work. There are, too, signs in the text that the choice of quotation was not always purely arbitrary but governed by some sort of genuine historical sense. An example of this is even provided by the notorious case, already mentioned, of the Sui emperor's edict attributed to an earlier Japanese emperor. The texts of the *Nihon Shoki* and the Sui History are almost identical at this point, except for trivial verbal discrepancies and for one brief but remarkable departure in the *Nihon Shoki* from the sense of the original. Where the Sui History says that the population at large is not abundantly provided with food and clothing, the *Nihon Shoki* says, 'In the capital and the country the clothing and caps have not yet attained to freshness and neatness' (tr. Aston). Eight characters have been substituted for the same number in the original, thus preserving the original rhythm. This bathetic item, in a dying edict, should almost certainly be connected with other items in the account of the same reign, which are concerned with sericulture and textiles and which are probably founded on the undoubted facts of Japanese intercourse with south China, during the fifth century, and the arrival of numerous Chinese artisans, including weavers. Again, the first mention of the activity of scribes or recorders is embodied in a phrase taken straight from the *Tso Chuan*, the commentary on the Spring and Autumn Annals. For that reason alone it is rejected out of hand by some critics as having no historical value. And yet the analogy of a neighbouring contemporary kingdom in Korea, combined with the inherent likelihood of the institution of some sort of recording at or about the date alleged (early fifth century), is at least sufficient to cast doubt on the validity of rejecting the entry on the sole ground of its provenance.

Detractors of the *Nihon Shoki* may find their surest ground in the failure of the compilers to make use of some Chinese historical sources. It seems almost certain that this failure was deliberate, since the relevant material must have been available in Japan. Patriotic motives must have been the reason for this. For the relevant Chinese materials naturally depict Japan not only as a barbarous country, but also as a vassal of China. For example, a Japanese sovereign of the fifth century is reported by the Chinese to have requested confirmation by them of his titles of 'King of the Wa and Generalissimo Who Maintains Peace in the East', etc.[14] Rather than try to tamper with records of such indignities, the Japanese chroniclers seem to have chosen simply to ignore them. However, the more formal and equal intercourse between the two countries, initiated by Prince Shōtoku, is less offensively treated in the Sui History, which, with a few modifications suggested by patriotic feeling, seems to have provided the basis of the *Nihon Shoki*'s account of the matter.

In their use of Korean sources, however, the Japanese were less circumspect. They not only used them but frequently quoted them, leaving unaltered a number of expressions which contradict the idea, fostered elsewhere in the work, of Japanese hegemony in Korea. Indeed, whatever may be thought of the objectivity of the *Nihon Shoki* as a whole, the valuable account of relations between Japan and the kingdoms of Korea during the fifth and sixth centuries is remarkably free from tendentiousness, while it contains numerous comments on matters of detail which clearly reflect a desire for accuracy. As was remarked above, not even the chronology of this subject appears to have been tampered with.

Meticulous examination of source material is, indeed, evident elsewhere in the work. It appears that entries concerning Buddhism at the end of the sixth and beginning of the seventh century were based on inscriptions of the period, while alternative accounts of an event or variant versions of a genealogy are frequently offered. Such variants are, unfortunately, usually introduced with some such phrase as', 'One document says . . .', 'Another document says . . .', etc., but, in addition, six native sources and three Korean ones are actually named. The greatest proliferation of variants occurs in the account of the legendary period or 'Divine Age', contained in the first two chapters of the work, where as many as eleven different versions of a story are offered, and almost every legend is presented in at least one alternative form. This elaborate treatment of the Divine Age, together with the continued appearance of the supernatural in the accounts of the reigns of the human emperors, is sufficient indication that the chroniclers were far from being so sophisticated as to distinguish between the divine and human periods in point of historical value; for different, but related, reasons, the modern historian must also avoid this distinction.

Doubtless many alternative variants were suppressed in the interest of clarifying dynastic claims, but at least no attempt was made to depict all the emperors as 'sage rulers', or, in general, to create in the past a golden age such as provided the pseudo-historical basis of Confucian political

[14] For the relevant Chinese materials fully translated, see Ryusaku Tsunoda and L. Carrington Goodrich, *Japan in the Chinese Dynastic Histories* (South Pasadena, 1951).

theory. Many of the early emperors are quite featureless, while to others are attributed acts of the grossest injustice and cruelty, presumably on the basis of strong tradition. Even in the matter of the war of succession of the Emperor Temmu himself, to which a whole chapter is devoted, the white-wash does not appear to have been very thickly applied. It is true that there exists no other source of information about this episode, but this conclusion may be justified by some of the wording; and, at least, the claims of the rival brother, Prince Ōtomo, are allowed to survive with sufficient clarity to have justified posterity in deciding that Prince Ōtomo did in fact reign as emperor.

Nothing is known of the personalities of those responsible for producing the *Nihon Shoki*. In any case, though revealing a natural bias, the work cannot be said to bear the impress of a single mind. It is truly a compila-tion, to which many hands appear to have contributed over a number of years. This is attested by variations in style, as well as suggested by incon-sistencies; and there even exists a draft of part of the work,[15] which, when compared with the finished product, helps to show how the compilers worked. The draft consists of a framework of purely dynastic items, lack-ing whole categories of information (concerning, for example, Korea, Buddhism, public works, etc.), considerably less precise in dating, less correct in Chinese grammar, less embellished with Chinese ornament than the final work. The editorial method emerges as 'scissors-and-paste', fol-lowed by assiduous polishing. The compilers' qualities as historians might be summed up by saying that they displayed, as almost all others in a like situation would display, an inability to distinguish between unreliable legend and reliable tradition; they had little aptitude for handling docu-mentary evidence, beyond either ignoring it, as in the case of much Chinese material, or reproducing it almost unedited, as in the case of the Korean material; though impelled in their work by a strong bias, they were not sufficiently skilful either to conceal their bias or to make the whole of their narrative consistent with it; finally, where the bones of a story were sus-ceptible of circumstantial or stylistic adornment, they revealed imagina-tion and skill in supplying these commodities.

In comparison with the ambiguities of the *Nihon Shoki*, the remaining five chronicles offer few points of interest in the present context. Certain formal aspects of these works were treated above; it now remains to make a few further comments on their contents.

The later chronicles are probably as reliable, within their narrow com-pass, as they are arid. Snellen concluded of the *Shoku Nihongi* (Chronicles

---

[15] For the existence of this draft, see G. W. Robinson, 'The Kuji Hongi: volumes 7, 8, and 9 considered as a draft of the Nihon Shoki', in *Memoirs of the Research Department of the Toyo Bunko*, No. 14 (Tokyo, 1955), pp. 81–138. A Japanese translation of this article appears in *Tōyō Gakuhō* xli, 1 (June, 1958), 67–127.

of Japan, continued) that, 'we can look confidently upon the *Shoku Nihongi* as a reliable, chronologically arranged record of events which had the attention of the Court of the Emperor of Japan in the eighth century A.D.'. This conclusion, *mutatis mutandis*, may be applied to the four subsequent chronicles also. What is important here is not only the reliability but the implied narrowness of scope. These chronicles cover a period, which, at the capital, was generally one of peace and tranquillity, enlivened by court intrigues and not seriously disturbed by the reports of the distant campaigns against the Ainu. Thus, these chronicles, representing as they do a selection from governmental archives, probably give an accurate reflection of the preoccupations of the central government of the day, when they record a prodigious proportion of triviality. The relative amount of space allotted suggests a deeper interest in the minutiae of court rank and dress than, for example, in provincial famines. Such items as the latter, too, are recorded strictly from the central point of view, as matters on which official action was taken. A few examples from Snellen's translation of the *Shoku Nihongi* well illustrate this: 'There was famine in seven provinces, Kawachi, Settsu, Izumo, Aki, Kii, Sanuki and Iyo, this was alleviated by sending presents'; or, 'Epidemic disease in Shinano, this was remedied by granting medicine'; or, even, 'Famine in Sanuki, this was lamented.' In the subsequent chronicles, even such items of provincial interest as these diminish almost to vanishing point. Yet the tendency of these compilations, as time went on, was to cover the ground in ever-increasing detail. Thus the last, the *Nihon San Dai Jitsuroku*, is a slightly longer work than the *Shoku Nihongi*, though it deals with only thirty years as compared with ninety-five.

It need hardly be emphasized that the use of the Chinese language no longer led, as it did in the case of the *Nihon Shoki*, to terminological anachronisms and general confusion. It was, on the contrary, the natural medium for recording the routine of a government of which all the departments and officials had Chinese titles. Grandiloquent edicts, loaded with Chinese quotations, recall the similar edicts recorded in the *Nihon Shoki*; but unlike most of those of the *Nihon Shoki*, these edicts were actually delivered. But the continuing preference of the compilers for transcribing selected material rather than attempting a summary, is, fortunately, responsible for the preservation of a form of ceremonial edict written in Japanese.

The predominance of members of one family, the Fujiwara, among the editorial staffs of these chronicles, might at first sight have sinister implications, and suggest that the reliability of these works may be more apparent than real. But this is no more than a reflection of the political situation, in which the principal government posts were gradually falling into the hands of this one family. To say that the chronicles accurately reflect the preoccupations of the central administration is to say that they reflect those of the Fujiwara. Moreover, the system by which the task of historical compilation fell to senior officials, was not a Fujiwara invention. They undertook the task in their capacities as officials of the bureaucracy. When, ultimately, they succeeded in shifting real authority away from the bureaucracy, leaving its machinery to turn over in undiminished elegance in a vacuum, and became themselves *de facto* rulers, the series of official chronicles came to an end.

G. W. ROBINSON

*Formerly Lecturer in the History of the Far East,
School of Oriental and African Studies, University of London*

*and*

W. G. BEASLEY

*Professor of the History of the Far East, University of London*[1]

(*a*) *The Historical Tales* (*rekishi monogatari*)

Japan made her first contribution in the field of historical writing during the eleventh century. Her previous essays in this field had been virtually confined to works of a purely annalistic type, written in Chinese by official committees and so consciously based on Chinese models as scarcely to exhibit, beyond their contents, any Japanese characteristics. The first section of this paper is concerned with the emergence and early development of the first histories to be written in Japanese prose.[2] Though the new genre soon decayed, without closely approaching perfection, it had cleared the way for other developments, equally remote from the Chinese tradition, which are discussed in section (*b*) below.

These early histories written in Japanese are now generally known as *rekishi monogatari* or 'historical tales', a term sufficiently indicative of their 'popular' and informal nature. The principal extant examples may be briefly listed, in the probable order of their composition, as follows:

*Eiga Monogatari* (Tale of Splendour). This relates in strict chronological order the history of the period 889 to 1092. The 'Splendour' is that of the statesman Fujiwara Michinaga (966–1028), to whose period of power the bulk of the work is devoted. There is no certainty concerning the authorship, but it is generally, though not universally, held that of the work's forty chapters the last ten, which deal with the period after Michinaga's death, were by a later hand.

*Ōkagami* (Great Mirror). The period covered is from 850 to about 1025, with most space devoted to the Fujiwara statesmen, especially Michinaga.

---

[1] The authors are each responsible for one section of this paper: G. W. Robinson for section (*a*), The Historical Tales; W. G. Beasley for section (*b*), The early feudal period.

[2] This subject has already been treated in English in Reischauer and Yamagiwa, *Translations from Early Japanese Literature* (Harvard U.P., 1951). The third section of the book is a translation of the most important part of the *Ōkagami* (Great Mirror), preceded by a lengthy introduction. This introduction contains some detailed argument concerning date and authorship as well as much bibliographical information on Japanese critical works, which will not be repeated here.

This is the first Japanese historical work to make use of the same arrangement of material as the Chinese Standard Histories: chronicles of emperors followed by biographies of statesmen and discourses on special topics. Date and authorship are both matters of conjecture. The most general view is that the work was written early in the twelfth century. It is universally held to be the finest of the genre, both as history and as literature.

*Imakagami* (Mirror of the Present Day). This continues the narrative of the Great Mirror to 1170, the date of its composition. The arrangement of the material is the same as that of the Great Mirror, of which it is in other ways also an imitation. Authorship is again uncertain.

*Mizukagami* (Water Mirror). This relates all Japanese history from Jimmu, the first emperor, to the beginning of the period covered by the Great Mirror, using a purely chronological arrangement. It is little more than a translation into Japanese of the relevant portion of a history called *Fusō Ryakki* (Abridged History of Japan), which was written in Chinese. The Water Mirror has long been attributed to a certain Nakayama Tadachika, who died in 1195, but this has recently been called in question and the work is held by some scholars to belong to the fourteenth century.

*Masukagami* (Pellucid Mirror). This covers, in chronological order, the period 1183 to 1333. Like the Tale of Splendour and Great Mirror, the work has a central theme, which in this case is the struggle between the court nobles and the military, following the foundation of the Kamakura Bakufu. The author has not been satisfactorily identified but was clearly an adherent of the Southern Court during the period of division. The work was written some time between 1333 and 1376.

Another work of this kind was written about the end of the twelfth century but has not survived. Two others appeared as late as the eighteenth century, but they are unnatural extensions of the series and as such fail to merit attention.

These works are as different as could well be imagined from previous historical writing in Japan. They differ in language, being written in Japanese instead of Chinese. They differ in authorship, being the work of private individuals (usually anonymous) instead of compilations by official committees. They differ in content and emphasis, being no longer confined to the fortunes of the throne and the central government, and are far less rigidly constructed than their predecessors. In so far as it is impossible to point to any transitional work the change appears not as gradual but sudden, so that it is important not only to examine the nature of such work but to inquire into the circumstances in which it came into being.

Of the series of official chronicles compiled from the early eighth century onwards,[3] the last to have survived was produced in 901 and con-

[3] On the subject of these earlier chronicles, see the paper by G. W. Robinson, above, pp. 213–28.

cludes its narrative with the year 888; a final work, which has not survived, probably continued the narrative to about 930. No definite reason can be assigned for the cessation of this series. It is true that in the ninth century Japan broke off official relations with China, where the T'ang power was on the decline, so that any considerations of prestige *vis-à-vis* China, that may hitherto have motivated the maintenance of these records, would cease to operate. But the cessation of the series was also probably in some way related to the change in the nature and tenure of political power, which began in the latter half of the ninth century. This change requires a brief description here, since, as well as being a likely partial cause of the discontinuance of the old type of history, it provided the inspiration and subject matter for the new.

The theoretical basis of the political system adopted and adapted by Japan from China in the middle of the seventh century was that the emperor should rule personally through the agency of his Great Council of State and its subordinate offices. In the course of time, one clan, the Fujiwara, managed to engross so many of the principal offices of state under this system, that further extension of their power could only come through some means of usurping that of the throne itself. This they contrived by marrying their daughters to emperors; then, soon after such a union had produced a son, the maternal grandfather would persuade the father to abdicate and would himself undertake the task of ruling as Regent (*Sesshō*) for the minor emperor. When circumstances made it necessary for an emperor of mature years to remain on the throne, his maternal grandfather would merely change his title from Regent to Chancellor (*Kampaku*) and retain his power unimpaired. This system persisted, with minor checks and variations, for some 200 years; and the Fujiwara reached the highest point of their power and splendour in the early years of the eleventh century, in the time of Michinaga. Though the Chinese form of bureaucracy was not discarded, it was often by-passed by the regents and chancellors, and many of its activities became more decorative than functional.

During the period of this oblique and peculiarly Japanese system of government, there gradually grew up in the peaceful capital a peculiarly Japanese literary and artistic culture. Until the ninth century, the chief literary use to which the Japanese language had been put was poetical. The development of a prose literature had had to wait on the evolution of a convenient method of writing Japanese; such a method having been devised, it was first exploited in the field of prose fiction. Though initially such work was written and read only by women, it was not long before male palates, also, surfeited with Chinese literature, learnt to savour the delicate Japanese dishes prepared by the ladies of the court. Western readers are happily in a position to obtain insight into the life and literature of tenth-century Japan through Dr. Waley's translation of The Tale of Genji (*Genji Monogatari*).[4] This long novel of court life was written by the lady Murasaki Shikibu in the early years of the eleventh century and is universally held to represent the highest point of development of this literary genre. The ensuing decadence was temporarily arrested or diverted, towards the end of the century, when the medium of Japanese prose and some of the techniques and ideas of fiction were applied to historiography.

Thus the Tale of Splendour and Great Mirror are substitutes for rather than successors to the official chronicles, while their true ancestry was The Tale of Genji and its predecessors. In the first place, the development of prose fiction had made the Japanese language available to the historian. It is commonly stated by modern critics that the authors of the new histories elected to use Japanese rather than Chinese as being more suitable for their chosen subject matter. For example, Yamagiwa says, 'The authors of the historical tales must have felt that in order to depict the elegant and charming life of the aristocracy of that era, the more easily manageable *kana* was clearly the more suitable medium. This might have been expected from the antecedent history of historical and narrative writing; still the joining of historical materials and narrative techniques expressed in syllabic characters shows the workings of a sound literary sense.'[5] But there is surely at least a suggestion here of the tail wagging the dog. The antecedent and contemporary history and popularity of prose fiction must have exerted a compulsive force on any literary aspirant at the turn of the eleventh to the twelfth century. The sound literary sense was at work, not in choosing Japanese as its medium, but in drawing history into the scope of that medium, a step naturally suggested by, *inter alia*, the realism of contemporary novels, short stories, and diaries.

Again, the most remarkable technical innovation in the historical tales, whereby the narrative is made to emerge in the course of a conversation between a number of fictitious characters, was presumably a borrowing, however indirect and unconscious, from the novelist's technique. This device appears as the invention of the author of the Great Mirror, by whom alone it was effectively used; in the subsequent 'Mirrors' it was so perfunctorily imitated as to add little to the exposition.

The Great Mirror purports to be a conversation which takes place among a small group of persons who happen to meet while waiting about at a monastery for a sermon to begin. The persons are: Ōyake Yotsugi, aged 150 (or 190 in some versions), who is the chief narrator; Natsuyama Shigeki, aged 140 (or 180), who generally acts as a kind of one-man claque to Yotsugi; together with Shigeki's aged wife, a young man and the author of the Great Mirror, who interject personal views, comments,

[4] Subsequent reference to this translation is made to the edition in one volume, published by Allen and Unwin (London, 1935).     [5] Reischauer and Yamagiwa, op. cit., p. 278.

and questions. The author tries to make his interlocutors real and human, and he is to some extent successful, especially with the old men. By means of the gentle fantasy of their fabulous age, he is able to suggest that his narrative is largely an eyewitness account; and often, indeed, especially through the descriptions of splendid garments, this illusion is remarkably well maintained. Further verisimilitude is sometimes subtly suggested by making the old men confess that they cannot remember with certainty. Some modern Japanese critics find themselves reluctantly obliged to object that violence is done to verisimilitude by the impossible length of the conversation, which could not have taken place within the stated time. But this is to confuse realism with naturalism; the objection, though true, is artistically irrelevant.

The conversational device is of special service to the author in two ways. It enables him to introduce alternative accounts of episodes with elegance and with graduated emphasis, in a manner impossible in the old official chronicles, with their direct formula, 'another book says . . .' Much more important than this was the convenient vehicle for the expression of criticism and censure which the device obviously affords. Such overt criticism was virtually without precedent in Japanese history.

It is a pity that this pleasant invention was never afterwards developed. It is true that old Yotsugi's granddaughter appears as one of the speakers in the Mirror of the Present Day (*Imakagami*), but in that work, as in the other 'Mirrors', the conversation is used only at the beginning and the end, and the speakers are conventionalized into lifelessness.

In one point of technique, however, the Great Mirror (and Mirror of the Present Day) borrowed, not from the writers of fiction, but from the Chinese historians. For the first time in Japanese historiography the material is arranged in the manner of the Chinese dynastic histories in chronicles of emperors and biographies of famous men, together with separate discussions of selected topics. But in this example of Japanese imitation of a foreign technique, the accusation of thoughtless mimicry will not lie. For, as has already been shown, the author of the Great Mirror was not uninventive. His object was to glorify a particular man, and this Chinese method of arrangement offered a means of devoting a specific portion of his work to that man, without so far departing from the conventional requirements of history as to ignore the august claims of the emperors to a place in the record. He saw clearly enough that Michinaga's splendour had to be understood in relation to the imperial court, which, in theory, he served; and he further explains or excuses his accounts of reigns much earlier than the time of his hero by means of the analogy of Buddha, who, before elucidating the Lotus Sutra, found it necessary to expound certain other sutras. It is true that in the Chinese dynastic histories, also, the chronicles of the emperors normally occupy only a small proportion of the whole, but none of those histories is so 'slanted' as is the Great Mirror. Moreover, though within this Chinese framework, the Great Mirror does not offer a rigid year-by-year account, such as faithful imitation of the Chinese model would involve.

In the Mirror of the Present Day no particular use is made of this arrangement, which is clearly derived, along with Yotsugi's granddaughter, directly and without positive purpose from the preceding work.

The arrangement of the other historical tales, being purely chronological, need not be assigned to any specific influence or example. Certain Chinese precedents had originally prompted the adoption of such an arrangement for the old official chronicles, and these in their turn may vaguely have influenced the authors of the Tale of Splendour (*Eiga Monogatari*) and Pellucid Mirror (*Masukagami*) in employing this natural if primitive arrangement. The author of the Tale of Splendour seems, at any rate, to have seen himself as continuing the official chronicles, when he started his own work at the point, the year 889, at which the last surviving chronicle (*Nihon San Dai Jitsuroku*) ceased. The chronological framework, though less rigidly used than in the chronicles, still constitutes an impediment to the fulfilment of the author's purpose, whereas in the Pellucid Mirror it is quite appropriate to the theme of the work. In both works the influence of fiction's modes of presentation can be seen at work in the chapter headings which allude in some way to the content, setting or, sometimes, poetry of the various chapters.

Even more important than the new technical equipment, made available to historians by the development of prose fiction, was the new conception of history, which was also engendered by fiction. This new conception embodied two salient ideas, an idea of the complexity of history and the consequent desirability of extracting from that complexity an historical theme.

It seems to have been appreciated that the past did not merely consist of a series of discrete and equally significant events, such as constituted almost the sole content of the old chronicles. The realism of fiction gave rise to the notion that the characters and everyday lives of the great men of the past were also 'history', just as much as the great events in which they played a part. There is a passage in The Tale of Genji which is of the greatest interest in this connection.[6] The hero, Prince Genji, is represented as 'vindicating the storyteller's profession as an art of real importance'. In the course of his vindication, he says, 'So you see as a matter of fact I think far better of this art than I have led you to suppose. Even its practical value is immense. Without it what should we know of how people lived in the past, from the Age of the Gods down to the present day? For history-books such as the Chronicles of Japan show us only one small

[6] Waley, op. cit., p. 501.

corner of life; whereas these diaries and romances which I see piled around you contain, I am sure, the most minute information about all sorts of people's private affairs. . . .' He goes on to emphasize that a novel must be true to life, realistic, and to show how this obliges the novelist to treat of vice as well as of virtue. Murasaki is concerned to make out a case for the seriousness of her art; but in so doing she also undoubtedly makes a good case for the importance of realism in historical writing and for the inclusion in an historical work of much that had hitherto lain outside its scope.

There were, of course, a number of forces acting to bring the historical tale into being, and it would doubtless be absurd to insist that the creation of the first of them, the Tale of Splendour, was directly due to the inspiration of the passage just quoted. But we can certainly affirm that The Tale of Genji was popular and influential and that it had been read by the author of the Tale of Splendour. The work, however, lacks a preface and nowhere turns aside from its theme to comment on the nature of history itself. The author of the *Ōkagami* is more articulate, both in his preface and through the mouths of his old raconteurs; while the name itself, 'Great Mirror', is probably connected with the new scope of history.

The name, Great Mirror, was not given to the work by its author, nor is it clear when and how the name arose. But in 1170 the *Imakagami* (Mirror of the Present Day) appeared under its present title, and the Great Mirror may by that date already have been known as a 'mirror', possibly as *Furukagami*, or 'Old Mirror', the words *ima* and *furu* being a common antithetical pair.

The term 'mirror' apparently implies that the work reflects reality. This is now, in various languages, a familiar use of the term, but these Japanese 'mirrors' seem to be the earliest examples of such titles in world literature. It should be noted that the usage is distinct from that in the title of the Sung historian Ssu-ma Kuang's *Tzu chih t'ung chien* (Comprehensive Mirror for Aid in Government). There, or in such works as 'A Mirror for Magistrates' or the 'Speculum Stultorum', the term implies a didactic or admonitory purpose, which is absent from the Japanese usage.

The topic is ventilated in the Great Mirror, in a passage translated by Yamagiwa.[7] When Yotsugi has completed his account of the emperors and is about to proceed with that of the ministers, an exchange takes place between him and Shigeki, which includes the following remarks:

Shigeki says, 'Although you have (already) held the mirror up to the circumstances of the many Emperors, now, in addition (to hear you speak of) the circumstances of the Great Ministers is to feel as if the morning sun were to burst brightly (upon us) . . . I am like the mirror that lies thrust in the comb-box . . . it hardly reflects anything . . .' A little later, Shigeki recites a poem, 'When I look upon a shining mirror, Both

[7] Reischauer and Yamagiwa, op. cit., p. 291.

those things already past and those still in the future do I see.' Yotsugi's poem in reply says, 'Oh, I am an old mirror that sees anew Both the remains of the Emperors (and their Great Ministers), one after the other, with no one hidden.'

Though the implications of these and a few further remarks would seem to be reasonably clear, some commentators believe that the Great Mirror was not without a didactic purpose, its aim being to show the future reflected in the past, and to indicate that the line of the emperors, already long, shall extend for ever into the future. This, they maintain, is even dimly implicit in the name of Yotsugi, which means 'succession of ages', and they adduce also the poem of Shigeki, quoted above. But, as for the poem, it has been plausibly suggested that the things 'still in the future' are simply those which Yotsugi is about to relate.

There is evidence from the titles of the other 'mirrors' too, and from their prefaces and epilogues. For example, the author of the *Mizukagami* chose his title, Water Mirror, in deference to the superiority of the Great Mirror, his idea being that water is an imperfect reflector. At the end of his work, the same author also gives a possible clue to the origin of the name Great Mirror and indicates the esteem in which that work was held, when he writes, 'Even the volumes of the Great Mirror, being as they are the work of an ordinary mortal, are far from matching the mirror of Buddha's Knowledge of the Great Round Mirror.' This latter expression refers to one of the Four Knowledges of Buddhism and is generally defined by saying that, just as in a great round mirror all phenomena might be displayed, so is there a knowledge which is the disclosure, in the round fulness of all virtues, of all the Laws.

This consideration of the term 'mirror' in this context, though far from exhaustive, may yet seem excessive. But the realization that the total of the past was a complexity beyond human knowledge and comprehension and at the same time a subject of deep interest seems to have been implicit in the use of the term. From this realization seems to have sprung the idea that an historical work could and should have a specific theme. Although the forms used by the new historians remained superficially those of China, the proportions of their works were quite different. A truly thematic treatment lies outside the traditions of Chinese historical writing, where a simple annalistic presentation is given even to a restricted topic or theme. Thus the authors of the Tale of Splendour and Great Mirror were breaking new ground when they attempted so to construct their works as to emphasize the glory of Fujiwara Michinaga, introducing other matter chiefly in order to give background or context to their main theme. Out of the first thirty chapters of the Tale of Splendour (which were probably the whole of the original work) no less than twenty-eight deal with the time of Michinaga; in the Great Mirror, also, more space is devoted to Michinaga than to any other single reign or minister. This disposition of space (assisted in the second work by the new arrangement of the material) constituted the principal means by which the authors fulfilled their ends. In trying to idealize his hero in much the same way as Murasaki's hero is idealized, the author of the Tale of Splendour, especially, is generally content to reduce his 'coverage' of any other subjects. Thus, in spite of the undoubted new consciousness of the complexity of the past and in spite of the inclusion of effects almost unthinkable in the old chronicles, we are given an account which omits much of political significance—much, indeed, which would have been included in the old chronicles. This criticism, applicable to the Great Mirror also, though to a lesser degree, is even more pertinent to the Pellucid Mirror; the author of that work, lacking the excuse which might be made for the other two authors of being almost more biographers than historians, is so interested in his theme of the struggle between civilian and military (Court and Bakufu) as scarcely to notice the matter of the Mongol invasion. This last fact, indeed, may remind the English reader of certain illustrious parallels in English letters, and may thus serve as a useful reminder that these histories are works of literature, not mere records. There are, of course, times when the effort to recast the matter of history in a literary or popular form breaks down, and we are given facts raw.

Apart from the Water Mirror (*Mizukagami*), which reproduces the many curious and erroneous anecdotes of its original, the *Fusō Ryakki*, these tales can be generally relied on to give accurate information. Such errors as are disclosed by collation with other sources appear to be those of mere inadvertence. The traditions of accuracy, taken over by the chroniclers from China, seem to have been respected also by the authors of the Historical Tales. It appears, for example, that the author of the Great Mirror was at pains to correct certain quite trivial errors he had discerned in the Tale of Splendour. Naturally we are in no position to check or verify all the information offered. But satisfactory verification of chronological or genealogical facts makes us the more ready to accept the wealth of more nebulous and less easily verifiable accounts of social and religious customs or personal descriptions.

It is generally accepted that a pervasive nostalgia for the peace and prosperity of the early years of the eleventh century was ultimately responsible for the appearance of the first of these tales in the more disturbed times which set in towards the end of the century. As Yamagiwa says, these tales 'record the high fortunes of Michinaga taken as the highest representative of the vanishing glories of the aristocracy'.[8] Thus, considering the nostalgic hero-worship which motivated the authors, their devotion to accuracy is the more creditable. Especially is this true of the Great Mirror,

[8] Reischauer and Yamagiwa, op. cit., p. 279.

in which, through the medium of the dialogue form, even the seamier side of certain transactions is reflected in the mirror of its pages.

The methods of these historians may have been crude and their success only partial. Their literary style was inferior in power and variety to that perfected by their predecessors in fiction. Nevertheless, historical writing in Japan had been freed by them from the Chinese chains. In the period which followed, partly under the influence of further political changes, it proceeded to develop along lines so various that, while recognizably Chinese in many of its elements, it could no longer be described merely as a local variant of Chinese historiography.

### (b) Historical writing in the early feudal period

By the twelfth century the power of the Fujiwara family had greatly weakened. In the Court itself it was being challenged by that of the so-called 'retired emperors', who made way for younger successors on the throne in order to free themselves for a more active intervention in politics. Outside the capital, a growing feudalism threatened the authority of the Court as a whole. After the middle of the century the leaders of the new *bushi* (samurai) class, having acquired control over vast areas of the country through a system of quasi-feudal relationships, were engaged in fierce disputes for political domination. Civil war between the two greatest of these, the Taira and Minamoto, resulted eventually in victory for the latter; and in the years 1185–92 Minamoto Yoritomo established at Kamakura a form of government, the Bakufu, variously described as 'feudal' or 'military', which assumed complete responsibility for the administration of Japan. At its head was Yoritomo himself with the title of Shōgun, ostensibly as the Emperor's military deputy, in practice a *de facto* ruler. In the provinces his nominees gradually took over the functions of the civil officials appointed by the Court, thereby increasing also their control over land and revenues, until in the thirteenth and fourteenth centuries both the economic and political position of the Court aristocracy was entirely undermined.

The system so created, with varying fortunes and under successive houses of hereditary Shōgun, persisted for nearly seven hundred years. In that period, two major attempts were made by the Imperial Court to resume its former powers. The first was under the Emperor Juntoku in the Shōkyū era (1219–21), the second under the Emperor Go-daigo in 1333–6. Neither was successful. Go-daigo came close to victory, for he overthrew the Hōjō at Kamakura, but they were soon replaced by a new line of Shōgun, founded by Ashikaga Takauji, and thereafter power remained firmly in feudal hands until 1868.

These far-reaching changes in the structure of Japanese society influenced also the nature of Japanese historical writing. The various 'mirrors', discussed above, had already moved some way towards a thematic treatment of history, especially in their emphasis on the great days of Fujiwara administration, and this was succeeded in the Bakufu period by a corresponding emphasis on the fortunes of the feudal class. The *Azuma Kagami* (Mirror of East Japan), for example, was a chronicle of events for the period 1180–1266, compiled by officials in Kamakura and presented from the *bushi* point of view. Despite its title, it did not follow the tradition of works like the Great Mirror. Rather, both in style and content, it invited comparison with the early Court chronicles—or with Chinese Veritable Records (*Shih-lu*)—being written in a language more Chinese than Japanese and dealing largely with official information and decrees. On the other hand, its preoccupation with the activities of the Shōgun and his ministers, as distinct from those of the Imperial Court, marked it off from all its predecessors. Different in kind, but equally concerned with feudal history, were books like the *Taiheiki*. This collection of tales of warfare from the fourteenth century, ironically entitled 'Records of Great Peace', is now regarded as a historical romance rather than as history, but its anecdotes and narrative, however unreliable, do constitute in some respects an account of the wars which brought about the fall of the Hōjō and the rise of the Ashikaga.

The outstanding historical works of this period, however, were Fujiwara Jien's *Gukanshō* (Miscellany of Ignorant Views), and Kitabatake Chikafusa's *Jinnō Shōtōki* (Records of the True Descent of the Divine Emperors).[9] It is significant that both were written at moments of crisis in Court-Bakufu relations. Most of the *Gukanshō* was drafted in 1220, at the time of Juntoku's abortive attempt to overthrow the Kamakura Bakufu, while the *Jinnō Shōtōki* dates from about 1340, soon after Go-daigo's brief period of personal rule, when the re-establishment of *bushi* power under Ashikaga Takauji had already forced Go-daigo into exile, as founder of a rival Southern Court in Yoshino. In these circumstances, it is not surprising that both books showed a marked interest in problems concerning the location of political authority. Their attempts to establish, through a discussion of past events, the proper relationship between an Emperor and his ministers (for example, the Fujiwara), or between Emperor and Shōgun, gave rise to an entirely new treatment of political history.[10] Moreover, in technique

[9] Subsequent references to these works are to the following editions: *Gukanshō*, ed. Nakajima Etsuji (Tokyo, 1935); *Jinnō Shōtōki*, ed. Miyaji Naokazu (Tokyo, 1934) [1929]. Parts of both works have been translated: of the *Gukanshō* by J. Rahder in *Acta Orientalia*, xv, 173–230; of the *Jinnō Shōtōki* by H. Bohner, under the title *Jinnō Shōtōki, Buch von der Wahren-Gott-Kaiser-Herrschafts-Linie* (Tokyo, 1935). Japanese discussions of the two books as historical writing are to be found in Kiyohara Sadao, *Nihon shigakushi* (Tokyo, 1928), pp. 57–71, 118–49, and Tsuda Sōkichi, 'Gukanshō oyobi Jinnō Shōtōki ni okeru Shina no shigaku-shisō', in *Hompō shigakushi ronsō* (2 vols., Tokyo, 1939), i, 491–524.

[10] It should be added that the Pellucid Mirror (*Masukagami*) also dates from the fourteenth century and shows a similar preoccupation with the struggle between Court and Bakufu: see section (*a*), above, p. 230.

and in their theoretical approach to historical writing they represented a considerable advance on anything which had gone before. For both reasons they merit more detailed consideration.

The author of the Miscellany of Ignorant Views (*Gukanshō*), the Buddhist priest Jichin (Fujiwara Jien, 1155–1225), was a son of the Chancellor Fujiwara Tadamichi and brother to Kujō Kanezane, who became Regent to the Emperor under the patronage of the first Shōgun, Minamoto Yoritomo. The complexity of political relationships which this implied was reflected in his writing. As a Fujiwara he viewed his family's record with some pride and justified it where he could, while the close link which his own branch of the family had established with the new feudal rulers disposed him to defend the Shōgun's assumption of authority. The arguments he advanced, which owed much to both Buddhist and Confucian theory, went briefly as follows. The history of Japan, he said, showed a progressive decline in moral standards from age to age. This both explained and justified political changes, for it was in the interests of good government that the Fujiwara had emerged to supplement Imperial power; and the breakdown of their authority in turn, with its resulting turmoil, made necessary the supremacy of 'military officials', by whom alone order could be restored. In other words, as Jichin saw it, the ideal situation was one in which an Emperor held a just balance among his ministers, but in periods of decadence it might be necessary for the country's sake that ministers should assume the leading role, as had happened in Japan first with the Fujiwara, then with the Minamoto.

There is clear evidence of Chinese influence in Jichin's thinking. His concept of moral values was not derived directly from China, but the connection which he described as existing between right behaviour on the part of rulers and the fortunes of the country or of the dynasty was thoroughly Chinese. So, too, was the cyclical theory which he applied to segments of Japanese history within the overall pattern of decline. Similarly, his argument that an ability to maintain order and provide effective government constituted the essential basis of legitimacy bears a strong resemblance to the Chinese doctrine of the Mandate of Heaven (*t'ien ming*), though Jichin applied it not to the rise and fall of dynasties—which was impossible in a Japanese context—so much as to the possession of hereditary power by ministers, like the Regent (*Sesshō*) and the Chancellor (*Kampaku*) or the Shōgun, and to the relationship between their authority and that of the Emperor.

In its application of these ideas, the *Gukanshō* followed a line of its own, as it did also in the method of their presentation. It did not adopt the standard pattern of arrangement of the Chinese dynastic histories, as the Great Mirror had done, for example, though its structure was in some ways reminiscent of them. Of its seven books, the first two, which seem to have been the last to be written, consisted of formal accounts of the Emperors from Jimmu to Go-horikawa (1222–33), dealing with such matters as the Emperor's parentage, marriage, children, principal officials, and the briefest possible list of important events during his reign. There followed the main substance of the work in Books III–VI. These, as the author stated in the preface to Book III, sought to expound the principles underlying historical change,[12] to explain the reasons for peace and civil war, for victory and defeat. Finally, in Book VII, the argument was brought together in theoretical terms and a policy indicated by which improvement might in future be achieved.

Books III–VI, although arranged chronologically by reigns of Emperors, also made use of a seven-part periodization of Japanese history. Its divisions may be summarized as, first, the reigns of the first thirteen Emperors from Jimmu to Seimu; second, Emperors Chūai to Kimmei (ending A.D. 572); third, from the accession of Bidatsu (572) to the great period of Fujiwara dominance under Go-ichijō, at the beginning of the eleventh century; fourth, from the early eleventh to the late twelfth centuries, ending at the reign of Go-toba (1186–99); fifth, the establishment of the Kamakura Bakufu in Go-toba's reign; sixth and seventh, the reigns of Tsuchi-mikado (1199–1211) and Juntoku (1211–21) respectively. Jichin himself described these periods[13] as stages in Japan's moral decline, but it is clear that the later ones, at least, relate more directly to political institutions. Moreover, it was to these that he devoted most of his attention, his narrative becoming more detailed as it approached his own time. The whole of Japanese history up to the early eleventh century was covered in Book III. Book IV carried the story to the reign of Go-shirakawa (1156–9), so that Books V and VI, or half the total space—the four books being almost exactly equal in length—were devoted to a mere sixty-odd years, approximately the years of Jichin's own life. This fact underlines the conclusions to be drawn from the nature of the views which he expressed. The *Gukanshō* was essentially purposive in its treatment of historical events. In appearance a general survey of Japanese history, its selection and arrangement of material, as well as its theoretical façade, were in fact geared to a discussion of conditions in its author's lifetime.

The Records of the True Descent of the Divine Emperors (*Jinnō Shōtōki*) by Kitabatake Chikafusa (1291–1354), just over a century later, shared many of the same characteristics, though it was less impressive as a piece of historical writing. The plan of its six books followed closely that of Books I and II of the Miscellany of Ignorant Views, on which they were clearly based, consisting for the most part of brief accounts of the Emperors, chronologically arranged and not apparently governed by any such rules

---

[12] 'yo no utsuri-yuku dōri': *Gukanshō*, p. 93. The same expression is used at the end of Book II (ibid., p. 90).    [13] Specifically in the early part of Book VII: *Gukanshō*, pp. 265–8.

of periodization as had distinguished its predecessor. Book I dealt with the Age of Gods, a period Jichin had chosen to ignore. Book II covered the reigns of the first twenty Emperors, Book III the following thirty, Books IV and V a further twenty each. Only Book VI broke the numerical pattern, since no more than six reigns were left for discussion.

Within this framework, however, Kitabatake Chikafusa occasionally broke new ground. The majority of his entries were similar to, though not usually so precise as, those of Jichin's Miscellany, Books I and II;[14] but he also adopted the practice, followed by many later writers as well, of interpolating more detailed surveys of events, or comments of his own, under whichever reign seemed most appropriate to them. In this way he succeeded, albeit rather clumsily, in making a single chronological series serve the purposes both of factual statement and interpretation. One might illustrate this by summarizing the longest entry, that for the reign of the Emperor Go-daigo (1319–39). It begins, after the usual formal prelimi-naries concerning the Emperor's parentage, upbringing, etc., with an account of the struggles against the Hōjō and the attack on Kamakura. Then comes a description of the honours and rewards bestowed on Ashi-kaga Takauji for his part in the Imperial victory. These, as Chikafusa points out, enabled him eventually to promote his own nominees and assume complete control of government, with the result that 'what was expected to become a *kuge* world has in fact become a *buke* world'.[15] At this point the narrative is halted while the author turns to a more general discussion of the background to these events. He starts by enunciating, in recognizably Chinese terms, the principles on which sound government must be based: first, the selection of suitable officials; second, the proper disposal of provinces and districts, which must not be allowed to fall into private hands; third, a just distribution of rewards and punishments. In all these Japan had failed, he said, in recent centuries. It was not merely that Takauji had been rewarded above his merits. The decline had begun as early as the Kankō period (1004–12), from which time on, under Fujiwara dominance, appointments to Court offices had too often been made because of family relationships or poetic skill rather than virtue and ability. As confusion grew, moreover, it became a frequent practice to make outright gifts of land by way of reward, instead of grants for limited periods, as had been the custom earlier, until by the beginning of the twelfth century no more than one per cent remained under the control of the central administration. Widespread disorder finally made necessary the emergence of a new military form of government, the Bakufu. This in its

[14] Compare, for example, the entries under Emperor Kammu: *Gukanshō*, pp. 34–35; *Jinnō Shōtōki*, pp. 131–3. The former gives much more precise data on such matters as the era-names (*nengō*) in use during the reign, with exact dates for their adoption, etc.

[15] *Jinnō Shōtōki*, p. 268, the whole entry for Emperor Godaigo being pp. 254–97. The terms *Kuge* and *Buke* denoted the Court and feudal nobility respectively.

turn enabled the *bushi* class to strengthen its hold on private land—the *shōen*, or manors—to the point at which even the Imperial prestige itself was threatened. The events of Go-daigo's reign followed as a natural consequence. Greed for land on the part of Court and feudal leaders brought a struggle for supremacy and inevitable civil war, in which the *bushi* were victorious. Here Chikafusa returns to his account of Go-daigo's reign, completing the entry with a description of the unsuccessful campaigns against Takauji in 1335-6 and Go-daigo's flight to the mountains of Yoshino.

Scattered in this way through the text of the Records of True Descent one also finds discussions of Fujiwara rule, of the role of the retired emperors, of the Hōjō's success in seizing control of Bakufu administration, and so on. Much of the interpretation, it seems, was derived directly from the Miscellany of Ignorant Views. Chikafusa, like Jichin, accepted the historical inevitability of rule by Regent, Chancellor, or Shōgun. At the same time, his book had a purpose of its own, originating, like that of the *Gukanshō*, in the political attitudes of its author. The Kitabatake family was traditionally connected with the great Shintō shrine at Ise, while Chikafusa himself was an adherent of Go-murakami, Go-daigo's successor as Emperor of the Southern Court. He was therefore concerned to urge the legitimacy of Go-daigo's line and to advocate its restoration to power in Kyōto. This task he undertook in the *Jinnō Shōtōki*. The book's very title, 'Records of the True Descent of the Divine Emperors', proclaimed what its emphasis was meant to be. Briefly, it insisted on the divine origins of the Japanese Imperial line, which ensured Amaterasu's eternal protection and guidance for it; but, it said, within the scope of the same Imperial line, there was nevertheless room for the operation of virtue as a determinant of the succession. In other words, an Emperor's actions, good or bad, might decide whether the succession passed to his own direct descendants or to another branch of the Imperial house. So stated, of course, the theory was in no way relevant to Go-murakami's claims, which Chikafusa actually argued on quite different grounds. Nor could it in its simplest form be reconciled with historical fact. This last difficulty was overcome by extending the effect of an Emperor's virtue so as to make it influence a number of generations, as well as by oblique references to the inscrutability of the will of the gods—a device which may have been useful politically but is singularly unconvincing in itself. However, it is not our concern here to examine the validity of Chikafusa's views. It is enough that they led him to impose a pattern on the writing of Japanese history.

By their use of purposive writing of this kind, linked to contemporary political problems, the *Gukanshō* and the *Jinnō Shōtōki* added a new element to Japanese historiography. In other respects they continued some of the traditions of works like the Great Mirror. Both were written in Japanese, for example, not in Chinese. The priest Jichin, in fact, at the end of Book II of the *Gukanshō*, specifically defended this choice as the only means of reaching a wider audience, while the last few pages of his work, setting out his views on future development, were presented as dialogue in a manner reminiscent of, for example, the Mirror of the Present Day (*Imakagami*). It is interesting to note, also, that in the preface to Book III Jichin gives as one of his reasons for writing the Miscellany the fact that there existed no histories like the Great Mirror (using the expression 'Yotsugi no monogatari') for the period after 1156–9. The Miscellany was thus linked consciously with the new style of historical writing. At the same time, of course, both the Miscellany (*Gukanshō*) and the Records of True Descent (*Jinnō Shōtōki*) represented new departures in point of arrangement. One might argue that the chronicle-narrative-conclusions pattern of the former was not unlike the Chinese arrangement of chronicle, biographies and monographs adopted in the Great Mirror; and that the arrangement of the *Jinnō Shōtōki*, a chronicle with interpolated passages of comment, could have been derived from examples of private historiography in China, such as Ssu-ma Kuang's Comprehensive Mirror (*Tzu-chih t'ung-chien*).[16] Chinese influence was clearly strong in both books, especially in philosophical assumptions and ideas of history, involving as they did the application to Japanese history of such concepts as the doctrine of the Mandate of Heaven, the cyclical view of dynastic rise and fall, or Confucian ethical-political theory. Yet one can point to no single Chinese model on which either could have been based in its entirety. They were more eclectic than earlier works, reflecting not so much a blind acceptance of Chinese practice as an ability to select and even modify what seemed most relevant from it. This could be described, on the one hand, as the result of greater familiarity with, and hence greater confidence in the handling of, things Chinese. On the other, it can be taken as an assertion of independence, manifesting itself in use of the Japanese language and in a concern with historical problems for which China offered no obvious parallel. It was not, of course, a rejection of the Chinese tradition. But the result was sufficiently un-Chinese to give substance to the argument that Japanese historians, by the fourteenth century, were evolving a tradition of their own. In large part this was because Japanese society was itself developing in a direction very different from that of China.

[16] On Ssu-ma Kuang's work, see the paper by E. G. Pulleyblank, above, pp. 151–66. The interpolation of comment was also a feature of the early Japanese chronicles, the *Rikkokushi*: see G. W. Robinson's paper, above, at pp. 220–1.

W. G. BEASLEY

*Professor of the History of the Far East, University of London*

*and*

CARMEN BLACKER

*Lecturer in Japanese, University of Cambridge*[1]

## 1. *General survey*

The traditions of prose writing, whether in the novel or in historiography, which had emerged in Japan in the eleventh to fourteenth centuries, did not continue to develop in the period immediately following. For over two hundred years the country was subject to almost constant civil war. In fact, it was not until the beginning of the seventeenth century that the establishment of Tokugawa rule restored law and order and thereby paved the way for a renewed interest in scholarly activity, an interest deliberately encouraged by the country's new rulers in an attempt to divert the attention of their followers from warlike to peaceful (and presumably harmless) activities. Not unnaturally, the writing of history found its place among the rest. The compilation of historical records was already regarded in Japan as one of the hallmarks of a civilized state. This tradition was strengthened by the example of Tokugawa Ieyasu, who studied the *Azuma Kagami* (Mirror of East Japan)[2] from a desire to learn something of the administrative methods of his supposed ancestors, the Minamoto. His grandson, Iemitsu, went further. In his later years he ordered the Confucian scholar, Hayashi Michiharu, to prepare an official history of Japan, thereby reviving a practice which had been abandoned several centuries earlier. The result was a chronicle entitled *Honchō Tsugan* (Comprehensive Mirror of Japan), dealing with the history of Japan from the earliest times to 1611, the first part of which, a summary of the early Court chronicles down to the ninth century, was completed in the lifetime of Iemitsu and Michiharu, while the remainder, after work had been resumed on Ietsuna's orders in 1664, was finished by 1670. Thirty years later another Hayashi prepared a shorter version under the title *Kokushi Jitsuroku* (Veritable

---

[1] The authors are each responsible for separate sections of this paper: W. G. Beasley for sections (1), General survey, and (2), Arai Hakuseki; and Carmen Blacker for section (3), Rai Sanyō.

[2] See above, p. 239.

Record of National History). Thereafter the Bakufu's historians, much like those who served the government of China, devoted part of their attention to the task of compiling the annals of their own time. The best-known product of their work was the *Tokugawa Jikki* (Veritable Account of the Tokugawa), written by the Hayashi family in the years 1809-49.

By no means all historical writing was official, however. Nor was it small in bulk. The most famous history of the age, the *Dai Nihonshi* (History of Japan), which was begun under the direction of Tokugawa Mitsukuni in 1657 and occupied the labours of several generations of scholars in the Mito fief, runs in its modern edition to seventeen volumes. There is a nineteenth-century continuation of it, compiled by Iida Tadahiko, which is of roughly equal size, and a number of other works which were quite substantial. One might cite Yamaga Sokō's *Buke Jiki* (Account of the Military Houses), of 1673, consisting of a brief sketch of Japanese political history before the sixteenth century, to which were added long sections of biographies of Shōgun and feudal lords, tables of officials, etc., in all fifty-eight books (*maki*), or about one-fifth of the number in *Honchō Tsugan*. Shorter works there were in plenty. If one includes as history all the collections of biographies—those of priests or artists or filial children, as well as those of feudal lords and famous rulers—together with minor chronicles concerning life in Edo or in the Imperial Court, the total is impressive.

It would be impossible to do justice to the whole of this literature in a brief paper. Moreover, most of it is now valuable as source material rather than as history. We shall therefore be concerned here chiefly with a few examples, which are of interest in themselves and help to illustrate the more important characteristics of Tokugawa historiography. Attention is concentrated on the works of two men in particular, each of whom is the subject of a separate section following this general survey. The first is Arai Hakuseki (1657-1725), whose most significant books in this context were *Dokushi Yoron* (Views on History), a study of Japan's history from the ninth to the sixteenth centuries, and *Koshitsū* (Survey of Ancient History), which deals with the earlier period. The second is Rai Sanyō (1780-1832), of small virtue as a scholar, but author of a book, *Nihon Gaishi* (Unofficial History of Japan), which most clearly reflects the kind of ideas influencing historical writing at the end of the period.

In an age when Confucian orthodoxy was officially encouraged in Japan, it is not surprising that the historians were Confucian scholars, most of them employed as such by the Bakufu or one of the great fiefs. The fact is reflected in their writing. It is to be seen particularly in the prevalent view of history as playing its part in the process of moral and political education. To some writers history was primarily a source from which lessons in government or administration might be drawn. To others, the historian's function was to apportion praise and blame in accordance with the dictates of Confucian ethics, as a means of teaching right behaviour. This duty was specifically enjoined on the compilers of the official chronicle, *Honchō Tsugan*, for example, in the rules laid down for their guidance in 1664.[3] They were instructed that the actions even of minor officials must be recorded if they would serve to encourage virtue or suppress evil and that mention should always be made of loyal subjects or filial sons, however humble their personal status.

Since Japanese Confucian scholars, even more than the rest of their countrymen, were steeped in the traditions of Chinese learning, it was natural that they would turn to China for literary models as well as for philosophical assumptions. The majority wrote in Chinese, or in a reasonable approximation to it. Many named the Chinese histories or historians they sought to emulate. The title of *Honchō Tsugan* (Comprehensive Mirror of Japan) was based on that of Ssu-ma Kuang's *Tzu-chih t'ung-chien* (Comprehensive Mirror for Aid in Government); Rai Sanyō specifically acknowledged part of Ssu-ma Ch'ien's Records of the Historian (*Shih chi*) as his model; while the same work apparently inspired Tokugawa Mitsukuni to begin the *Dai Nihonshi*, if the latter's preface is to be believed. The *Dai Nihonshi*, in fact, was the first Japanese attempt to include the full range of material to be found in the Chinese dynastic histories.[4] Its first section comprised a chronicle of events down to the fourteenth century, arranged chronologically by reigns of Emperors. The next, and longest consisted of biographies of Empresses, Imperial Princes, famous men, poets, rebels, etc., categories which for the most part followed Chinese practice. This much was completed by 1709, when the book first received its present title. Monographs on such subjects as religion, geography and military affairs were added later, together with tables of officials. At almost all points the arrangement was Chinese, both in general conception and even in detailed organization.

Nevertheless, not all the similarities between Chinese and Japanese historiography are to be explained in terms of imitation. Many were due to similar traditions, themselves the product of Chinese influence in a wider sense, or to the existence of similar problems. In both countries, for example, the acceptance of history as a source of moral tales or of political and bureaucratic precedent lent itself to an anecdotal and annalistic treatment. Perhaps for this reason, neither developed a serial chronology. Years were identified by their place in Imperial reigns or by reference to era-names (Japanese, *nengō*; Chinese, *nien-hao*), with a consequent blurring of

---

[3] These rules are stated in full in Kiyohara Sadao, *Nihon shigakushi* (Tokyo, 1928), pp. 173–5.

[4] It was the first attempt, at least, to do so in terms of form, if not of content; compare, on this point, the observations by G. W. Robinson on earlier historical writing in Japan, especially with reference to the *Nihon Shoki* and *Ōkagami*, above, pp. 219–21, 233–4.

temporal relationships.[5] This fact has been of immense importance in both China and Japan, where the chronicle remained the normal vehicle of historical statement long after scholarship had in other respects reached a high level of development.

This perpetuation of the chronicle form is particularly evident in official histories and such private works as were planned on a similar scale. Here, however, the Tokugawa historians faced certain disadvantages. For over six hundred years the compilation of official histories had ceased to be a function of the Imperial Court, while, except for one brief period, which saw the completion of the *Azuma Kagami*, the Bakufu had not assumed an equivalent responsibility. As a result, there was a gap of centuries for which there existed neither histories nor a central archive on which they could easily be based. The first step for Japanese historians of the seventeenth century, therefore, was the actual collection of material, much of it scattered throughout the country in private hands; and one might well trace back to this time the preoccupation with the editing and publication of historical sources, which has figured so largely in Japanese scholarship ever since.[6] Certainly it accounts for Tokugawa interest in the *Shih chi* and the earlier Chinese private histories. Works like the dynastic histories of the Sung and Ming, though more nearly contemporary, were being produced by a machinery which found no parallel in Japan.

Perhaps because of its very difficulty, the mechanical task of assembling information tended to overshadow all others for many Japanese historians of this period. The Mito scholars, especially, in preparing the *Dai Nihonshi*, went to enormous trouble in collecting books and records. Moreover, they produced work which was in many respects accurate to the point of being meticulous, however tedious it may be to read. Sources were carefully examined and collated; textual errors and variants were pointed out; and specific references were frequently inserted, even for details of comparative unimportance. In the modern printed text (Tokyo, 1929), there are three notes dealing with such matters in the first two lines alone, while there are few pages which do not contain at least one, sometimes of considerable length.

On the other hand, this represents little more than a refinement of the

---

[5] The era-name system, particularly, with its multiplicity of unrelated labels, each referring to only a few years, must be held largely responsible for this. It takes a prodigious effort of memory to be able to recognize at sight that the third year of Bunroku and the second year of Bunka—by Western reckoning, 1594 and 1805 respectively—are over two centuries apart and fall in two different 'periods', politically. It is difficult enough to remember even their chronological order. On the other hand, it would be dangerous to assert that such a system of recording dates entirely prevented Chinese and Japanese scholars from being aware of temporal sequence when dealing with long periods of time. Both, after all, depended heavily on memorizing texts and data in other respects and succeeded remarkably in so doing.

[6] Though it is also relevant to note that Japanese records are more subject than most to destruction by natural disaster. Fire, earthquake, and flood are not infrequent.

techniques used in editing the *Nihon Shoki* (Chronicles of Japan), centuries earlier.[7] The passion for accuracy of statement was not matched by any attempt to analyse or explain. And even in the shorter narrative histories, which occasionally made their appearance, such qualities were rare, though it is here, if at all, that one would expect to find them. In fact, it is only in the work of Arai Hakuseki that one can detect anything approaching a modern attitude to methodology and subject-matter. In the preface to his *Koshitsū* (Survey of Ancient History) he not only advocated advanced techniques of historical investigation, but also urged that their purpose was to make possible a reinterpretation of the period studied. In *Dokushi Yoron* (Views on History), a few years earlier, he had already abandoned the strict chronicle form for a system of periodization based on political characteristics. This did not take him far from the traditional labels, it is true.[8] Yet he made it part of a study of the transfer of power from Court to Bakufu, then from one line of Shōgun to another, which is quite unlike the work of his contemporaries in its awareness of causation and development.

It is a little surprising that Hakuseki was virtually alone in this, for in other ways the feudal period of Japanese history was an important influence on Tokugawa writing. At the very least it enforced a number of departures from the regular Chinese pattern. It was obvious that in Japanese history there were whole series of events, concerned with the Bakufu and feudal leaders generally, which did not fit into the standard categories of Chinese historiography. On these subjects information had nevertheless to be included. Thus in *Dai Nihonshi*, biographies of Shōgun and their officials were introduced as additional headings, while the entries in the tables of officials and the nature of some of the monographs both served to modify the emphasis on Imperial government. Many private works, like Yamaga Sokō's *Buke Jiki* (Account of the Military Houses), were concerned almost exclusively with feudal history. Even Rai Sanyō's Unofficial History of Japan, despite its fame as an expression of loyalty to the Imperial tradition, was in form a study of the feudal houses.

In this connexion there is added significance in the widespread interest shown in the *Shih chi* (Records of the Historian) of Ssu-ma Ch'ien.[9] This was not merely because that work had great prestige as the first of the Standard Histories. Nor was it simply that its author had faced a number of problems (in assembling his material, for example) which were shared by Tokugawa scholars. It was also that he had to some degree been dealing

[7] See above, pp. 224-6.

[8] The traditional divisions of Japanese history in the feudal period, which are still in general use today, are based on the names either of the successive lines of Shōgun and other feudal rulers (Minamoto-Hōjō, Ashikaga, Oda-Toyotomi, Tokugawa) or of the centres from which they governed (Kamakura, Muromachi, Azuchi-Momoyama, Edo).

[9] For a discussion of the *Shih chi*, see the paper by A. F. P. Hulsewé, above, p. 34-37.

with a comparable period in Chinese institutions. In taking account of the existence of Chou feudalism, particularly in its biographical sections, the *Shih chi* exhibited a model of arrangement which in later centuries was more applicable to Japan than China.

However, it was not only in details of arrangement that feudal history influenced Tokugawa writing. While it had little effect on basic ideas of methodology or on general outlook—even for Arai Hakuseki the rise and fall of feudal houses did not raise questions any different in kind from those which applied to dynasties in China: both were phenomena explicable by Confucian theory, conforming to cyclical patterns individually and not requiring discussion as a series—yet it was of far-reaching importance in providing scope for differences of interpretation. One might say, indeed, that Japan's feudal history made interpretation unavoidable. Its theme was the transfer of power from Imperial to feudal hands. Specifically, it recorded the emergence, side by side with a titular Emperor, of an hereditary *de facto* ruler, the Shōgun, in whose person was concentrated all administrative authority. How far was this process justifiable? Not all accepted it as such, at any time. From the beginning there had been voices raised to question the legitimacy of government by Shōgun.[10] Moreover, once the question had been put it was impossible for the historian to evade it, if only because his decisions on points of fact must themselves commit him to one side or the other. In the fourteenth century, for example, which was the true Imperial line? Was it the Northern Court, whose emperors reigned in Kyōto with the support of the Ashikaga Shōgun? Or was it the Southern Court, which held the Imperial regalia and was eventually restored? The choice between them involved a judgement not only on the actions of the Ashikaga but also on the wider issue of Court-Bakufu relations. Yet a choice had to be made, even in compiling a chronicle. There could be only one Court and one Emperor.

This kind of dilemma, although inherent in their subject-matter, was in practice something forced on Tokugawa writers by the age in which they lived. There was still a Shōgun in Japan. There was still an Emperor, who reigned but did not rule. Hence the relationship between the two was as much a matter of contemporary politics as of academic interest. Historians, for their part, were usually members of the feudal class and often men of affairs as well as scholars, with the result that political circumstance largely determined both the direction of their studies and the nature of their findings. Tokugawa historiography not only showed a marked preoccupation with feudal history. It also produced interpretations of it which were more often imposed on, than derived from, the evidence.

In the late seventeenth and early eighteenth centuries, when the Toku-

---

[10] Concerning earlier treatment of the theme, see, for example, the section dealing with Fujiwara Jien and Kitabatake Chikafusa, above, p. 238–44.

gawa Bakufu was at the height of its power, scholars were in some ways under less political compulsion in their treatment of feudal history than those of later generations. This is not to say that it was safe to criticize the regime, however indirectly. Still less was there any inclination to attack feudal rule in general. On the other hand, not every historian found it necessary to extend his acceptance of contemporary conditions to the point where it involved justification of all the actions of all Shōgun, past as well as present. Official works, of course, like *Honchō Tsugan*, inevitably assumed the rightness of the Bakufu's position. So did Arai Hakuseki, in the sense that his *Dokushi Yoron* (Views on History) is a reasoned defence of the necessity for feudal government. Yet Hakuseki, although a member of the Shōgun's entourage, did not allow personal loyalties to blind him entirely to historical fact or lead him into falsification of the story. He accepted the legitimacy of the Southern Court. He could be critical of feudal as well as of Imperial leadership. For things like this, indeed, he was later applauded by historians of the Imperialist tradition, though they were details which did nothing to weaken his essential argument.

Departures from the standard Bakufu interpretation were still more apparent in the Mito fief's History of Japan (*Dai Nihonshi*). Despite the fact that it was prepared by scholars in the service of one of the senior Tokugawa branch houses, its avowed purpose was to expound the principle of loyalty (*taigi-meibun*) in Japanese history, that is, to glorify the Imperial line. This is evident in the wording of its preface, in particular. For the rest, apart from the assertion of the Southern Court's legitimacy in the main chronicle section, the theme found detailed expression largely in the volumes of biographies.

It was on such points that the book's later reputation in the *sonnō* ('honour-the-Emperor') movement came to depend. Even so, its reputation was not entirely deserved.[11] To read into the *Dai Nihonshi* an advocacy of direct Imperial rule is to give it a meaning which its authors would certainly have denied. For them, an attempt to restore some part of the Court's prestige did not necessarily imply an attack on the Bakufu as an institution any more than Edo's occasional moves towards reconciliation with Kyōto modified the Shōgun's claim to absolute authority. Much the same might be said of other early writers, men like Yamaga Sokō (1622–85) and Kumazawa Banzan (1619–91). It was not until the nineteenth century, as Tokugawa control weakened and the Emperor became a focus of opposition to it, that historians began consciously to take sides in a debate over Court-Bakufu relations. Only then did Imperial prestige

---

[11] It seems to be rather too readily assumed that the book was read, as distinct from being discussed, by later generations. Quite apart from the forbidding size of the work, it did not become at all widely available until after 1852 and can have influenced directly only a very narrow circle. In fact, none of the early Tokugawa books were really published in the modern sense. This makes it difficult to assess their effect, whether on politics or on scholarship.

and Bakufu authority become mutually exclusive, in scholarship as in politics. By that time, the anti-Tokugawa movement had been provided with some sort of a theoretical basis by the work of the so-called 'national scholars', or *kokugakusha*.

The *kokugakusha* drew inspiration both from the *Dai Nihonshi* and from the writings of Arai Hakuseki. With the former they shared an attitude towards the Imperial Court and views on certain incidents in Japanese history, while from the latter they derived much in methodology, particularly in their careful reappraisal of the early chronicles. It is difficult to treat them as historians in the strict sense, for their work was more religious and linguistic than historical; but the new emphasis they put on the position of the Emperor, as well as their strictures on the dynastic confusion of China as compared with the continuity of the Imperial line in Japan contained the seeds of historicism if not of history. Motoori Norinaga (1730–1801) was the outstanding figure of the group, famous chiefly for his studies of the *Kojiki* (Records of Ancient Matters). These still constitute a major contribution to our understanding of the earliest periods in Japan, though Norinaga did not himself make use of them primarily as a historian. Nor, on the other hand, did his insistence on the divinity of Imperial descent lead him in practice to challenge the authority of the Shōgun. In this he differed little from his predecessors. It was later events, in fact, which made Norinaga in restrospect a leader of political reform and gave him his importance in historiography. Once the *sonnō* movement gained momentum as an expression of anti-Tokugawa feeling, the ideas of the *kokugakusha* were developed into a full-fledged school of historical interpretation.

One can see this process beginning in the work of Rai Sanyō (1780–1832). Sanyō was not only a Confucian scholar, writing in Chinese, but was also influenced by the *kokugakusha* through the person of Hashimoto Inahiko, one of Norinaga's pupils. Frequently the comments which he inserted at various points in the text of his Unofficial History of Japan (*Nihon Gaishi*) (1829) were made in terms of loyalty to the Emperor, though the book itself was a study of the feudal rulers of Japan from the Minamoto to the Tokugawa. His comments also showed some interest in causation and a great deal of concern about right behaviour; but their historical value suffers from a general disregard for factual accuracy. In scholarship, indeed, Sanyō cannot rank high. His importance is to be found rather in the attitudes and ideas which he expressed. He reflected the views of the *sonnō* movement, the significance of which was in essence political and contemporary. Moreover, he reflected those views more accurately than some later commentators might lead one to expect. Neither Sanyō nor his Mito contemporaries attacked feudalism or the Bakufu as such—any more than the authors of the *Dai Nihonshi* had done before them. There are even parts of the *Nihon Gaishi*, such as the account of the rise to power of the Minamoto, which closely parallel the work of Arai Hakuseki, who was ostensibly a Bakufu apologist. In part, no doubt, this was due to a fear that open criticism might bring punishment by Tokugawa officials. It has usually been so interpreted. Equally, however, it serves to emphasize that it was not till a later stage that either political leaders or their historian allies were actively contemplating a radical break with the political traditions of the past. Once they did so the slogan *sonnō* changed its meaning, becoming a symbol of Imperial restoration in a new sense, and this meaning in turn was read back into earlier writings. It was by this process that Rai Sanyō acquired a continuing influence out of all proportion to his merits.

With Rai Sanyō, Tokugawa historiography properly so called comes to an end, for the influence of western ideas, though it first becomes apparent in the last few years of the regime's existence, belongs to the story of modern Japan, as also does the final evolution of the Imperial tradition in historical writing. We therefore turn now to a more detailed consideration of the work of Arai Hakuseki and Rai Sanyō. Before doing so, however, it seems desirable to indicate briefly some general conclusions that emerge.

First, it is clear that all historians of the time were strongly influenced by Chinese ideas and Chinese historical writing, even though these did not always prove exactly applicable to Japanese problems of methodology and interpretation. Secondly, the attitudes they expressed were closely linked with social status and political affiliation: history was backward-looking, motivated by a desire to seek an answer to questions of contemporary importance and frequently taking the form of a search for material to support existing prejudice. Consciously or unconsciously, writers imposed interpretation in this sense even on the chronicle form. Finally, by so doing, some of them bequeathed to modern Japan the rudiments of what later scholarship has turned into the 'national' school of historical writing. Even now the importance of this cannot be ignored as an influence on our knowledge of the Japanese past.

## 2. *Arai Hakuseki* (1657–1725)

The Confucian scholar Arai Hakuseki is perhaps better known as a statesman than as a historian. He entered the service of the Tokugawa lord of Kōfu in 1693 and soon established his position as one of the latter's chief advisers, so that when his lord became Shōgun under the name of Ienobu in 1709, Hakuseki was able to exert considerable influence on Bakufu policy. With Ienobu's death in 1712 he again retired into relative obscurity, but his experience as an official had left its mark upon his outlook. Recognition of this is vital to any understanding of his historical writing.

Hakuseki's reputation as a historian rests chiefly on three books,[12] each of them produced at a different stage in his career. The first, his *Hankampu* (Account of the Feudal Domains), was completed in 1702 while he was still no more than *jusha* (official Confucian scholar) of the Kōfu fief. It was a study of the history of the great feudal families of his day, each house being treated in turn and a special emphasis being given to its relations with the Tokugawa. Yet, although it was the longest of his works, it adds little to our knowledge of his methodology or outlook, for which reason it will receive no detailed treatment in this paper. The other two books are more important. *Dokushi Yoron* (Views on History) comprised Hakuseki's drafts for lectures he delivered to the Shōgun in 1712 and took the form of an outline history of Japan from the middle of the ninth to the end of the sixteenth century. *Koshitsū* (Survey of Ancient History), which he finished in 1716 after his retirement, turned its attention rather to the earliest years of Japanese history, re-examining and re-assessing the records on which a study of that period must be based. In modern terms, indeed, *Koshitsū* might be described as a monograph, an example of Hakuseki's use of historical techniques, whereas *Dokushi Yoron* was more a survey history. Its concern was with interpreting rather than establishing facts, which makes it a better starting point for a discussion of its author's outlook and ideas.

In his youth Hakuseki had been a *rōnin*, one of many thousands of lordless samurai who had fallen victim to Tokugawa policies which involved frequent transfers of feudal lords and confiscation or rearrangement of their fiefs. Like others, he sought a career in one of the few ways open to him in a society which was becoming increasingly static, by becoming a Confucian scholar. It was good fortune that brought him to Kōfu and made his lord successor to the Shōgun Tsunayoshi; and though he never entirely lost his resentment against those whose power was based on birth alone, success none the less made him a supporter of the existing order of things. The Bakufu had given him some wealth and much prestige. The Bakufu, therefore, deserved his loyalty, not only as an official, but also as a historian.

*Dokushi Yoron* might well be described as a defence of the role of the feudal class in Japanese history.[13] Book I traces the decline of Imperial authority, beginning with the period when Fujiwara control at Court

[12] All three are to be found in *Arai Hakuseki Zenshū*, 6 vols. (Tokyo, 1905–7). *Hankampu* comprises vol. i; *Dokushi Yoron* is given in iii, 399–584; *Koshitsū* in iii, 210–316. Unlike the works of most *jusha*, the three books are written in Japanese.

[13] For a discussion of this point see especially Nakamura Kōya's excellent article, 'Shika to shite no Arai Hakuseki', in *Hompō shigakushi ronsō* (Shigakkai: 2 vols., Tokyo, 1939), ii, 963–72; also Izu Kimio, *Nihon shigakushi* (revised edition, Tokyo, 1947), pp. 220–41. The most detailed study of Hakuseki's historical writing is Katsuda Shōnen, *Arai Hakuseki no rekishigaku* (Tokyo, 1939), in which pp. 130–81, 278–85 deal more specifically with *Dokushi Yoron*.

became institutionalized by the creation of the offices of Regent (*Sesshō*) and Chancellor (*Kampaku*), ending with the period of the Namboku wars in the fourteenth century, which saw the final transfer of power into the hands of feudal rulers. Books II and III describe the rise of this new ruling group and the process by which authority passed successively from the Minamoto to the Hōjō, the Ashikaga, Oda Nobunaga, Toyotomi Hideyoshi, and finally the Tokugawa. Hakuseki's first object in this was to show that the breakdown of central administration in the hands of the Emperors and Fujiwara made the rise of the new military rulers both necessary and logical. Only thus, he argued, could law and order have been restored to Japan. His second object was to show how the rise of each new house of Shōgun followed inevitably from the mistakes and weaknesses of its predecessor. The process, he asserted, had continued down to the sixteenth century. It had there been halted by the Tokugawa, whose virtues and ability gave their regime a permanence no other had achieved before it. It was at this point that his narrative came to an end, ostensibly because it was here that feudal rule had reached its climax.

To this picture of Hakuseki as a Bakufu apologist, however, one must add other elements, derived from his outlook as a Confucian scholar. The whole purpose of *Dokushi Yoron* was didactic in the Confucian sense. On the one hand it was designed as part of Ienobu's political education, pointing out the lessons to be learned from history and the mistakes to be avoided. In this sense it can be treated as part of the admonitory literature with which Tokugawa scholars so often bombarded their patrons. Equally, it retained something of the moral purpose which was so common a feature of the 'praise-and-blame' type of historical writing. The fall of the Ashikaga, for example, as Hakuseki saw it, was explained as much by their ethical failings as by political incompetence. In his eyes, again, lack of loyalty or of filial piety on the part of men like Nobunaga and Hideyoshi seemed enough to account for their inability to found a ruling house. Everywhere he expressed himself in such Confucian terms. Often, indeed, he came close to applying Chinese concepts of legitimacy and 'the will of Heaven' to the history of Japan. He did this not in relation to the Imperial line itself,[14] but with reference to the succession of *de facto* rulers who overshadowed it, both by implying that an ability to unite the country and restore order gave a Shōgun a certain *right* to govern, which he lost when his administration weakened, and by linking the possession of such abilities with both lineage and virtue (*dōtoku*). It was characteristic of him that he condemned the Fujiwara for the disorder which their moral failings

---

[14] The existence of a single Imperial line in Japan, except for the brief period of the Northern and Southern Courts during the fourteenth century, meant that the problem of legitimacy did not arise there in the same form as in China. Hence Chinese discussions of the basis of legitimate rule had little direct influence on Japanese historiography.

brought: because of it, he said, 'the way of Heaven inclined towards those who had shown merit',[15] namely, the feudal class.

*Dokushi Yoron*, therefore, was coloured by Hakuseki's Confucian training as well as by his feudal background. To put it differently, he wrote both as a Tokugawa official and as a Confucian scholar, facts which determined the purpose of his writing and in large part the nature of it. In this he differed little from others of his period, though his ability and wide interests mark him off from most. It is rather in his methodology, however, that we find the qualities which made him a true historian in an age of chroniclers and moralists.

Hakuseki never quite succeeded in freeing himself from the traditions of a scholarship which regarded exposition of the classics as its proper function. Both in *Dokushi Yoron* and in *Koshitsū* passages of comment are interpolated in, rather than being made part of, his narrative. On the other hand, he moved a long way towards abandoning another deep-rooted custom, especially in the former, when he departed from the strict chronicle form which his contemporaries (and most of his successors) still regarded as the normal vehicle for historical writing. It is true, of course, that the things he wished to say did not lend themselves to a technique which treated history as a series of discrete events. It was not possible to expound causation efficiently, to analyse the collapse of Fujiwara power or the rise and fall of feudal rulers, without some kind of topical arrangement. To that extent his method was dictated by his purpose. Nor was it entirely original, even in Japanese terms. The first three books of Yamaga Sokō's history of the feudal houses (*Buke Jiki*), completed in 1673, had in their general structure used a similar chronological arrangement to that of *Dokushi Yoron*, tracing the history of the Imperial Court down to the fourteenth century and then going back to the beginning of the Kamakura Bakufu to pick up the story of feudal rule. Some of the detail of Hakuseki's periodization can be found even earlier, in Fujiwara Jien's *Gukanshō* (Miscellany of Ignorant Views), written during the Kamakura period.[16] None the less, though these works may have helped to shape his ideas, Hakuseki himself must be given the credit for elaborating a systematic periodization of Japanese history in a form which has continued to influence political historians even in modern times.

*Dokushi Yoron* falls into two main parts. The first (Book I) deals with the decline of Imperial authority, the second (Books II and III) with the rise and development of feudal rule. Each is subdivided in its turn. In the history of the Imperial Court Hakuseki identified nine periods, or rather, nine 'changes', each of which marked the beginning of a new era with

---

[15] *Dokushi Yoron*, in *Arai Hakuseki Zenshū*, iii, 541.

[16] So also can a similar attitude towards the relationship between Emperor and Shōgun: see above, p. 240.

political characteristics recognizably different from what had gone before. These can be summarized as follows: first, the age of true Imperial rule, ending in the middle of the ninth century; second to fifth, successive stages in the rise and decline of Fujiwara control and of government by retired Emperors; sixth and seventh, the Kamakura Bakufu, being the periods of Minamoto and Hōjō dominance respectively; eighth, the Emperor Go-daigo's brief assumption of power in 1333–6; ninth, the victory of the Ashikaga. With the last of these, power finally passed to the feudal class and the Court ceased to be the centre of Hakuseki's interest. However, to trace the rise of feudal rule he found it necessary to go back to the Kama-kura period and beyond, so his treatment of this subject (Books II and III) overlapped in time much that he had already covered. For his study of the feudal period he made use of five divisions. The first three of these, dealing with the Minamoto, Hōjō and Ashikaga, corresponded with periods six to nine of the earlier part of his book, now treated from a different viewpoint. Of the remainder, period four covered Oda Nobunaga and Toyotomi Hideyoshi; period five, which was identified but not dis-cussed, the Tokugawa.

There are obvious weaknesses in such a system of periodization, quite apart from any objections which modern scholars might make to points of detail. Its complete preoccupation with political criteria, of course, is not surprising. Few Confucian scholars had any real awareness of economic causation, and in this respect, as in much else, Hakuseki was a man of his age. Like most of his contemporaries, moreover, he showed a proper dis-cretion in avoiding any discussion of the age in which he lived. His essentially feudal outlook did not prevent him from criticizing feudal rulers —his condemnation of Minamoto Yoritomo for his attitude to the Im-perial Court and his strictures on Hideyoshi's land reform might both be cited—but he failed to apply similar standards of judgement to Tokugawa Ieyasu, logical though it might have been to do so. Yet this is a mild and not unusual form of intellectual dishonesty. Nor does it weaken his funda-mental argument that feudal rule was logical and necessary in Japan, despite its imperfections. The actions of Ashikaga Takauji, for example, are accepted by him as inevitable, even when they are stigmatized as morally unsound. The Emperors, too, though not personally attacked, do not escape their share of responsibility for the decline of Court prestige, which to Hakuseki provides both the cause and justification of government by Shōgun. This, indeed, is the essential theme of *Dokushi Yoron*. To it, the book's periodization is remarkably apt.

In his Views on History, therefore, Hakuseki largely succeeded in break-ing free from the annalistic form, which a chronological system based on era-names (*nengō*) and Imperial reigns imposed on so much of Chinese and Japanese historical scholarship. By so doing he revealed an awareness of the historical process which could not otherwise have been developed. To Hakuseki, history was not just a series of discrete events, a random collection of tales to be used for the moral or political edification of his readers. It involved a movement through time, which could be analysed and explained. It is true that his analysis is rudimentary and his explanation in part tendentious. Neither can one escape the conclusion that his justification of feudal rule stemmed from the man himself rather than from the facts he studied. On the other hand, he at least avoided dangers of a different kind. Nowhere does he describe history as a continuous decline from a golden age in the ancient past or as an inevitable progression towards a glorious future. To this extent he achieved realism and detachment.

These qualities were even more in evidence when Hakuseki turned his attention to the early history of Japan. In the introduction to *Koshitsū* (Survey of Ancient History),[17] he advocated an approach to the problems and techniques of historical investigation for this period which is unique in Tokugawa historiography. 'History', he said, 'is to narrate events in accordance with the facts and show men the lessons thereof.'[18] The second part of this statement reflects his Confucian training; and the first part, if taken in isolation, might seem no more than the sort of pious hope which usually found its way into the preface of a work of scholarship. A striving for accuracy was a virtue Hakuseki shared with others. What distinguished him, however, was his statement of the methods by which accuracy might be attained. In studying early history, he urged, Chinese and Korean records should be used in addition to those of Japan. Moreover, it was necessary to attempt a re-examination of the language of the early chronicles, stripping it of connotations acquired in later centuries and so restoring its original meaning. Finally, by these means, it would be possible to achieve a satisfactory explanation of events without recourse to a theory of 'divine mysteries': the *kami* could be treated not as gods but men, whose actions were human and explicable.

The Survey of Ancient History, like so many books, does not live up to the promise of its introduction. Yet it was not without influence. The *kokugakusha* of the eighteenth century carried out much of the language study which it recommended, while others have sought to make a detailed correlation of the Japanese, Chinese, and Korean records. In this sense Hakuseki was one of the founders of a branch of historical scholarship which still survives today. At the same time, the political and religious elements in the Shintō revival long prevented the rational re-interpretation of the Age of the Gods which he envisaged as the result of using these tech-

---

[17] For discussion of *Koshitsū* see Katsuda, *Arai Hakuseki no rekishigaku*, pp. 44–85, 262–8; Nakamura, 'Shika to shite no Arai Hakuseki', pp. 983–92; Kiyohara Sadao, *Nihon shigakushi*, pp. 214–24.

[18] 'Shi wa jitsu ni yotte ji wo kishite, yo no kankai wo shirusu mono nari': *Arai Hakuseki Zenshū*, iii, 212.

niques. Even now the subject is hedged about with prejudice. Indeed, while it is true to say that his studies of feudal history have long since been outdated, both in method and in content, the principles which he enunciated for the study of earlier periods have only recently been accepted and applied in full.

## 3. *Rai Sanyō (1780–1832)*

Rai Sanyō's fame as a historian rests neither on any very exhaustive or original historical research nor on any startlingly new interpretation of history. It rests rather on one piece of writing which happened to express, more forcefully and persuasively than any previous work, an old current of thought and feeling which, at the time Sanyō wrote, was beginning to acquire a new importance and significance.

This work, the *Nihon Gaishi* (Unofficial History of Japan), first published in 1829, purported to record the vicissitudes of the various military houses of Japan from the time of the rise to power of the Taira and Minamoto down to the final pacification of the land under the Tokugawa. Its obvious underlying thesis was, however, that the rise of the powerful military families was in itself deplorable; that the ruling power in Japan should rightly and properly belong to the Emperor alone; and that the military governments of the various shogunal families had hence all been by definition illegitimate.

There was, of course, nothing particularly new about these views. The medieval work *Taiheiki* (Records of Great Peace)[19] had expressed much the same sentiments of reverence to the Emperor—and indeed several passages in the Unofficial History are virtually *kambun* paraphrases of passages in the *Taiheiki*. The writings of the Mito school of historiography, from the huge compilation *Dai Nihonshi* down to the essays of Fujita Yūkoku, Fujita Tōko, and Aizawa Seishisai, had advanced very much the same Imperialist views as those of Rai Sanyō. Both Sanyō and the Mito scholars had in common, moreover, a background of Confucian philosophy in terms of which, unlike the equally Imperialist but more rabidly nationalist *kokugakusha*, like Motoori Norinaga, they sought to justify their yearnings for Imperial restoration. Both Sanyō and the Mito scholars used a vocabulary which was later to take on great emotional significance. Words such as *taigi-meibun* (loyal duty) and *kokutai* (national essence), first popularized by these writers, came to be invested, in the late Tokugawa and early Meiji periods, with virtually talismanic power.

The Unofficial History of Japan was, however, much more widely read than the Mito works. Whereas the *Dai Nihonshi* was huge, bulky, and inaccessible, and Aizawa's famous essay *Shinron*, for example, was at the time only privately circulated, the *Nihon Gaishi*, written in a *kambun*

[19] See above, p. 239.

(Chinese) style which Sanyō's contemporaries evidently found peculiarly attractive, was before long in most educated people's hands. Its particular virtue was that it expressed these old persistent sentiments in a manner which contemporary readers found deeply moving and inspiring.

Born into a Confucian family of some repute—his father, Rai Shunsui, was a fairly well-known Chu Hsi scholar—and educated on Confucian lines, Sanyō naturally looked to Confucian historiography for sanction and justification of his views. The form of the *Nihon Gaishi*, he was therefore careful to state, was modelled on the section of Ssu-ma Ch'ien's *Shih chi* (Records of the Historian) called *shih chia*, or histories of the various feudal lords of China; and certainly the basic thesis of the work could well be interpreted as an application to Japanese history of the principle, so much stressed in Chu Hsi's *T'ung-chien kang-mu*, of *sonnō-sempa* or 'revere the Emperor and despise the military ruler'.

In the *Nihon Gaishi*, moreover, the military families are treated in terms of what would at first sight appear to be the conventional Confucian apparatus of praise and blame. The families who supported the Throne, particularly emperors such as Go-Toba and Go-Daigo who made abortive attempts to regain the lost Imperial authority, were good. The families who unashamedly appropriated the Emperor's rightful functions and powers, thus reducing the Throne to an empty shell, were all bad—though some were very much worse than others. The Minamoto family, for example, though bad in so far as they were the virtual originators of shogunal government, were yet not entirely culpable since their rise to power was virtually necessitated by the hopeless incompetence of Fujiwara rule, itself made inevitable by the growing luxury and incompetence of the Emperors themselves. Had not Minamoto Yoriyoshi and Yoshiie, for example, stepped in when they did, far more unscrupulous rascals might have plunged the whole land into chaos. As it was, these Minamoto did excellent work on behalf of the Emperor, but were so absurdly inadequately recompensed for their services that it was inevitable that their descendent Yorimoto should have reaped the rewards they themselves had been denied.[20]

Very bad indeed, on the other hand, was the Hōjō family. With the possible exceptions of Hōjō Yasutoki and Hōjō Tokimune, they were none of them better than devils and reptiles. Their guilt lay in the fact that they, a family of very inferior lineage, had, quietly and without any expenditure of military violence, appropriated the power which had rightfully belonged to the Minamoto family, just as the Fujiwara had, quietly and insidiously, appropriated the rightful power of the Throne. The plea put forward by so many former historians that Hōjō rule was fully justified by success was

---

[20] *Nihon Gaishi*, in *Dai Nihon Shisō Zenshū* (Tokyo, 1931), xv, 25–27. This attitude to the Minamoto closely parallels that of earlier works like the *Gukanshō* and *Dokushi Yoron*; see above, pp. 240, 242–3.

entirely invalid. Even Hōjō Yasutoki's rule, though customarily held up as exemplary, in no wise atoned for the crimes of his family. Indeed, the so-called 'good' rule of the Hōjō, Sanyō went so far as to assert, was undertaken from the purely selfish motive of warding off censure for their initial crime of usurpation.

In the case of Hōjō Tokimune, his achievement in driving off the Mongol invasion was certainly, Sanyō grudgingly admitted, 'sufficient to atone for the crimes of his ancestors'. Indeed, his defensive tactics—relying on small and easily manœuvrable ships instead of large, cumbersome ones, and on swords instead of guns—were exemplary enough to serve as a model for all times. Victory was determined more by men than by weapons, Sanyō declared—thus parting company with contemporary Mito scholars such as Aizawa Seishisai, who insisted that predatory foreigners could only be repelled by large battleships and guns.[21]

Bad also was the Ashikaga family, particularly Ashikaga Takauji, whom Sanyō dubbed a dog, sheep, fox, and rat for the nefarious part he had played in frustrating Go-Daigo's attempt to restore the fallen fortunes of the Throne.

Good, by contrast, was the Nitta family, particularly Nitta Yoshisada, who chose to support the hopeless cause of the Throne rather than pursue his own ends, in which he would undoubtedly have been successful.

But most glorious of all was the Kusunoki family. By supporting the Throne and even giving up his life for it at a time when it was at its weakest and most discredited, shunned by almost everyone else for fear of the overwhelming power of the Hōjō, Kusunoki Masashige had set a shining example of supreme loyalty and heroism. It was tragic that Go-Daigo should have been so foolish as to fail to reward Masashige with titles and honours worthy of the great services he had rendered, for thereby he laid the way open for the wicked Ashikaga Takauji to stain the history of the Throne by seizing power. Nevertheless, tragically unsuccessful though Masashige's career was, his noble example of loyalty would, Sanyō declared, last through the ages as eternally as mountains and rivers.[22]

The Tokugawa family Sanyō could not, of course, openly condemn. Since he could scarcely include them explicitly in his general censure of military rule, he contented himself with praising Ieyasu for bringing peace to the land after so many years of civil war, taking pains to clear him of all imputation of malice and treachery towards the unfortunate Hideyori, and leaving his readers to infer for themselves that Tokugawa rule was in his eyes no more legitimate than that of the Minamoto, Hōjō, Ashikaga or ,any other family he had earlier condemned.

Though Sanyō in this way used the orthodox Confucian framework of praise and blame in presenting his particular view of the Japanese past, he

[21] Ibid., pp. 29–36.          [22] Ibid., pp. 37–44.

could scarcely use it in the orthodox Confucian way, for in those terms his thesis was simply not tenable. He could hardly make out that 'good' rulers brought peace and prosperity and 'bad' ones turmoil and decline, if most of the persons he wished to praise had been remarkable for their failures and early deaths, while those on whom he heaped most abuse had been rather conspicuously successful as rulers and long-lived as dynasties. He was hence constrained to look for some explanation of historical causation other than the usual one of the moral character and conduct of individual rulers. This he found in an idea which he called alternatively *jisei, jiun, sedō,* or *sei,* a 'force' or 'movement of the times', comparable to water bursting through a dyke, against which mere human effort, however moral, glorious, or heroic, was powerless. It was owing to this irresistible force, he could then make out, that all his heroes had been failures and all his villains successes. The initial rise to power of the military class and decline of the Throne, deplorable and tragic though these had been, were yet inevitable because of *jisei*.[23] The emperors Go-Toba and Go-Daigo had failed in their attempts to restore the Throne to its rightful power, for the reason that *jisei* was weighted against the Throne at those particular times.[24] Inevitable for similar reasons was the defeat and death of Nitta Yoshisada, good and loyal though he was, and the strength and longlasting success of the Ashikaga family, bad and disloyal though they were.[25]

Sanyō nowhere precisely defined *jisei*, or explained what generated the force or caused it to decline or accumulate or change its direction. It would seem, however, that he regarded it as a kind of legacy of the past, a force generated not by one's own moral actions but by those of one's predecessors. Thus Yoritomo's rise to power was due to inevitable *jisei* because it was the proper requital of the meritorious services rendered by his forbears Yoriyoshi and Yoshiie, who themselves had been deprived of their due reward. Go-Toba and Go-Daigo were both powerless against a *jisei* weighted against the Throne through the accumulated weakness of their predecessors.

*Jisei* was at any rate a limitation on the power of mere individuals to influence the course of history, and as such proved a useful germ of an idea for later historians to develop and elaborate. Early Meiji historians of the school known as *bummeishi*[26] certainly used the term *jisei* in their attempts to explain the Japanese past in terms of the fashionable positivist school of Buckle, Guizot, and Herbert Spencer, and it may well have been from Sanyō's ill-defined ideas that they gained at least the words to express their new view of historical causation.

But the real importance of the *Nihon Gaishi* as a work of history lies undoubtedly in the emotions it inspired. Dull, intemperate, and historically

---

[23] Ibid., pp. 12–13.
[25] Ibid., p. 48.

[24] Ibid., pp. 38–39.
[26] See introduction, p. 15.

inaccurate as so much of it appears today, to many samurai of the late Tokugawa and early Meiji periods it read as a profoundly inspiring expression of neglected truth. It is difficult to believe, wrote B. H. Chamberlain in 1890,[27] 'that a book so intolerably dry could ever have fired a whole nation with enthusiasm. That it did so is one of the curiosities of literature'. It seems clear, indeed, that the book not only, as Chamberlain wrote, 'contributed in no small measure to bring about the fall of the Shogunate', but that the moral lessons from the past it sought to inculcate continued to inspire the Japanese for many years afterwards. The cult of Kusunoki Masashige (*nankō-sūhai*) as a paragon of supreme loyalty and heroism, in particular, persisted well into the Meiji period and seems to have been revived, together with indiscriminate praise of Sanyō, during the 1930's. Certainly the writers of articles in the numerous special numbers of journals at that time devoted to such subjects as 'Reverence for the Emperor', record the tears of emotion which they shed over the Kusunoki passages in the *Nihon Gaishi* and the reverence with which they made the pious pilgrimage to Sanyō's grave. One writer, determined to absolve Sanyō from any modern criticisms of inadequacy as a historian, declares him to have had an unusually penetrating insight into economic influences on the course of history, citing as evidence a few of Sanyō's Chinese poems in which cereals and prices are given passing mention.[28] Another declared that the *Nihon Gaishi* had without any doubt become world famous, for was there not a partial English translation of the work by Sir Ernest Satow, and had he not found Sanyō's name inscribed on a plaque in a library in Boston, marking him among the great literary figures of the world?[29]

Sanyō may well have been more gifted as a poet than as a historian,[30] but it may have been his very poetical talents which commended his history so well to the Japanese.

[27] *Things Japanese*, p. 257.

[28] Nakayama Kyūshirō, 'Nihon Jusha Rai Sanyō no Shigaku', in *Hompō shigakushi ronsō*, ii, 1037.

[29] Sakamoto Miyama, 'Rai Sanyō to Nihon Gaishi', in *Rekishi Kōron*, vol. v, No. 7 (1936), p. 121.

[30] Most Japanese articles purporting to treat of 'Sanyō as a Historian' quote with great tedium and irrelevance numerous lines of his Chinese poetry. He is said to have excelled at the composition of Chinese poetry from a very early age.

## 15. SHIGENO YASUTSUGU AND THE MODERN TOKYO TRADITION OF HISTORICAL WRITING

### JIRO NUMATA[1]

*Assistant Professor, Historiographical Institute*
*(Shiryō-hensanjo), Tokyo University*

## 1. *Introduction*

Two distinct types of historical writing are discernible in the early Meiji period. The first is, of course, that known as *bummeishi-ron* or essays in the history of civilization; the second is that which was based on the work of the *kōshō-gaku*[2] school of textual collation. The first, in common with all other activities in the cultural sphere at the time, was influenced by, or even modelled on, the productions of the West. Examples are afforded by the work of such men as Fukuzawa Yukichi or Taguchi Ukichi.[3] The individual writers differed in their viewpoints, but nearly all tended to work with some aim in view other than that of pure academic research, such as understanding of western Europe, or the purveying of knowledge useful in the political exigencies of the time—the popular rights movement (*jiyū-minken undō*), for instance—or, again, the introduction of Western rationalism, and so forth. Much of their work, therefore, consisted of translations of Western historical writings or of books based on those writings. Their mission, in short, was enlightenment rather than academic study. In this paper I shall confine myself to consideration of the development of the second type mentioned above, the Japanese tradition. For a time in the early years of Meiji, this tradition was little more than a survival from the immediately preceding age, the Tokugawa period. Then, however, with the impetus of governmentally sponsored historiographical undertakings, the traditional methods of research began to move forward again, making contact with those of the West and presently bringing into

---

[1] This paper was written originally in Japanese and has been translated by Mr. G. W. Robinson.

[2] The term kōshō (Chinese, *k'ao-cheng*) refers to the techniques developed by Chinese scholars for criticial study of the texts of the Confucian classics, subsequently applied also to historical texts (see the papers by E. G. Pulleyblank and P. Demiéville, above, pp. 159–60, 168–9). They were adopted by Japanese Confucianists in the Tokugawa period and used extensively. They became so closely linked with historiography in Japan that some modern dictionaries translate *kōshōgaku* simply as 'historical research', but a more accurate rendering would be 'investigation of texts' or 'collation'. The object of *kōshō*, as applied to historical writing, was to attain factual accuracy by a close critical examination of original or early texts. By extension, it came also to include the comparison of different accounts of any given incident. See also below, pp. 268–73.

[3] See introduction, p. 15.

being through assimilation with them the Japanese 'academic' school of research and historiography.

In view of the large part thus played by government historiographical undertakings in the development of this 'academic' school of historical research and historiography, I propose to deal principally with those undertakings and with Shigeno Yasutsugu, who played a leading role therein.

## 2. *Historiography sponsored by the Meiji government*

The task of the new Meiji government was ultimately the modernization of Japan. Even so, however, the political revolution that was the Meiji Restoration began with the object of 'restoring' Imperial rule, so that a spirit of return to the past appeared in fact to be its guiding inspiration. Though this spirit dwindled in due course, its very considerable strength, at least in the early days of the new regime, may be deduced from the revival, as organs of the central government, of the Jingi-kan or Department of (Shintō) Religion and Dajō-kan or Great Council of State, for which provision had originally been made under the Taihō Code in the eighth century.

It is not surprising, therefore, that very soon after the new government had been set up, even before military operations in the civil war had been brought to an end, the government should have taken in hand the task of compiling a national history, and that its professed object should have been to provide sequels to the *Rikkokushi* or Six National Histories.[4] We might say, in other words, that the new government's object was to emphasize its own legitimacy.

In 1869 there was set up within the old *Wagaku kōdanjo* (Institute of Japanese Studies)[5] an office known as the *Shiryō Henshū Kokushi Kōsei Kyoku*, or Office for the Collection of Historical Materials and Compilation of National History. The Meiji Emperor then gave to his chief minister, Sanjō Sanetomi, a rescript written by his own hand, commanding him to initiate an historiographical project. In effect, this was an instruction for the compilation of an official history which should carry on from the last of the Six National Histories, the *Nihon Sandai Jitsuroku*, that is, from the year 887, the object being 'to set right the relation between monarch and subject, to make clear the distinction between civilization and barbarity, and to implant the principle of virtue throughout the empire'. This was shortly followed by the establishment within the former Bakufu school, the

[4] The *Rikkokushi*, the series of official chronicles ending in the ninth century, are the subject of the paper by G. W. Robinson, above, pp. 213–28.

[5] The *Wagaku Kōdanjo* was a school set up at Edo in 1793 by Hanawa Hokiichi with the permission of the Bakufu; it came subsequently under the control of the Hayashi family. Lectures were given on the history and laws of Japan. The school was also responsible for the compilation of the *Hanawa Shiryō*, of which more is said below, p. 270.

*Shōhei-kō*,[6] of an office known as the *Kokushi Henshū Kyoku*, or Office for the Compilation of National History. When, presently, the *Shōhei-kō* and two other schools[7] were amalgamated to form the nucleus of a university, this history office was also incorporated in the university and devoted to the compilation of a national history. This represents the first institution of a permanent office for historiography, such as did not exist even when the Six National Histories were compiled. At this university, Chinese studies, which had hitherto occupied the main place, were joined by Japanese studies, or, rather, the Japanese side was strengthened; those now entrusted with the work of historical compilation at this office included scholars in both fields. But in the course of time historians of the Chinese tradition came to occupy a dominant position in the historiographical project.

It was decided to start on the task of continuing the Six National Histories by using as a basis the chronologically arranged collection of historical material assembled at the *Wagaku Kōdanjo* during the Tokugawa period by Hanawa Hokiichi and known as the *Hanawa Shiryō* (Hanawa Historical Materials);[8] but it was not long before this course was abandoned, and, after a number of further changes, a *Shūshi-kyoku* or Office of Historiography was set up in 1875, becoming, in 1877, the *Shūshi-kan* or College of Historiography, at which the work of compilation was properly put in hand.

Four types of compilation were undertaken at the College of Historiography. The first involved the editing of historical material and Imperial genealogies for the period of the Northern and Southern Courts and after, under the direction of Kawada Tsuyoshi. The second was the editing of material relating to the Tokugawa period, under the direction of Shigeno

[6] The *Shōhei-kō* was originally a private school belonging to the Confucian scholastic family of the Hayashi, within the Tokugawa Bakufu. It was established in 1630 by Hayashi Razan with the help of Tokugawa Iemitsu. It was at first located at Ueno Shinobugaoka, in Edo, being moved later to Yushima, after which it came under the direct control of the Bakufu.

[7] One was the *Kaisei-jo*, a school established in Edo in 1857 by the Bakufu for the purpose of study and instruction in *rangaku* or Dutch studies. It was originally called *Bansho-shirabe-jo*, the name being changed in 1863 to *Kaisei-jo*. The other was the *Igaku-sho*. In 1857 doctors who used Dutch medical methods joined together to set up the *Shutō-jo* or Institute for Vaccination in Edo. This was transferred to the control of the Bakufu in 1860, and in the following year renamed *Seiyo Igaku-sho* or Western Medical Studies Institute.

[8] Hanawa Hokiichi was a *kokugakusha*, or scholar of Japanese studies, of the latter half of the Tokugawa period. Though blind, he pursued studies in Japanese literature and history, and, in 1793, set up the *Wagaku Kōdanjo*. In about 1779 he started work on the compilation of the *Gunsho Ruijū* (a classified compendium of numerous works on many subjects of many periods), and in 1819 all the 670 volumes were published. In addition, he also collated and published the texts of a number of ancient works. The *Hanawa Shiryō* was a compilation which followed on from the *Rikkokushi*, presenting in chronological order material for the period from 889 onwards. Work began in 1806 and continued until it was abandoned in 1861, by which time a draft in 430 fascicles is said to have been produced. A portion of the work is preserved at the Shiryō Hensanjo at the present time.

Yasutsugu. The third was the compilation of the *Fukko-ki* (Record of the Restoration) and of the *Meiji Shiyō* (Outline of Meiji History).[9] Fourth was the compilation of local topographies.

Such was the organization within which the editorial work proceeded. In due course there emerged the view, which steadily hardened from July 1879 onwards, that an official history should be compiled from the material on which work was in progress. There was, however, an unreconciled opposition of ideas between Shigeno and Kawada, the former being in favour of compiling an official history, while the latter held that it would be better to postpone the attempt until the material for it was as complete as possible. In 1881 however came the transfer of Kawada to the Department of the Imperial Household. There ensued a reorganization of the College of Historiography, whereby, with Shigeno as Deputy Chief Editor (the Chief Editor being Ijichi Masaharu) and Kume Kunitake, Hoshino Hisashi and others as editors, work was at length begun on the *Dai Nippon Hennen Shi* (Chronological History of Japan). By this time the *Fukko-ki* had been completed, while the work on the genealogies and local histories had been transferred to the Department of the Imperial Household and the Ministry of the Interior respectively.

It was planned that the Chronological History of Japan should be written in Chinese in annalistic form and should cover the period 1392 to 1867. It was thus to be mainly annalistic in form, but provision was also made for ten sections of monographs on selected topics. The editorial rules, of January 1882, provided as follows:[10]

(1) The form of the Tso Tradition (*Tso Chuan*) and Ssu-ma Kuang's Comprehensive Mirror (*Tzu Chih T'ung Chien*)[11] would be followed generally, with suitable modifications, every effort being made to explain the development of events.

(2) Accordingly, though the form would be annalistic, there would be no necessity to adhere strictly to chronological arrangement; cause and effect should be shown with clarity, and material on particular subjects should be grouped separately.

(3) Further, important matters connected with the administrative system or finance and economics or shifts in the state of politics or the life of the people should receive the most detailed treatment possible.

The above points seem to make it clear that the intention was to combine

[9] The *Fukko-ki* is a chronologically arranged record of the period from Keiō 3 (1867), 10th month, 10th day to Meiji 1st year (1868), 10th month. There are 289 chapters in 15 volumes. The *Meiji Shiyō* is a chronologically arranged record which starts at the same point as the *Fukko-ki* and continues to December 1874, a continuation carrying the record down to 1882: 7 volumes, including appendix.

[10] According to *Shiryō Hensan Shimatsu* (Account of the Compilation of Historical Materials), a draft preserved at the Shiryō Hensanjo (Historiographical Institute of Tōkyō University).

[11] See above, pp. 26 and 151–9.

the two traditional forms, the annalistic and the annal-cum-monograph, to produce a new vehicle for Japanese history. The points have much in common with the plan, to be described below, for taking into account Western historical methods. Yet while they demonstrate that there was a desire to respond to the needs of a new epoch, they still belonged in general terms to the main thread of Chinese-style historiography in Japan, carrying on the traditions of the *Rikkokushi, Honchō Tsugan*, and *Dai Nihonshi*.

In this way, then, the compilation of the Chronological History of Japan (*Dai Nippon Hennen Shi*) was begun and carried on (until its abandonment in 1893) by the combined endeavours of the group of compilers named above, centred round Shigeno. Part of the draft of the work is still preserved in the Shiryō Hensan-jo (Historiographical Institute) of Tokyo University.

The above is only a brief account of the inception and development of these official historiographical projects, but it will be clear even from this account that the heart of the project and its leading figure was Shigeno Yasutsugu.

3. *Shigeno Yasutsugu and his historical studies: history of the* kōshō-gaku *tradition*

Shigeno Yatsusugu was a samurai of Satsuma during the feudal period. He was born in 1827 in a samurai family of low rank in that fief. After attending the college of the fief, the Zōshikan, he proceeded to Edo (now Tokyo) in 1848 to continue his studies, entering the *Shōhei-kō* and studying Chu Hsi philosophy. It may be supposed that it was during this perioa that he came in contact with the scholastic tradition of textual collation known as *kōshō-gaku* (Chinese: *k'ao-cheng*) which was subsequently to become the basic ingredient of his character as an historian. After seven years at this school, he left to become a teacher at the fief school in the official residence of the lord of Satsuma in Edo. Then in 1863 he was deputed to conduct peace discussions with the British naval squadron, which had bombarded Kagoshima, and he concluded these discussions at Kanagawa. In the following year, 1864, on the instructions of Shimazu Hisamitsu, he compiled an historical work calle.' *Kōchō Seikan*. In 1865 he translated and annotated *Bankoku Kōhō* (Law of All Countries).[12] After the Restoration, in 1878, he went to Tokyo and worked in the new government's Ministry of Education, and then, by way of the Great Council of State, entered the *Shūshi-kyoku* (Office of Historiography).[13] Finally, after the formation of

---

[12] *Bankoku Kōhō* (Chinese, *Wan-kuo Kung-fa*) was a book on international law written in Chinese by the American missionary in China, W. A. P. Martin. Shigeno was ordered by his feudal lord to translate the book and the first three voiumes were published in 1869.

[13] According to *Seisai Sensei Gyōjō Shiryō*, in *Shigeno Hakase Shigaku Rombunshū*, vol. i (Tokyo, 1938). (The latter work, which is a collection of Shigeno's articles on historical subjects, will be referred to below as *Rombunshū*.)

the *Shūshi-kan* (College of Historiography), he became, though nominally only Deputy Chief, the actual director of the government's historiographical undertakings.

Such was Shigeno's career. His knowledge of, and attitude to, history were, therefore, inevitably based on Chu Hsi philosophy, but in his case there was in addition the influence of that scholastic tradition known as *kōshō-gaku*, which had been developing during the latter half of the Tokugawa period.

*Kōshō-gaku* was a modern phenomenon in China also, having flourished there from the second half of the seventeenth century until about the beginning of the nineteenth, during which time it had been adopted by a number of scholars. Introduced into Japan, these methods of textual study were used there also from the late seventeenth and early eighteenth centuries for the study of the Chinese classics, and were also applied to the field of *kokugaku* (i.e., the study of Japanese history and classical literature). As a result there appeared among the scholars of Japanese subjects a number who used the methods of *kōshō-gaku*, among whom were several, such as Kariya Ekisai, Oyamada Tomohiko, and Fuji Teikan, for whose scholarly achievements Shigeno himself professed a high regard.

Chinese studies in Japan at the end of the Tokugawa period were no longer, as they had been at the beginning of the period, studies of ideas and philosophy, but had come to be largely concerned with the field of Chinese literature as such or with textual studies of the *kōshō-gaku* kind. Such influences would presumably have been important in the work of the *Shōhei-kō*. Certainly it is true that the *kōshō-gaku* school had made very great progress indeed by the middle of the nineteenth century. As Shigeno himself pointed out,[14] the vogue for *kōshō-gaku* may be said to have arisen less among the scholar-officials of the Bakufu or the fiefs than among the independent *rōnin* (lordless) scholars or rich townsmen, who had time and leisure for it. It was a mode of study of such a character as to permeate such sections of society and was intimately bound up with the cultural life of Edo and the other great cities. Shigeno spent a long time studying in Edo at the Shōhei-kō, where he came in contact with the cultural life of the city and was subjected to the influence of the prevalent *kōshō-gaku* school.

Moreover, at the time of strong anti-foreign sentiment at the end of the Tokugawa period, Shigeno was responsible for such matters as conducting peace discussions with Britain and translating and annotating the *Bankoku Kōhō*, experiences which, we may suppose, brought him into what was for a Chinese scholar a comparatively new atmosphere.

Then again, as has been mentioned above, Shigeno had some experience

[14] See Shigeno's article, 'Gakumon wa tsui ni kōshō ni ki su', published 1890 (*Rombunshū*, i, 35–46).

of historical compilation in Satsuma. In 1864 Shimazu Hisamitsu of that fief undertook the compilation of an annalistic history, but it was Shigeno who was in charge of the work. This history was subsequently named *Kōchō Seikan*. It covered Japanese history from the Emperor Jimmu to A.D. 1393. I shall not go into Hisamitsu's motives in undertaking the work or into the course of its development or into Shigeno's part in the enterprise,[15] beyond remarking that the original intention was to produce a chronicle history of Japan modelled on Ssu-ma Kuang's Comprehensive Mirror (*Tzu Chih T'ung Chien*), but that in fact the project ended in rewriting in chronological order the Tokugawa period work, *Dai Nihonshi*, in which the material had been arranged as annals, biographies, and monographs. At the end of 1865 a draft of forty-one fascicles was completed. When he embarked on the task, Shigeno adopted the chronological arrangement because of the inconvenience which, in a work arranged like the *Dai Nihonshi*, resulted from having to look for information in a number of different places. It was this argument which later made him choose the same arrangement when he undertook the compilation of the Chronological History of Japan (*Dai Nippon Hennen Shi*). His work on the *Kōchō Seikan* also made him thoroughly familiar with the *Dai Nihonshi* and brought some of its shortcomings to his attention; he later began systematic examination of its text, which led him eventually to criticism of the work as a whole.

When the official history project was initiated in 1869, the original intention was to continue from where the Six National Histories had left off (A.D. 887), but when the work began on the *Dai Nippon Hennen Shi* in 1881, the starting point was the year 1392.[16] For the plan of continuing the Six National Histories had been substituted that of continuing the *Dai Nihonshi*. The reason was, of course, that in its scope and in the underlying thoroughness of its collation and presentation, the *Dai Nihonshi* was regarded as the greatest achievement of its time and was considered to rank with works compiled by Imperial decree. However, as has been said above, textual study based on *kōshō-gaku* methods had made considerable progress during the period before Meiji. For example, one compilation of that period, the *Hanawa Shiryō*, was of such high quality that it was possible to incorporate part of it without alteration in the *Dai Nihon Shiryō* (Chronological Source books of Japanese History: described below), when that series was compiled and published. Shigeno and his fellow editors, therefore, though claiming to be following the *Dai Nihonshi*, did not do so slavishly by any means, but followed their model in a critical manner.

[15] On this subject, see Ōkubo Toshiaki's article, 'Shimazu-ke hensan Kōchō Seikan to Meiji shoki no shūshi jigyō', *Shigaku Zasshi*, vol. 1, No. 12, pp. 1–45.

[16] In fact, on this occasion, he went back a little from 1392 and started from 1318. He then checked the text of the *Dai Nihonshi* for this period and rearranged the material in chronological order.

Shigeno himself, especially as a result of his contact with the *kōshō-gaku* school of the late Tokugawa period, had come to have a high regard for that kind of study and later went so far as to maintain that all scholarship resolves itself into *kōshō-gaku*.[17] Thus, as his researches progressed, he became critical of statements made in the *Dai Nihonshi*. What principally provided him with the basis for his criticism was the material assembled by the Office, later College, of Historiography and his study of it. As a part of their preparations for writing an official history, these offices had made a collection of material which they arranged in chronological order and called *Shiryō* (Historical Materials). To this end every opportunity was taken to search out ancient documents and other materials and add them to the collection. This activity was carried out on a particularly large scale from 1885 onwards, and during the years 1886–8 Shigeno and his colleagues went all over Japan energetically assembling documents. The ancient documents and other evidence thus assembled were then applied to the purpose of re-examining accounts which had become accepted and correcting errors in them. This new kind of re-examination first made its appearance when the compilation of the Chronological History of Japan began. As a result of collation with the newly discovered primary materials, the opportunity arose to find and correct errors not only in the *Dai Nihonshi* but in other earlier historical works as well. Consequently, the fruits of these *kōshō-gaku* studies carried on in the Office of Historiography began to attract the attention of people at large.

The reason for this was that, as their researches progressed, Shigeno and his colleagues discarded the conscious purpose which had informed all previous historical writing and began to adopt an objective attitude which aimed at discovering objective facts. Such moral purposes as 'the clarification of relations between monarch and minister' were, of course, at work not only in the *Dai Nihonshi* but also in the spirit in which the Meiji historical project was first undertaken; but the activities of Shigeno and his colleagues constituted a repudiation of the hortatory or moralistic history, which had come to dominate the historical thinking of former periods, and might be said, in other words, to have established the independence of history, or of scholarship, from politics and ethics. Most active in this respect was Shigeno, and, under him, Kume and Hoshino. When Shigeno said, 'Those who engage in historical work must be fair and impartial in their hearts',[18] and when Kume said, 'Let us see history purged of the old usages of exhortation',[19] they proclaimed their new view with the

---

[17] In his article 'Gakumon wa tsui ni kōshō ni ki su', *Rombunshū*, i, 35–46.

[18] Shigeno's article thus entitled, i.e. 'Shigaku ni jūji suru mono wa sono kokoro shikō shihei narazarubekarazu' (published 1889), *Rombunshū*, i, 30–32.

[19] Kume Kunitake's article thus entitled, i.e. 'Kanchō no kyūshū wo araute rekishi wo miyo' (published 1891), *Shigaku Zasshi*, vol. ii, No. 19, pp. 1–17.

utmost clarity, but it may be worth giving here one or two instances of their activities.

As early as 1873–4, Kawada Tsuyoshi had written a paper entitled *Nihon Gaishi Bengo* (Examination of the Unofficial History of Japan) in which he criticized Rai Sanyō's *Nihon Gaishi*.[20] In 1884 Shigeno delivered a lecture in Tokyo entitled 'The view that many current historical accounts are factually erroneous',[21] criticizing the *Nihon Gaishi*, after which he continued to make public new views of his own. Kume Kunitake was particularly bold in putting forward new views on all kinds of questions, and on one such occasion, in 1891, when he went so far as to publish an article entitled 'Shintō as a primitive custom of sacrifice to heaven',[22] he came under such heavy attack from all sides, especially from Shintoists and nationalists, that he was obliged to leave the university.

But most public attention was aroused when Shigeno denied the existence of Kojima Takanori and expunged him from the pages of history. Kojima Takanori had been recorded even in the *Dai Nihonshi* as a loyal minister of the Southern Court and had originally figured in the famous *Taiheiki*. Shigeno, however, came to the conclusion, as a result of his researches in ancient documents and records, that it was impossible to regard Kojima as an actual person and he omitted him from the Chronological History of Japan. It appears that his researches in this connection were based on work of Kume Kunitake;[23] but, however that may be, when in 1890 Shigeno delivered his lecture entitled 'A Study of Kojima Takanori'[24] and so made his views public, he attracted widespread attention. Shigeno published a number of other articles, in addition to this, in which he corrected erroneous views from the past and denied the validity of traditional material. For all this the public rewarded him with the nickname 'Doctor Expunger', his handling of the Kojima Takanori question remaining one of his most famous achievements.

In these examples we see at work the criticism of historical sources and the research based thereon which Shigeno and Kume evolved from *kōshō-gaku*. The extreme rigour and minuteness of their methods contain elements comparable with the source criticism employed by modern Western historians in their researches. Armed with these weapons, Shigeno and his

[20] Ōkubo Toshiaki, *Nihon Kindai Shigaku Shi* (Tokyo, 1940), p. 253. On the *Nihon Gaishi*, see above, pp. 259–63.

[21] Shigeno's article thus entitled, i.e. 'Sejō rufu no shiden ōku jijitsu wo ayamaru no setsu', *Rombunshū*, i, 9–19.

[22] This article was published in *Shigaku Zasshi* in 1891 and subsequently became a controversial topic. When in 1888 the work of historical compilation was transferred to the Imperial University, Shigeno and Kume had been made professors, but Kume found himself obliged to relinquish his post in 1892 because of this article.

[23] Ōkubo Toshiaki, *Nihon Kindai Shigaku Shi*, pp. 254–5. Kume's studies of this subject are supposed to have been carried on about 1882 to 1884.

[24] Shigeno's article thus entitled, i.e. 'Kojima Takanori Kō', *Rombunshū*, ii, 577–90.

colleagues addressed themselves to their task of compiling a chronicle history. In addition, by way of bringing together the results of these researches of theirs, they published in 1890 from Tokyo Imperial University a work called *Kokushi Gan* (A Survey of Japanese History). This book was also intended as a pointer in the teaching of Japanese history and was long used as a university textbook and as a standard in other ways in the field of Japanese historical education, exercising considerable influence.

The foregoing constitutes a brief account of the work of Shigeno and his colleagues at the College of Historiography based on *kōshō-gaku* methods; but it is also true that during the same period these men were beginning to take an interest in the historical methods of the West.

### 4. *The growth of Shigeno's interest in Western historical methods*

Shigeno's interest in Western historical methods began quite early, but it manifested itself not so much in his attitude to the collation and criticism of historical materials, described in the previous section, as in his desire to apply Western methods to his style of presentation in the Chronological History. This probably arose from the trend towards 'history of civilization' which had become pronounced after the beginning of the 'Period of Cultural Enlightenment' (the term applied to the early Meiji period), or, indeed, in a more general way, from the wider cultural influences of the West at the time. As early as May 1875 a document concerning the work of the Office of Historiography, presented by that office to the Great Council of State, included the following passage:

> The form of Western historiography is such that it incorporates within a chronological arrangement a causal treatment of events; sometimes argument is introduced, sometimes maps, diagrams or statistics are provided, and the work is carried out in such a way that the outline is comprehensible at a glance. It is essential therefore that in our future compilations we introduce headings into our chronological scheme, that from time to time we give some account of the causation and development of events, and that, when geographical descriptions are involved, we insert maps.[25]

As Professor Ōkubo has pointed out,[26] we may suppose that this was drafted by Shigeno. Again, in December 1879, in the course of a lecture in Tokyo 'On the method of compiling a national history',[27] Shigeno gave expression to almost exactly the same opinion. Shigeno could not read European languages, of course, but translations enabled him to give attention to western historical works. He was in a position, for instance, to

[25] *Shiryō Hensan Shimatsu*, in the Shiryō Hensanjo.
[26] In his article in *Shigaku Zasshi*, vol. i, No. 12, pp. 1–45, cited above. [27] *Rombunshū*, i, 1–8.

read Jean Crasset's *Histoire de l'église du Japon*,[28] which was published in translation by the Great Council of State, as well as a Chinese history of the Franco-Prussian War.[29] Most suggestive of all seems to have been *The Satsuma Rebellion* by Augustus H. Mounsey.[30]

Soon after the end of the Satsuma rebellion, in about December 1877, the College of Historiography began collecting material for a history of the rebellion, and rules for the compilation were ready in the following April. A draft work entitled *Seisei Shimatsu* (Account of the Pacification of the West) was prepared in due course. It happened that at just this time a certain Suematsu Kenchō, who was well known as a young and brilliant journalist and man of letters, proceeded to take up an appointment as a secretary at the Japanese Legation in England, and in February 1878 the College of Historiography accordingly entrusted him with 'the investigation of British and French historical methods'.[31] The terms of their request to him were briefly as follows: most Japanese historical works, from the Six National Histories onwards, had been annalistic in form, giving chronological accounts of reigns and of the words and deeds of Emperors; not until the *Dai Nihonshi* had the material been rearranged in the form of chronicle, biographies, and monographs; then, while the essential facts concerning government, political, and administrative systems, and warfare had been recorded in them, neither Japanese nor Chinese histories had ever described in adequate detail the fluctuations of the economy of the country as a whole, or changes in social and religious customs, or the cause and effect of these things, or the conditions of life of the people at large; it was therefore essential to examine and take cognisance of the forms of European historiography.

On his arrival in England, therefore, Suematsu applied to the British historian, George Gustavus Zerffi, whom he persuaded to write *The Science of History*,[32] which, on its appearance in 1879, he sent to the College of Historiography. But before this, Mounsey's *The Satsuma Rebellion* ap-

[28] Published in translation in 1878 by the Great Council of State, under the title *Nihon Seikyō Shi*. The original work was published in Paris in 1689, but the translation was made from the second edition of 1715.

[29] This history was written by Wang T'ao, rendered into colloquial language by Chang Tsung-liang, and published in 1871. It was published in Japan in 1878 and 1887.

[30] I have been unable to find detailed biographical information on Mounsey, but for the following points I am indebted to Mr. Edwin G. Beal, of the Library of Congress, through the good offices of my friend, Professor Robert K. Sakai, Assistant Professor in the University of Nebraska. It appears that Mounsey was a British diplomat, who, after serving in various places, was appointed a secretary at the British Legation in Japan in 1876. He was transferred to Athens in 1878. In April 1881 he was made British Minister in Columbia, and died at Bogota in the following year. He was a Fellow of the Royal Geographical Society and wrote, in addition to the work under consideration, *A Journey through the Caucasus and the interior of Africa* (1872).

[31] *Shiryō Hensan Shimatsu.*

[32] The letter in which Suematsu conveyed his request to Zerffi, dated 6 March 1879, is printed at the beginning of the book. Zerffi (1821–92) was a Hungarian refugee teaching in London: see *Dictionary of National Biography*, xxi, 1323–4.

peared in England,[33] and Suematsu appears to have been responsible for sending a copy of it to the College. This organization seems immediately to have had the book translated, and the draft translation in three volumes, called *Satsuma Hanran Ki*, is still preserved at the Shiryō Hensanjo (Historiographical Institute).

When in the same year Zerffi's book was completed and sent to Japan by Suematsu, the College of Historiography applied to the celebrated scholar of the time, Nakamura Masanao (Keiu), for a translation. Nakamura was too busy to produce a complete translation and gave up after doing only a part, and the work was finally completed in 1887 by Saga Shōsaku. The draft, entitled *Shigaku* (History), survives at the Shiryō Hensanjo.

To describe Zerffi's book briefly, it is a large volume of 773 pages, divided into seven chapters. The first chapter, which might be described as an introduction to historical scholarship, discusses such questions as the nature of historical scholarship and, as it were, the terms of reference of the historian. Chapter 2 deals with the ancient history of the Orient and Greece; Chapter 3, Greece; Chapter 4, Rome; Chapter 5, Christianity; Chapter 6, the Middle Ages; Chapter 7, the Modern Period. Each chapter constitutes a general cultural history of its subject. Each chapter also contains some description and discussion of the historiography of the period concerned. The work thus provided a suitable model of western historical research of the time.

The content of the work has been criticized in the following terms by the late Professor Imai, a specialist in English history:[34]

> The treatment is detailed for the ancient period, whereas for the medieval and subsequent period it is bare. In particular, so excessively brief is it on the subject of the historical studies of the most advanced period of all, the nineteenth century, that it can hardly be termed a satisfactory introduction to the subject. For example, in dealing with England the author mentions so recent a work, at the time, as J. R. Green's *A Short History of the English People*, but in treating German and French historians he mentions only E. Curtius and T. Mommsen in connection with ancient history, contenting himself merely with listing the names of B. G. Niebuhr, L. v. Ranke and H. v. Sybel under historical studies of the nineteenth century; and he never mentions at all such men as H. v. Treitschke, J. Burckhardt, F. de Coulanges and G. J. J. Monos. Again, though the work is comparatively rich in references to India as well as to China and Japan, presumably inserted for the benefit

[33] The preface to *The Satsuma Rebellion* is dated 28 February 1879 and that of Zerffi's book 15 October 1879.
[34] Imai Toshiki, 'Seiyō shigaku no hompō shigaku ni ataetaru eikyō', in *Hompō Shigaku Shi Ronsō* (2 vols., Tokyo, 1939), ii, 1439–69.

of Japanese scholars, there is no description of German, French or English work in the field of historical editing and compilation. The work cannot therefore be said to satisfy the terms of Suematsu's request.

Moreover, again according to Professor Imai, Zerffi gives pride of place to German historical scholarship, so that in this respect also the work failed to satisfy the desire of the College of Historiography to examine English and French historical methods. It is true that the book is unbalanced in these ways, but considering that it was produced within about six months of Suematsu's request, it was inevitable that it should to some extent fail to conform to its terms.

When Suematsu requested the production of this work, he laid down twelve conditions as to the form it should take. These are reproduced in the book as an appendix entitled 'Instructions', together with Suematsu's letter of request. Comparison of these conditions with the terms of the request addressed by the College to Suematsu, which were outlined above, suggests that although Suematsu's Instructions did, in fact, approximately cover the requirements of the *Shūshi-kan*, there were also certain points of difference between the two in their ideas of history, and that the latter was interpolating his own views when he asked, for example, for an account of philosophical historical writing or of problems concerning historicism. It seems, in short, that Suematsu's ideas were close to those of the contemporary writers of 'history of civilization'.

Three hundred copies of Zerffi's book were printed in London, of which one hundred were sent to Tokyo, and delivered, it appears, early in 1880 at the latest. As already described, the College of Historiography took steps to translate it and planned to circulate it generally. However, this plan was never realized.

We cannot determine the extent to which Shigeno and others may have read and digested this work, but in the course of his lecture 'On the method of compiling a national history', Shigeno remarked, 'We have asked Mr. Nakamura Masanao for a translation, and when it appears, I hope it will prove a most useful work of reference for us.' Moreover, the College paid for the expenses of the production of the work what seems, from its budget at the time, a considerable sum of money.[35] Again, the number of passages in the extant copy of the draft translation, *Shigaku*, which have been subjected to correction and interpolation, attests both the hopes reposed in the work and the considerable amount of study which was devoted to it.

Shigeno thus showed a great interest in Western historical studies, but I

---

[35] According to the *Shiryō Hensan Shimatsu*, the annual budget of the *Shūshi-kan* at this time was about Y30,000, and when Suematsu went to England the *Shūshi-kan* gave him Y1,500 for his expenses in connection with the book, etc. Moreover, when the printing of the book was finished, they paid another £348 (in payment for the writing and printing). They paid yet a further Y591 for the expenses of the translation.

am inclined to think that it was Mounsey's *History of the Satsuma Rebellion* from which he received the greatest stimulus. As a native of Satsuma, who was even acquainted with Saigō, it was natural that he should have felt a great interest in Saigō's rebellion. Doubtless, therefore, it was with great interest that he engaged in the compilation of the *Seisei Shimatsu* (Account of the Pacification of the West) and, if only for that reason, he would naturally be greatly interested in another work which handled the same theme. In his lecture 'On the method of compiling a national history', he said:

> This book [Mounsey's *Satsuma Rebellion*] begins with an account of the Bakufu and the fiefs; next it deals with the circumstances of the overthrow of the Bakufu by Saigō and his colleagues; then it discusses such questions as when Saigō and his colleagues first began to feel dissatisfied with the new government and the circumstances which planted the first seeds of rebellion. The course of the rebellion itself is then given only in outline, followed by detailed treatment of the political situation after the rebellion and the effect of the rebellion on public opinion and so on. Whether each individual conjecture is correct or not may be open to question, but it is only by attention to such points that we can arrive at the truth. The *Nihon Seikyō Shi* (*Histoire de l'église du Japon*) and other Western histories are similar. Unlike Japanese and Chinese histories, which confine themselves to factual statement, Western histories inquire into causes and consider effects, provide detailed accounts of their subjects and vivid pictures of conditions of the time with which they are concerned. There can be no doubt that their form and method embody many points of value to us.

Such was the interest Shigeno felt in the methods of Western historical writing. Nevertheless, in spite of his intention of examining cause and effect, giving detailed accounts of his subjects, and painting vivid pictures of conditions at various times, in so far as he was committed to the production of the Chronological History (*Dai Nippon Hennen Shi*) in Chinese, he was confronted with a practical problem of extreme difficulty. So even in the *Seisei Shimatsu*, the detail is principally to be found in the chronological account of the warfare itself, and it can hardly be said that he applied the methods of narration which he so much admired in *The Satsuma Rebellion*.

Consequently, in spite of his intention of learning Western methods of historical writing, no definite influence of this kind is visible in his own historical writing, least of all in the Chronological History.

5. *Contact between* kōshō-gaku *and Western historical methods: the emergence of modern historical scholarship in Japan*

From about 1878 to 1887, Shigeno and the other scholars at the College of Historiography were thus intending to learn the historiographical methods of the West, but their intention was not so far fulfilled as to affect either the method or the style of the Chronological History of Japan.

However, the fulfilment of this purpose of introducing Western historical method was approached at about the same time from another direction. In 1887 the German historian, Ludwig Riess,[36] was invited to come to Japan as professor of history in the newly-established department of history in the College of Literature at Tokyo Imperial University. On arrival in Japan, he began to give instructions in the regular methods of historical research employed in the West, especially those of Germany.

There was no particular connection between the employment of Riess and his introduction of German historical scholarship, on the one hand, and the movement towards Western historical scholarship on the part of the College of Historiography, on the other. Rather it was the general tendency at this time, in all fields of scholarship in Japan, for German scholarship to occupy the most prominent position. Riess belonged as a historian to the school of Ranke. Through him, the regular German historical method which had begun with Ranke was first introduced into Japan. Shortly afterwards, two Japanese who had been studying in Europe returned to Japan, Tsuboi Kumazō in 1891 and Mizukuri Gempachi in 1892, and both began to lecture on German historical scholarship at the Imperial University in Tokyo. In this way began instruction in the methods of Western historical research and writing, in particular the rigorous criticism of sources, and the Imperial University of Tokyo became the centre from which these studies developed.

When in 1889 a department of Japanese history was established at the Imperial University, Riess submitted a memorandum in which he explained the necessity of such ancillary disciplines as diplomatics and the collection of sources, and further explained the necessity of learning the European techniques in these disciplines.[37] In addition to the lectures which he subsequently delivered, he also published a number of studies in

---

[36] Ludwig Riess (1861–1928). Studied history and geography at Berlin University. Doctoral thesis, *Geschichte des Wahlrechts zum englischen Parlament* (1885). Went to Japan in 1887 and lectured on history at the Imperial University of Tokyo. Returned home in 1893 and collected European material on relations with Japan at The Hague and elsewhere. Returned home again in 1902 and became a lecturer at Berlin University, subsequently becoming an associate professor. In his later years worked on the revision of George Weber's history of Germany. His published works include *Lectures on English Constitutional History* (1891), and *Allerlei aus Japan* (1904).

[37] The text of this memorandum appears in *Tōkyō Teikoku Daigaku Gojūnen Shi* (Tokyo, 1932), i, 1928.

the history of the intercourse between Japan and Europe, which provided Japanese scholars with practical examples.[38]

In the year immediately before that of the establishment of a department of Japanese history, that is, in 1888, the work of compiling the Chronological History of Japan, which had been going on at the College of Historiography, was transferred to Tokyo Imperial University. Shigeno and Kume and other colleagues thereupon became professors, delivering lectures at the university besides continuing their editorial work. These men, as explained above, had been engaged in applying critical methods to the examination of the former fruits of Japanese historical labours—the *Dai Nihonshi*, for example—and incorporating their results in the Chronological History (*Dai Nippon Hennen Shi*); and in the university they were now thrown into contact with the new imported Western historical theories and research methods. There were two aspects of these new ideas to which they responded readily: first, the idea of the independence of history as a pure science; second, in terms of method, that of subjecting sources to rigorous criticism.

Even in the West, history as a distinct discipline had only quite recently freed itself from the sphere of applied knowledge. Since Ranke had propounded his principles of research and writing 'Wie es eigentlich ist', history had become established as a separate science independent of ethical or political implications; and this theory was one which was readily comprehensible to, and indeed in accord with, that of Shigeno and his colleagues, who, however crudely, had already argued that history should be independent of hortatory or admonitory purpose (in Confucian terms).

In 1889 members of the department of history and of the department of Japanese history at the Imperial University, together with those who had been working at the College of Historiography, formed the Historical Society of Japan (*Shigakkai*), of which Shigeno was made president. His opening lecture at the inaugural meeting was entitled 'Those who engage in historical work must be fair and impartial in their hearts.'[39] In the course of it he said:

> History presents a picture of conditions as they were. It is the examination of these circumstances and the reasoned explanation of them which constitute the prime function of historical scholarship. There does indeed exist the view that the main concern of history is to instruct men about moral relationships or conduct; and among those who write with this in mind, there are some who are inclined to distort the facts. This is contrary to the true meaning of history. History only results if the moral lessons—the encouragement of good and discouragement of evil, the

---

[38] e.g., *History of the English Factory at Hirado* (Tokyo, 1898); *William Adams und sein 'Grab' in Hemimura* (Tokyo, 1900), etc.   [39] *Rombunshū*, i, 30–32.

clarification of moral relationships—emerge as a natural product of a faithful account of the facts. This is what I mean when I speak of an impartial view and impartial pen.

The critical methods of Western historical science as applied to sources also met with a ready response from these men, trained as they were in the tradition of *koshō-gaku*. For these methods corresponded in some ways with the techniques of collation and criticism used by these Japanese scholars when they applied the methods of *koshō-gaku* to the study of ancient documents and records. But there was a sense in which they gained from the West, even in this connection. Or, rather, it might be fairer to say that the realization that their own existing methods corresponded with those of the West strengthened their self-confidence. Certainly the existence of common ground between the two schools resulted in a fusion of the traditional historical scholarship of Japan with that of the West, or, to express it another way, the Japanese were able, by building on the basis of *koshō-gaku*, to learn and apply the methods of the West.

When, in March 1890 Shigeno addressed the Gakushi Kaiin on the theme, 'Scholarship ultimately resolves itself into *koshō*',[40] he said in the course of his lecture:

> *Koshō* corresponds broadly to what is called in the West, Induction. In the study of history, also, we collate a piece of evidence, 'A', with pieces of evidence, 'B' and 'C' and so arrive at our conclusion; in fact, we use induction.

He also said:

> I believe, in brief, that all the world's scholarship must ultimately resolve itself into induction, that is to say, into *koshō-gaku*.

Again, in an article published in March 1890 entitled 'The method of historical research',[41] he made the following emphatic assertion:

> History always and everywhere involves the weighing of evidence. Among the evidence some may be true and some false. It is the judgment of the historian that determines which is true and which false.

Such, then, was the order of Shigeno's comprehension of the methods of Western historical study. There were a certain number of points in common between the methods of *koshō-gaku* and those of Western historical science in connection with source criticism, and it was through these common points that he was able effectively to learn the methods of the West. In his lecture at the inaugural meeting of the Historical Society, which was cited above, he said in conclusion:

---

[40] *Rombunshū*, i, 35–46.　　[41] The original title is 'Rekishi Kenkyū-hō', *Rombunshū*, i, 66–68.

It is my hope that, *when we have subjected to the processes of Western historical scholarship* the material which the Office of Historiography and its successors have collected and when we have in that light examined the evidence of our country's past and compiled a history therefrom, the formation of this Historical Society will have proved to have done the state some service.

Here again we have a glimpse, clear if brief, of Shigeno's attitude to the methods of the West.

Gradually, then, in this way, the methods of Western historical scholarship were superimposed on the traditional methods of Japan and began to be taught in the departments of history and of Japanese history at the Imperial University, while the journal of the Historical Society of Japan, known as the *Shigakkai Zasshi* (later, *Shigaku Zasshi*) or Historical Journal of Japan, became the most authoritative organ of publication.

As a result of this superimposition of Western historical methods on the existing ones of *kōshō-gaku*, there was established a positivist method according to which only facts verified in reliable original sources could be regarded as objective historical facts; and this it would be fair to call the birth of modern historical science in Japan.

### 6. *Influence of the new methods on historiographical projects*

Once the methods of Western historical scholarship had been taken into use, it was natural that the traditional historiographical method, which consisted of writing an annalistic history in Chinese, should have gradually lost its attractions and become obsolescent.

I suppose it need hardly be said that the distinguishing feature of annalistic history is the opportunity it affords through its arrangement of events in their natural chronological sequence for extreme objectivity of statement. But if a method is desired by means of which causal relations may be explored and events treated synthetically or synoptically—and it was this potentiality that Shigeno and his colleagues were seeking in Western historical method—the annalistic form is unsuitable. When, therefore, Japanese historical studies began to move forward under the influence of those of the West, the old mode of annalistic presentation in Chinese began to lose significance.

But also, quite apart from this natural tendency, annalistic history was being subjected to criticism and attack from outside. This took various forms, among which we may distinguish the following three varieties.[42]

First, there was opposition to the writing of Japanese history in Chinese, which arose from the tide of nationalist feeling that had surged up in Japanese society generally after about 1887—one ingredient in this movement

[42] Miura Hiroyuki, *Nihon Shigaku Shi Gaisetsu* (now contained in *Miura cho Nihon Shi no Kenkyū dai ni shū*, Tokyo, 1930); Ōkubo Toshiaki, *Nihon Kindai Shigaku Shi*.

being a reaction against the Europeanizing policies pursued by the government since early Meiji and against the general mania for Western things. The opposition on the part of the *kokugakusha*, who pursued Japanese studies, was a powerful motive force in this. Because the projects undertaken by the Office of Historiography, etc., had become the preserve of such men as Shigeno and Kawada, who were Confucian scholars, the *kokugakusha* conceived a strong antipathy towards the projects, and, by way of resistance, initiated a movement for writing Japanese history in Japanese. In 1883 they formed a body called the *Shigaku Kyōkai* or Historical Association and treated the College of Historiography virtually as though it were an enemy country. The opposition of these men—among whom were professors and lecturers at the same Imperial University—was of appreciable strength.

Second, there was resentment at some of the results to which the *kōshō-gaku* methods of the Office of Historiography and its successors had led, and, hence, animosity towards *kōshō-gaku* itself. This arose from the reaction of a section of society to the denial of factuality to certain well-known and venerated historical personages or events, as in the case of Kojima Takanori which was described above. A further aspect, too, was the friction caused by the fact that history, as practised by Shigeno and his colleagues in their work of compilation, was becoming divorced from moral aims.

Third, there was opposition to the very fact of historiography being undertaken by the government, it being maintained by some that any governmental activity in this field should be confined to the collection and ordering of material and that the actual writing of history should be entrusted to the unfettered researches of the people at large.

Amid this diversity of opposition, the work on the Chronological History, which had been going on at the Imperial University, was discontinued in March 1893, Shigeno was relieved of his professorship, and Hoshino was left at the university to clear up what business remained.[43]

In this way the historiographical project initiated by the government was brought to an end. Nevertheless, as has been described above, the new method of historical research involved in the collection and study of ancient documents and other basic source materials had come to be regarded in the world of contemporary historical scholarship in Japan as an indispensable element in historical research. The technique of the collection, study and editing of material, which had been carried on by the government agencies like the Office of Historiography, had by this time advanced to the point at which it could fulfil that need. Hence the his-

---

[43] *Tōkyō Teikoku Daigaku Gojū-nen Shi*, ii, 1192. *Tōkyō Teikoku Daigaku Gakujutsu Taikan* (Tokyo, 1942), i, 250 et seqq. A further brief word on Shigeno may be of interest. From 1879 onwards he was a member of the *Tōkyō Gakushi Kaiin* (Tōkyō Academy); in 1890 he became a member of the House of Peers. He represented Japan at the third international congress of academies at Vienna in 1907. He died in 1910.

toriographical undertaking so suddenly discontinued was soon revived in a new guise as 'compilation of historical material' (*shiryō no hensan*). In 1895, Tokyo Imperial University set up an institution called Shiryō Hensan-gakari to undertake the compilation of historical materials, and so the work began again. It is this institution which has become the Shiryō Hensanjo, or Historiographical Institute, of the present day.[44]

But there were points of difference between the new project and its predecessor. At the head of the new project was Hoshino, who had served in the *Shūshi-kyoku* and *Shūshi-kan*, but the new project no longer involved writing an annalistic history in Chinese. It was solely devoted to the compilation of *shiryō*, or 'historical materials', from which history might be written. The reason advanced was that circumstances had changed and the time for writing Japanese history in Chinese was now past. It was felt, moreover, that if history is written by only two or three people, the subjective views of those two or three may distort the facts. It would therefore be better to make a compilation of materials as they stand, and then to make this available, by publication, to the scholarly world in general. But since this would be a task quite beyond the capacity of an individual, it was considered best to make it a state undertaking. This would have the desirable result of enabling historians in general to make use of the material to write their own political, economic, religious, or other kind of history. The compilation of material, which had hitherto been a means to the production of an annalistic history in Chinese, now became an end in itself.[45]

The man principally responsible for drawing up the new plan was Mikami Sanji,[46] an assistant professor at the College of Literature of the Imperial University, and one of those who participated in the historiographical undertaking. Mikami had of course received instruction from Shigeno and had also come under the influence of Riess and Tsuboi, of whom, as an assistant professor, he was also a colleague. He was of course one of those who had come to an understanding of the new Western science of history, and I am inclined to think that, through Riess and Tsuboi, he may have derived some inspiration from the compilation and publication of the famous *Monumenta Germaniae Historica*.

In this way began the compilation of the *Dai Nihon Shiryō* (Chronological Source Books of Japanese History) and *Dai Nihon Komonjo* (Old Documents

---

[44] I follow the *Shiryō Hensan Shimatsu*. Cf. also *Tōkyō Teikoku Daigaku Gojū-nen Shi*, vol. ii, and *Tōkyō Teikoku Daigaku Gakujutsu Taikan*, vol. i.

[45] Tsuji Zennosuke, 'Hompō ni okeru shūshi no enkaku to kokushigaku no seiritsu', in *Hompō Shigaku Shi Ronsō*, i, 1–25.

[46] Mikami graduated from Tōkyō University in 1889. In 1890 he became a member of the staff responsible for compiling the Chronological History. In 1892 he was made an assistant professor, becoming a full professor in 1899, at which time he became Director of the Shiryō Hensan-gakari.

of Japan), which are being published today by the Historiographical Institute. Publication began in 1901. The period then selected to be covered by the *Dai Nihon Shiryō* ran from the accession of the Emperor Uda in 887 to the Meiji Restoration of 1868. This period was divided into sixteen parts, and compilation began simultaneously on each part. The basis of the first part was formed by the *Hanawa Shiryō*, mentioned above; and this fact shows how highly we should regard the level attained by the historical researches of the Tokugawa period, based on *kōshō-gaku*, which produced the *Hanawa Shiryō*.

At present, the *Dai Nihon Shiryō* Part IV (covering the period 1185 to 1221, the so-called Kamakura Period) has been completed; Parts XIII, XIV, XV, and XVI have not yet been started; but the remaining parts are all in process of compilation and publication. Even so, it is likely to be some decades yet before the work reaches completion.

The arrangement of the Chronological Source Books (*Dai Nihon Shiryō*) is that of the chronicle. Outline accounts of events are given in brief paragraphs arranged by date. Where the day of an event is known, year, month, and day are recorded; where the day is unknown, year and month are given; where the month is also unknown, the year alone is given. In certain cases, all material relating to a given event may be brought together under the one head, while, in the case of notable personages, a detailed biography is appended under the date of death. In all cases, whatever material constitutes the source for a given item or event is cited in standard form under the appropriate entry. All kinds of material, assembled by the industry of the Office of Historiography and its successors, ranging from ancient documents, diaries and other records, to genealogies, drawings, sculptures, war tales, romances and private histories, if properly relevant, are quoted verbatim. The frequent use of ancient documents and diaries is a particular feature of the work.

Thus the form of the *Dai Nihon Shiryō* owes something to the influence of its predecessor, the uncompleted Chronological History of Japan, in so far as it is annalistically presented. At the same time, as was indicated above, by bringing together under one head all material relating to certain events, it has been found possible to incorporate material which would have been intractable in the pure annalistic form and to treat episodes in such a way as to make their course comprehensible as a whole.

The Old Documents of Japan (*Dai Nihon Komonjo*) differs from the Chronological Source Books. It prints in a form as near as possible to the original such ancient documents as have survived. It starts with the oldest surviving documents, that is to say, those of the Nara Period (eighth century A.D.), the present principle of arrangement being chiefly according to the institutions or persons by whom the documents are preserved, that is to say, shrines, temples, monasteries and private houses.

In addition to the above two compilations, certain others are now being issued. These include the *Dai Nihon Kokiroku* (Old Diaries of Japan), which is a publication of the edited texts of important diaries, as faithful as possible to the originals; and the *Dai Nihon Kinsei Shiryō* (Materials for the Early Modern—i.e. Tokugawa—History of Japan), which publishes the edited texts of important materials bearing on the Tokugawa period, including collections of laws, material on economic history and fief administration, and so forth. The availability of these works, the *Dai Nihon Shiryō*, *Dai Nihon Komonjo*, *Dai Nihon Kokiroku*, and *Dai Nihon Kinsei Shiryō*, has provided Japan's present day historians with valuable facilities for their work.[47]

### 7. *Conclusion*

As will have become clear in the foregoing pages, the historiographical undertaking of which Shigeno was in charge never saw completion in the form in which it was initiated; but, altered in form and arrangement, it has been carried on in the compilation and publication of such works as the *Dai Nihon Shiryō*, so that Shigeno may well be described as the father of the projects for the compilation of historical materials which exist at the present time.

But it is not only in such connections that Shigeno's influence is to be found. It was also considerable in the field of historical studies generally, as will have emerged from the foregoing. First of all, there is the independence of history as a discipline in itself, which was mentioned above. The efforts of Shigeno and his successors to escape from the moral view of history and adopt an objective viewpoint have been continued. Of course, the example of men like Kume Kunitake gives rise to some slight doubt whether they were always able to maintain such a standpoint whatever the circumstances, but it remains generally true that throughout this period the independence of history as a discipline was growing steadily greater. Secondly, it need hardly be said, there was the fact that Shigeno and his colleagues succeeded in bringing together the critical methods of Western historical scholarship and their own *kōshō-gaku* methods, and in transmitting this syncretism to the rising generation of scholars. We may cite as an example of this the organization of the science of diplomatics as a recognized ancillary branch of historical studies in Japan, carried out principally by Kuroita Katsumi; for the basis of this was the collection and study of ancient documents by the Office of Historiography and its successors, and such studies as those of Kume in this field had a considerable influence on Kuroita's work. Naturally it is not suggested that *kōshō-gaku* can be exactly equated with Western historical science, but there were points

[47] Up to the end of March 1956 the total number of volumes issued in these four series had reached 354.

in common between the two, principally in the method and technique of criticizing sources; and these points made it possible for Japanese scholars to understand Western historical science with ease and rapidity. But also for this reason, as was said by the late Professor Imai, 'since there existed in Japan an individual historical scholarship (i.e. that based on *kōshō-gaku*) which had already made fairly considerable progress, it cannot be said on the whole that the influence of the west in the field of history was so fundamental as in most other branches of science'.[48]

The fruits of research thus gained have been continuously embodied in the *Dai Nihon Shiryō* and other compilations, while in another direction they have also formed the matter of a number of independent books and articles.

We are today still influenced by these developments through numerous channels. At Tokyo University, in the Department of History, the Department of Japanese History, and the Historiographical Institute, we have been directly influenced by such historians as Professors Mikami Sanji, Kuroita Katsumi, and Tsuji Zennosuke.[49] Then there have been the various professors at Kyōto and other universities. Many of these were, on the one hand, heirs to the tradition of Shigeno and his colleagues, and, on the other, students of Western historical scholarship, in which they were instructed by Riess or Tsuboi. Thus the 'Tokyo tradition of historical writing' is, in other words, a tradition of objectivity or of an attempt to adopt an objective standpoint in historical research and writing; or, again, it could, perhaps, be called positivist research and writing. It is this that constitutes the main stream of academic historical scholarship in Japan. In its development it has been closely connected with the work of historical compilation.

This is not to say, of course, that this tradition is the whole of historical research and writing in Japan. Already, as early as the days of Shigeno, the rival school of *bummeishi* (history of civilization)[50] had become established, possessing excellent characteristics of its own. As time went on, yet other kinds of history came into being: cultural history was born and the materialist view was introduced, while at one time there was the ultra-nationalist Imperialist view of history. From these various standpoints criticism and indeed attacks were directed against the objectivist school. For instance, in the early days Taguchi Ukichi argued that 'the annalistic method is no more than chronological tabulation'.[51] Again, proponents of the materialist or Imperialist ideas objected that the writing and method of the academic school embodied no 'view of history' or that they constituted no more than the arrangement of historical material. Again, there

---

[48] Imai Toshiki, from his article in *Hompō Shigaku Shi Ronsō*, ii, 1439–69.
[49] Kuroita and Tsuji followed Mikami as successive heads of the Shiryō Hensan-gakari (later Shiryō Hensanjo).     [50] See introduction, p. 15.     [51] *Nihon Kaika Shōshi*, ch. 7.

were those who argued that in the task of compiling and editing materials it would have been better to have adopted German methods.

Notable progress is being made in historical scholarship today. This may be seen simply by looking at the expansion of the field of study, where we find not only political history, but also economic history, social history, and the history of ideas, all advanced in their writing and methods and all highly specialized. Thus, even in terms of historical compilation, there are circumstances in which the needs of such advanced studies are not adequately met simply by the chronological form chiefly adopted in the Chronological Source Books (*Dai Nihon Shiryō*). It was with a view to providing as satisfactory an answer as possible to such needs that the Old Documents of Japan (*Dai Nihon Komonjo*) was put in hand alongside the *Dai Nihon Shiryō* and that at the present time the Old Diaries of Japan (*Dai Nihon Kokiroku*) and Materials for the Early Modern History of Japan (*Dai Nihon Kinsei Shiryō*) are being compiled and published.

In method and in form there is doubtless room for future improvement. We ourselves acknowledge that. And it is our hope and intention to effect all possible improvements in these matters, and to offer still better material, better presented, to students of history.

# 16. MODERN JAPANESE ECONOMIC HISTORIANS

HUGH BORTON

*President, Haverford College; formerly Director,*
*East Asia Institute, Columbia University*

As Dr. Arnold Toynbee has recently pointed out, the stupendous progress in technological skills has vastly reduced the comparative size of the world and made it a single unit. At the same time, the conflicts between classes have been inflamed and are capable of causing the irrevocable disintegration of society. Furthermore, the destructive power of warfare is such that civilization can be destroyed. These developments have awakened economic historians to a new interest in problems of economic growth. They note that within the past century and a half, economic output has increased fivefold, but that this growth has been at an unequal rate in various parts of the world. Both of the World Wars, particularly World War II, revealed in striking fashion the close correlation of economic and military strength. The economic stagnation caused by the world depression of the 1930's further aroused their interest and made them ask why this came about and how it could be avoided in the future.

Faced with these stupendous problems, economic historians have come to recognize the obvious limitations of traditional studies in the field of economic growth and are seeking a broader approach to the problem. They are perfecting the procedures which will permit them to investigate profitably those changes which are conducive to growth. They are analising those factors in society which militate against or contribute towards change. They are attempting to isolate those factors which stimulate the growth process, which force new economic ways on under-developed areas or which result in new economies surpassing the old ones. Some scholars, notably W. W. Rostow, have concluded that the rate of growth and change in a society is determined by certain factors or propensities. These include the propensities of a society to develop fundamental science, to apply science to economic ends, to accept innovations, to seek material advance, to consume, and to have children. Finally, he believes that the strength of the propensities and their course of change are determined by the long-run interrelationship of the economic, social, and political forces of a society.[1]

[1] For a summary statement of the findings of two recent conferences on economic growth viewed in historical perspective see Shepard B. Clough, 'Strategic Factors in Economic Growth: A Social Science View', *Political Science Quarterly* (New York, March 1953), lxx, 19–27. For a critique of Toynbee's thesis and a study, from the point of view of an economic historian, of why shifts

This interest in a broader study of the growth of different societies increases the importance of an analysis of the work which already has been carried on by Japanese economic historians. In the first place, the new hypotheses will need to be tested in different societies and these tests can be made only if reliable, factual studies are available. Because of the large amount of material involved, such comparisons will have to be based on fundamental research already carried on by Japanese scholars. In the second place, our analysis will clarify a basic difference of interest among Western scholars of Japan and other parts of Asia and among a large segment of contemporary Japanese historians. Whereas the former are beginning to analyse the contrasting factors in the modernization of Japan and China, a large group of Japanese historians are devoting their efforts to an interpretation of the modernization of their country in terms of economic determinism.

As for the latter, Tōyama Shigeki, one of the most widely read historians of Japan's modernization, claims that the spontaneous change of Japan from feudalism to absolutism prevented it from becoming a victim of the same fate which China received at the hands of European and American capitalist oppressors. Furthermore, the power of the modernization of the Japanese was, he maintains, superior to the Chinese because the peasant uprisings in Japan were a struggle against feudalism. He then concludes, without the benefit of facts to prove his point, that this type of struggle made the internal development of absolutism inevitable within Japan. Hani Gorō, another influential proponent of this school of thought, maintains that only the materialist school is able to analyse correctly all of the historical facts of the Meiji Restoration of 1868. Despite the existence of overwhelming evidence which shows that the initiative for the Restoration came from the middle-class samurai of the more advanced clans, Hani claims that its basic motive force came from the lower classes, the peasantry and the propertyless townsmen. He concludes that these groups, though politically immature, rapidly developed leadership and the knowledge of modern ideology and would have produced a successful proletarian revolution if the samurai and capitalists had not staged a counter revolution.[2]

and changes in civilizations have taken place, see Shepard B. Clough, *The Rise and Fall of Civilisation* (McGraw-Hill, New York and London, 1951). Other studies which indicate a broader approach are Colin Clark, *Conditions of Economic Progress* (1951); League of Nations, *Industrialisation and Foreign Trade* (Geneva, 1945); and Walter W. Rostow, *The Process of Economic Growth* (New York, 1952).

[2] See Tōyama Shigeki, *Ishin Shi* (Tokyo; Iwanami) pp. 45 et seq. Hani Gorō, 'Meiji Ishin', in *Nihon Shakai no Shiteki Kyūmei*. For recent studies by Western scholars bearing on this subject see William W. Lockwood, *The Economic Development of Japan, Growth and Structural Change 1868–1938* (Princeton: Princeton University Press, 1954); Simon Kuznets et al, editors, *Economic Growth, Brazil, India, Japan* (Durham: Duke University Press, 1955); Rushton Coulborn, editor, *Feudalism in History* (Princeton: Princeton University Press, 1956); Marion J. Levy, 'Contrasting Factors in the Modernization of China and Japan', *Economic Development and Cultural Change*, vol. 2 (October: 1953).

Fortunately, both for Occidental and Japanese scholarship, a group of scholars at Kyōto University, under the leadership of Professor Honjō Eijirō (b. 1888), have largely remained aloof from this controversy, and through their research and study have made valuable contributions to both our general and specific knowledge of Japan's economic history. Hence, this paper will concentrate on the work of this body of scholars. Before doing so, however, it will be necessary to give a brief description of the early growth of the study of economic history in Japan, of the availability of materials, the perfection of techniques, and the importance of other groups, especially the Marxists.

### Economic writings in the Tokugawa period

Prior to the Imperial Restoration of 1868, some attention had been given by Japanese writers to economic problems. This was particularly true of scholars of the Tokugawa period, but they should not be considered as economic historians. For example, such men as Arai Hakuseki (1657–1725) and Kumazawa Banzan (1619–90) were products of their times and were concerned with the improvement and perpetuation of the feudal system. Hakuseki, as the chief adviser to the Shogun Ienobu in 1709, studied the currency problem for practical reasons. He wished to strengthen the power and strength of the Shogunate. In his proposals for recoinage as a means of stopping inflation, he advocated the restoration of the quality of the coins to their value in the early seventeenth century. Banzan, while a harsh critic of the government, was looking for ways to alleviate some of the economic ills of society. In his *Daigaku Wakumon*, written at a time when luxurious living at the Shōgun's court and among the people was condoned, if not encouraged, he admonished the rulers to inaugurate a benevolent government (*jinsei*). It should select competent ministers, store rice to meet the minimum needs of the people, prevent waste in its production, improve the methods of flood control, and release the warriors from attendance at court so that they could return to the land.[3]

While the popular literature of the late seventeenth and early eighteenth century is best known for its realism in depicting the life of the townsmen, one of the 'novelettes of the floating world' (*ukiyo no sōshi*) is of special interest to the economic historian. 'The Vicissitudes of the Farmers' (*Hyakushō Seisuiki*) first appeared in 1713 as one of the books printed at the Kyōto shop known as Hachimonji-ya. Under the proprietorship of

---

[3] For a translation of Hakuseki's proposals see N. Skene Smith, 'An introduction to Some Japanese Economic Writings of the 18th Century', *Transactions of the Asiatic Society of Japan* (second series, 1934), xi, 32–105. A discussion of some of Hakuseki's other writings appears above, pp. 253–9. Banzan's *Daigaku Wakumon* is in Galen M. Fisher, 'Kumazawa Banzan, His Life and Ideas', *Transactions of the Asiatic Society of Japan* (second series, 1938), xvi, 223–58. Selections of writings on economics of these and other Tokugawa Confucian scholars are treated in Honjō Eijirō, *Nihon Keizaishi Shisō Shi* (Tokyo, 1948).

Andō Jishō (1662–1745), this publishing house soon became the most famous of its kind. Ejima Kiseki (1667–1736), who wrote in a semi-humorous, semi-pornographic style, was hired as a ghost writer. Thus it is impossible to determine which of these novelists was the author of 'The Vicissitudes of the Farmers'. The significant point to note, however, is that the author wrote on one of the most pressing subjects of the times, namely, the hardships of the peasants resulting from the abuses of the managers of the fiefs.

Though the characters in the novel are doubtless fictitious, the customs and conditions which it vividly describes were prevalent in the early eighteenth century in many parts of Japan. The action is placed in the province of Harima. It describes the exorbitant taxes exacted from the peasants in the following manner:

> Any who were unable to pay them sold their daughters in Osaka. Everything was recorded for tax purposes, including the fruit trees, as well as the poles used for pulling water buckets out of the well. Not a single tree was to be cut down without permission. All were ordered taxed according to their position for is not a farmer like a wet towel which gives forth more water the more it is squeezed?

When the chief retainer of the feudal baron forced the peasants to buy tickets for an itinerant theatrical performance and brothel, because the fief was to receive a handsome portion of the profits, the farmers revolted. The retainer was forced to flee and the farmers were placated only after they received a written promise that extra taxes would not be imposed on them. When the older brother of the Lord of Harima returned to the fief, he concluded the officials should be exonerated because:

> 'Without doubt the troubles in the fief are the fault of my brother and though he is my only one, bring him here immediately and hold him in custody. Exact not a single grain in taxes over that of ordinary years from the people. Open up my treasury and repay them their due.' Thus was justice established and all were thankful that the time had come when the lord truly was the boat and his ministers the tranquil water.[4]

Later writers, such as Honda Toshiaki (1744–1812) and Satō Nobuhiro (1769–1850), advocated foreign trade but within the framework of the existing economy. Thus, whether written by government officials, philosophers, or novelists, the economic writings of the Tokugawa period may have been critical of some aspect of the feudal regime but were not seeking its overthrow.

*Earliest economic historians*

After the Imperial Restoration of 1868, interest in economic history as

---

[4] 'Hyakushō Seisuiki', in *Ukiyo Sōsho, Yedo Jidai Bunkei Shiryō*, iii, 265 et seq.

a subject worthy of study did not appear for nearly thirty years. In the interim, however, the new government sponsored the collection and publication of documentary materials, individual scholars translated Western works on economics and political economy, and some writers began to deal with the development of Japanese culture on the basis of their knowledge of European affairs. One of the foremost of these was Professor Taguchi Ukichi (1855–1905).[5] In 1877 he began the publication of *Nihon Kaika Shōshi* (A Short History of Japan's Modernization) in which he dealt with Japan's development in the light of his knowledge of the West. He pointed out the necessity of determining the special interests of Japan and then establishing a policy consistent with these needs. Before the final section of his history was completed in 1882, at which time it was published in a single volume, he had translated Leon Levi's *History of British Commerce*. In general, Taguchi supported free trade and the liberal thought of the British classical school.

On the other hand, there were several advocates of protectionism who took issue with Taguchi. One of these scholars was Ōshima Sadamasu, who is important both in his own right and for the translations he made of Malthus in 1876 and of List's *National System of Political Economy* in 1889. In his two best-known works, *Jōsei Ron* (1891) and *Keizai Sanron* (1900), Ōshima argued that national characteristics, law and the economy of countries vary. Consequently, it could not be assumed that *laissez-faire*, which might be good for England, would be equally applicable to Japan or other parts of Asia. This position was argued more strongly by Maeda Masana (1850–1921), an official in the Department of Agriculture and Commerce, in 1892, in a work entitled *Shoken*, in which he claimed Japan was slavishly following foreign ways and forgetting its own unique heritage. He deplored the subordination of industrial development to foreign theories, whether protectionism or *laissez-faire*, and believed that a study of the special requirements of Japan would reveal the necessity to protect some industries and leave others to develop by themselves.

The next period of economic writings, from about the beginning of the twentieth century, was characterized by the first scientific efforts in economic history. The two pioneers in this field were Uchida Ginzō (1872–1919) and Fukuda Tokuzō (1874–1930). Uchida graduated in 1896 from the College of Literature of Tokyo Imperial University and began graduate studies in economic history. Two years later he published an article in the Journal of History (*Shigaku Zasshi*) on the nature and scope of economic history under the title of 'Keizai Shi no Seishitsu to Han'i ni tsuite', in which he clearly differentiated between the history of economics and 'economic history'. About the same time he was appointed lecturer in economic history at Tōkyō Imperial University and in 1902 went to

[5] See introduction, p. 15.

Europe to study. Shortly after his return, he became a professor of economics at Kyōto University, where his special interest in economic history was to be enthusiastically championed by a new generation of scholars. In his writings he emphasized the influence of racial heritage, climate, natural resources, population growth, and foreign relations on Japan's history and probed into the reasons for its development. His *Keizai Shi Sōron* (A General Treatise on Economic History), published in 1912, became the guide-book for all students in this field. Based largely on his lectures at Kyōto, it covers such topics as the nature and sphere of economic history, methods of research, and general economic development. This study was incorporated in his later and more comprehensive *Nihon Keizaishi no Kenkyū* (Study of Japanese Economic History, 1921).

The second of the earliest economic historians, Fukuda Tokuzō, studied in Germany and reflected the influence of Brentano and Beucher and later taught at the Tōkyō University of Commerce. He claimed that the time had arrived for inductive studies and turned his attention to a reexamination of foreign theories and their significance for Japan's development. In his *Die Gesellschaftliche und Wirtschaftliche Entwicklung in Japan*, published in Stuttgart in 1900, he emphasized the dictatorial aspects of the Tokugawa government and was the first to describe it as an absolute police state. He then pointed out many parallel developments in Japan and Europe. In 1907, this study, which had a strong influence on the economic and political thought of later writers, was translated into Japanese and appeared under the title *Nihon Keizai Shi Ron* (Treatise on Japanese Economic History).

### Different groups of economic historians

Simultaneously with this advance in the study of Japanese economic history, new materials were appearing in accessible form for use of students and scholars. The various ministries of the government, such as Finance and Agriculture, sponsored numerous official publications. Important scholars edited numerous writings on the modern period. For example, by 1917 Professor Takimoto Seiichi (1857–1932), Professor of Economics at Keiō University, had edited and published a vast collection of economic writings, largely from the Tokugawa period, in a thirty-six volume collection entitled *Nihon Keizai Sōsho*. In another decade, he was to begin to edit the even more comprehensive *Nihon Keizai Taiten* (Compendium of Japanese Economics).

But the most significant development following World War I was the proliferation of centres of study of economic history. By 1922 a professorship specifically for the economic history of Japan was established at Kyōto University and within a decade a similar post was created at Tōkyō Imperial University.

At the same time, heated controversies arose between certain schools of thought. Simultaneously with the post-World War I growth of socialism, a group of socialist economists emerged who interpreted Japan's economic development in terms of theoretical Marxism. One of the first and most important of these Marxists was Kawakami Hajime (1879–1946). Originally appointed a lecturer in the Economics Department of Kyōto University, he was promoted to the rank of professor in 1915. In 1928, he resigned to enter politics and to establish the Labour Farm party (*Rōnōtō*). In the interim his early writings in the press on social problems had attracted wide attention. His *Keizai Taikō* (Principles of Economics), published in 1928, included a history of the development of capitalism as interpreted by Marx. This work had a wide appeal among the intellectuals. His arrest and the suppression of all radicals in the 1930's did little to wipe out his influence.

One of the direct results of Kawakami's writings, as well as that of the impact of the widespread post-war interest in socialism, was to stimulate, both among Marxists and their opponents, the study of Japanese capitalism and its growth. Naturally, such studies concentrated on developments after Japan was opened to the West and after the process of industrialization had gained momentum. Professor Takahashi Kamekichi (b. 1894) of Waseda University was one of the outstanding economic historians who challenged the Marxist interpretation of Kawakami. In his 'Meiji Taishō Sangyō Hattatsu Shi' (History of Industrial Growth, 1868–1926), published in 1928 as the first part of *Nihon Sangyō Shi* (History of Japanese Industry), and *Nihon Shihonshugi Hattatsu Shi* (History of the Development of Japanese Capitalism), he emphasized the difference between Japanese imperialism and that of the advanced Occidental countries. While the latter had depended on colonial areas for raw materials and markets for their manufactures, Japan looked to its colonies to solve the population problem. He also clearly indicated that Japan's industrial age was in its infancy when the Restoration took place. In his analysis of industrial growth, he was far more interested in setting forth an accurate account of economic events and problems than trying to make them fit into an ideological pattern.

But the group of economists under strong Marxist influence took violent exception to this position. In 1932 they published their view in a collection of special studies (*Kōza*) and hence have come to be known as the Kōza group. The numerous articles in *Nihon Shihonshugi Hattatsu Shi Kōza* (Symposium on the History of the Growth of Japanese Capitalism) fall into four categories: an analysis of the history of the Meiji period, the development of Japanese capitalism, the actual state of Imperialistic Japan, and an extensive bibliography. Their ideas, which were elaborated later by many of the members, reflected the official

Communist view.[6] One of the most significant essays was by Hattori Shisō on what he described as the Revolution and Counter Revolution of Meiji ('Meiji no Kakumei to Han-Kakumei'). He argued that Japan's independence from foreign domination, as compared with China's subordination, was the result of the advanced state of manufacturing in Japan at the end of the Tokugawa period. Thus the inherent pressure from within for foreign markets created a state strong enough to withstand the expansion of Western capitalism.

The controversy was partially quieted by the strong measures taken by the government to suppress the leftists. Furthermore, Takahashi and Professor Tsuchiya Takao of Tōkyō Imperial University continued to show in their writings that the Kōza group oversimplified the analysis of capitalism. At the same time, in the field of political theory, Professor Koizumi Shinzō of Keiō University led the opposition to the Marxist school, rejected their value theory, and wrote on Adam Smith, Malthus, and Ricardo. As noted below, however, the controversy is far from settled and some of the old Kōza members are actively publishing in the post-World War II period.[7]

### The Kyōto group under Honjō Eijirō

While the controversy continued as to how Japan's economic modernization should be interpreted, a well-trained group of economic historians was developing at Kyōto Imperial University which devoted its time and energies to analysing specific problems in the Tokugawa and Meiji periods. Under the leadership of Professor Honjō Eijirō, it became one of the outstanding centres of the study of economic history in Japan. Appointed to teach in the Department of Economics in 1922, he began to give courses in Japanese economic history. By 1926, he offered a seminar on the financial problems of the Tokugawa government and had as his students several persons who later became noted scholars in the field. The next year the lectures and research topics centred around the land system and in 1928 it shifted to the Meiji period. At the same time, Professor

---

[6] The chief editor of the Kōza series was Noro Eitarō. Other important contributors included Hani Gorō, Yamada Mōritarō, and Hirano Yoshitarō. Yamada and Hirano amplified and solidified the thinking of the Kōza group in books published in 1934 in which they analysed Japanese capitalism from a Marxist standpoint. The subsequent debates among the Marxists, including the unorthodox interpretations made by Inomata Tsunao and his followers, caused a split in the ranks. Since the latter group published their views in the Labor and Farmer Journal they came to be known as the Rōnō (Labor-Farmer) group. This complicated, ideological split is referred to as the Kōza-Rōnō controversy.

[7] In the descriptive material on their recently published annotated bibliography on Japanese economics, Remer and Kawai have given a brief survey of this controversy and have listed under a separate heading most of the chief studies by members of the opposing groups. This bibliography is also a most helpful reference for the key works on economic history. Charles F. Remer and Saburo Kawai, *Japanese Economics: A Guide to Japanese Reference and Research Materials* (Ann Arbor: University of Michigan, 1956), especially pp. 13-34. The most extensive bibliographies on Japanese history are those published by Professor Honjō and described below on pp. 300-1.

Kokushō Iwao (1895–1949) was teaching in the Department of Agriculture with special emphasis on agricultural economics. Shortly thereafter, the results of these studies began to appear in print.[8]

In the first place, both Professors Honjō and Kokushō were active in publishing general analytical studies. For example, in 1928, Professor Honjō published under the title of *Nihon Keizai Shi Gaisetsu* (Outline of Japanese Economic History), the lectures on Japanese economic history which he had been giving at the university. In this volume, building and expanding on the work of Uchida Ginzō, he defined the problems of economic history in Japan, the natural conditions of the country, the changes which had taken place in its political and social organizations, and population and agrarian problems. In his *Kinsei Hōken Shakai no Kenkyū* (Studies in Modern Feudal Society), he concentrated on the changes which had occurred in society in the Tokugawa period with a more detailed explanation of the conditions which brought about the collapse of feudalism. At the same time, he assisted in the editing of a valuable collection of Tokugawa writings on social and economic conditions. These appeared in a twelve-volume set entitled *Kinsei Shakai Keizai Sōsho* (Documentary Series on Modern Society and Economics).

Three separate monographs by Professor Kokushō, which appeared in 1928, are indicative of the special interest which he had in agricultural problems and especially in peasant uprisings. The most famous of these, *Hyakushō Ikki no Kenkyū* (Studies in Peasant Uprisings), treats of the causes, forms, conditions of growth, and nature of more than five hundred such outbursts. He concludes, to the disgust of the Marxists, that they were local, unplanned phenomena without revolutionary characteristics and were not directed at changing the basic political and social structure of the feudal regime.[9]

But an analysis of two separate volumes of monographic studies, both edited by Honjō and containing contributions by himself and his colleagues, will give a clear picture of the research undertaken by the Kyōto group. In the first of these, *Nihon Kōtsū Shi no Kenkyū* (Studies in the History of Japanese Communications), seven authors have investigated many crucial problems connected with transportation and communications after

[8] The most outstanding students of these seminars were Horie Yasuzō (b. 1904), currently Chairman, Department of Economics, Kyōto University; Egashira Tsuneharu (b. 1900), Chairman, Department of Economics, Shiga University; Kuroha Hyōjirō, Professor of Economics, Naniwa University; Ōyama Shikitarō (b. 1902), Professor of Economics, Ritsumeikan University. For an authoritative history of Kyōto University's Economic History Research Institute, see Honjō Eijirō, *Nihon Keizai Shi Kenkyūjo Shi* (1953).

[9] The other studies by Kokushō published in 1928 were *Hōken Shakai no Tōsei to Tōsō* (Unity and Strife in Feudal Society) and *Hyakushō Ikki Shidan* (Historical Talks on Peasant Uprisings). Another specialist on peasant uprisings was Ono Takeo. For an extensive bibliography on this subject see Hugh Borton, *Peasant Uprisings in the Tokugawa Period, Transactions of the Asiatic Society of Japan* (second series, vol. 16, 1938).

1600. These investigations, based largely on new material, including local, primary sources, clarify many aspects of Japan's historical development since that time. Five of the studies centre around the problems created by the special corvée (*sukegō*) levied on villages along the highways to supply horses and men for the use of official messengers or missions. The remaining chapters are careful, detailed accounts of the post-stations and barriers, the ford across the Ōigawa River, and shipping.

In his introductory survey of travel along the five chief highways, Honjō, by the use of sources on local regulations and institutions, clarifies the different institutions and customs in the villages in the eastern and western sections of the country. He also gives detailed information on items such as transportation and lodging fees along the highways.[10]

The chapter in the monograph by Professor Ōyama Shikitarō (b. 1902), on 'The *Sukegō* and Village Life' is particularly valuable. It shows that while some groups in society profited from the extensive travel along the highways, the villagers who were required to render *sukegō* services suffered severely. The system had originated from a need for the Tokugawa government to obtain support for the relay stations necessary for the transmission of official messages. As the responsibilities of the new centralized dictatorship expanded, however, the communication needs became heavier and the corvée more severe. By 1694 the extent of assistance required in men and horses for *sukegō* was settled at two horses and two men for each 100 *koku* of rice income of the village. During the next century and a half, official traffic along the highways increased, and with it greater levies were extracted from the villagers. The peasants were expected to be available for these services during three months of the spring and three months of the fall. In addition, they were subject to the regular tax in rice of half of the crop. Hence to meet their taxes many farmers sold their children or wives as slaves in the city.

One of the interesting sources used by Ōyama in his study is that entitled *Minkan Seiyō*, written in the early eighteenth century by Tanaka Kyūgu. Tanaka had been assigned by the Bakufu to prevent water damage along some of the rivers such as the Arakawa. Appalled by the poverty and misfortune of the peasants which he saw about him, he recorded his observations of the people, of the operation of government at the local level, and of the questionable activities of the officials. He also included in his writings some suggestions concerning the control of waterways and the improvement of the transportation system. His book made such an impression on other officials that it was finally presented to the Shōgun. Yoshimune, who was eager for any suggestions on how to improve rice production and the economic conditions of the country, rewarded Tanaka

---

[10] Honjō Eijirō, ed., *Nihon Kōtsū Shi no Kenkyū*, Kyōto Keizai Shi Kenkyū Kai Kiyō (Tokyo: Kaizo Sha, 1929), i, 5 et seq.

with a stipend sufficient to supply thirty men and appointed him as supervisor of two domains.[11]

But like the other Tokugawa writers on economic and social problems, Tanaka sought to improve the system of centralized feudalism, not to abolish it or change it radically. While the Bakufu knew of the difficulties which faced the villages responsible for *sukegō* services, it apparently did little to help them. In fact, the Shōgun's basic policy of compulsory alternate attendance of the feudal barons at the Shōgun's court at Edo (*sankin-kōtai*) had created conflicting economic conditions. This system had stimulated land transportation, the circulation of money throughout the various domains, and the general development of the national economy. This increased use of the highways had contributed especially to the prosperity of such groups as the innkeepers, the public porters and livery men. At the same time, the Bakufu found that the travel requirements of its own officials had increased, which meant that the villages must supply greater *sukegō* services. Thus the peasants from the villages responsible for the corvée were penalized still further. In extreme cases, they revolted in protest.

Professor Kokushō has written a chapter in this monograph on the peasant disputes which arose from these extra demands made on the *sukegō* villages. The most noteworthy examples of such uprisings were those of 1764–5. The farmers first declined to meet the requirements for an official Korean embassy. Then they refused to supply the manpower and horses for the Bakufu's envoys going to Ieyasu's mausoleum at Nikkō. They revolted and forced the authorities to promise that no extra taxes would be imposed in the future. From the manuscript material for one district in Shinano, covering the period from 1749–1843, Professor Kokushō found thirteen cases in which the farmers raised objections to the corvée by legal means, namely, by an appeal to the authorities. He concludes that, while comparatively few of these incidents turned into revolts or uprisings, the complaints increased notably after the middle of the Tokugawa period and were most frequent along the Eastern Seaboard and Central Mountain Highways (Tōkaidō and Nakasendō). He also notes that they were not revolutionary in character in the sense that they were limited to villages along these highways, involved comparatively few persons, and were directed against a single abuse.

Finally, the study of Kuroha Hyōjirō (b. 1904), on the policy of the Meiji government towards *sukegō*, reflects the confusion which faced the young imperial reformers. According to profuse quotations from contemporary manuscripts, there was extensive distress after 1859 in the villages responsible for *sukegō*, particularly along the Eastern Seaboard Highway. After the Restoration, the new government issued regulations

[11] Honjō, *Nihon Kōtsū Shi*, pp. 27–192.

designed to relieve the peasants from this service but much confusion resulted. Even the creation of a Land Transportation Office did not settle the problem and the system continued until 1871.[12]

Similarly, the new government suffered from the extension of an old policy, adopted for strategic reasons, which prohibited the construction of bridges or even the use of boats across the Ōigawa. From the detailed material which Hiramatsu Hiroi has collected on the fording of this river, it is clear that the policy was designed for a static society. Furthermore, since every person and every object was carried across this river either by man or beast, and since this ford was on the most important highway in Japan, one sees in graphic relief the primitive character of land transportation. When it is realized that boats were not used regularly until 1871 to cross the Ōigawa, one wonders how the new Imperial government was able to unify the country so readily after 1868.

The second collection of reports resulting from the work of the seminars in economic history at Kyōto University appeared in 1930 as *Meiji Ishin Keizai Shi Kenkyū* (Studies in the Economic History of the Meiji Restoration).[13] As in the case of the previous volume, it was edited by Honjō, but the topics covered are of a much wider range. The three sections written by him deal with the new policy of the Bakufu in its closing years, the 'forced loans' (*goyōkin*) of the Meiji government, and reactionary thought of that period. Kanno Watarō (b. 1895) has four articles on different economic institutions such as the commercial companies (*shōsha*), transportation companies (*tsūshō kaisha*), exchange houses (*kawase kaisha*), and national banks (*kokuritsu ginkō*). Kikkawa Hidezō (b. 1898) has written on the new government's policy of sponsoring work for the gentry, whose annual rice stipends were commuted into government bonds. Horie Yasuzō has a chapter on early financial problems. Finally, Kokushō has made four contributions, three of them on subjects relating to agricultural problems. In the first, he outlines the farm policy of Matsukata Masayoshi (1835–1924) and in the last two he surveys the peasant uprisings at the time of the Restoration which arose from various economic, social, and religious causes. He maintains, as he did in his other studies of uprisings in the earlier periods, that they were not a social revolutionary movement. The farmers were fighting neither for the Tokugawa government nor for the Imperial cause but for the elimination of specific abuses. Kokushō notes that there were nearly two hundred of these revolts during the decade from 1868 to 1878. Most of them were the result of such factors as the general disorder of the times, the ignorance and obstinacy of the farmers, the

---

[12] Kokushō Iwao, 'Sukegō ni Motozuku Nōmin no Funsō', Honjō, *Kōtsū Shi*, pp. 225–49; and Kuroha Hyōjirō, 'Meiji Seifu no Sukegō Seisaku', ibid., pp. 251–78.

[13] Honjō Eijirō, ed., *Meiji Ishin Keizai Shi Kenkyū*, Kyōto Keizai Shi Kenkyū Kai Kiyō, vol. 2 (Tokyo: Kaizo Sha, 1930). The volume also contains a useful chronology of economic history and a bibliography.

weakness of the new government, and the rise in commodity prices. Others were precipitated by the issuance of new decrees which abolished the classes, which permitted the eating of beef, or which inaugurated universal conscription. The uprisings caused by religious motives arose from the compulsory separation of Buddhism and Shintoism and the legalization of the propagation of Christianity.

*Journal of Economic History and research aids*

Simultaneously with their research on specific problems of the Tokugawa and Meiji periods, in July 1929, the Kyōto group of economic historians, under the leadership of Honjō and Kokushō, organized their own Society for the Study of Economic History (Keizai Shi Kenkyū Kai) and four months later published the first issue of the society's organ, *Keizai Shi Kenkyū* (Journal of Economic History). As outlined in the first volume, the purpose of the journal was to have at least one learned periodical specializing on economic history, and to publish historical documents, special studies, chronologies and bibliographical material. It was also hoped that it would serve as a co-ordinating medium between local historians working on local problems and persons working on national problems. Many of the writings of this group were first published in *Keizai Shi Kenkyū* and were collected later in book form. This monthly periodical continued to appear regularly until May 1944, when several issues were combined prior to the final issue of January 1945.[14]

Professor Honjō also had been active in compiling bibliographical information on Japanese economic history. His first bibliography was published in 1924 as *Nihon Keizai Shi Bunken* and a supplement was issued three years later. These two volumes were combined, new material was added, and a revised and enlarged edition of an annotated list of the chief works on Japanese economic history published before 1931 appeared two years later as *Kaihan Nihon Keizai Shi Bunken*. Divided into three sections of general works, source materials and monographs, with appendices on local histories and works in European languages, it has become the standard work in the field. Although subsequent special issues of *Keizai Shi Kenkyū* have kept the bibliography up to date, it was not until 1942 that the second volume of the bibliography appeared in book form. Under the title of *Nihon Keizai Shi Shin Bunken*, it contained works published from 1932 through 1940. The latest volume in this series, covering the period from 1940 through 1950, appeared three years later as *Nihon Keizai Shi*

---

[14] The May 1944 issue contained the May and June issues; the July and August issues were combined with January 1945 and published as the 1943 issue of *Keizai Shi Nenkan* (Yearbook of Economic History): *Nihon Keizai Shi Kenkyū Jo Shi*, pp. 7–9.

*Dai San Bunken.* Thus, these three volumes are indispensable references for the economic historian of Japan.[15]

*Institute for Research in Japanese Economic History*

After several unsuccessful attempts in 1931 to combine the Economic History Society and the Social History Society, Professor Kokushō visited the various centres of economic history in Europe in anticipation of establishing a similar institute in Kyōto. Upon his return, he contributed the funds for the grounds and building for the Institute for Research in Economic History of Japan (Nihon Keizai Shi Kenyū Jo) which was formally opened in May 1933. Its purposes were (1) research by individual members, (2) co-operative research, (3) publication of books and periodicals, (4) the collection of books and materials, and (5) holding special lectures, exhibits, and meetings. As will be noted below, the appearance of sixteen volumes in the special series published under the Institute's auspices is clear proof that the first three objectives were achieved. Fortunately the Institute was able to secure the library of Professor Takimoto Seiichi, which formed the nucleus for its collection. Finally, the lectures and exhibits continued for the first two years of the Institute's existence. After 1935, with Professor Kokushō and others no longer able to continue to support it as in the past, much of the work was curtailed. The research of those who had been connected with it has continued and has been appearing in the form of significant monographs.[16]

As early as 1929, Professors Honjō, Kokushō, and Kanno and others had concluded that the few economic dictionaries which already existed were not adequate to meet the reference needs of the economic historian. Hence they devised a plan with eight other scholars to examine the general and local histories, economic writings and dictionaries on social, economic, and historical subjects for topics to be included in an encyclopaedia. About 10,000 items were chosen but circumstances forced the suspension of the work.

With the formation of the Institute for Research in Economic History of Japan, the encyclopaedia project was taken over as an Institute project.

[15] As Professor Honjō acknowledged in the preface to the first volume, he was assisted in this compilation by other members of his group such as Yugi, Ueda, Horie, Ōyama, and Matsuo. Full bibliographical information on these volumes follows: (1) Honjō Eijirō, compiler, (*Kaihan*) *Nihon Keizai Shi Bunken* (Tokyo: Nihon Hyōron Sha, 1933), 908 pp.; (2) Honjō Eijirō, *Nihon Keizai Shi Shin Bunken* (Tokyo: Nihon Hyōron Sha, 1942), 722 pp.; (3) Honjō Eijirō, Kikkawa Hidezō, and Matsuyoshi Sadao, compilers, *Nihon Keizai Shi Dai San Bunken* (Tokyo: Nihon Hyōron Sha, 1953), 612 pp.

[16] The Directors of the Institute were Honjō Eijirō, Kyōto University Department oι Economics; Kokushō Iwao, Kyōto University Department of Agriculture; Nakamura Naokatsu, Kyōto University Department of Literature; and Kanno Watarō, Ōsaka University Department of Commerce. *Nihon Keizai Shi Kenkyū Jo Shi*, pp. 11–62.

The four directors of the Institute (Honjō, Kokushō, Kanno, and Naka-mura) acted as supervisors over the dozen scholars assigned to write the encyclopaedia articles. The 10,000 titles, which were originally selected, were reviewed and new topics were added. By the latter half of 1935, the compilation had progressed sufficiently to warrant holding regular meetings with the compilers. At these sessions, which were held weekly after October, the manuscripts were revised, new topics were added and charts and illustrations were chosen. The first of ten sections was printed in 1936 and the final section was completed in 1939. In 1940 these were bound into permanent book form in three volumes and published as *Nihon Keizai Shi Jiten*. The first two volumes contained the subject matter, the last volume the indexes.

The explanatory texts for the entries are written in a clear style and contain both the historical significance of the subject and an explanation of the derivation of the terms. Thus, in explaining a term such as *men* (rice tax), the literal meaning of 'to exempt, pardon or relieve from office' is noted. At the same time, an explanation is given as to how the word came to be used for the tax a person paid in order to be exempt from further obligation. Hence the term came to be synonymous with 'taxes'. Both regional and universal terminology were included in the dictionary. Consequently one finds under *nanushi* the definition of 'a village chief' and the term *shōya* given as an equivalent for western Japan. Finally, appropriate illustrations, book titles, and chronological and other charts are included. All important entries are signed by the contributor. In view of the fact that the items are listed alphabetically on the basis of their reading (a, i, u, e . . . order), the last volume is exclusively an index.

Another lasting contribution of the Institute for Research in Economic History of Japan was the seventeen volumes published over a period of ten years as part of the Research Series (*Kenkyū Sōsho*) by nine different authors. For the most part they are monographs devoted either to a specific subject such as the system of monopoly sales among the feudal fiefs, the new policy of the Bakufu, and the efforts to find work for the new gentry, or to a single province, feudal principality or city.[17]

One of the most important monographs on special subjects is that by Professor Horie on the monopoly sales system. Entitled *Waga Kuni Kinsei no Sembai Seido* (The Monopoly Sales System in Modern Japan), it is the first volume in the series and sets a high standard of scholarship. Based on general as well as local source materials, the first part of the volume analyses the main features of the problem. The author believes that this

[17] Three of these volumes are economic histories of Western countries (United States, France, and Germany). Two of them, Honjō Eijirō, *Keizai Shi Gairon* (Outline of Japanese Economic History), and Horie Yasuzō, *Kinsei Nihon no Keizai Seisaku* (Economic Policies of Modern Japan) are general studies. For a list of authors and titles, see *Nihon Keizai Shi Kenkyū Jo Shi*, p. 40.

system of monopolistic sales in the various fiefs, which developed to assist their shaky finances, is the most important aspect of their modern development. This feudalistic form of controlled economy was one of the chief factors which transformed the semi-independent economies of the various feudal domains into a national economy.[18] For example, in order to obtain the goods to sell as a clan monopoly, the clan government first developed their own commercial agencies and then actively sponsored production of that product. Outlets for the sales were controlled within the fiefs and 'exports' to Osaka and other areas were encouraged. In Yamaguchi, salt balls were 'exported' under fief auspices as early as 1780, Kōriyama in Mino shipped out silk after 1860 and Kagoshima was a source of sugar.

This study then proceeds to show how these elaborate activities required the circulation of the currency of the fiefs throughout important commercial centres such as Osaka, the formation of special offices for these monopolistic sales (*kaisho*) and for the encouragement of the production of local products (*kokusan kaisho*). Special clan warehouses and commercial offices were formed in Osaka and other important centres. From the opinions of contemporary writers quoted in this study, there was general approval of the system. A dissenter such as Hayashi Shihei of Sendai, however, memorialized his feudal baron in 1781 pointing out that profits from such transactions only benefited the *daimyō* sponsoring it.[19]

The second part of Horie's work, which resulted from his having visited various local areas to ferret out pertinent source material, is devoted to special studies such as the way monopolies operated in Tottori, Uwajima, and Yamaguchi, or ginseng sales and iron manufacturing in Matsue. As for the ginseng, it was particularly significant because it was exported to China through Nagasaki. In 1873 the 'industry' was sold to the Meiji government. Thus in this important volume, the author has increased our knowledge of the operation of both the local and national economy during the past two centuries. He has also outlined clan-sponsored sales, distribution, and production methods which were easily and naturally transferred after the Meiji Restoration to the national scene by the clan oligarchs who had become familiar with them in their old domains.

Another study, which underlines the tendency in Japan's economic institutions towards centralized, monopolistic controls, is that by Miyamoto Mataji (b. 1907) on the trade associations or corporations (*kabu nakama*).[20]

[18] See Horie Yasuzō, *Waga Kuni Kinsei no Sembai Seido*, Nihon Keizai Shi Kenkyū Jo Kenkyū Sōsho (Tokyo: Hyōronsha, 1933), i, 3 et seq. Professor Horie Yasuzō is, in many ways, the successor to Professor Honjō. He is currently Chairman of the Department of Economics at Kyōto University, where he has been a professor since 1945.     [19] Ibid., p. 126.
[20] Miyamoto became one of Honjō's graduate students in 1931. He was appointed an assistant shortly thereafter and specialized in commercial history. He is concurrently professor at Kyūshū University and Ōsaka University. He recognized the importance of the subject when he saw the materials being used in the compilation of the *Ōsaka Shi Shi* (History of the City of Ōsaka). His

After a description of their predecessors and the manner in which they were formed, Miyamoto takes up their organization and method of operation. Formed to protect the interests of members in the same business, they were clearly monopolistic in character. Their membership was restricted, they prohibited external or internal competition and controlled the market. They protected the members' interests because of their special strength. His study concludes with sections on the efforts of the Bakufu to abolish them, the economic confusion which ensued and their final dissolution in 1871–2 when the Meiji government permitted warriors and even farmers to participate in trade.

These rather cursory and inadequate accounts of some of the volumes in the Institute's special Research Series will give an idea of its contribution to our knowledge of Japan's recent economic history. As for most of the other volumes in the series, they are either of a general nature or concentrate on a single locality. In the latter category are the monographs on the economy of the Matsue fief, the tax-free domains of the famous Buddhist stronghold of Kōya San, modern Osaka, and the merchants of Ōmi.[21] Another volume, a symposium edited by Honjō, typifies the interest of the Kyōto group in local problems and in specific subjects. Thus its contents range from the Japanese-British coal mine operation on Takashima Island to the rice taxes and levies at the end of the Tokugawa period.[22]

---

work relies heavily on this history as well as that of Nagasaki. His volume is *Kabu Nakama no Kenkyū* (Studies of the Trade Corporations), Kenkyū Sōsho, vol. 9 (Tokyo: Yuhi Kaku, 1938).

Another special study in the series which should be mentioned is Kikkawa Hidezō, *Shizoku Jusan no Kenkyū* (Studies on Encouragement of Employment for the Gentry), Kenkyū Sōsho, vol. 3 (Tokyo: Yuhi Kaku, 1935). Professor Kikkawa (b. 1898), now Chairman of the Department of Commerce, Dōshisha University, has analysed this problem which was of such social importance from 1868 to 1890. He describes the various methods, such as special loans, reclamation projects and support from the banks, used to help the former warrior class.

[21] For authors and titles of these works see *Nihon Keizai Shi Kenkyū Jo Shi*, pp. 40–41.

[22] Egashira Tsuneharu (b. 1900), one of the group of early graduates of Kyōto University in economic history and now Chairman of the Department of Economics at Shiga University, prepared the sections on the Takashima Coal Mine and on the industrialization of the Saga and Kōchi fiefs. Miyamoto, Horie, Ōyama, and Kanno, familiar members of the Kyōto group, were also contributors. See Honjō Eijirō, *Bakumatsu Keizai Shi Kenkyū*, Kenkyū Sōsho, vol. 6 (Tokyo: Yuhi Kaku, 1935). For material in English based on these studies, see Thomas C. Smith, 'The Introduction of Western Industry to Japan during the Last Years of the Tokugawa Period', *Harvard Journal of Asiatic Studies* (1948), xi, 130–52, and Hugh Borton, *Japan's Modern Century* (New York: Ronald Press, 1955), pp. 22–66.

Some mention must be made of Honjō's two volumes in English. His *Social and Economic History of Japan* (Kyoto: Institute for Research in Japanese Economic History, 1935), and his *Economic Theory and History of Japan in the Tokugawa Period* (Tokyo: Maruzen Co., 1943) are translations of articles which appeared in the *Keizai Shi Kenkyū* or as chapters in his various general studies such as *Nihon Keizai Shisō Shi*, *Nihon Keizai Gaisetsu* or *Bakumatsu no Shin Seisaku*. Since there is much overlapping of subject matter in the original material in Japanese, a common feature of modern Japanese scholarship, the reader may find the lack of organization and contents in the volumes in English somewhat confusing. They are, however, the most recent general studies available on the subject.

*The dissolution of the Institute and post-war studies*

Even before no more than six volumes of the Research Series had been published, the very existence of the Institute was threatened because of lack of funds. The Directors vainly sought help from new groups. As noted above, as early as 1936 its activities were restricted. It continued, however, to publish the monthly journal *Keizai Shi Kenkyū* and the annual bibliographical list known as *Keizai Nenkan* (Yearbook on Japanese Economics). In 1942, when Professor Honjō became president of Osaka University of Commerce and moved to Sakai, the management of the Institute was left to Professor Horie. With the scarcity of newsprint during the latter part of the war, publication of even the journal and yearbook ceased in early 1945. With key members of the Institute scattered and the requisition of the building by the Allied Occupation authorities after Japan's surrender, it ceased to exist. Professor Kokushō died suddenly in Okayama in 1949. The library, which it had hoped would be kept intact, was divided, although the main portion of it went to Osaka University of Economics where Kokushō had been President. But the training and experience, which the early directors and research staff of the Institute had received, continued to pay generous dividends. In 1954 six of the familiar figures under the leadership of Honjō, collaborated to compile the *Keizai Shi Nenkan* or bibliography on economic history for the period 1951 to 1953. All of them, except Professor Honjō who had been editing the *Ōsaka Shi Shi* (History of the City of Osaka), were holding teaching posts in important universities.[23]

On the other hand, the post-war obsession of many historians, not necessarily just economic historians, with interpreting Japanese history by Marxist terminology has made them seek verification for their doctrine rather than seek out the facts and let them speak for themselves. The preoccupation of many of the most productive members of the Rekishi Gaku Kenkyū Kai (Society for the Study of Historical Scholarship) with this problem, as well as with reviving the old Rōnō-Kōza controversy, has not added to their objective scholarship. On the other hand, their writings seem confused and dogmatic and do not compare favourably with the objective, thorough work of the Kyōto school.

By comparison, the work of the Kyōto group gains in stature. Their investigations will prove to be invaluable to scholars, Japanese or foreign, who may wish to use their material in connection with a broad approach to the whole question of Japan's economic growth. For Professor Kokushō to be condemned by the Marxist-inclined members of the Rekishi Gaku Kenkyū Kai as a leader of the unenlightened 'akademizum' group because

[23] Kikkawa is at Dōshisha, Egashira at Shiga University, Horie at Kyōto University, Kuroha at Naniwa, and Miyamoto at Osaka.

of his position on the peasant uprisings, does not prove his conclusions to be false.[24] Rather, it is a challenge to objective scholars everywhere to present the facts of Japanese history and of the history of the peoples of Asia as they are, not as they appear to be, to seek the truth, not isolated events to be used to verify some political and economic philosophy.

[24] See Tōyama Shigeki, 'Meiji Ishin Kenkyū no Seika', in the work which he edited entitled *Nihon Shi Kenkyū Nyūmon* (Tokyo: Daigaku Shuppan Kai, 1951), pp. 201 et seq. For a review article on the writings of several influential members of the *Rekishi Gaku Kenkyū Kai* and comments thereon see: John W. Hall, 'Review of Rekishi Gaku Kenkyūkai, *Nihon Shakei no Shiteki Kyūmei*', *Far Eastern Quarterly* (November, 1951), pp. 97 et seq., and George B. Sansom, 'Notes on John W. Hall's Review . . .', *Far Eastern Quarterly* (August, 1952), pp. 506–7.

C. R. BOXER

*Camoens Professor of Portuguese,University of London*

For most of the period covered by this paper, Western historical writing on
the Far East can conveniently be divided into two kinds: that produced
by the Jesuits, and that produced by anybody else. The reasons for this
are fairly obvious. As regards China, with few and fleeting exceptions, the
Jesuit missionaries (and mandarins) were the only Europeans who could
move with any degree of freedom throughout the Middle Flowery Kingdom. They studied the language, and they were in close touch with
Chinese books and scholars, particularly those connected with the Court
of Peking. They alone had access to the fountain-head of Chinese scholarship, and they could (as a rule) count on the help of qualified Chinese
collaborators and interpreters. As regards Japan, the Jesuits were only
able to function freely in that country between 1550 and 1614, during
which time they had facilities for studying Japanese books comparable to
those which they enjoyed in China—although the turmoil of the *sengoku-
jidai* was hardly conducive to historical research before Hideyoshi's unification of the island-empire in 1590. During the two centuries of the *sakoku-
jidai*, the Dutch traders cooped up in Deshima had little incentive to study
Japanese history or culture, although Kaempfer, Titsingh, and Von
Siebold showed what could be done by those who had a mind to try.

As a broad generalization, it can be said that the European merchants
who traded to the East had neither the incentives nor the opportunities to
study the Asian races with whom they came into contact, compared with
the advantages which the average missionary enjoyed in this respect. The
trader went out East to make money as quickly as possible, and he then
returned home; or perhaps he settled down at Macao, Batavia, or Calcutta, when he had achieved (or failed to achieve) that object. The missionary went out East to save souls, prepared to live for the rest of his life
in his chosen mission-field. He had perforce to learn the language, and he
was not, like the trader, confined to the coastal towns. The missionary
could meet all sorts and conditions of men in the interior, whereas the
merchant's contacts were usually limited to his 'opposite numbers' and to
the officials, coolies, and whores of the ports which he frequented. Finally,
the missionary was often, although by no means invariably, a better
educated and more cultured man than the merchant, who was inclined to

seek relief from the tedium of the counting-house in wine, women, and song.

The Italian Jesuit, Valignano, wrote of the position of the Portuguese in Macao at the end of the sixteenth century: 'The Chinese never have friendship with foreigners; so that although the Portuguese have dealt with them for many years, yet there is no single recorded instance of mutual friendship and correspondence between them, as there is between the Portuguese and the other peoples with whom they have contacts.'[1] Writing of the position of the Portuguese in Japan about the same time, Valignano noted that they seldom went further inland than the Kyūshū ports, 'and because of the great difference in language, manners and customs, the Japanese think very little of them, and they still less of the Japanese'.[2] The same remarks apply, *mutatis mutandis*, to the other European traders in the East. When Isaac Titsingh suggested in 1781 that the Dutch factors at Nagasaki should be encouraged to study Japanese culture, the governing-council at Batavia wrote with disarming complacency: 'this is easier said than done, since it is a general rule in these parts to sacrifice to Mercury but never to Pallas'.[3] Readers of William Hickey's inimitable *Memoirs* will readily recall how little attraction Oriental studies had for the jolly topers of John Company. There were exceptions of course (the Asiatic Society of Bengal was founded in Hickey's day), but broadly speaking, when we want historical information about the peoples of the Far East in the sixteenth to eighteenth centuries, it is to the missionaries, and above all to the Jesuits, that we must turn. Tachard and Gervaise in Siam; De Rhodes in Tongking; Rada, Chirino, and Delgado in the Philippines; Martini, Gaubil and De Mailla in China; Frois and Rodriguez in Japan. For that matter, it is primarily to the Calvinist ministers, Baldaeus and Valentyn, that we have to turn in Dutch historical writing for similar information about Ceylon, Malabar, and Indonesia. It may be added that one Western prejudice which was shared by missionary and merchant alike was their conviction that Christianity was the only true revealed religion and that all other forms of worship were derived from the Devil.

Having stated this much by way of introduction and explanation, I must begin this paper with an exception to the general rule. The first European historian to collect Chinese books, and to acquire an educated Chinese slave for the sole purpose of translating them, was neither a missionary nor a trader, but the Portuguese crown official and chronicler, João de Barros (1496–1570). Barros had several outstanding merits as a historian. He strongly criticized the practice of minimizing the casualties of one's own

[1] P. M. D'Elia, S.J., *Fonti Ricciane. Documenti originali concernenti Matteo Ricci e la storia delle prime relazioni tra l'Europa e la Cina, 1579–1615* (Rome, 1942), i, 202 n.

[2] C. R. Boxer, *The Christian Century in Japan, 1549–1650* (California University Press, 1951), p. 189.　　　[3] C. R. Boxer, *Jan Compagnie in Japan, 1600–1850* (The Hague, 1950), p. 141.

side and absurdly exaggerating those of the enemy. Alluding to the common Chinese accusation (repeated in the *Ming-shih*) that the Portuguese kidnapped Cantonese children in order to roast and eat them, he remarks that this belief is not surprising since the Portuguese were only newcomers to China, and they themselves believed equally silly stories about strange peoples in distant lands. His approach to China was frankly one of admiration, and he rated the achievements of the Chinese as high (or higher) than those of the Greeks and Romans—praise indeed from a Renaissance Humanist, such as the Portuguese chronicler was.[4]

Although the bulk of the information which João de Barros gathered from his Chinese slave, Chinese books, and from Portuguese who had visited Canton, was embodied in his unpublished *Geography* which disappeared after his death, certain facts about Chinese history which struck him and his contemporaries can be gathered from their published works. These were (i) the construction and maintenance of the Great Wall, (ii) the stability and efficiency of the Chinese governmental system, (iii) Chinese priority in the invention of printing and gunpowder, and (iv) the Chinese maritime expeditions to the Indian Ocean during the late Yuan and early Ming period. The identity of Ming China with Marco Polo's Cathay was not recognized, perhaps because *Il Milione* made no mention of such outstanding Chinese products as the Great Wall, printing, and tea. The sixteenth-century Portuguese chroniclers were not widely read in the rest of Europe; but even if their eulogies of the Chinese empire made no great impression, they did something to prepare the ground for the ready acceptance of the Jesuits' pro-Chinese propaganda in the next two centuries.

The sum of knowledge available to educated Europeans about China's past was thus distinctly limited until the publication of Gonzalez de Mendoza's *Historia de las cosas mas notables, ritos y costumbres del Gran Reyno de la China* (Rome, 1585). This famous work ran through thirty editions in the principal European languages before the end of the sixteenth century, and its contents were a revelation to the learned world of Europe. The historical portions of this book (and much of the rest) was derived from a 'Relación' by Fr. Martin de Rada, O.E.S.A., who had visited Fukien in 1575, and brought back to Manila a large collection of Chinese books, including many historical works. With the aid of local *Sangley* interpreters, Rada made a remarkably accurate digest of Chinese dynastic history, although he inadvertently omitted the Shang and Chou dynasties from his otherwise complete lists. Rada had a strong scientific bent, and apart from being the first European to give an outline of Chinese history

---

[4] For further details on João de Barros as a pioneer Orientalist and embryo sinologue, cf. C. R. Boxer, 'Three historians of Portuguese Asia', *Boletim do Instituto Português de Hongkong* (Macao, 1948), i, 18–25.

exclusively from Chinese sources, he was the first to identify China with Cathay.[5]

Despite the popularity of Gonzales de Mendoza's book, most of the European works which were published about the Far East during the last quarter of the sixteenth century and the first decade of the seventeenth were primarily concerned with Japan, where the Jesuit missionaries were obtaining far more spectacular success than in China. This state of affairs was not at first altered by the prohibition and persecution of Christianity enforced by the Tokugawa Shōgunate from 1614 onwards. The numerous martyrdoms gave rise to an equally numerous pamphlet-literature about them, which only began to taper off when Japan was effectively closed to the R.C. missionaries in the sixteen-forties. All of these works more properly belong to Mission-history than to the history of the Far East itself, and the same can be said of Trigault's *De Christiana Expeditione apud Sinas* (Augsburg, 1615). This book, which was based upon the famous Jesuit Matteo Ricci's papers, achieved a comparable popularity[6] to Gonzalez de Mendoza's *Historia*, but it does not add anything to the historical section of the older work. The honour of taking the first great step forward in the study of Chinese history since Fr. Martín de Rada's pioneer effort in 1575, belongs not to Ricci, but to another Italian Jesuit, Padre Martino Martini (1615–61).

Martini was the author of a little *History* of the conquest of China by the Manchu Tartars which achieved an astonishing popularity, and must have been one of the most widely-read books in contemporary Europe.[7] He also compiled an *Atlas of the Chinese Empire*, based on the *Kuang-yü-t'u* and other Chinese sources, which at once became and for long remained a standard work. Of more lasting importance, however, was his *Sinicae Historiae Decas Prima*, first published at Munich in 1658, which amplified the work that Rada had begun. This book, based exclusively on Chinese chronicles, gave a much more detailed account of Chinese dynastic history from P'an-ku down to the Western Han.[8] Martini accepted the authenticity of the official Chinese chronology (a point which both Rada and Ricci had evaded), and stated that Chinese authentic history went back to 2952 B.C., or some six hundred years before the Flood according to the Vulgate version of the Bible. He did not state outright that this proved the authenticity of the Septuagint version of the Scriptures, but he clearly implied that either this was the correct chronology, or else that the Flood had not

---

[5] *South China in the sixteenth century, 1550–1575* (Hakluyt Society, vol. cvi, 1953), 260–310, where Rada's 'Relacion' of 1575 is translated in full.

[6] Eleven editions in various languages during the decade 1615–25.

[7] Streit, *Bibliotheca Missionum* (1929), v, 796–7, lists 21 editions in 20 years, but has omitted an illustrated edition (Utrecht, 1655).

[8] A second Latin edition was published at Amsterdam in 1659, and a French translation at Paris in 1692.

extended as far as East Asia. In either case, the authenticity of Holy Writ was thereby impugned, since the Vulgate Version had been accepted as orthodox Catholic doctrine by the Council of Trent, and most Protestant divines were in agreement with Catholic chronology on this point.

Martini's exposition of early Chinese history met with a mixed reception in Europe. Some scholars, such as Isaac Vossius, accepted his viewpoint as supporting their own arguments in favour of the Septuagint, while others, such as George Horn, warmly attacked his theory as undermining the infallibility of the Christian Bible. The Papacy compromised by allowing the Jesuit missionaries to follow the Septuagint chronology in China, despite the ruling of the Council of Trent in favour of the Vulgate.[9] As a result of Martini's work, however, it became increasingly evident to many European scholars that China had a civilization far older than that of Greece and Rome, and perhaps even older than that of Egypt and Babylon, thus making Eastern Asia rather than the biblical lands of the Middle East the cradle of civilized mankind.[10]

Although Martini's writings made a considerable stir among thoughtful European scholars, we must not exaggerate their influence. As late as 1681, when Bossuet published his celebrated *Discours de l'histoire universelle*, he never mentioned the Orient, contenting himself with that 'Europe-centric' approach which still unbalances so much Western historical writing. Nor was Martini without his critics even among the China missionaries of the Society of Jesus. If the waspish Spanish Dominican, Fr. Domingo Fernandez Navarrete, is to be credited, the Portuguese Jesuit Gabriel de Magalhães and the Italian Luis Buglio said that it was arguable whether Marco Polo or Martino Martini had made the most mistakes in their respective accounts of China.[11]

Navarrete was anything but an impartial critic of the Jesuits, but his *Tratados* deserve more attention from historians than they have usually received. Although he profoundly disagreed with the Jesuits' efforts to find a *modus vivendi* between Confucianism and Christianity, Navarrete was otherwise as staunch an admirer of Chinese culture and civilization as was any Jesuit. He also had very definite views on Chinese history which he aired in his *Tratados*. He ridiculed the assertion of the Portuguese chroniclers that the Chinese had ever voyaged as far as Ceylon, India, and Mada-

---

[9] 'And because that according to the version of the Holy Scripture called the Vulgar, it would of necessity follow that *Fohi* and *Yao* must have been born and reigned before the Deluge, therefore we are forced in this country to follow the version of the Seventy' (Magalhães, *A New History of China*, London, 1688, p. 252).

[10] For the impact of Martini's *Sinicae Historiae* on the learned world of Europe, cf. V. Pinot, *La Chine et la formation de l'esprit philosophique en France, 1640–1740* (Paris, 1932), pp. 200–5, 289–90.

[11] Fr. Domingo Fernandez Navarrete, O.P., *Tratados Historicos, politicos, ethicos, y religiosos de la monarchia de China* (Madrid, 1676), p. 24. Mr. James Cummins has completed for publication a London Ph.D. thesis on this Spanish friar which includes a great deal of unpublished material and stresses the pro-Chinese nature of the *Tratados*.

gascar, maintaining that such a 'weak, cowardly and peaceful nation' had never had the enterprise to go further than the straits of Sunda and Singapore. He freely admitted that in many respects the heathen Chinese were more civilized, better governed, and better behaved than the nations of contemporary Christendom, adducing some interesting experiences of his own to prove as much. He accepted the contention of the Chinese chroniclers that there had been twenty-two dynasties with a total of 208 emperors from the time of the legendary Five Rulers, although, being a staunch supporter of the Vulgate chronology, he refused to accept the Chinese dating. He gives a large number of Chinese historical anecdotes, similar to those published later in Giles' *Chinese Biographical Dictionary*, and he also alludes to the provincial and regional gazeteers with their wealth of historical and topographical information. He argues that more attention should be paid to what one Chinese scholar said about the historical meaning of a Chinese character than to the views of thirty missionaries on that subject, severely criticizing the Jesuits for their endeavours to reinterpret certain passages in the Chinese classics 'in a sense contrary to that received [in China] during the last three or four thousand years'.[12]

The interest in Chinese history among European scholars, whether China Jesuits or stay-at-home historians, for long centered round the vexed question whether the official Chinese chronology could be reconciled with that of the Christian Bible. Roman Catholics, Protestants and Free-thinkers, all took part in this debate, originally touched off by the publication of Martini's *Sinicae Historiae Decas Prima*, and the discussion waxed exceedingly acrimonious at times. This problem soon became closely involved with the famous dispute over the Chinese Rites which aroused even bitterer feelings, but which also contributed greatly to popularizing works on China among the educated public of Europe. Another offshoot of this historical discussion which later aroused considerable interest in Europe, was whether Chinese characters and Egyptian hieroglyphics had a common origin, and, if so, what deductions could be drawn therefrom.

In the course of the eighteenth century, three schools of thought developed among the Jesuits who concerned themselves with Chinese history. The first school, represented by the Jesuits at Peking, regarded the Hsia, Shang, and Chou dynasties as historical, and considered that the length of Chinese history could be reconciled with the chronology of the Septuagint. Fathers Régis, Gaubil, Parrenin, and De Mailla, were the foremost exponents of this group. The second school, represented by the Jesuits of Canton and Macao, denied the authenticity of Chinese history before the

---

[12] *Tratados Historicos*, i, pp. 3–8, 14, 17, 24, 28–29, 36, 49, 53, 65, 80–81, 91–128, 174–85, 250–4, 290 ff. A second volume of the *Tratados* was printed but not published at Madrid in 1679, being suppressed on account of its violent attacks on the Jesuits of the China mission.

fifth century B.C. They claimed that the Chinese classics were esoteric books announcing the advent of a Messiah, which had originally been transmitted by the biblical Jewish patriarchs, but to which the Chinese had lost the key. The most audacious of this group was Père Foucquet, who eventually had to leave the Society on this account. He believed that Fu Hsi was identical with the Patriarch Enoch, the Greek Hermes and the Latin Mercury. The third school was composed of the Paris Jesuits who edited the works which their confrères forwarded from China. The most prominent of this group was the celebrated Père Du Halde. He sought to reconcile the views of his Peking and Canton colleagues as far as possible, drastically editing their manuscripts before publishing or utilizing them in the *Lettres Edifiantes et Curieuses* (34 vols., 1702–76), and in his *Description géographique, historique, chronologique, politique et physique de l'Empire de la Chine* (4 vols., Paris, 1735).[13]

Du Halde upheld the chronology of the Vulgate, and maintained that authentic Chinese history began with the Emperor Yao in 2357 B.C. He was also determined to prove that the Confucian Rites were not idolatrous in origin or in actuality, and that the Chinese empire in 1735 was still remarkably free from vicious superstitions. He accordingly suppressed or softened all passages in the original writings of the China Jesuits which tended to depict the Chinese in an unfavourable light. Hence the flattering impression given of China and the Chinese in the voluminous works which he edited. These works, together with Le Comte's *Nouveaux Mémoires sur l'état présent de la Chine* (Paris, 1696), were the principal sources for all Europeans who wrote on China in the eighteenth century. Leibniz, Voltaire, Gibbon *et al.*, relied heavily on them, although Du Halde's depiction of the Chinese as paragons of virtue did not find such ready acceptance in England as in France.[14] From the strictly historiographical point of view, Du Halde's work added little to the material previously published by Gonzalez de Mendoza, Martini, and Couplet.[15] As a contemporary French critic noted, in Du Halde's otherwise encyclopaedic account of China, 'l'histoire fût reduite à de singles notes chronologiques'.

Undoubtedly the greatest of the French Jesuit sinologues and the finest historian among them was Antoine Gaubil, who reached Peking in 1733 and lived there until his death in 1759. Humboldt rightly called him 'le plus grand savant des missionaries'; and Ting Tchao-ts'ing, who considered the missionaries pretty poor sinologues on the whole, is unqualified in his

[13] By far the best documented review of this subject is V. Pinot's work cited in note 10 above.

[14] Cf. C. S. Ch'ien, 'China in the English Literature of the eighteenth century', *Quarterly Bulletin of Chinese Bibliography* (New Series), vol. II, Nos. 1–4 (June–December 1941).

[15] P. Couplet, S.J., *Tabula chronologica trium familiarum imperialium monarchiae sinicae* (Paris, 1686), and idem, *Confucius Sinarum Philosophus* (Paris, 1687). Couplet's *Tabula chronologica* begin with Huang Ti (2697 B.C.) and end with K'ang-hsi.

praise of Gaubil.[16] Only a small part of his work was published in his lifetime,[17] and he more than once complained that his Paris colleagues made insufficient use of the historical works which he sent them. He made no pretence at being an original author,[18] but explained that he was trying to give Europeans some exact and critical notions of Chinese history as related by the most reliable Chinese historians.[19] He offered to send to Paris a complete set of the *Ming-shih* soon after its publication, and he envisaged the possibility of bribing some of the Peking Palace officials so as to get a sight (or better still, a copy) of the *Shih-lu* (Veritable Records).

Gaubil realized that the 'dry and abstract' nature of the historical material which he sent home was partly responsible for the delay in publishing his learned but daunting treatises. Despite all that has been written on the Chinese vogue in Europe, especially in France, during the eighteenth century, the reading public wanted above all 'de quoi s'amuser généralement', as Gaubil wrote. Du Halde was well aware of this trend, and this helps to explain why he abridged, bowdlerized or omitted so many contributions by his learned colleagues at Peking. Even so, his massive *Description de la Chine* was widely criticized as being too diffuse, too dull and too expensive, although it at once became and for long remained the standard work on China.[20] Naturally, these views were not shared by the more learned European scholars. French savants such as Fourmont and Fréret eagerly corresponded with the Jesuits at Peking and avidly read all the historical information which these could supply.

Fréret complained that the historical part of Du Halde's work was little more than a re-hash of material already published by Martini and Le Comte; but he found it difficult to find a publisher for Gaubil's works, as commercial publishers fought shy of historical disquisitions with a strictly limited appeal. This was also the principal reason for the delay in publishing Moyriac de Mailla's *Histoire Générale de la Chine*, which was based entirely on Chinese historical works and completed in 1737, but which only found a publisher thirty-four years later through the efforts of the

[16] Ting Tchao-ts'ing, *Les Descriptions de la Chine par les Français, 1650–1750* (Paris, 1928), pp. 33–34, 49–50, 61 ff. Much of what he says about Gaubil is taken without acknowledgement from Abel-Rémusat's biographical sketch in *Nouveaux Mélanges Asiatiques* (Paris, 1829), ii, 277–90.

[17] Gaubil's principal historical works include the *Histoire abrégée de l'astronomie chinoise* (Paris, 1729); *Histoire de Yen-tchis-can et de la dynastie des Mongou* (1739); *Le Chou-king, un des libres sacrés des Chinois* (1770); 'Abrégé de l'histoire Chinoise de la grande dynastie Tang', published serially in the *Mémoires de Pékin*, xv (1791), and xvi (1814); *Traité de la chronologie Chinoise divisé en 3 parties* (1814). A full list will be found in L. Pfister, S.J., *Notices biographiques et bibliographiques sur les Jésuites de l'ancienne mission de Chine, 1552–1773* (Shanghai, 1934), ii, 676–93.

[18] 'Ici, nous ne piquons pas d'être auteurs, et auteurs originaux' (letter of Gaubil d. 28, viii, 1752, *Lettres Edifiantes et curieuses* [ed. 1843], iv, 66).

[19] 'Je tâche de donner des notions exactes et critiques de l'histoire chinoise et des historiens chinois anciens et modernes' (*Lettres Edifiantes*, iv, 61).

[20] *Lettres Edifiantes* (ed. 1843), iv, 75; V. Pinot, *La Chine et la formation de l'esprit philosophique en France*, pp. 142–5, 159–67, 170–8.

Abbé Grosier.[21] At the same time, it must be admitted that the Jesuits'
*Lettres Edifiantes et Curieuses* (34 vols., Paris, 1702–36), became increasingly
inclined to dwell on the curious rather than on the edifying, thus reversing
the tendency which had prevailed for most of the sixteenth and seventeenth
centuries. The Jesuits' crowning achievement was the magnificent series
of *Mémoires* which form a fitting close to the literary labours of their missionaries in China.[22] They are of a much higher standard than the *Lettres
Edifiantes*, and reflect the new spirit which was abroad in the 'Enlightenment', being intended to satisfy the curiosity of savants and historians, and
not for the edification of the faithful.

Before taking leave of the Jesuits, we may briefly consider the extent to
which they were indebted to their Chinese collaborators and interpreters.
Padre Gabriel de Magalhães claimed that the language was easier to learn
than either Greek or Latin, and implies that he and his colleagues wrote
their numerous works in Chinese unaided.[23] Doubt was rightly cast on
these assertions by Père Louis Le Comte, who stated that on the contrary
no European could ever become really fluent in Chinese.[24] The Dominican
Fernandez Navarrete boasted that he knew over ten thousand Chinese
characters; but he admitted that neither he nor any of the missionaries
who were concentrated at Canton in 1669, could understand the wording
of a memorial which was submitted to the Dragon Throne on their behalf.[25]
It seems obvious that the missionaries relied much more heavily on their
Chinese collaborators than they were often prepared to admit. Martini,
Couplet, and others were studiously vague in citing their Chinese authorities; but Gaubil and De Mailla were much more punctilious in this respect,
and likewise acknowledged more freely the indi pensable help which they
had received from native interpreters and scholars.[26]

How did the Jesuits' work affect the development of historical writing on
China in Europe? The answer is easy. Whereas in 1681 Bossuet took no
account whatever of Chinese history, a century later both Gibbon and
Voltaire showed themselves acutely conscious of its importance. As C. S.

---

[21] Moyriac de Mailla, *Histoira générale de la Chine* (12 vols., Paris, 1777–83). Based originally on
the *T'ung Chien Kang Mu* of Ssu-ma Kuang, as edited by Chu Hsi, but continued down to the
Ming and early Ch'ing period. Mr. O. B. van der Sprenkel points out that H. Cordier's *Histoire
générale de la Chine* (4 vols., Paris, 1920), has incorporated whole sections of De Mailla's work
without acknowledgement.

[22] *Mémoires concernant l'histoire, les sciences, les arts, les moeurs, les usages etc., des Chinois, par les
missionaires de Pékin* (17 vols., Paris, 1776–1814). Though published after the suppression of the
Society of Jesus, most of the papers printed in this invaluable series had been written before 1760.

[23] G. Magalhães, S.J., *A New History of China* (London, 1688), pp. 77–82.

[24] L. Le Comte, S.J., *Memoirs Historical* (ed. London, 1738), pp. 177–85.

[25] D. Fernandez Navarrete, O.P., *Tratados Historicos* (1676), i, 111, 169, 252–4.

[26] Gaubil on occasion complained that he could not get sufficiently erudite and capable
assistants, probably because Chinese scholars of the first rank no longer cared to be so closely
associated with the Jesuits as they had been in late Ming and early Ch'ing days (*Lettres Edifiantes*,
iv, 59).

Ch'ien has remarked of the *Decline and Fall*: 'From the Pisgah height of his universal historical learning, Gibbon could clearly see how the East and West affect each other, and co-relate in a causal nexus events apparently unrelated.'[27] With the publication of Voltaire's *Essai sur les Moeurs* in 1764, China attained to the summit of her glory among the French, but many of Voltaire's other works bear ample testimony to his abiding interest in Chinese history.[28] Admittedly, his study was not purely dis-interested, for Chinese history furnished him with much ammunition for his attacks on the *ancien régime*. Where the Jesuits hesitated between the Septuagint and the Vulgate in their efforts to reconcile Chinese with biblical chronology, Voltaire boldly asserted that the length of authentic Chinese history proved the fallibility of the Bible. This was an ironical end to the pioneer labours of the Jesuit missionary historians, for their work was now done. After the suppression of the Society of Jesus in 1773, and the successive deaths of the last survivors of the Peking mission, the torch of Sinological learning in the West passed into other hands. Nothing, however, can deprive the sons of Loyola of the credit which is due to them for holding it aloft for so long.

Western historical writing on Japan during the sixteenth, seventeenth, and eighteenth centuries was, for obvious reasons, far more meagre than that on China. It was soon realized that Japanese civilization was derived from China; and hence Japanese history hardly entered into the heated discussion about Chinese and biblical chronology which aroused such interest in Europe. Inevitably, the Jesuits had a virtual monopoly of this field for over a century. João de Barros consulted the celebrated traveller, Fernão Mendes Pinto, when collecting material about Japan, but the Coimbra Jesuits dissuaded him from doing so when they heard of it, pointing out that the correspondence of their missionaries formed a much more reliable source. Barros' successor, Diogo do Couto, took the same line; for he tells us that he left the history of Japan to the Jesuit missionaries who lived in that country and who were studying Japanese history from the original sources.[29] Padre Luis Frois (1532–97) wrote a lengthy *Historia do Japam*, but the title is a misnomer since the book was a history of the Jesuit mission in Japan. It did contain a preliminary historical sketch of

[27] C. S. Ch'ien, 'China in the English Literature of the 18th century', pp. 37–38. Mr. Victor Purcell has written an erudite and entertaining work, 'Gibbon and the Far East', which I hope will be published soon.

[28] P. Martino, *L'Orient dans la littérature francaise au XVIIe et au XVIIIe siècle* (Paris, 1906), pp. 141, 181.

[29] Letter of Cipriano Soares, S.J., 1569, in *Anais da Academia Portuguesa da Historia*, II Série, i, 140 (Lisbon, 1946); Diogo do Couto, *Decada V* (Lisbon, 1612), Livro 8, cap. xii, fl. 182 v.

the island-empire prior to the arrival of St. Francis Xavier in 1549, but unfortunately this section has been lost.[30]

The outstanding Jesuit historian of Japan was undoubtedly Padre João Rodriguez (1561–1634), nicknamed 'Tçuzzu' (*Tʋʯi*) or 'interpreter', who had quite exceptional qualifications for his task. He had come out to Japan in his 'teens and campaigned with old Ōtomo Sōrin of Bungo before entering the Society of Jesus. He became court-interpreter (and to some extent confidant) of Hideyoshi and Ieyasu, moving in the highest circles of the land before he was banished to Macao in 1612. On reaching China, he threw himself into the study of the Chinese language, classics, and history, travelled widely in the interior, and served in some of the north-east frontier campaigns against the Manchu Tartars. A prolific and polemical writer, he took the opposite viewpoint to Ricci and most of his colleagues on the question of the Confucian Rites, and he was still engaged on his massive 'Historia da Igreja do Japão' at the time of his death. Unfortunately, only a part of this work has been published, but we can see from this section that Rodriguez must have made a very good job of the whole. His knowledge of Chinese enabled him to check the Japanese chronicles as no other European was able to do effectively until the nineteenth century; and hence he took a wider and a deeper view than either Frois or Kaempfer.[31]

Rodriguez, like all of us, had his limitations. At one time he propounded the view that both Japanese and Chinese were descended from the lost ten tribes of Israel, but he abandoned this theory later. He then suggested that Japan was originally peopled by two main streams of emigrants from the mainland, one composed of the aboriginal (pre-Chinese) inhabitants of Chekiang and the eastern seaboard, and the other from (or via) Korea. He also suggested that the Ainu came originally from N.E. Tartary and Siberia. He very clearly distinguished between the origins of the Tennō and the Shōgun, explaining the significance of the rise of the Taira and Minamoto and of Ashikaga Takauji. He gives a most interesting account of the growing prosperity of Japan as a whole from 1588 onwards, although stressing that the peasantry were being increasingly burdened with taxes

[30] G. Schurhammer, S.J., and E. A. Voretzsch, *Die Geschichte Japans, 1549–1578 von P. Luis Frois, S.J.*, *nach der Handschrift der Ajudabibliothek in Lissabon, übersetzt und kommentiert* (Leipzig, 1926); *Segunda Parte da Historia de Japan começando pela conversão del Rey de Bungo, 1578–1582*, ed. J. A. Abranches Pinto and Y. Okamoto (Tokyo, 193⁸); *La première ambassade du Japon en Europe, 1582–1592. Le Traité du Père Frois*, ed. J. A. Abranches Pinto and Y. Okamoto, H. Bernard-Maître, S.J. (Tokyo, 1942); J. F. Schütte, S.J. (ed.), *Luis Frois, S.J. Kulturgegensätze Europa-Japan, 1585* (Tokyo, 1955).

[31] G. Schurhammer, S.J., 'P. Johann Rodriquez Tçuzzu als Geschichtschreiber Japans', *Archivum Historicum Societatis Iesu* (Rome, 1932), i, 23–40; C. R. Boxer, 'Padre João Rodriguez Tçuzzu, S.J., and his Japanese grammars of 1604 and 1620', *Miscelânea de filologia, literatura e história cultural à memória de F. Adolfo Coelho* (Lisbon, 1950), ii, 338–63; J. L. Alvarez-Taladriz, 'Perspectiva de la Historia de Japon segun el P. Juan Rodriguez, S.J.', *Tenri Daigaku Gakuho* (1952), iv, 165–84.

to support the *daimyō* and the *samurai*. A perusal of Rodriguez' unfinished 'Historia', shows that this tireless Portuguese Jesuit was a worthy precursor of Siebold, Chamberlain, and Satow.[32]

The extinction of the Jesuit mission by the bloody persecution of 1614–40, left the Dutch at Deshima as the only means of contact between Japan and the Western world for over two centuries. The Dutch have often been criticized for their indifference to the rich cultural panorama of Tokugawa Japan, and for concentrating on profit and loss accounts rather than on art and belles-lettres. But what else could have been expected from the representatives of a commercial company closely and jealously guarded by a suspicious and arrogant bureaucracy? To search for an account of *kabuki* or of Japanese history in the files of the 'Deshima Dagh-Register' is like looking for an appreciation of Peking Opera or of the *Shu-ching* in the ledgers of Jardine, Matheson & Co. It is hardly surprising that there were not many potential historians to be found among the 'merchants of light' on Deshima, but two of these deserve brief consideration here.

Dr. Engelbert Kaempfer (1651–1716) was only in Japan for two years as against the twenty spent in Dai Nippon by Padre João Rodriguez, S.J. It is therefore understandable that the latter's grasp of Japanese history was superior to that of the worthy Westphalian; but Kaempfer's *History of Japan* was soon published, thus entitling him (and not Rodriguez) to be described as the scientific discoverer of Japan to the Western world. Considering the handicaps under which Kaempfer worked, and the fact that his personal knowledge of the country was limited to Nagasaki, Kyōto, Yedo, and the Tōkaidō, the amount of valuable and accurate information to be found in his *History* is astonishing. McClatchie has commented on the surprising accuracy of Kaempfer's description of the baffling and intricate layout of Yedo castle;[33] and a still more impressive tribute was paid by Aoki Okikatsu in his *Tōmon Jusaku* of 1804. 'The presence of this Holland Factory [at Deshima] has called into being books like Kaempfer's, which depicts our country's situation so well, that I, never having been in the Kwantō, still know what that district is like, because I have read this Dutch book, and so the Europeans know. Is it not terrible?'[34]

It must be admitted that the purely historical section of Kaempfer's *History* is not the most valuable part of his work; but it represents a great

---

[32] *Historia da Igreja do Japao pelo Padre João Rodriguez Tçuzzu, S.J., 1620–1633. Transcricão do Códice 49-IV-53 (fls. 1–181) da Biblioteca do Palácio da Ajuda*, ed. J. A. Abranches Pinto (2 vols., Macao, 1954–6). Some sections have been printed in Spanish translation with notes by J. L. Alvarez-Taladriz, 'La Pintura japonesa vista par un europeo a principios del siglo XVII', *Mas y Menos* (Osaka, 1953), xiv, 32–43; Idem, *Juan Rodriguez Tçuzu, S.J., Arte del Cha* (Tokyo, 1954). Cf. also preceding note.

[33] T. R. H. McClatchie, 'The Castle of Yedo', *Transactions Asiatic Society of Japan* (1888), pp. 119–54, especially p. 138.

[34] J. Feenstra Kuiper, 'Some notes on the foreign relations of Japan in the early Napoleonic period,' *Transactions Asiatic Society of Japan*, II Series (1924), i, 77.

advance on anything which had appeared in print before, being based on extracts from the *Nippon-Ōdaiki* and the *Nippon-Okaitsu*.[35] Like his Jesuit contemporaries in China, Kaempfer tried his hand at reconciling traditional Sino-Japanese chronology with the Book of Genesis. He was convinced that the Japanese were descended from the Babylonians, and he traces their migration from the Tower of Babel across Central Asia, China, and Korea, to Japan. He adds with disarming ingenuousness: 'Now if anybody knows how to bring them either thro' the Eastern Tartary and the country of Yezo (which way perhaps the American colonies went) safer and speedier, I am very willing to submit.'[36] Kaempfer's *History* immediately became the standard European work on Japan just as Du Halde's *Description* did on China, and it maintained this position down to the arrival of Commodore Perry and the publication of Von Siebold's researches.

If Kaempfer's somewhat misnamed *History* remained the standard general work on Japan for over a century, the purely historical section was replaced by the labours of Isaac Titsingh (1745–1812), to whom belongs the honour of compiling the first major European work exclusively devoted to a survey of Japanese history in the strict sense of the term. Unlike most of the Deshima Factors, Titsingh, who came of an Amsterdam patrician family, had received a good University education in both medicine and law.[37] Fortunately for him, his years in Japan coincided with the dictatorship of the Tanuma, who, corrupt and inefficient as they may have been, were relatively farsighted and liberal-minded as regards foreign contacts.[38] Whereas Kaempfer's Japanese collaborators had been confined to 'prentice interpreters and petty officials who could be tempted by bribery and the bottle, Titsingh was able to consort with *daimyō* such as Shimazu Shigehide and Kuchiki Samon. He even maintained a correspondence with these nobles, and with his friends among the senior interpreters, for years after he left Japan. His work has thus the great merit of being based almost exclusively on Japanese sources.

Titsingh's guiding principles in his historical researches were defined by him in a letter to his friend, William Marsden, as follows: 'in order to form a proper idea of the spirit, the character and the customs of a nation,

[35] Mr. G. W. Robinson informs me that Kaempfer's copy of the (*Dai*) *Nippon Ōdaiki*, published in 1684, is in the British Museum Library, but it has not been possible to identify the *Nippon Okaitsu*, which Kaempfer gives as another of his principal sources in his preface.

[36] E. Kaempfer, *The History of Japan, giving an account of the ancient and present state and government of that empire* (2 vols., London, 1728), i, 91. The title is rather a misnomer since the major portion of the work comprises a description of Japan as Kaempfer knew it.

[37] For a bio-bibliographical sketch of Titsingh, see C. R. Boxer, *Jan Compagnie in Japan* (ed. 1950), pp. 135–72. Dr. W. J. Van Hoboken informs me that Titsingh entered as a law student at Leiden in December 1764.

[38] An attempt has been made recently to rehabilitate the Tanumas by J. Whitney Hall, *Tanuma Okitsugu, 1719–1788* (Harvard University Press, 1955).

almost unknown in Europe, I deemed it preferable to represent them in their own dress. To obtain this end, I applied during my stay in Japan to some friends, reputed as men of learning, and free from all national prejudices; they procured me such works on various topics as enjoyed with them the highest regard; having succeeded in this, a literal translation appeared to me more congenial with the purpose, and likely to be more satisfactory to the desire for more distinct notions on a people almost unknown, though fully deserving the attention since a number of years so profusely lavished on the Chinese.'[39] In dedicating the manuscript of his Chronology of the Japanese and Chinese' to Kuchiki Samon in 1807, Titsingh reminded the daimyō of Fukuchiyama: 'you will remember my solemn promise not to mention in the least but what has been extracted from your most esteemed works, or was grounded on undeniable authorities [and] on the accounts of people deserving of all credit, nothing in consequence of my own will be added to the principal'.[40] This method of relying exclusively on the best native sources and commentators was very similar to that employed by Gaubil in his historical researches at Peking.

Titsingh's published work, again like that of Gaubil, was criticized on account of its 'dry and abstract' nature, but there is no doubt that both of them were working on the right lines in endeavouring to 'put over' the work of Chinese and Japanese historians to their Western colleagues. For years after he had left Japan, Titsingh tried to continue as he had begun. He took two Chinese interpreters with him to Bengal, but they were not scholars and they soon died. He visited the Court of Peking in 1795, as the last envoy from the Dutch East-India Company, and started to learn Chinese in Java. He also envisaged the possibility of getting Japanese historical works for the libraries of Europe through the medium of the Chinese traders at Nagasaki, but this project, too, came to nothing.[41] Most of the material which he amassed was dispersed after his death, but his posthumously published works were still found useful by James Murdoch in his standard *History of Japan*. Murdoch also points out that Titsingh, despite his exclusive reliance on native materials, had a sounder and more critical estimate of traditional Japanese chronology than either Kaempfer, Von Siebold or Rein.

One characteristic of Western historical writing on the Far East during this period remains to be mentioned. This writing was virtually all the work of amateurs. Even João de Barros, although his *Decadas* enjoyed royal

[39] C. R. Boxer, *Jan Compagnie in Japan* (ed. 1950), p. 170.  [40] Op. cit., p. 183.
[41] *Asiatic Review* (May–August, 1832), viii, 17–30. Titsingh's principal historical works were published posthumously. *Mémoires et Anecdotes sur la dynastie régnante des Djogouns*, ed. A. Rémusat (Paris, 1820), English edition, *Illustrations of Japan* (London, 1822); *Nipon o Dai Itsi ran, ou Annales des Empereurs du Japon*, ed. Klaproth (Paris, 1834), this last volume being published for the Oriental Translation Fund of Great Britain and Ireland.

patronage, produced his great work in the scanty leisure hours which his official post as Factor of the India House at Lisbon afforded him. We may suspect that Antoine Gaubil, S.J., devoted more time to his historical researches at Peking than to proselytizing among the heathen Chinese, but it remains true that his primary object was the conversion of souls and not the study of Chinese history for its own sake. Keampfer and Titsingh were both employees of a great commercial trading company when they first engaged in their historical researches.

About the turn of the eighteenth century a marked change of approach occurred. A new generation of scholars made their appearance, the younger De Guignes, Abel-Rémusat, Klaproth and others, all of whom may be termed professional Orientalists. These men no longer depended on the works of others, whether missionaries, merchants, or travellers, for their material, but could go direct to the original literary sources themselves. Inevitably the old order changed, yielding place to new, a process hastened by the ferment of ideas during the time of the French Revolution and the Napoleonic wars. Consideration of their work consequently falls outside the scope of this paper, since the results of their labours were published in the nineteenth century. But it is worth noting that they paid high tribute to the work of their amateur predecessors, and particularly to the learned Jesuit missionaries of Peking.

# 18. BRITISH HISTORICAL WRITING ON JAPAN

G. F. HUDSON

*Director of Far Eastern Studies, St. Antony's College, Oxford*

Down to 1854 British contact with Japan had been limited to the brief period of trade at Hirado at the beginning of the seventeenth century and to occasional visits of British ships which merely caught glimpses of the coasts and seaports of the closed country. For the rest, information about Japan came from Dutch sources, supplemented for the 'Christian Century' by Portuguese, Spanish, and Latin records. Discussions in Britain about the desirability of trying to reopen commercial intercourse with Japan drew on the stock of knowledge then available and put together in such a work as Pratt's *History of Japan*, published in 1822, but the sum total did not amount to much, and in the eighteen-fifties ideas about both the geography and the history of Japan were vague in the extreme. The British warship carrying Lord Elgin to Japan to negotiate a treaty in 1858 could not take refuge in Kagoshima Bay when struck by a storm off the south end of Kyushu because the coast was entirely uncharted, and its captain in his memoir of the voyage refers with the excitement of a traveller on the utmost fringes of the known world to the mysterious Suwo-nada Sea about which information could be gathered only from 'the itineraries of the Dutch envoys and others who have passed from Nangasaki to Yedo by the native routes'. The Shogun in Elgin's conception was the 'Temporal Emperor' of Japan, while Kyoto was the 'spiritual capital', the seat of merely ecclesiastical dignitary, an idea which reflects the memory of relations between the Papacy and Empire in medieval Europe and was a striking example of the danger of trying to fit a little-known historical development into categories of thought that were not applicable to it. The mistaken interpretation of Japanese history according to which the relations between the imperial dynasty and the Bakufu were those between spiritual and temporal power had important consequences in practical politics, for the Western powers assumed that the Shogun had complete authority for the making of treaties and were taken by surprise when they found that the refusal of the imperial sanction was widely held in Japan to deprive them of validity.

After the opening of Japan to foreign travel and residence, a British community grew up in Japan including a number of persons, by profession diplomats, consuls, business men, teachers, journalists or missionaries, who learned to read Japanese and who developed special interests in some field of Japanese studies. The Asiatic Society of Japan fostered these studies and published their results, which contributed in the next generation to serious attempts to write political and cultural histories of Japan. W. G. Aston, who served in the British Legation in Tokyo, declared in his preface to *A History of Japanese Literature*, published in 1899, that 'forty years ago no Englishman had read a page of a Japanese book' and that even at the time of his own writing 'there is no body of critical opinion on Japanese books in any European language', so that 'the historian of their literature is thrown mainly upon his own resources and must do his best, by a direct examination of those works which the verdict of posterity has marked out as most worthy of notice, to ascertain their character and place in literature, and to grasp as far as possible the ideas which inspired them'.

On the political side the flood of books of travel and interpretative comment on contemporary Japan inevitably focused attention on her adaptation to contact with the West and emergence alone among Eastern peoples as a strong national state of Western type. The Anglo-Japanese alliance of 1902 not only greatly stimulated British interest in Japan but also caused a generally favourable view to be taken of Japanese institutions and their development. The Japanese themselves were at this time busy rewriting the history of their own country under the influence of Western methods of historical scholarship and they were also interested in what Western writers had to say on the subject. They were not, however, greatly impressed by the earlier Western ventures in this field if we may judge by the foreword written in 1912 by Baron Kikuchi to Brinkley's *A History of the Japanese People*, in which he himself also collaborated; after claiming that 'the sudden rise of the Japanese nation from an insignificant position to a foremost rank in the comity of nations has startled the world' and denouncing the idea that 'we were a people but little raised above barbarism trying to imitate Western civilization without any capacity for really assimilating or adapting it', he goes on to say that 'among so many books there has not yet been, so far as I know, a history of Japan, though a study of its history was most essential for a proper understanding of many of the problems relating to the Japanese people'. This was indeed a little unkind to Murdoch, the two volumes of whose work covering the history of Japan to 1651 had already appeared in 1903 and 1910 respectively. It is possible, however, that Murdoch's treatment of the Japanese past, with its robust prejudices, lively polemics, and philistine attitude towards Japanese traditional cultural values disqualified his work in Baron Kichuchi's eyes as a serious interpretation of national history. Murdoch, with all his defects, must nevertheless be regarded as the principal pioneer in the large-scale writing of Japanese history in the English language, and his massive volumes are still readable, as much for the opinions of their author on men and events as for the substantial research that went into them.

Murdoch had the collaboration of a Japanese scholar, Yamagata Isoh, and it is not easy to ascertain how much of the factual record should be attributed to the latter, but the general outlook and commentary are stamped unmistakably with Murdoch's peculiar, sharp-edged personality. He was a political radical and a wholehearted devotee of progress, so that the Meiji era appeared to him a wholly glorious and desirable culmination of the national history; 'the history of modern Japan', he writes, 'now entered upon that astonishing career which has gained for her not merely admission into, but such a unique and distinguished position in, the Comity of Nations, begins to assume towards the record of the Tokugawa Age a relation analogous to that of the fecund efflorescence of the spring landscape to the seemingly rigid and monotonous torpidity of frost-bound winter'.

This outlook led Murdoch to regard the whole of Japanese history as an approach, unfortunately too often slowed down, to this happy climax and to make movement towards it the only criterion of value in the story; his complete lack of any aesthetic sense confirmed him in a view which deprived ancient and medieval Japanese culture of almost all its significance. Thus he finds the Japan of the late sixteenth-century full of 'pulsing, vigorous, lusty life', but he cannot find a good word to say for Yoshimasa, whose patronage of the arts he regarded merely as a frivolous waste of time. His judgments were also strongly influenced by his intense dislike for both Buddhism and Confucianism—emotions only surpassed by his still greater dislike of Christianity; this general anti-religious bias, however, at least had the advantage of making him pronounce a completely impartial plague on both houses in the period of Japan's 'Christian Century'.

Brinkley had a much more sympathetic attitude towards the Japan of the past than Murdoch and a much more sensitive appreciation of Japanese culture; as a historian, however, he was more of a compiler and tended merely to array facts rather than to analyse or explain them. A journalist by profession, with a far-ranging curiosity about all aspects of Japanese life, he was always a historical reporter rather than a historian; his great merit, as compared with Murdoch, was in linking together the political and cultural sides of Japanese history. The cultural history was meanwhile being advanced by enthusiasts for various branches of Japanese art who strove to establish the sequence of periods and styles in their respective fields and thus became to a greater or lesser extent historians of Japan. In this art-history the most distinguished British figure was Lawrence Binyon, whose history of Far Eastern painting, covering both China and Japan, must remain a classic, even though some of its generalizations, based on the connoisseur's rather than the researcher's approach, have had to be modified by later and more detailed studies. Of very great value also for the understanding of Japanese cultural history was the work of Arthur

Waley, who, like Binyon, was concerned with the literature and art of both China and Japan, but for this very reason was able in his brilliant essay on 'The Originality of Japanese Civilization' to deal effectively with a question which can never be treated adequately by a scholar too narrowly specialized on things Japanese.

The year 1931 saw the publication of a book which may be regarded as the outstanding British contribution to the writing of Japanese history— Sir George Sansom's work in the Cresset History Series, described in its sub-title as a Short Cultural History. Sansom was uniquely qualified to write a comprehensive history of Japan in which the political, economic, and cultural factors should be combined in due balance, for during his long residence in the country he was at once Commercial Counsellor of the British Embassy, with a remarkable knowledge of current economic conditions, and a connoisseur and collector of Japanese art. In this book the economic foundations of society in each period are treated with a thoroughness which had not been approached by Murdoch or Brinkley, and which reflected both the development since their time of studies in economic history, particularly by the Japanese themselves, and also the influence of theories of the economic interpretation of history, whether Marxist or non-Marxist, on historical thinking between the two world wars. With Sansom's work the history of Japan was made far more intelligible and significant in economic terms than it had been before; at the same time the literature and arts of Japan were presented, not as self-contained developments within a barely related historical framework, but as characteristic manifestations of each period.

With regard to the problem which had loomed so large for the pioneers of British historical writing about Japan, that of the explanation for Japan's rapid self-modernization in the Meiji era, Sansom's book was in accord with the tendency among the Japanese themselves to emphasize the forces making for change in the late Tokugawa period and to minimize the effects of the forced opening of the ports by the Western powers. The earlier view had represented the transformation as so sudden and unprepared as to be almost miraculous; later and more detailed studies, on the other hand, greatly modified the picture of a completely stagnant and archaic society in the years before Perry's visit and brought out the significance of the activities of the Rangakusha, the spread of money economy within the feudal structure and certain beginnings of large-scale enterprise in finance and industry. It seems now, however, that the pendulum has swung too far the other way, and that a corrective is needed for the extreme 'internalist' view of Japan's evolution expressed by Sansom in the phrase that 'what opened the doors was not a summons from without but an explosion from within'. This interpretation has proved very acceptable, though for different reasons, to Japanese nationalists as reducing the role of the West in altering the course of Japanese history, to Marxists as asserting the universality of the movement from feudalism to capitalism and the unimportance of regional time-lags, and to Western minds as minimizing the West's responsibility for the coercion of seclusionist countries in an age when the activities of the Elliotts and Perrys no longer appear in restrospect quite as beneficial or as justifiable as they did fifty years ago. There are, nevertheless, no adequate grounds for believing that either China or Japan would have developed a real capitalist economy or engaged in large-scale international trade during the nineteenth century but for the application of force by the Western powers. What is needed today is a more thorough and more comprehensive study of seclusionism as a social and political system, not only in Japan but also—and comparatively—in China, Korea, and Vietnam, so that its importance as a historical factor may be better estimated and understood.

To the same period as Sansom's great work belongs another more specialized study of Japan's cultural history which ranks as a major contribution in its field—Sir Charles Eliot's account of Japanese Buddhism. Eliot, like Sansom, had experience of Japan as a diplomat, and his volume on the religion called by another writer 'the creed of half Japan' was written at Nara after his retirement from official life. But Eliot saw Japanese Buddhism in a much larger context of *Kulturgeschichte*; the Japanese volume is only the fourth of his large-scale work on Hinduism and Buddhism, of which the first three cover the development of Indian religion in India itself, South East Asia, Tibet, and China. Since Buddhism, despite its immense importance for the social and cultural, and even for the political history of Japan, was imported fully grown from the mainland of Asia and cannot be adequately understood without detailed reference to its Indian and Chinese antecedents, the range of Eliot's cultural interests was essential to the success of his undertaking in the Japanese sector of the subject. Eliot's work finely complements from a Western point of view the work of Anesaki, Suzuki, and other Japanese scholars who have endeavoured to interpret to the West a religious development the study of which presents special difficulties because it straddles the cultural histories of India, China, and Japan.

In a much narrower, and yet perhaps more intimate field of Japanese historical study another Englishman who made a name for himself during this period was Ponsonby Fane, whose eccentric and romantic expertise had much in common with the cultural dilettantism of Backhouse in China. Ponsonby Fane fell in love with the city of Kyoto and his assimilation to the Japan of a past age was such that on a N.Y.K. liner he was the only man wearing Japanese dress. His knowledge of the history and genealogies of Japanese aristocratic families was proverbial, and his history of Kyoto, if not a major historical work, was at least evidence of how far it was possible for an Englishman to become a Japanese.

In extreme contrast to the attitude of Ponsonby Fane with its extreme emotional attachment to a traditional Japan was a new kind of British writing about Japan—for the most part about the country's recent history—which appeared in the nineteen-thirties and reflected the revulsion of British sentiment against Japan in the period which followed the termination of the Anglo-Japanese alliance and saw the growth of a Japanese imperialism trampling on liberal ideals and encroaching on British interests in the Far East. Typical of this 'debunking' school, with its emotional overtones of hostility towards Japan, was Morgan Young's *Japan under Taisho Tenno*. The earlier sentimental, if somewhat condescending, British enthusiasm for the modernized social and political order of the Meiji era was now replaced by a sombre picture of corrupt and oppressive administration, tyrannical police power and irresponsible militarism. It was a picture which represented an inevitable reaction from the sentimentality of the previous generation, and it received plenty of confirmation from Japanese actions between 1931 and 1945, but it was not conducive to fairness in the interpretation of Japanese history, and the requirements of anti-Japanese propaganda during the Pacific war were for the time being even more adverse to the quest for historical truth about Japan.

Among British historical works on Japan which have appeared since the end of the Pacific war three may be mentioned as of outstanding importance. The first is Sansom's *The Western World and Japan*, a sequel to his earlier work in which Japanese history is viewed in a world-historical perspective with the tracing of movements of diffusion of culture to Japan first from Asia and then from Europe. All the old questions about Japan's responses to the West are reviewed and answers given which are always stimulating and relevant. On one of Sansom's main themes, that of Japanese-European contacts in the period between the Portuguese arrival in Japan and the final closing of the country, his book was followed shortly afterwards by Professor Boxer's *The Christian Century in Japan*, which, with its author's special ability to combine both Japanese and Portuguese sources, has superseded all previous accounts of the subject in English.

The third book, Professor Allen's *A Short Economic History of Modern Japan*, was begun before the war, but completed with hind-sight of Japan's new situation after her defeat and surrender. The work of a leading British economist with a special knowledge of Japan, it remains unrivalled as a lucid and concise account of Japan's economic evolution since Tokugawa times. Its importance, however, far transcends the purely Japanese context; at the present time, when the industrialization of Asian and African countries has become a central issue in world affairs, there is, as the author suggests, 'some general interest in tracing the evolution of a modern industrial system within a society so differently constituted from that of Western nations'.

# 19. THE SOCIAL HISTORY OF MONGOL NOMADISM

OWEN LATTIMORE

*Lecturer in History, The Johns Hopkins University*

At the end of the eighteenth century when he wrote his *Decline and Fall*, Gibbon subjected the problem of the barbarian invaders of Roman civilization to the scrutiny of the new rationalism of his age. The material that he had before him included the Greek and Roman writers from Herodotus onward, the thirteenth-century narratives of Plano de Carpini, Ascelin, and William of Rubruck (of whom Carpini and Rubruck were extremely realistic observers, who travelled through much wider stretches of the steppe homeland of the pastoral nomads than did Marco Polo), and the works of the great French pioneers, clerical and lay, who first began to present to the West the historical records of China—in part, through translations of the Manchu translations from the Chinese. He was also able to draw on translated Persian and Arabic material.

In putting his hand to this widely diversified material, Gibbon was not satisfied with reconstructing the sequence of events. He was interested also in causation. In the passage in which he attributes the attack of the Goths on the western provinces of Rome to the impact of the Huns on the Goths themselves, along the Danube, some forty years earlier, he speaks for example of 'the original principle of motion', and sets out to discover its 'latent cause' among the nomad peoples. In the pages that follow there is an interesting mixture of rational, essentially scientific thinking about environment and social structure and function, in which Gibbon was in advance of his time, and of thinking in which the still current assumptions of his time did not allow him to be adequately scientific.

Gibbon makes his inquiry under three headings—Diet, Habitation, and Exercises, and it is instructive to run through his treatment of these topics, for in our own time many concepts about nomadic society and its relation to its environment have become stereotyped and unimaginative. Gibbon, by comparison, is refreshingly individual.

On Diet, Gibbon commendably does not accept at full value 'the common association of carnivorous and cruel'; he puts his emphasis on the fact that herds are a mobile and self-increasing food reserve, as compared with stored grain, and therefore especially valuable for campaigning.

On Habitation, he points out that a herding people can be more quickly mobilized than farmers who are dispersed over the countryside in permanent homes, and that in a settled civilization the society is divided into urban and rural components. He considers the townsmen to be inferior military material. Among nomads, on the other hand, the dwellings are portable, matching the mobile food reserve, and when nomads break camp and move to a new pasture they naturally 'introduce, in the distribution, the order, and the guard of the encampment, the rudiments of the military art'. In fact, 'The connection between the people and their territory is of so frail a texture that it may be broken by the slightest accident. The camp, and not the soil, is the native country of the genuine Tartar.' (Gibbon uses tribal names like Tartar and Scythian indiscriminately; he is not here concerned with the histories of tribes, but is trying to generalize his ideas about a kind of society.)

On Exercises, he notes that the pastoral life provides much leisure. He attributes this leisure in large part to the use of captives as herdsmen; had he known any nomadic people at first hand, he might have added that in times of peace also the men have much leisure, because the work around the camp is done by the women, and much of the herding by children. The leisure, he says, 'is usefully spent in the violent and sanguinary exercise of the chase', which is 'an instructive exercise for their numerous cavalry'.

Gibbon then makes a distinction between the Germanic tribes, who were of course not nomads, whose society, he says, 'has the appearance of a voluntary alliance of independent warriors', and the Inner Asian tribes which 'assume the form of a numerous and increasing family'. He draws attention to the importance of genealogy among them, as a result of which 'whatever distinctions of rank may have been introduced by the unequal distribution of pastoral wealth, they mutually respect themselves and each other as the descendants of the first founder of the tribe'. He then makes the shrewd comment that 'the custom . . . of adopting the bravest and most faithful of the captives, may countenance the very probable suspicion that this extensive consanguinity is, in a great measure, legal and fictitious'.

Here it may be commented that adoption and other devices for by-passing blood kinship did not in fact distinguish the Inner Asian from the Germanic tribes; these devices were known from one end of Eurasia to the other, but they appeared with different frequency in different periods of changing social history. Gibbon did not know, and at the time he lived could not find out, how much of what he thought was Germanic can be duplicated in the social history of the Mongol and Turkish peoples. Following Tacitus, he notes the Germanic 'voluntary alliance of independent warriors'; but without his voluntary independent warrior, his *nukud* (sing. *nukur*) Chingis Khan could never have made his career. The Mongol *nukur*, the Slavic *druzhinnik*, and the French *antrustion* are all the same social phenomenon.

Although he has previously emphasized the mobility of these tribes, Gibbon goes on to say that 'the limits of their peculiar territories were gradually fixed by superior force or mutual consent'. Tribes were compounded with each other because 'the weak were desirous of support, and the strong were ambitious of dominion'. There resulted a political superstructure headed by a supreme military chief. This office was hereditary in his family, but not necessarily by primogeniture. 'As it is the indispensable duty of a Tartar sovereign to lead his warlike subjects into the field, the claims of an infant are often disregarded, and some royal kinsman, distinguished by his age and valour, is intrusted with the sword and sceptre.' The khan collects a tribute both of ordinary property and of spoils of war and because of this and his own wealth in flocks and herds is able 'to reward the most deserving or the most favoured of his followers, and to obtain from the gentle influence of corruption the obedience which might be sometimes refused to the stern mandates of authority'.

'The immediate jurisdiction of the khan,' says Gibbon in his summing up, 'is confined within the limits of his own tribe', and is modified by the 'Couroultai' (*khuruldan*) or assembly of all the princes and chiefs of tribes, who assemble on horseback 'with their martial and numerous trains, and the ambitious monarch who reviewed the strength, must consult the inclination, of an armed people. The rudiments of feudal government,' Gibbon concludes, 'may be discovered in the constitution of the Scythian or Tartar nations, but the perpetual conflict of those hostile nations has sometimes terminated in the establishment of a powerful and despotic empire. The victor, enriched by the tribute and fortified by the arms of dependent kings, has spread his conquests over Europe or Asia; the successful shepherds of the North have submitted to the confinement of arts, of laws, and of cities; and the introduction of luxury, after destroying the freedom of the people, has undermined the foundation of the throne.'

Gibbon is worth quoting at this length because he sets out so many of the facts, and raises so many of the questions, that must still be considered by the social historian who deals with such a people as the Mongols. These are:

1. The mobility of property, food resources, dwellings.

2. A form of life in times of peace which provides training for periods of war.

3. A compound society which includes slaves and other subordinate individuals or groups, but which by the device of adoption, or the free adherence of warriors to a chosen chief, permits an individual to be taken up from a subordinate group into the ruling group.

4. The problem of tribe and territory. It seems clear that Gibbon held that the tribe is primary, that 'the camp, and not the soil, is the native

country', and that it is only subsequently that 'the limits of their peculiar territories were gradually fixed'.

5. The limitation on arbitrary power when the people is an armed people. Gibbon sees in this the 'rudiments' of feudalism, but he does not seem to believe that a true feudalism ever developed. What happened instead was, from time to time, a conquest of civilization, the consequences of which eroded the nomadic society from within—and I think that we may assume that Gibbon believed that after this the cycle began all over again.

Some further developments, however, lie between Gibbon's thinking and the schools of history of our time. Gibbon stood at or near the beginning of the rationalist tradition. During the nineteenth century there stemmed out of this tradition two different materialistic approaches to the study of society in its relation to environment. The non-Marxist materialism, developed especially by geographers (notably Ratzel in Germany), tended to treat nature as if it were animated and even purposeful. We find with interesting frequency such expressions as 'the environment permits'—or 'forbids', or 'encourages'. (I must admit that I have all too frequently slipped unconsciously into this manner of writing myself.) This tendency, leaving out intermediate names for the sake of brevity, reached an extreme in Ellsworth Huntington's theory of 'climatic pulsation' fifty years ago, which gave changes of climate as the cause of nomadic migrations, leading to conquests. As a dry cycle progressed and pastures dried up, nomads in search of new pastures clashed with other nomads and with settled peoples, setting in motion a chain of military and political events. Man is ultimately at the mercy of gross natural forces. Huntington even extrapolated environmental theory into racist theory: certain kinds of climates produced superior races.

Huntington's climatic explanation was largely accepted by Toynbee in his *Study of History*; although Toynbee also printed a long note by Geoffrey Hudson, pointing out that in Mongolia, for instance, if 'desiccation' were to dry up the pastures, the same desiccation would lower the precipitation in Siberia, to the north, so that trees would no longer grow, but grass could still grow. The Mongols would then only to have to move north and would not have to go west to bother the world.

The Marxist materialism is different. (I write this with hesitation, conscious of the shallowness of my knowledge in this field.) It begins with the idea that man is an animal who, like any other animal, tries to keep himself alive by taking from nature whatever is available. But man is also a social animal; he therefore, from the time that he is distinguishable as man in the scale of evolution, takes from nature not only as an individual but as a member of a society.

Assuming that up to this point I have not made any mistake that makes what I have to say entirely irrelevant, I offer the following non-Marxist rephrasing of the Marxist concept of 'the mode of production': since man lives both as an individual and as a member of a group, he wins his living from nature through a complex process in which his abilities as an individual interact with his position as a member of a group. This combination, at any given historical level, is given a strong set by the prevailing mode of production (pre-industrial, industrial), out of which arise further complications involving the means of production (who controls them?) and the relations of production (who gets more, who less?). The more evolved the technique, the more sophisticated the combination of technical skill and social organization, the more complex the system of what one might call 'gears' or processes between man the individual and the raw natural environment from which he draws, but can draw only as a member of society, what he needs to keep himself alive.

By the time the industrial mode of production has been reached, society has interposed a whole series of primary and secondary processes between the individual man and the environment. Society operates these processes through an intricate organization which involves, notably, a great deal of division and specialization of labour. The industrial mode of production results in the highest degree of control over the environment that man has thus far achieved. One result is that industrial man is able to fly to the Arctic and to live there clothed in industrially-made fabrics, eating packaged, industrially-produced foods. Even his housing is industrially produced and imported. In describing this phenomenon, one should not say that 'the Arctic encourages the white man to supersede the Eskimo', any more than one should say that 'the Arctic encourages the Eskimo manner of life'. The only commonsense way to put it is to say that 'until the industrial age, the best way that man had evolved for living in the Arctic with a good deal of security and comfort was that of the Eskimo'.

Similarly in discussing pastoral nomadic society and its history the approach that brings the best results is to avoid thinking of what the climate, the vegetation, and the fauna of the steppe 'permitted', 'encouraged', or 'forbade', and to try to analyse, instead, what combinations of economic practices and social organization enabled men to live successfully as herders in the steppe, and what the consequences were in the relations between peoples of the steppe and agricultural and urban peoples.

For the historian it is worth knowing what the life and society of the nomads of Inner Asia really were, and what really was the significance of Gibbon's 'principle of motion' of this society in such conquests as those of the Mongols. For the present, and probably for a long time to come, field research on this life and society can only be done in territories controlled or dominated by either Russian or Chinese Communists. For this reason it is essential for non-Marxist social historians to work out methods through which they can put to use, according to their own understanding, the materials which are available only through Marxist publications.

On the other hand, field research among nomads of the Near and Middle East can still be done principally by non-Marxists. This opportunity should be followed up. In a paper published two years ago ('The frontier in history', *Relazioni*, X Congresso internazionale di Scienze Storiche (Roma), Firenze, 1955, i, 105–38), I suggested that the Inner Asian nomads were 'excluded' from civilizations like that of China by fortified frontiers like the Great Wall. As the agriculturally-based, urban-centred civilization of China grew, it took up all the land that could best be exploited by Chinese farming. On the arid northern margin of this land, where there was neither sufficient rainfall nor sufficient irrigation water for a prosperous farming society, primitive farming was anciently combined with primitive herding. As the herding became more skilled and more profitable, groups of these people abandoned their farms and took to living entirely in the steppe. Other components of the Eurasian steppe society, between the Black Sea and China, derived from the Inner Asian oases on the south and from the forests on the north (by a transition from forest hunting to steppe herding).

'In the Iranian-Mesopotamian-Arab world,' however, 'the geographical and social pattern is much more confused . . . a major phenomenon being that pastoral nomads were not only excluded on the north but enclosed in blocks of desert, semi-desert, steppe, and highland country within the general sweep of civilization.' Both the contacts and the conflicts with civilization of these 'enclosed' nomads were different from those of the 'excluded' nomads. Since permanent internal 'Great Wall' frontiers could not be maintained, political interaction was more intimate and economic symbiosis more complicated. By comparing 'excluded' and 'included' pastoral nomadisms and noting the differences it might be possible, by analysis of what they have in common, to work out a model of 'pure' nomadism, which of course never existed in history but would be useful for the clarification of problems of social theory.

It would also, I think, help to clear up some of the confusions in Soviet discussion of nomadic society and history. In the 1930's there was a discussion of pastoral nomadic society among Soviet scholars. The only publication from this period that has been available to me is N. N. Koz'min, *On the question of Turco-Mongol feudalism*, Moscow-Irkutsk, 1934 (in Russian). It appears to have represented the orthodox view of that time. It is based largely on non-Marxist authorities, such as Fustel de Coulanges. The central argument is that control of territory controlled society: *nulle terre sans seigneur*. The weak side of the book is that in pursuit of this feudal theory it treats the herdsman as merely a peasant. Indeed, this weakness pervades much Marxist discussion of nomadism. In earlier publications the term 'peasant' is actually used; in recent years there is a tendency to beg the question by borrowing terms from the languages of pastoral peoples (such as Mongol *arad*, 'a commoner'); but such terms are semantically too vague, in the language which borrows them, to solve the real problems of terminology.

The Chinese sources do not provide the Russian-Marxist emphasis on territory with firm support. Like all civilized peoples, the Chinese have their own stock of clichés about nomads. Probably the most frequently repeated of these may be rendered, in its average form, 'they have no fixed abodes, but move about, following water and grass'. It would be useful to compile a list of the terms which the Chinese copy from book to book, and with the help of this list to sort out terms which are more likely to preserve for us the direct descriptions of observers.

The strongest support for the emphasis on territory in a really old Chinese text is in a passage in the chapter on the Hsiungnu or Huns in the *Shih Chi* (Ch. 110). The passage is part of a recital which, as I suggested a good many years ago (*Inner Asian frontiers of China*, New York, 1940, p. 463), may echo an underlying epic of the Hsiungnu people themselves. It describes how Mao-tun murdered his father and made himself ruler. The Tung-hu, neighbours of the Hsiungnu, then demanded from Mao-tun as tribute first a famous horse and then one of his favourite wives. Against the advice of his officials, Mao-tun granted each of these tributes in succession. The Tung-hu then demanded that he surrender a tract of abandoned or unused land lying between the Hsiungnu and the Tung-hu. This time some of the officials advised surrender, as it was abandoned land, but Mao-tun was angered. 'Land', he said, 'is the root of the nation'; he decapitated those of his officials who had advised surrender, and went to war against the Tung-hu.

It would be a useful enterprise to collate this and a number of other passages from Chinese documents with passages which can be found in Mongol documents and in the narratives of medieval travellers. As the matter now stands, 'land is the root of the people' can be taken by a Koz'min and equated with *nulle terre sans seigneur* as if that were all there is to it. But that most certainly is not all there is to it. There are a great many other passages to support the argument that in a mobile society sometimes the best use that can be made of mobility is to abandon territory. The chief may find that it is better to abandon territory, if by so doing he can still hold his following together. Thus T'u-men, father of Mao-tun and founder of the Hsiungnu imperial line, 'migrated away' from the Ordos to escape being subordinated to the frontier drawn by Ch'in Shih-huang-ti, the Great Wall Emperor (*Shih chi*, 11d). Given the alternatives—holding the territory together or holding the tribe together—it looks as though the following working hypothesis could be proposed: in the history of pastoral nomads there are some crises in which it is better to defend territory, even if by doing so some of the people may be lost; other crises in which what matters is to hold the people together, even if that means abandoning territory.

Recently discussion has been renewed in the Soviet Union. One author, L. Potapov, 'On the nature of patriarchal-feudal relations among the nomadic peoples of Central Asia and Kazakhstan', *Voprosy Istorii* (1954), 6, reasserts the old emphasis on territory. Another, S. E. Tolybekov (who appears to be himself a Kazakh), 'On the patriarchal-feudal relations among nomadic peoples', *Voprosy Istorii* (1955), 1, asserts that ownership of livestock is the source of power and the criterion of class-differentiation. There are a number of other articles, some of them in journals that are not easy to find, and I have by no means read the whole of the discussion, but fortunately there is a summing-up article by the editors in *Voprosy Istorii* (1956), 1.

A number of points are made. Some of them are valid and advance the discussion. Others reveal the continuing limitations of Soviet thought in this field. A bow is made to Vladimirtsov, a great scholar who bridged the Tsarist and Soviet periods and whose important work on *The Social structure of the Mongols* (Leningrad, 1934) is now available in a French translation, but it is stated that Soviet historians do not agree with his understanding of 'nomadic feudalism'. I myself find that Vladimirtsov must be used with care because, though he was one of the great scholars of the Mongol language and provided valuable explanations of terms, and established the historical periods in which various terms came into use, his understanding of social and political institutions was not equally deep.

A reference to the discussion of the 1930's is made. Apparently the recent discussion began with a review of the publications of the 1930's at a joint session of the Academies of Science of the Republics of Central Asia and Kazakhstan at Tashkent, in 1954. The current views of Potapov and Tolybekov are then taken up, with the prefatory warning that the social and economic history of nomad peoples has been insufficiently studied in detail, and that we should not apply the data of one people to another or of one period to another. I should accept this as a sound warning but not as an absolute prohibition—for how else are the processes of history to be studied?

The editorial opinion is that land is dominant as the 'means of production', and that Tolybekov and others are wrong in suggesting that under nomad conditions there is so much land, and that it can be productively used with so little labour, that it 'loses its character as a means of production'. There is a hint here that perhaps Tolybekov and others may represent the views of Kazakhs and other peoples that actually have nomadic histories and a carry-over of nomadic traditions, while the Potapov school represent a Russianizing Marxism, of European derivation, projecting its theories into the source materials of the Inner Asian peoples. It is inevitable that situations of this kind should exist, and it is inevitable that they should take the form of Inner Asians saying, in effect, 'you Russians think you know everything, but why cannot you open your eyes to the fact that there are things in our history that are different from the historical materials on which your theories are based, and deserve fresh and independent consideration?' while the Russians reply, 'do not be so provincial and bourgeois as to think that these differences of yours are real differences, and not mere variations of the well-established data, gathered from world history, which assure the universal validity of Marxist theory'. It may be true that the 'particularists' are at times too narrow and too limited, but unfortunately it is also true that in the past accusations of 'bourgeois nationalism' have led to severe repressions, sterile orthodoxy, and the paralysis of new and fresh thinking.

At any rate, the main point of the orthodoxy of the 1930's is reaffirmed. It is asserted that among Mongols, Kazakhs, and others, those who became the feudal nobles did so by seizing the right of allocation of land for use. An expression repeatedly used is that the land was 'in practice', or 'virtually' (*fakticheski*) the property of the nobles.

Tolybekov holds that the specific characteristic of patriarchal feudalism is that the land remains communal property, while the feudal property is cattle. (Perhaps I may be permitted to interject that this is rather close to my own views, at the stage of development which they had reached in the 1930's.) This view the editors reject. If this were all, they say, the feudal class would simply have more cattle and the commoners less, and the contrast would not be one of exploiters and exploited. The truth is that the feudal classes *fakticheski* own the land and also the majority of the cattle.

It is wrong, the editors say, to assume that the big cattle owner assigned a portion of cattle to poor men for temporary use, thus making them dependent and creating 'feudalism' and 'serfdom'. That would imply that those not forced into dependence by lack of livestock would remain outside the feudal order. But a real feudal nomadism would not be interested in cattle-less dependents. The feudal lord was not interested in impoverishment, but in exploitation of the maximum number of households economically able to maintain themselves. Marx is cited in support. To clinch the argument, the editors use the following formula: one must not think of personal dependence without economic content. Underlying personal dependence is dependence of the workers on the feudal class who are *fakticheski* owners of the pastures.

This conclusion is weak, because an expression like 'virtual' or 'practical' or *fakticheski* ownership of the land gives us no description, much less an analysis, of the institutions and sanctions of pasture ownership or use. The editors of *Voprosy Istorii* indirectly admit as much. They have, they say, only taken up certain questions that arose in the course of the discussion; they have not taken up the evolution of feudal land property when nomads are included under non-nomad governments, as the Mongols were under the Manchus and the Kazakhs under Tsarist Russia, and there was a penetration of commercial, money, and capitalist relations into the economy of the nomads. They commendably call for research on such problems, and also on the 'commune' (*obshchina*), the significance of survivals of the commune as the core of later resistance to the aristocracy, the forms of land dependency and feudal rent, and other matters. (Without going into detail at the moment, it appears to me that what is meant here by the 'commune' is what Western writers would call the 'tribe'.)

Some of this 'further work' had, as a matter of fact, already been done. V. V. Bartol'd (W. W. Barthold), some of whose work, such as *Turkestan down to the Mongol invasion*, is well known in translation, and who like Vladimirtsov bridged the Tsarist and Soviet periods, noted that in their Middle Eastern conquests some of the Mongol nobles, especially those of the imperial line, preferred the nomadic life. They considered themselves permanent warriors, even though encamped among a conquered, settled population. Conquered people were to be recklessly taxed, even if it led to the destruction and disappearance of settled life; peoples not yet conquered were to be raided and plundered at opportunity. An opposite tendency was for members of the Mongol ruling class to ally themselves with families of the administrative, bureaucratic, and land-owning class of the conquered countries and thus to take up and continue the previously existing methods of administration and taxation. Bartol'd's work has been continued, with the addition of new material and a Marxist working out of details, by his Soviet successors, among whom outstanding names are those of A. Yu. Yakubovskii and S. P. Tolstov. There is a brief but valuable note on this field of Russian historiography in I. Petrushevskii's general introduction to Vol. I of the works of Rashid-ad-Din. (Vol. I, Moscow-Leningrad, 1952; Vols II and III had appeared previously.)

Parallel work of the highest quality on Inner Mongolia, primarily the Ordos region, is being done by Father Antoine Mostaert, whose most recent publication is 'Matériaux ethnographiques relatifs aux Mongols ordos', in *Central Asiatic Journal* (1957), ii, 5. As a philologist, Father Mostaert ranks with such great names as Vladimirtsov, Ramstedt, and Pelliot; but none of these spent so many years living in a Mongol society as he did. One of the least-known fringe regions is being intensively documented by Father Louis M. J. Schram. Vol. I, 'The Monguors of the Kansu-Tibetan frontier: their origin, history, and social organization', appeared in *Transactions of the American Philosophical Society* (Philadelphia, 1954, xliv, 1); Vol. II,

'Their religious life' (1957, xlvii, 1); Vol. III will be a translation, with commentary, of the family chronicles of one of their noble families. We are, in fact, in the process of acquiring a mass of new material which will make possible a thorough review of older ideas of the nature and history of nomadic society. In Germany, W. Heissig is working on a general Mongol history, based on Mongol documents.

It is not too early to make some tentative suggestions.

(1) Gibbon is clearly still entitled to great respect. He had a natural eye for the essential characteristics of both social and political institutions and for their interaction with economic and geographical factors. In his time separate 'disciplines' of sociology, economics, and so on had not yet been constituted, claiming 'methodologies' of their own. This has its advantages, for it also means that Gibbon is free of many preconceptions that have since arisen, and much of the habitual thinking that now makes review both more necessary and more difficult.

(2) Non-Marxist materialism easily reduces itself to absurdity when it subconsciously treats nature as an active, quasi-purposeful force which 'imposes' limitations on a society, 'reducing' it to terms of survival within a materialistically described environment. The student of society should treat material conditions with the greatest respect, but his working method should be to treat a society as a complex—a body of people, a body of knowledge, skills, and practices, and a body of institutions which regulates the working of the whole; and he should treat this complex as representing the degree of mastery which the society has attained, within the historical period being dealt with, in asserting its control over the environment.

(3) Marxist materialism, as demonstrated in the Soviet material from which I have cited, is too narrow and too doctrinaire. Certain of its conceptions, like means of production, modes of production, and class conflict, are useful working tools, but there is a tendency to use these tools as mere tests of orthodoxy. Certainly the student of society should be strict in analysing and differentiating the elements of a complex, but he should not let classification become so rigid that it masks the functioning of the complex as a whole.

Working from these preliminary observations I think it should be possible to set up a model of nomadic life and society which could enable us to understand better what happened, and why it happened, in the history of such peoples as the Mongols.

(1) *Mobility.* Livestock are mobile. This is what sets the herdsman apart from the peasant. The amount of mobility varies a great deal according to kinds of livestock, geographical region, and historical period, but the important thing about a nomad people is not so much that they *do* move as that they *can* move (Lattimore, 'The geographical factor in Mongol history', *Geog. Journ.*, xci, 1938). The movable dwellings and the possession

of means of transport distinguish the nomad from the farmer who grazes cattle as a supplementary activity. The importance of this difference in times of war or natural calamity is obvious.

(2) *Title to land.* At one period the land may be thought of as collectively owned, and divided only for allocation of use; at another time it may be permanently divided and exclusively owned. At times the right of passage, rather than occupation, may be critical.

Mention has been made of the 'abandoned' land between Hsiungnu and Tung-hu. Such tracts can be of great importance in regulating peaceful passage between seasonal pastures, and in institutionalizing the customs of raiding and desultory warfare, as contrasted with war for the purpose of conquest; for even raiding and desultory warfare can be institutionalized, as we know from a wide range of historical examples. Perhaps the last surviving illustration of this 'abandoned' land (the term is one that is used by Chinese and other outsiders; it is really no-man's land) is, or was recently, the wide fringe of pasture, rich in itself but unused, surrounding the core territory of the Ngoloks, a pastoral robber tribe in Northeastern Tibet. For the most recent mention, unfortunately all too brief, see André Migot, *Tibetan marches* (New York, 1955).

*Control of land and people.* In trying to determine whether ownership of land or of cattle is primary, the recent Marxist writers have got themselves into a blind alley. The question is one of historical period. In the far outlying steppe, in periods when the nomads are neither within reach of the projected power of a civilized empire nor attached as retainers to the barbarian conquerors of an empire, Gibbon is right in saying that 'the connection between the people and their territory is of so frail a texture that it may be broken by the slightest accident'.

In the *Secret history of the Mongols,* in a passage referring to an undated legendary period, some Mongol heroes go out into an unclaimed wilderness where they live by hunting. One day they see a small body of people in migration. They capture these people, and thus they have the beginning of a tribe with which to assert control over territory.

Conversely, in time of defeat it may be preferable to hold together a group of people in flight and retreat rather than try to hold on to a particular tract of land (see above, pp. 334–5). With even a very small group of people it may be possible in time to recuperate, to subordinate other people, and to lay claim to wider territory. The *Secret history* gives a perfect description of a situation of this kind (including the defection of most of the family retainers) in its account of the troubled boyhood of Chingis, after the death of his father, when the family fortunes were at their lowest.

The emphasis changes when nomads are brought into relations with an empire. The situation has two variants: in one, a civilized empire extends its fringes into nomad territory, in the other, the nomads are retainers of a barbarian of their own stock who has captured a few border provinces or a whole empire. In either case a strong empire wants to know where people are, who is to be charged with guarding what sector of the frontier, what is the size of the military contingent that can be summoned from each area. It therefore allocates territories, and in them it institutionalizes authority, rights, and duties. Here we have Gibbon's second instance: 'the limits of their territories were gradually fixed by superior force or mutual consent.' Or, as William of Rubruck noted of the Mongols in the thirteenth century, 'Each captain, according to whether he has more or fewer men under him, knows the limits of his pasturage and where to feed his flocks in winter, summer, spring, and autumn.' (For a convenient modern edition, but thinly annotated, see Christopher Dawson, ed., *The Mongol mission*, 1955.)

At this point we are certainly entitled to talk of feudalism, or of the beginnings of feudalism. A very symmetrical example is given by Father Louis M. J. Schram, in his work on the Monguors already mentioned. The Monguors were established as a frontier feudal group under the Mongol conquests of China; on the fall of the dynasty they transferred their allegiance to the new Chinese Ming dynasty; with the fall of the Ming they continued in the same status under the Manchu or Ch'ing dynasty.

In the Soviet discussion cited above Potapov gives data from the history of the Bukeev Horde of the Kazakhs to show the dominance of land property in Kazakh feudalism. On the basis of the material just presented I think that Tolybekov is clearly right in criticizing Potapov on the ground that this did not arise from 'feudalizing' tendencies within the Kazakh society itself, but from the fact that 'the whole land of the Inner Horde was granted by Paul I [the Russian Tsar] to the Sultan Bukei. Consequently Bukei and his heirs in the Inner Bukeev Horde obtained the right of proprietors over these lands on the basis of Russian state legislation and not through the ancient customs of a nomad society'. (Tolybekov, as cited, 83.)

(4) *Subordination.* The stratification of chiefs and subordinates varies according to the periods described in the preceding section and there is a corresponding difference between power based on control of a group of followers, and status and power governed by allocation of territory. Here we must return to the factor of mobility, which has already been stressed. The serf could not change lords at any advantage to himself. If he fled, he had to abandon the land he cultivated. He could not come to some other lord and ask for service, combined with protection, with any assets that gave him bargaining power. The nomad who was subordinate within his own tribe, or who had been captured by another tribe, had the advantage that he could steal horses and flee to another tribe. There he could ask for service as a warrior, equipped with remounts. Of course the chief to whom

he appealed could simply kill or enslave him and take his horses; but if he happened at the time to be building up his forces and looking for recruits he would not do so, because it would discourage others from coming to him as adherents.

A passage in William of Rubruck shows how formidable the nomad or the escaped captive of nomads could be. 'For their Ruthenian, Hungarian, and Alanian slaves, of whom there is a very large number . . . band themselves together in groups of twenty or thirty and run away by night and they have bows and arrows, and whomsoever they come across by night they kill. By day they stay in hiding, and when their horses are tired they come during the night up to a large group of horses on the pasture lands and change their horses; they also take away one or two of them so that they can eat them when the need arises.' What makes this instance the more striking is that it dates from the period when the authority of the Mongol empire, and its ability to enforce regulations, were at their height.

Within the nomadic society defection could be controlled—within limits —by the device of group responsibility. We have an instance in the *Secret history*. As a youth Chingis was captured by hereditary enemies. He escaped, hid, then crept to a tent where he heard mare's milk being churned. The household were subordinates of his enemies, and this was part of their required work. The head of the family hid Chingis, and he eventually got away. Later, when Chingis had begun to rise in the world, this man came and joined him. He explained that he had wanted to come earlier, but could not because of his family; in other words, he could not defect until the whole group was able to escape, for fear of group responsibility.

I have here been speaking of 'subordination', because terms like 'slavery' and 'serfdom' are inadequate to cover all the varieties. Not all of these varieties are to be found in any one period or region, but they include: the individual slave; families which might be called 'retainers', attached to the families of rulers or chiefs (such families could own and inherit property); and subordinate clans or even tribes which were partly in the service and partly under the protection of an overlord tribe; these larger groups could have their own hereditary chiefs, and individuals and families could own and transmit property; it was the group collectively that paid tribute in kind and in services. Some of these forms of subordination are discussed in Wolfram Eberhard, *Conquerors and rulers: social forces in medieval China* (Leiden, 1952); in Schram, as already cited above; and in Lattimore, Introduction to Schram, op. cit. The process of stratification bears out Gibbon's acute observation, 'the weak were desirous of support, and the strong were ambitious of domination', for the part played by the search for protection was more important than is usually acknowledged, and not all subordination was due to capture or conquest.

Subordination and sub-subordination of this kind was most likely to take place in long periods of chronic warfare, as described for instance in the passages of the *Secret history* that deal with tribal history, before Chingis began the conquest of settled lands. It involved the disintegration of tribes linked by real or fictitious blood kinship as well as the institutionalizing of the new forms of subordination. In the Soviet literature, the most original contribution to this part of the field of discussion that I have seen is S. Yushkov, 'On the question of the pre-feudal ("barbarian") state', *Voprosy Istorii* (1946), vii. This article led to no real discussion among Russian historians, which is a pity.

After tribal territories became attached to the frontiers of major empires conditions became more feudal and, as one might expect, the forms of subordination were modified. Among the Mongols, in addition to the ordinary 'commoners' who carried out routine general service, aristocratic families continued to have subordinate families attached to them for personal services. In the Russian literature, all commoners are frequently referred to, indiscriminately, as 'serfs'; I think wrongly, although Father Mostaert also occasionally uses the term.

It would be more accurate to say that under the Manchu empire the Mongols were divided among a great number of territories or 'banners'; the process is succinctly described in Father Mostaert's latest article, cited above; see also Owen Lattimore, *The Mongols of Manchuria* (New York, 1934). In the 'banners', all men of military age nominally had the status of hereditary warriors, but it is certainly true that, with long-continued peace, their condition did tend in many ways to approximate to that of serfs. One indication of this trend is the virtual disappearance of clan names, except among nobles; a man became known, not as So-and-so of Such-and-such clan or tribe, but as So-and-so of Such-and-such Banner. This is noted by Father Mostaert in his most recent article and also earlier in his 'Les noms de clan chez les Mongols ordos', in *Ordosica*, reprint of *Bulletin*, ix (Catholic University of Peking, 1934). This phenomenon recalls the lack of family names among European serfs.

We now come to a final question, that of evolution and devolution. Enough has been said to show that in the social history of such peoples as the Mongols there is (*a*) internal evolution of the society itself; (*b*) combined evolution when the society becomes attached to the frontier of an empire and its institutions must be adjusted accordingly; (*c*) devolution, when the empire disintegrates and the nomads—or some of them—become detached from its frontiers and fall back into the steppe.

In a great empire like that of China the historical cycle had alternating phases of centralization and decentralization. Since decentralization historically precedes centralization, we can call the shift of phase into centralization 'evolutionary', and the return to a phase of decentralization 'devoluntionary'. In the devolutionary phase the Chinese were still a people belonging to the same kind of society. They simply fell back to an earlier condition of that society, from which they were capable of evolving once more, along the patterns inherent within their own society (leaving out the question of reunification by conquest from the outside), up to the phase of unification.

When, on the other hand, Mongols became attached to the frontier of a settled empire they began to evolve along patterns not necessarily inherent in their own society; when they became detached from that frontier they devolved, not to an earlier stage of this conjunct society, but to their own earlier society, which was a quite different kind of society. For want of better terms I propose to call one a frontier-feudal society and the other a steppe-tribal society. Centralization by war and conquest within the steppe-tribal society was the result of a quite different process from that which centralized the empire to which the tribes might become attached in the frontier-feudal stage.

We know, for example, that the family of Chingis Khan were at one time frontier feudatories of the Chin or Jurchid empire of barbarians ruling in North China. They then fell away from that frontier, reverted to the steppe, and within the steppe engaged in the politics and warfare of a nomadic society, out of which in the course of time Chingis emerged as first the unifier of the steppe tribes and then the founder of conquest empires in settled lands. Unfortunately the devolutionary part of the record is only fragmentarily documented, but there are many parallels— one of them being the clan-history of the founder of the Manchu dynasty. This is the aspect of the social history of the Mongols and other nomads that most needs new research.

# INDEX
## Chiefly of Historians and Histories